MEXICAN FOOD

The Ultimate Cookbook

MEXICAN FOOD

The Ultimate Cookbook

GABE ERALES, LUIS ROBLES, BALO OROZCO, AUGIE SAUCEDO, LORI SAUER, AARON MELENDREZ & JOSÉ LUIS HINOSTROZA

With **VANESSA CECEÑA**

Photographs by
JIM SULLIVAN

CIDER MILL PRESS

BOOK
PUBLISHERS
KENNEBUNKPORT, MAINE

CONTENTS

Introduction   13

Meat   27

Poultry   97

Seafood   135

Vegetables   209

Soups   287

Masa   351

Antojitos   399

Sauces, Salsas & Sides   439

Desserts   541

Cocktails & Beverages   651

Index   812

FOREWORD

By Vanessa Ceceña

I was raised along the US-Mexico border, in San Diego, with Tijuana sitting just a few miles to the south. For my family, the border was fluid: we would cross it to shop for groceries, to soothe cravings for tacos, and to visit our loved ones during holidays. Some of the strongest memories from my youth are those connected to my fascination with the countless cookies and pastries in Mexican grocery stores, those confections dazzling me until I inevitably got lost wandering around the aisles.

On family trips down the coast to the state of Baja California, I would indulge in the lobster from Puerto Nuevo, which is served with large, handmade flour tortillas, refried beans, and Mexican rice. I enjoyed eating cocteles—requesting more octopus with tentacles whenever possible—at the fish market in Ensenada. At the age of four I was ordering a dozen fresh oysters for myself, and dressing them with a bit of lime juice, red salsa, and a pinch of salt.

After traveling more extensively throughout Mexico as an adult, I have come to realize how magical the food of my parents' home country is, capable of transporting me back to moments with loved ones that have passed. To the days where we prepared tamales for Christmas Eve dinner; to my uncle making sure my carne asada was extra crispy; to those times I watched my grandmother make my beloved buñuelos, the fritter from Chihuahua.

By continuing to use indigenous techniques and ingredients to preserve these traditional recipes, we can honor the generations past and approach cooking as an homage to our ancestors, who saw food as a way to display their pride in their culture.

Cooking is a tool for storytelling, for cultural preservation. It has the power to create space for strangers to dialogue within, which is why it so often serves as the introduction to another culture. Being offered a plate of food that involved hours of labor is a gift filled with love and dedication. Each dish tells its own story of its people, its history.

The recipes developed for this book are a compilation of dishes that show the ornate gastronomy of México and the unique story of each contributing chef.

¡Buen Provecho!

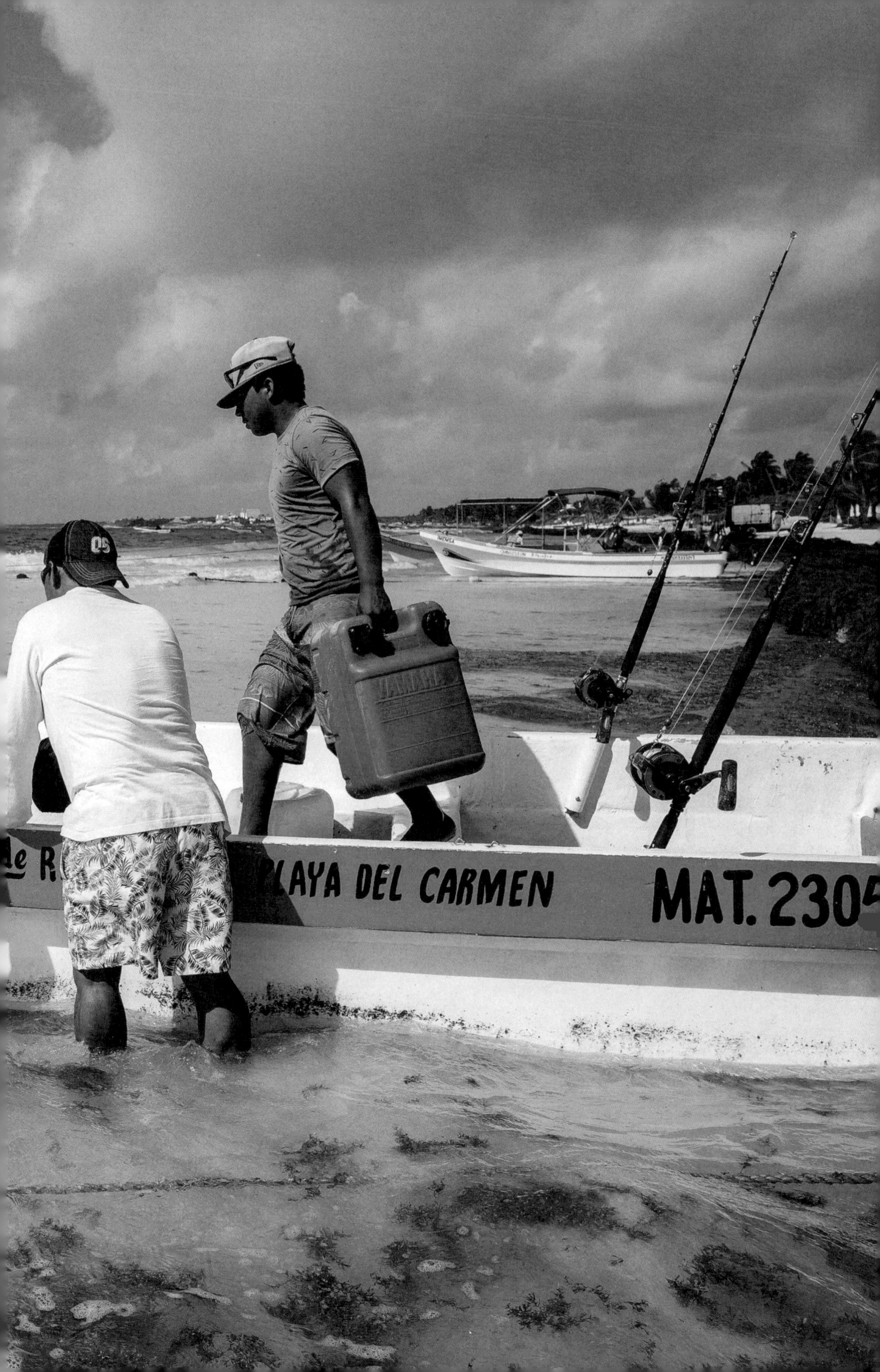
LAYA DEL CARMEN
MAT. 230

INTRODUCTION

By Vanessa Ceceña

The indigenous people of Mexico have a close connection to agriculture, and to nature. This connection is apparent in the beautiful huipiles that have hand-embroidered designs symbolizing corn, for example.

Mexico's gastronomy is grounded in indigenous ingredients, dishes, and techniques.

Despite efforts to erase indigenous practices and ways of life during the colonial era, many indigenous peoples of the region have maintained strong traditions, passing down family recipes from generation to generation. As a result, the food from southern Mexico is considered to be the most traditional, because it has managed to maintain its indigenous roots via the continued use of traditional ingredients.

Complex and arduous dishes are reserved for large celebrations like weddings and Day of the Dead. Preparing mole from scratch, for example, is a process that can last several days.

Mexican food is intricate, beautiful, and delicious because all parts are used—every bit of livestock and produce, even the fungus that grows on corn (known as huitlacoche). Those pieces that others disregard are considered essential in Mexican cuisine, such as the pork tripe in the comforting menudo (see page 293), where it adds texture and a sense of adventure.

HISTORY OF MEXICAN CUISINE

Prior to the arrival of the Spanish, the use of meats in Mexican dishes was uncommon, and corn, beans, and squash formed the foundation of most dishes. The Conquest introduced livestock such as cows, pigs, chicken, goats, and sheep to the country, and these were then incorporated into the existing dishes, resulting in the recipes we recognize as Mexican cuisine today.

Colonization also introduced spices and plants foreign to the region at that time. Dutch merchants traveling along Caribbean trade

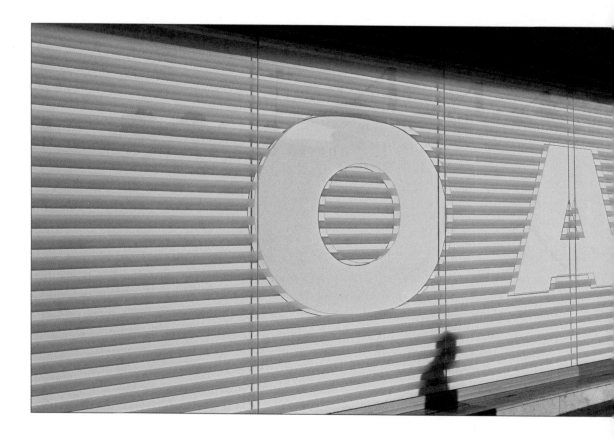

routes arrived on the coast of Veracruz, and also left their mark on regional cuisine. The most notable influence from the Dutch is the use of queso de bola (Edam cheese), which is hollowed out and stuffed with meat and nuts; and crispy crêpes that are filled with Nutella or cheese.

From 1519 to 1580, the Spanish brought the first African slaves, from Angola and the Congo, to the two main ports in Veracruz and Campeche. The demand for slaves in Mexico continued until the early 1800s. Consequently, Mexican cuisine includes traces of African cooking. Ingredients native to Africa include rice, plantains, sesame seeds, hibiscus flower (which is used to make

the popular agua de jamaica, see page 784), and watermelon. Afro-Mexican communities continue to thrive in the Costa Chica of southern Guerrero and Oaxaca, and also in Veracruz.

It is believed that produce from Asia arrived in Mexico starting in the sixteenth century. During these years mango, tamarind, dried, salted plums and apricots, and chamoy were introduced and became commonly used, particularly in Northern Mexico. Mexicali, a border town in Baja California, is known for its Chinese food, with over 200 Chinese restaurants in the city.

During the eighteenth and early nineteenth centuries, people from Lebanon

migrated to Mexico, initially arriving in Veracruz and later settling in towns throughout the republic. While Lebanese immigrants only accounted for a small percentage of the overall population of Mexico, their culinary traditions became intertwined with native dishes. Tacos de adobada or tacos al pastor are a result of the collision between these two cultures. The red marinade that contributes much to making these tacos what they are is a combination of Middle Eastern and Mexican spices. The method of cooking the meat, where it is placed on a vertical spit (trompo) and slowly cooked is an adaption of the shawarma that is featured in Middle Eastern cooking.

The occupation of Mexico by the French during the 1800s introduced French culinary techniques into the existing culture. Dishes that incorporated the use of reduced sauces, like baño maria, were labeled as a la francesa. There were efforts by those with higher socioeconomic status to view native dishes, like tamales, as lower class and unrefined. While efforts to erase the existing cuisine ultimately failed, French inspiration can still be found in the sweet breads and empanadas that are popular throughout the country.

THE REGIONAL CUISINES OF MEXICO

The geography, topography, and climate of Mexico heavily influences the ingredients that are accessible to people in its various regions. The northern part of the country consists of long stretches of desert with tall and looming saguaro cacti. Mountain ranges can be found all around the country, but are particularly common in the central part of Mexico. The southern and eastern parts of the country—Veracruz, Chiapas, and the Isthmus of Tehuantepec in Oaxaca—are full of vegetation and tropical greenery. Baja California has the Pacific Ocean to the west and the Sea of Cortez on its eastern coast. And of course, Mexico's eastern coast cradles the Gulf of Mexico.

Many dishes, like tacos and tamales, can be found in every state in Mexico. But each region has its own take on these dishes. Mole, a sauce or paste that is made out of ground chocolate, nuts, and spices, is a prime example of the country's regional diversity. While the sweeter moles featuring rich, velvety chocolate, are more widely known, in central and southern Mexico mole can be spicy and/or textured, pairing with turkey, beef, or seafood.

In addition to their own takes on the traditional dishes, every state within Mexico has dishes that are unique to it. A breakdown of these regions and some of what you can expect from each cuisine follows.

North (Baja California, Chihuahua, Durango, Coahuila, Nuevo León, Sinaloa, Sonora, and Tamaulipas): The northern states of Mexico are arid and dry. In this region dried meats are commonly incorporated into dishes. Chilorio, dried pork, is wrapped in flour tortillas to make burritos. Machaca, dried beef, is sautéed with onion, tomatoes, and fresh chile peppers, and served with refried pinto beans. Machaca can easily be converted into a breakfast dish by adding it to scrambled eggs. The use of dried meats hints at the past scarcity of animal protein in the region, with curing and drying used to make the most of what was available.

Baja California is recognized for its mariscos, or seafood, like the lightly battered and fried fish tacos, and ceviche, raw fish or shrimp cured in lime juice. The lobster from Puerto Nuevo has become iconic in its simplicity, with

warm, melted butter served over the top and Mexican rice, refried beans, and flour tortillas on the side.

Central (Aguascalientes, Colima, Guanajuato, Jalisco, Mexico City, Michoacán, Nayarit, Queretaro, San Luis Potosi, Puebla, and Zacatecas): In Jalisco, the bolillo is a sour and salted bread similar to a baguette. Its crunchy outer layer is ideal for making tortas ahogada, a sandwich made with lean pork and topped with a red chili sauce. Bolillos can replace spoons when eating beans and birria (see page 67), a rich meat stew made with goat, beef, or mutton. Carne en su jugo, beef in its juice (see page 90), is the typical dish of Guadalajara, the capital of Jalisco. The beef is slow-cooked in broth until extremely tender, and then served with a side of frijoles de la olla (see page 257). On hot days, it's customary to drink tejuino (see page 789), a cold drink made out of fermented masa.

The state of Michoacán is the birthplace of carnitas, cuts of pork braised in lard. Pork shoulder is the cut of choice because of its fattiness, but it is common to add all cuts of the pork, like the liver and intestines, to the brass cauldron, the traditional vehicle for cooking carnitas. The tender meat that results is served in tacos fashioned from double tortillas and garnished with finely chopped cilantro, onion, radish, lime, and red salsa. Guisados of chicken, potato, carrot, and onion topped with green cabbage, as well as gorditas, are sold by street food vendors in the region.

Puebla is renowned for its mole poblano (see page 119), chiles en nogada, and rompope, a type of eggnog with white rum. To prepare the chiles en nogada (see page 85), the chile is roasted, peeled, and stuffed with beef picadillo (see page 73). It is then topped with a creamy walnut sauce and pomegranate seeds.

South (Campeche, Chiapas, Guerrero, Oaxaca, Quintana Roo, Tabasco, Veracruz, and the Yucatan): The diversity of Mexico's cuisine is most apparent in its southern states, a result of both the ethnic diversity in the region, and the preservation of its indigenous cultures. Oaxaca, for example, has seven ethnic regions, each with its own language, culture, and cuisine. Similarly, in the Yucatan, Mayan cooking techniques and ingredients can still be found in modern-day kitchens.

As one moves south, and draws closer to the equator, the geography and climate drastically change, becoming lush and tropical in the humid weather that is ideal for the cultivation of coffee beans, which Chiapas, Oaxaca, and Veracruz are known for. The climate of the region has lent itself to the cultivation of an assortment of tropical fruits, such as guanabana (soursop), papaya, starfruit, and mango.

The food hailing from Oaxaca, the land of the seven moles, is one of the most recognized internationally, an appreciation that is in part due to the preservation of indigenous cooking techniques and native crop cultivation. Common ingredients found in Oaxacan cuisine include huitlacoche (corn smut), chocolate, hoja santa (Mexican pepperleaf), black beans, the aromatic herb epazote, and flor de calabaza (squash blossom). These ingredients are found in tetelas (see page 382), tlayudas, enmoladas, and quesadillas (see page 251).

The tlayuda is a large, crispy handmade tortilla smeared with asiento, the fat left over after deep-frying pork, refried black beans, and cheese (Oaxacan quesillo), layered with slices of tomato and avocado, and topped with a smoky red salsa. Tlayudas can be served with tasajo (beef that has been air-dried and pounded thin), cecina (thinly sliced pork), chorizo, or a combination of all three.

A variety of insects are also part of the region's gastronomy. Chinicul (red worm), chicatanas (flying ants), and hormigas de miel (honeypot ants) are consumed, at times in chile salsas, at others in tacos. Chapulines (grasshoppers), either small or large, are seasoned with lime, salt, and chiles, and can be ordered with a side of guacamole and totopos (tortilla chips) to accompany a beer or a mezcal cocktail (for a recipe, see the Cocktails & Beverages chapter). Traditional drinks include chilacayote water (fig-leaf squash) and tejate, a cold beverage made with maize, cacao, and mamey sapote.

Further south is the state of Chiapas, another ethnically diverse area with high regard for its native customs and ways. The subtropical climate and lush vegetation foster the various fruits and vegetables used in the region's recipes. Tamales on the Pacific coast of Chiapas

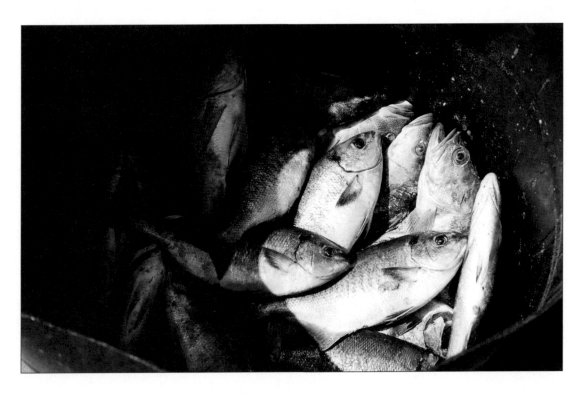

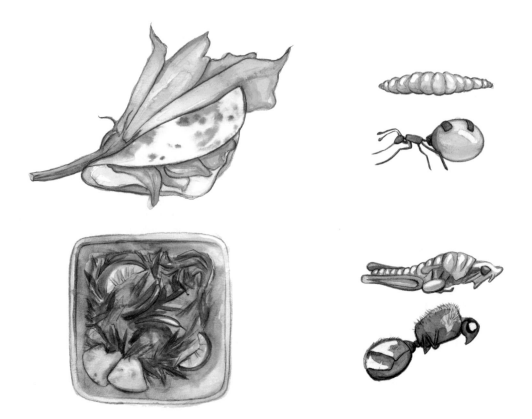

are prepared with seafood, such as the longnose gar and jellyfish, and reptiles including iguanas. Tamales from the highlands of Chiapas are made with meats, beans, and chiles. Tamales juacanes stand astride these two regions, and are made with dried shrimp, pumpkin seeds, and black beans. Banana leaves are frequently used to wrap the tamales for cooking. Tacos de cochito, pork marinated in saffron sauce, or fish tacos made with gar, a local fish that has a texture similar to poultry when cooked, are other dishes frequently enjoyed in Chiapas.

In this southernmost state, fermented maize-based drinks, such as pozol made with cacao, or tascalate, a thick drink made from cacao, toasted nixtamal corn, piloncillo, cinnamon, vanilla, and achiote, are popular. These drinks predate the arrival of the Spanish, and are packed with nutritional value; they were consumed by indigenous peoples, especially those who needed to travel for long periods of time, like merchants.

The Yucatan's gastronomy is unique because it preserves the Mayan cooking traditions, but combines them with Spanish, Dutch, and Lebanese influences, a marriage that leads to a unique combination of flavors and aromas. The core of Yucatecan cuisine is formed by achiote, habanero chiles, citrus, like the sour orange, and smoke, which is created either by roasting or barbecuing ingredients. Deer, turkey, pork, quail, armadillos, and other game meats are the proteins of choice in the Yucatan.

The quintessential dish of the Yucatan is cochinita pibil, a slow-roasted pork marinated in a red chile sauce (see page 28). To maximize the rich, smoky flavor of the chiles and spices, pibil is cooked in an underground pit and covered with banana leaves. The pork is served with pickled red onions and habanero chiles, and handmade corn tortillas (see page 352). The use of banana leaves for roasting protein, or for wrapping and steaming tamales, adds a subtle sweetness and earthiness.

Recados, or spice mixes used as pastes or rubs for protein or vegetables, are uniquely Yucatecan and are responsible for the rich flavor palette of some regional dishes. Preparing recado rojo, a popular paste, requires roasting achiote (or using a premade achiote paste), combining it with lime, orange, and grapefruit juices, oregano, marjoram, habanero chiles, garlic, cinnamon, and salt (see page 497). The resulting paste features a delicate balance of citrus and spice that Yucatecans have mastered better than most.

Veracruz, the vibrant southern state known for its Son jarocho music and coffee, is a tropical region with its coastline on the Gulf of Mexico, resulting in gastronomy that is rich in flavors and textures. The Spanish conquest began in Veracruz, and its ports quickly became important. European ships would dock along the coast and bring spices and other goods, like the olives found in arroz a la tumbada, a popular dish similar to Spain's famed paella. The seafood sourced from the coast of Veracruz consists of shrimp, crab, oysters, snails, red snapper, and cod, among others.

STAPLE INGREDIENTS

While Mexico is abundant in native herbs and produce, beans, chiles, and maize are the three ingredients that form the backbone of the country's cuisine.

BEANS

Beans originated in South and Central America and are one of the earliest cultivated plants, with the known variants now numbering around 40,000. These legumes are high in nutritional value and consumed throughout Mexico, in households at every socioeconomic level.

Pinto and black beans are the most commonly used legumes in Mexico; however, rio zape, ayocote, and flor de mayo beans are also part of the country's diet, most typically in central Mexico. In northern Mexico, people eat whole beans cooked in their broth (frijoles de la olla), topped with queso fresco and chile. Refried pinto beans are served as sides to chilaquiles and other popular dishes. Frijoles charros are typical of north central Mexico and its border towns.

In southern Mexico, black beans replace pinto beans and are served in similar ways. Epazote, a native edible green with a strong, earthy flavor, is commonly added to black beans while they're cooking. Traditionally, beans are cooked in an earthen clay pot over low heat with onion, garlic, and, at times, lard. While the use of pure clay pots is believed to enrich the flavor of beans, metal pots and pressure cookers are now often used.

Each variety of bean has a distinct consistency and flavor. Rio zape beans are similar to the pinto bean, but are described as having notes of coffee and chocolate. Black beans are known for their earthy flavor, while pinto beans are creamier and mild. Ayocote beans, originating in Oaxaca, are potato-like in flavor and starchiness. Flor de mayo beans are similarly starchy, but feature a smoky taste.

CHILES

Chile peppers originated in Mexico (Mesoamerica) around 5000 BCE in the Tehuacán Valley. The word *chile* originates from the Nahuatl word *chilli*, meaning hot pepper. With colonization, chile peppers were introduced to other countries. Each chile has a different taste, a different level of spice.

Our ability to feel spiciness is due to mammals having a receptor in their brains that tells the body their "mouth is on fire." Birds are not able to feel this burning sensation when eating chiles, allowing them to spread chile seeds far and wide.

When chiles are green, they are considered immature. If left on the vine, they will eventually turn red. Chiles that are to be dried are often left on the vine until they are red. Once chiles are dehydrated, they are called by another name. For example, the fresh chilaca pepper is called the pasilla negro in its dry format.

Fresh and cooked chiles, with their varying levels of spice, can be found in numerous Mexican recipes. The seeds of the peppers, either fresh or cooked, can be removed prior to consumption to reduce the level of spice.

Chiles can be dried, roasted, smoked, or completely charred. One can roast chiles first, and then dry them. Or they can be hung to dry when they are green or red. Some of the native chiles found in Mexico are:

Poblano: They are commonly found in their dry, smoky format, when they become the ancho. They are used in making adobo or chile pastes and have a light to medium spice level, and an earthy flavor.

Chilaca: Mildly hot; when dried, it is referred to as pasilla negro.

Chipotle: These are dried and then smoked jalapeño peppers, with medium to hot spiciness.

Chile Pasilla: Slightly sweet, smoky, and a low amount of spice. This chile is cultivated in Oaxaca.

Guajillo: This chile is the dried form of the mirasol pepper, and has a sweet, fruity flavor and mild spice.

Drying chiles is a way to preserve their flavor and ensure longevity. Smoked chiles are commonly used in recipes like mole. Roasting chiles, either over an open fire, on a grill, or on a stovetop, is common throughout Mexico. Dishes that involve stuffing chiles with cheese, like in chiles rellenos, will call for roasted chiles. This method softens the pepper and loosens the chile's skin, which needs to be removed prior to stuffing it. Roasting chiles alters their flavor profile, making them sweeter, and the smokiness retained is, in chiles rellenos, beautifully balanced by the light batter and the creamy melted cheese.

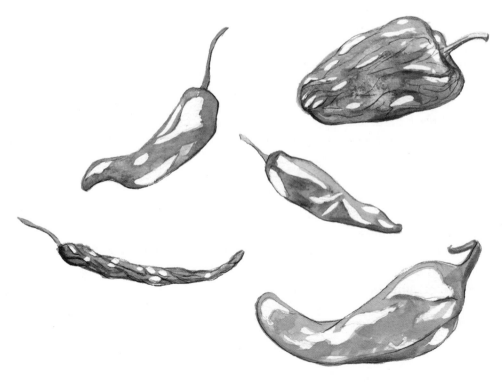

Charring and roasting a variety of chiles, and then mixing them with other ingredients, is a common method in various Mexican dishes like the Mayan recado negro from the Yucatan. This strongly flavored paste requires chiles de arbol and ancho chiles to be toasted until they are blackened and then ground with garlic, oregano, achiote seeds, and other spices until the mixture is the preferred consistency.

The method in which chiles are prepared when making marinades, stews, and salsas can be telling as to the geographical origin of the dish, or of the cook. They are ground along with chocolate and nuts on the metate to make mole, and mixed with tomatillos and garlic to make a chunky salsa verde using a molcajete, a mortar and pestle made out volcanic rock.

MAIZE

Corn, or maize, is one of the most prominent food staples in Latin America, and provides the foundation for many Mexican dishes, such as tortillas, sopes, and empanadas. The earliest traces of corn cultivation go back to Mesoamerica, and there are now 59 corn variants unique to Mexico and grown by small-scale farmers. There are over 28,000 distinct seeds and species of corn throughout the world.

Preparing and cooking corn to be used for masa (dough), for example, is a slow and intricate process that requires precise technique. To make masa, maize is cooked and prepared according to the pre-Hispanic nixtamalization technique that uses the three main ingredients: corn, water, and calcium oxide (quicklime or burnt lime). In this preparation, dried corn kernels are placed in water and cooked over low heat. Pure calcium oxide is added to the water during this initial cooking process; this step is key to making a dough that can produce the perfect tortilla. Adding the right amount of calcium oxide allows for the thin outer layer of the corn kernel to fall off as it boils. As the corn cooks, it begins to change color; the parts of the kernel that were white prior to cooking become a light yellow.

Overcooking the kernel will result in overhydration of the corn, creating a dough that has a gum-like consistency. Dough made with overcooked corn will not be adequate for making tortillas. But it can be used to make other corn-based dishes, like tamales or memelas.

Every step in the nixtamalization process is important, including the rinsing of the corn after boiling. While the calcium oxide is required in the cooking process, it must be fully washed off prior to grinding the maize on the metate—a rectangular grindstone with a concave upper surface—as this step preserves the corn's true color.

To grind the corn on the metate, small amounts of water need to be poured on the cooked kernels. However, using the water that the corn was cooked in will change the color of the dough, making it brown in spots. The water that the corn was cooked in will have high alkalinity, with a pH level around 13.

Metates are most commonly made out of volcanic stone or limestone, and used throughout Mexico to finely grind the corn used to make masa. A pestle, usually made out the same stone as the grindstone, is a heavy piece of stone with rounded edges. When grinding the corn, one must angle the pestle in such a way that it allows one to pull up the corn and push it down while adding pressure. Adding a small amount of water during this process will allow the ground kernels to slowly turn into a paste and, eventually, a dough.

Elasticity is key to making the perfect tortilla. One must be able to crumple the freshly made corn tortilla in the palm of one's hand without breaking or cracking it when one opens one's fist. When trying to judge ideal tortilla, remember that the tortilla in its Platonic form will always bounce back to its perfectly round shape.

MEAT

The limitations created by Mexico's topography and climate mean that every animal, and every cut from it, must be stretched as far as possible. The people of Mexico have met these challenges admirably, painstakingly developing techniques and borrowing liberally from other cultures (such as the rotating spit, adapted from Lebanese cooking, that keys al pastor tacos) to ensure that nothing goes to waste, and everything hits at the height of flavor.

These inventive dishes, from the birria that has saved the day for many a carouser (see page 67) to the crackly carnitas (see page 46 and 76) and cochinita pibil (see page 28) that have elevated Mexican cuisine into a global phenomenon, and many others are collected here.

COCHINITA PIBIL

YIELD: 4 TO 6 SERVINGS / **ACTIVE TIME:** 30 MINUTES / **TOTAL TIME:** 3 HOURS

This dish of slow-cooked pork is the signature dish of the Yucatan. It is somewhat similar to barbecue, but, in reality, is unlike any other dish in the world.

1. Place the pork shoulder in a large mixing bowl and season generously with salt. Pour the Recado Rojo over the pork and rub it all over. Place the pork in the refrigerator and let it marinate 1 to 2 hours. If time allows, marinate for up to 24.

2. Preheat the oven to 300°F. Remove the spines from the banana leaves and gently toast them over an open flame until pliable and bright green. Line a Dutch oven with the banana leaves, place the pork on top, and cover the pork with the onion. Fold the banana leaves over the pork to create a packet. Cover the Dutch oven, place it in the oven, and roast until the pork is fork-tender, 2 to 3 hours.

3. Remove the lid from the Dutch oven and open up the banana leaf packet. Raise the oven's temperature to 400°F and roast for another 20 minutes. Serve with lime wedges, tortillas, X'nipek, cilantro, and Salsa de Chiltomate.

INGREDIENTS:

5-7 LBS. PORK SHOULDER, CUBED

1¾ LBS. RECADO ROJO (SEE PAGE 497)

1 PACKAGE OF BANANA LEAVES

1 LARGE WHITE ONION, JULIENNED

LIME WEDGES, FOR SERVING

CORN TORTILLAS (SEE PAGE 352), WARM, FOR SERVING

X'NIPEK (SEE PAGE 487), FOR SERVING

FRESH CILANTRO, CHOPPED, FOR SERVING

SALSA DE CHILTOMATE (SEE PAGE 477), FOR SERVING

CHILIBUL

YIELD: 4 SERVINGS / **ACTIVE TIME:** 30 MINUTES / **TOTAL TIME:** 1 HOUR

This Yucatecan dish of shredded beef sautéed with achiote, chipotle, and black beans is typically served with tortillas, to be eaten as tacos, or in tortas.

1. Place the steak in a large saucepan with the onion, garlic, bay leaves, marjoram, oregano, thyme, and dried chipotles. Season with salt, cover the steak with water by 2 inches, and bring to a gentle simmer.

2. Cover the pan and simmer for 1 to 2 hours, until the steak is tender and easy to shred with a fork. Let the steak cool in the liquid.

3. Remove the steak from the cooking liquid and shred it.

4. Place the steak, beans, and pureed chipotles in a saucepan, bring to a gentle simmer, and cook until everything is warmed through, 15 to 20 minutes.

5. Season with salt and serve with tortillas, the salsa, and Escabeche.

INGREDIENTS:

2   LBS. SKIRT STEAK, CHUCK ROAST, OR BRISKET

1   WHITE ONION, QUARTERED

1   HEAD OF GARLIC, HALVED

2   BAY LEAVES

1   TEASPOON DRIED MARJORAM

1   TEASPOON DRIED MEXICAN OREGANO

1   TEASPOON DRIED THYME

2   CHIPOTLE CHILE PEPPERS, STEMMED AND SEEDED

    SALT, TO TASTE

1   LB. COOKED OR CANNED BLACK BEANS, MASHED

8   OZ. CHIPOTLES EN ADOBO, PUREED

    CORN TORTILLAS (SEE PAGE 352), WARM, FOR SERVING

    SALSA DE CHILTOMATE (SEE PAGE 477), FOR SERVING

    ESCABECHE (SEE PAGE 518), FOR SERVING

32 | MEXICAN FOOD

MILANESA DE RES Y MOLE BLANCO

YIELD: 4 SERVINGS / **ACTIVE TIME:** 30 MINUTES / **TOTAL TIME:** 1 HOUR

The creaminess of the mole complements the crunchiness of the milanesa de res, a breaded cutlet. Crushed saltines can be substituted for the bread crumbs, just remember to adjust the amount of salt you're going to use in the dish.

1. Place the eggs, pepper, and garlic in a mixing bowl, season with salt, and whisk until combined.

2. Place the bread crumbs in a shallow bowl and season with salt. Place the flour in a separate shallow bowl. Dredge the steak in the flour, followed by the egg mixture, and finally the bread crumbs. Repeat until the steak is fully coated and place it on a parchment-lined baking sheet.

3. Add canola oil to a Dutch oven until it is about 1 inch deep and warm it to 350°F over medium heat. Working in batches, add the steak to the oil and fry, turning once, until cooked through and golden brown, about 6 minutes. Transfer the cooked steak to a paper towel–lined plate.

4. To serve, spread about ½ cup of the Mole Blanco on a plate, top with the steak, and serve with the lime wedges and salpicon.

INGREDIENTS:

3   EGGS

1   TABLESPOON BLACK PEPPER

2   GARLIC CLOVES, GRATED

      SALT, TO TASTE

3   CUPS BREAD CRUMBS

2   CUPS ALL-PURPOSE FLOUR

2-3   LBS. TOP ROUND STEAK, SLICED INTO ¼-INCH-WIDE PIECES

      CANOLA OIL, AS NEEDED

      MOLE BLANCO (SEE PAGE 458), WARMED

      LIME WEDGES, FOR SERVING

      SALPICON DE RABANO Y CHILE HABANERO (SEE PAGE 486), FOR SERVING

COSTILLA CORTA DE RES
CON CHILE COLORADO

YIELD: 4 SERVINGS / **ACTIVE TIME:** 30 MINUTES / **TOTAL TIME:** 2 HOURS

This smoky short rib stew is Mexican comfort food at its peak. As there is plenty of goodness to sop up, flour tortillas are superior to corn here.

1. Preheat the oven to 300°F. Season the short ribs generously with salt and pepper.

2. Place the oil in a Dutch oven and warm it over medium heat. Working in batches to avoid crowding the pan, place the short ribs in the skillet and cook, turning occasionally, until browned on all sides. Remove the seared short ribs from the pot and set them aside.

3. Add the onion to the pot and cook, stirring frequently, until translucent, about 3 minutes. Stir in the stock and half of the Chile Colorado and bring to a simmer. Return the short ribs to the pot, return to a simmer, and cover the pot.

4. Place the Dutch oven in the oven and braise until the short ribs are tender and falling off the bone, about 1½ hours.

5. Remove the short ribs from the pot. Add the remaining chile to the Dutch oven and cook the liquid over high heat until reduced by half, skimming off any fat as desired.

6. Return the short ribs to the sauce and serve with tortillas, lime wedges, and Escabeche.

INGREDIENTS:

- 4-6 **LBS. BONE-IN SHORT RIBS**
- **SALT AND PEPPER, TO TASTE**
- 2 **TABLESPOONS EXTRA-VIRGIN OLIVE OIL**
- 1 **WHITE ONION, JULIENNED**
- 8 **CUPS BEEF STOCK (SEE PAGE 342)**
- 8 **CUPS CHILE COLORADO (SEE PAGE 452)**
- **FLOUR TORTILLAS (SEE PAGE 444), WARM, FOR SERVING**
- **LIME WEDGES, FOR SERVING**
- **ESCABECHE (SEE PAGE 518), FOR SERVING**

CECINA DE CERDO

YIELD: 6 TO 8 SERVINGS / **ACTIVE TIME:** 30 MINUTES / **TOTAL TIME:** 2 HOURS

This marinated and grilled pork loin is best as a filling for tacos, accompanied by nothing more than lime and cilantro.

1. Place the guajillo peppers in a dry skillet and toast over medium heat until they darken and become fragrant and pliable. Submerge them in a bowl of hot water and let them sit for 30 minutes.

2. Place the seeds and bay leaf in the skillet and toast until fragrant, shaking the pan frequently. Grind to a powder using a mortar and pestle or a spice grinder.

3. Place the oil in a Dutch oven and warm it over medium heat. Add the garlic, cook until fragrant, and then add the chiles de arbol. Fry for 30 seconds and then remove the pan from heat.

4. Drain the guajillo peppers and reserve the soaking liquid. Place the guajillo, chiles de arbol, spice powder, and garlic in a blender and puree until smooth, adding the vinegar and soaking liquid as needed to attain a "nappe" consistency, meaning smooth and thick enough to evenly coat the pork. Season the puree with salt.

5. Place the pork tenderloin in a baking dish and pour the puree over it. Stir until coated and marinate in the refrigerator for at least 30 minutes. If time allows, marinate the pork for up to 24 hours.

6. Preheat a charcoal or gas grill to medium-high heat (about 450°F). Clean the grates and lightly brush them with oil. Place the tenderloin on the grill and grill until the interior is 145°F, 2 to 3 minutes per side.

7. Remove the tenderloin from the grill and serve with tortillas and lime wedges.

INGREDIENTS:

7	OZ. GUAJILLO CHILE PEPPERS, STEMMED AND SEEDED
1	TEASPOON CUMIN SEEDS
1	TEASPOON CORIANDER SEEDS
1	BAY LEAF
2	TABLESPOONS EXTRA-VIRGIN OLIVE OIL, PLUS MORE AS NEEDED
4	GARLIC CLOVES, MINCED
10	DRIED CHILES DE ARBOL, STEMMED AND SEEDED
	SALT, TO TASTE
7	TABLESPOONS APPLE CIDER OR CHAMPAGNE VINEGAR
2	LBS. PORK TENDERLOIN, SLICED AND POUNDED ¼-INCH-THICK
	CORN TORTILLAS (SEE PAGE 352), WARM, FOR SERVING
	LIME WEDGES, FOR SERVING

LOMO Y MANCHAMANTELES

YIELD: 4 SERVINGS / ACTIVE TIME: 30 MINUTES / TOTAL TIME: 24 HOURS

A stew that is traditionally made with pork loin and fruit like bananas, pineapples, and the peaches that are featured in this recipe.

1. Fill a large saucepan with cold water and add 1¾ oz. of salt for every liter of water. Place the pork in the brine and let it sit in the refrigerator for 24 hours.

2. Remove the pork from the brine, pat it dry, and let it come to room temperature. Preheat a grill to medium-high heat (450°F).

3. Place the tenderloin on the grill and grill until the interior is 145°F, 3 to 4 minutes per side. Remove from the grill and let it rest for about 10 minutes before slicing.

4. Brush the cut sides of the peaches with honey and season them with salt. Grill until deeply charred, but not falling apart, about 6 minutes.

5. Spread ½ cup of the mole on each plate, top with slices of pork and the grilled peaches, and serve with tortillas.

INGREDIENTS:

SALT, AS NEEDED

1 LB. PORK TENDERLOIN

2 PEACHES, PITTED AND QUARTERED

¼ CUP HONEY

2 CUPS MOLE MANCHAMANTELES (SEE PAGE 455), WARM

CORN TORTILLAS (SEE PAGE 352), WARM, FOR SERVING

MICHOACÁN-STYLE CARNITAS

YIELD: 6 TO 8 SERVINGS / **ACTIVE TIME:** 30 MINUTES / **TOTAL TIME:** 2 HOURS

Avocado leaves, beer, and plenty of citrus feature in this specific version of the famed dish.

1. Place the lard, bay leaves, and avocado leaves in a Dutch oven and warm over medium-high heat. When the lard comes to a simmer, stir in the beer, charred onions, and garlic.

2. Warm à skillet over medium heat and season the pork shoulder liberally with salt. Working in batches to avoid crowding the pan, add the pork shoulder to the skillet and sear until browned all over, turning occasionally.

3. Add the seared pork to the lard and simmer until it begins to get tender, about 2 hours.

4. Stir in the lime juice and orange juice and continue to cook the pork over low heat until the pork is extremely tender, another 30 to 45 minutes.

5. Remove the pork and chop it into bite-sized pieces for tacos. Serve with the white onion, tortillas, lime wedges, cilantro, and salsa verde.

INGREDIENTS:

1	LB. LARD
5	BAY LEAVES
5	AVOCADO LEAVES
3	CUPS NEGRO MODELO BEER
2	YELLOW ONIONS, HALVED AND CHARRED
2	HEADS OF GARLIC, HALVED AND CHARRED
5-7	LBS. PORK SHOULDER, CUBED
	SALT, TO TASTE
1	CUP FRESH LIME JUICE
1	CUP ORANGE JUICE
1	WHITE ONION, BRUNOISED
	CORN TORTILLAS (SEE PAGE 352), WARM, FOR SERVING
	LIME WEDGES, FOR SERVING
	FRESH CILANTRO, CHOPPED, FOR SERVING
	SALSA VERDE TATEMADA (SEE PAGE 480), FOR SERVING

DZIK DE RES

YIELD: 6 SERVINGS / ACTIVE TIME: 30 MINUTES / TOTAL TIME: 1 HOUR

This is a Yucatecan dish of diced brisket braised with habanero chiles and a host of other flavorful ingredients, most of which are contained within a sachet to make for easy prep and cleanup.

1. Season the brisket with salt and place it in a large saucepan with the stock. Bring to a simmer over medium heat.

2. Using a piece of cheesecloth, create a sachet with the garlic, bay leaves, thyme, onion, cinnamon stick, oregano, and marjoram. Secure the sachet with kitchen twine and add it to the saucepan.

3. Simmer the brisket until it is very tender, 1 to 2 hours. If time allows, let the meat cool in the broth.

4. Strain the liquid and reserve for another use. Shred the brisket into thin strands, place them in a mixing bowl, add the lime juice and orange juice, and stir to combine. Season with salt and then fold in the radish, habanero, red onion, avocados, and tomatoes.

5. Serve with cilantro, tortillas, and lime wedges.

INGREDIENTS:

- 2 LBS. BEEF BRISKET, TRIMMED AND QUARTERED
- SALT, TO TASTE
- 8 CUPS BEEF STOCK (SEE PAGE 342)
- 3 GARLIC CLOVES
- 2 BAY LEAVES
- 4 SPRIGS OF FRESH THYME
- ½ ONION, CHARRED
- ½ CINNAMON STICK
- 1 TEASPOON DRIED MEXICAN OREGANO
- 1 TEASPOON CHOPPED FRESH MARJORAM
- 1 CUP FRESH LIME JUICE
- 1 CUP ORANGE JUICE
- 3 OZ. RADISHES, SLICED THIN
- 3-4 HABANERO CHILE PEPPERS, STEMMED, SEEDED, AND MINCED
- 1 LARGE RED ONION, JULIENNED
- 2 AVOCADOS, PITTED AND SLICED
- 8 OZ. ROMA TOMATO, SEEDED AND BRUNOISED
- 1 SMALL BUNCH OF FRESH CILANTRO, CHOPPED
- CORN TORTILLAS (SEE PAGE 352), WARM, FOR SERVING
- LIME WEDGES, FOR SERVING

BEEF CHEEKS WITH SALSA VERDE

YIELD: 4 SERVINGS / **ACTIVE TIME:** 15 MINUTES / **TOTAL TIME:** 2 HOURS AND 30 MINUTES

Beef cheeks are a tough part of the cow that require long and slow cooking methods such as a braise in this recipe, which is a great use of offal. Once cooked properly, beef cheeks provide a good amount of very tender, flavorful meat. When you go to buy them at the local butcher, ask them to clean the beef cheeks for you and remove any connective tissue.

1. Fill a large saucepan with water and add the beef cheeks, onion, garlic, and dried chiles.

2. Season the water very generously with salt, add the cinnamon stick, and bring to a boil. Reduce the heat to low and simmer the beef cheeks until tender, about 2 hours.

3. Remove the beef cheeks and reserve 1 cup of the cooking liquid. Chop the beef cheeks into ½-inch cubes and stir them into the salsa.

4. Stir in the reserved cooking liquid, taste, and adjust the seasoning if necessary. Serve with warm tortillas, cilantro, and lime wedges.

INGREDIENTS:

2   LBS. BEEF CHEEKS

1   WHITE ONION, HALVED

3   GARLIC CLOVES, CHOPPED

6   DRIED CHILES DE ARBOL, STEMMED AND SEEDED

4   GUAJILLO CHILE PEPPERS, STEMMED AND SEEDED

    SALT, TO TASTE

1   CINNAMON STICK

2   CUPS SALSA CRUDA VERDE (SEE PAGE 525)

    CORN TORTILLAS (SEE PAGE 352), WARM, FOR SERVING

1   BUNCH OF FRESH CILANTRO

    LIME WEDGES, FOR SERVING

HIGADOS EN SALSA CHIPOTLE DE ADOBO

YIELD: 4 SERVINGS / **ACTIVE TIME:** 30 MINUTES / **TOTAL TIME:** 45 MINUTES

A plate of liver and onions bolstered by the smoky flavor of chipotle chiles is a nostalgic dish for many Mexican families.

1. Place the chicken livers, flour, garlic powder, chili powder, cumin, salt, and pepper in a mixing bowl and stir until the chicken livers are coated.

2. Place the lard in a skillet and warm it over medium heat. Shake the chicken livers to remove any excess flour, add them to the skillet, and briefly fry for 10 seconds on each side. Add the onion and garlic and cook until the onion is translucent, about 2 minutes.

3. Stir in the chipotles and stock, reduce the heat to medium-low, and let the mixture simmer until the sauce has emulsified and the chicken livers are cooked through, 5 to 10 minutes. Serve immediately and garnish each portion with cilantro.

INGREDIENTS:

- 1   LB. CHICKEN LIVERS
- 3   TABLESPOONS ALL-PURPOSE FLOUR
- 1   TABLESPOON GARLIC POWDER
- 1   TABLESPOON CHILI POWDER
- 1   TABLESPOON CUMIN
-   SALT AND PEPPER, TO TASTE
- 1   TABLESPOON LARD
- ½   WHITE ONION, DICED
- 2   GARLIC CLOVES, DICED
- 2   TABLESPOONS CHOPPED CHIPOTLES EN ADOBO
- ½   CUP CHICKEN STOCK (SEE PAGE 341)
-   FRESH CILANTRO, CHOPPED, FOR GARNISH

LENGUA EN SALSA ROJA

YIELD: 6 SERVINGS / **ACTIVE TIME:** 20 MINUTES / **TOTAL TIME:** 4 HOURS

Lengua, or tongue, is another form of offal that provides great flavor and yield for any recipe where you want very tender meat, and exceptional flavor.

1. Place the tongue in a large pot and cover it with cold water. Season generously with salt, stir in half of the onion and garlic, the cinnamon, and cloves and bring to a boil.

2. Reduce the heat to low and simmer until the tongue is very tender, about 3 hours. Weight the tongue down with a heavy plate as it simmers.

3. While the tongue is simmering, warm a dry skillet over medium heat. Add the tomatoes, jalapeños, and remaining onion and garlic and cook until charred (you can also roast these in the oven if that's your preferred method). Transfer the charred vegetables to a blender and puree until smooth.

4. When the beef tongue is tender, remove it from pan and reserve 2 cups of the cooking liquid. Remove the outer connective membrane from the tongue while it is still warm and then slice the tongue into thin slices or cubes.

5. Place the olive oil in a large skillet and warm over high heat. Add the pureed salsa, season it with salt, and cook for 3 minutes.

6. Stir in the tongue and cook for 5 minutes. Serve with tortillas, cilantro, and radishes.

INGREDIENTS:

3-4	LBS. OX OR BEEF TONGUE
	SALT, TO TASTE
1	WHITE ONION
6	GARLIC CLOVES, CHOPPED
1	CINNAMON STICK
6	WHOLE CLOVES
5	LARGE TOMATOES
4	JALAPEÑO CHILE PEPPERS
1	TABLESPOON EXTRA-VIRGIN OLIVE OIL
	CORN TORTILLAS (SEE PAGE 352), WARM, FOR SERVING
1	BUNCH OF FRESH CILANTRO, CHOPPED, FOR SERVING
1	BUNCH OF RADISHES, TRIMMED AND SLICED THIN, FOR SERVING

CARNE ASADA

YIELD: 4 SERVINGS / **ACTIVE TIME:** 30 MINUTES / **TOTAL TIME:** 3 HOURS

A marinade capable of doing all the heavy lifting. The grill is also an option for cooking the steak, but a cast-iron skillet produces the best results.

1. Place all of the ingredients, except for the steak and the tortillas, in a baking dish or a large resealable plastic bag and stir to combine. Add the steak, place it in the refrigerator, and let marinate for at least 2 hours. If time allows, marinate the steak overnight.

2. Approximately 30 minutes before you are going to cook the steak, remove it from the marinade, pat it dry, and let it come to room temperature.

3. Place a large cast-iron skillet over high heat and add enough oil to coat the bottom. When the oil starts to shimmer, add the steak and cook on each side for 4 minutes for medium-rare.

4. Remove the steak from the pan and let rest for 5 minutes before chopping it into cubes, making sure to cut against the grain. Serve with the tortillas and your favorite taco fixings.

INGREDIENTS:

1   JALAPEÑO CHILE PEPPER, STEMMED, SEEDED, AND MINCED

3   GARLIC CLOVES, MINCED

½   CUP FINELY CHOPPED FRESH CILANTRO

¼   CUP EXTRA-VIRGIN OLIVE OIL, PLUS MORE AS NEEDED

    JUICE OF 1 SMALL ORANGE

2   TABLESPOONS APPLE CIDER VINEGAR

2   TEASPOONS CAYENNE PEPPER

1   TEASPOON ANCHO CHILE POWDER

1   TEASPOON GARLIC POWDER

1   TEASPOON PAPRIKA

1   TEASPOON KOSHER SALT

1   TEASPOON CUMIN

1   TEASPOON DRIED OREGANO

¼   TEASPOON BLACK PEPPER

2   LBS. SKIRT STEAK, TRIMMED

    CORN TORTILLAS (SEE PAGE 352), WARM, FOR SERVING

TOSTADAS DE CUERITOS

YIELD: 6 SERVINGS / **ACTIVE TIME:** 15 MINUTES / **TOTAL TIME:** 1 HOUR AND 15 MINUTES

Tostadas are a great way to use fried and crispy tortillas as a vehicle for any topping of your choice. This variation uses pork skin, which when pickled can be a great appetizer or snack. As this recipe can be served at room temperature, it's a great way to stay cool in the warmer months.

1. Bring a large pot of water to a boil. Add the salt, chiles, vinegar, onion, and oregano, reduce the heat so that the liquid simmers, and add the pork skin. Cook for 30 minutes.

2. Turn off the heat and let the pork skin sit the pickling liquid for another 30 minutes.

3. The pork skin will have expanded and absorbed some of the liquid. Transfer the skin and remaining pickling liquid to a sterilized mason jar and store in the refrigerator for up to 2 weeks.

4. Add oil to a Dutch oven until it is about 1 inch deep and warm it to 350°F. Add the tortillas, taking care not to crowd the pot, and fry until crispy, about 2 minutes. Transfer the tostadas to a paper towel–lined plate to cool.

5. To assemble the tostadas, spread some of the beans on the tostadas and top with the pickled pork skin, Escabeche, lettuce, and cotija cheese.

INGREDIENTS:

- 2 TABLESPOONS KOSHER SALT
- 3 DRIED CHILES DE ARBOL
- 1 CUP WHITE VINEGAR
- ½ WHITE ONION, SLICED THIN
- 1 TEASPOON DRIED MEXICAN OREGANO
- 1 LB. SKIN FROM PORK BELLY, CUT INTO ¼-INCH-WIDE STRIPS
- CANOLA OIL, AS NEEDED
- CORN TORTILLAS (SEE PAGE 352)
- 1 CUP FRIJOLES NEGROS REFRITOS (SEE PAGE 254), WARM
- 1 CUP ESCABECHE (SEE PAGE 518)
- ½ CUP SHREDDED LETTUCE
- 1 CUP COTIJA CHEESE (OPTIONAL)

CHICHARRON EN SALSA ROJA

YIELD: 6 SERVINGS / **ACTIVE TIME:** 25 MINUTES / **TOTAL TIME:** 1 HOUR AND 15 MINUTES

Chicharron, or pork rind, appears in many guises and can be used with any of the recipes in the Masa chapter. If you happen to live near a Mexican market, you can also make the sauce ahead of time and buy chicharron there, where it is likely fried daily.

1. Place a cooling rack in a rimmed baking sheet. Season the pork belly with the salt.

2. Place the lard in a Dutch oven (make sure it doesn't reach more than halfway up the sides of the pot) and warm over medium-high heat. Add the pork belly and cook until golden brown and crispy, about 1 hour.

3. Place the pork belly on the cooling rack and let it drain. When the pork is cool enough to handle, chop it into ½-inch cubes.

4. Fill a medium saucepan with water and bring it to a boil. Add the tomatoes, serrano peppers, and garlic and cook until tender, about 10 minutes. Drain, transfer the vegetables to a blender, and puree until smooth.

5. Return the puree to the saucepan, add the pork belly, and simmer for about 20 minutes, so that the chicharron absorbs some of the sauce. Serve with tortillas and beans.

INGREDIENTS:

1	LB. PORK BELLY, CUT INTO 1-INCH-WIDE AND 6-INCH-LONG STRIPS
1½	TABLESPOONS KOSHER SALT
4	CUPS LARD OR CANOLA OIL
4	LARGE TOMATOES
3	SERRANO CHILE PEPPERS
3	GARLIC CLOVES
	CORN TORTILLAS (SEE PAGE 352), WARM, FOR SERVING

BIRRIA DE CHIVO

YIELD: 8 SERVINGS / **ACTIVE TIME:** 4 HOURS AND 35 MINUTES / **TOTAL TIME:** 24 HOURS

One of the most beloved dishes from the state of Jalisco, birria is a stew traditionally made of mutton or beef. It relies on the method of slow cooking tough cuts of meat to achieve the tender and flavorful quality of the stew. The rich broth or "consomme" is the cooking liquid that is produced by the meat and chiles as they slowly cook, providing an amazing depth of flavor.

1. Cut the meat into 3-inch cubes and place them in a baking dish.

2. Place the guajillo peppers in a dry skillet and toast over medium heat until they darken and become fragrant and pliable. Submerge them in a bowl of boiling water and let them sit for 15 minutes.

3. Place the peppercorns and cinnamon stick in the skillet and toast until fragrant, about 1 minute. Combine with the oregano, allspice, and cumin and grind the mixture into a fine powder with a mortar and pestle or a spice grinder.

4. Season the meat with salt and the spice powder. Drain the guajillo peppers and place them in a blender along with the garlic and white vinegar. Puree until smooth and then rub the puree over the meat until it is coated. Marinate in the refrigerator overnight.

5. Remove the meat from the refrigerator an hour before you intend to cook.

6. Preheat the oven to 350°F. In a large Dutch oven, warm the olive oil over medium heat, add the onion, and cook until translucent, about 3 minutes.

7. Stir in the tomatoes, bay leaves, meat, marinade, and 1 cup of water and bring to a boil. Cover the pot, place it in the oven, and braise until the meat is very tender, about 3 hours.

8. Check the meat every hour to make sure it has enough liquid. You don't want to skim off any of the fat, as this will remove liquid from the pot and flavor from the finished broth.

9. Remove the meat from the pot and shred the pieces that haven't fallen apart. Stir the meat back into the liquid.

10. When serving birria, it is customary also serve a cup of the strained broth as an appetizer with warm tortillas. The stew can also be served with tortillas, cilantro, and pickled onions.

INGREDIENTS:

5	LBS. GOAT OR LAMB MEAT FROM THE LEG OR SHOULDER
10	GUAJILLO CHILE PEPPERS
1	TEASPOON BLACK PEPPERCORNS
½	CINNAMON STICK
1	TABLESPOON DRIED MEXICAN OREGANO
1	TEASPOON ALLSPICE
½	TEASPOON CUMIN
	SALT, TO TASTE
5	GARLIC CLOVES
2	TABLESPOONS WHITE VINEGAR
2	TABLESPOONS EXTRA-VIRGIN OLIVE OIL
1	ONION, FINELY DICED
3	LARGE TOMATOES, DICED
2	BAY LEAVES
	CORN TORTILLAS (SEE PAGE 352), WARM, FOR SERVING
1	BUNCH OF FRESH CILANTRO, CHOPPED, FOR SERVING
	PICKLED RED ONION (SEE PAGE 515), FOR SERVING

COSTILLITAS DE PUERCO EN CHILE ROJO

YIELD: 6 SERVINGS / **ACTIVE TIME:** 25 MINUTES / **TOTAL TIME:** 1 HOUR AND 25 MINUTES

This tender pork rib recipe leans considerably on a blend of chiles, and results in a simple and delicious dish that can be enjoyed as is, with tortillas, or any side you like.

1. Fill a large saucepan with water, season it generously with salt, add the ribs, onion, garlic, and bay leaves, and bring the water to a boil.

2. Reduce the heat to medium and cook until the ribs are tender but not falling apart, about 1 hour.

3. Place the chile peppers in a dry skillet and toast over medium heat until they darken and become fragrant and pliable. Submerge them in a bowl of hot water and let them sit for 20 minutes.

4. Place the cumin seeds in the dry skillet and toast until fragrant, about 1 minute. Transfer to a small dish.

5. Drain the chiles, place them in a blender, and add the thyme, toasted cumin, onion, garlic, and 2 cups of the cooking liquid. Puree until smooth, taste the puree, and season with salt.

6. When the pork is tender but still intact, remove the ribs and drain them on paper towels.

7. Place the lard in a deep skillet and warm over medium heat. Add the ribs and sear, turning occasionally, until browned all over.

8. Drain any excess fat from the pan, strain the puree over the ribs, and cook over low heat for 10 minutes. Serve with warm tortillas or rice and beans.

INGREDIENTS:

	SALT, TO TASTE
4	LBS. PORK RIBS, CUT INTO 3-INCH-WIDE PIECES
1	WHITE ONION
4	GARLIC CLOVES
2	BAY LEAVES
4	GUAJILLO CHILE PEPPERS, STEMMED AND SEEDED
2	PASILLA CHILE PEPPERS, STEMMED AND SEEDED
4	CHIPOTLE MORTIA CHILE PEPPERS, STEMMED AND SEEDED
2	TABLESPOONS CUMIN SEEDS
1	TABLESPOON DRIED THYME
½	CUP LARD OR EXTRA-VIRGIN OLIVE OIL
	CORN TORTILLAS (SEE PAGE 352), WARM, FOR SERVING (OPTIONAL)
	WHITE RICE, COOKED, FOR SERVING (OPTIONAL)
	FRIJOLES DE LA OLLA (SEE PAGE 257), FOR SERVING (OPTIONAL)

PIERNA DE PUERCO

YIELD: 6 SERVINGS / **ACTIVE TIME:** 30 MINUTES / **TOTAL TIME:** 2 HOURS AND 30 MINUTES

Ahomestyle recipe that is a delicious way to take advantage of the slow cooker.

1. Place the chiles in a bowl of hot water and let them sit for 20 minutes.

2. Place the black peppercorns, coriander, and cumin in a dry skillet and toast until fragrant, shaking the pan frequently.

3. Drain the chiles and place them in a blender along with the toasted spices, cinnamon, cloves, garlic, vinegar, and mezcal. Puree until smooth and season the puree generously with salt.

4. Place the pork shoulder in a large baking dish, rub the puree over it, and let it marinate for 1 hour.

5. Place the pork shoulder and marinade in a large saucepan, add water until the pork is covered, and add the onion and bay leaves. Bring the water to a boil, reduce the heat so that the water simmers, and cook the pork until it is fork-tender, about 1 hour.

6. Stir in the flour and cook until the sauce has thickened slightly. Taste, adjust the seasoning as needed, and serve with white rice.

INGREDIENTS:

2	ANCHO CHILE PEPPERS, STEMMED AND SEEDED
1	DRIED CASCABEL CHILE PEPPER, STEMMED AND SEEDED
1	CHIPOTLE MORITA CHILE PEPPER, STEMMED AND SEEDED
1	GUAJILLO CHILE PEPPER, STEMMED AND SEEDED
½	TEASPOON BLACK PEPPERCORNS
1½	TEASPOONS CORIANDER SEEDS
1	TEASPOON CUMIN SEEDS
½	TEASPOON CINNAMON
½	TEASPOON GROUND CLOVES
8	GARLIC CLOVES
½	CUP WHITE VINEGAR
1	CUP MEZCAL
	SALT, TO TASTE
8	LBS. PORK SHOULDER
½	WHITE ONION, CHOPPED
4	BAY LEAVES
1	TABLESPOON ALL-PURPOSE FLOUR
	WHITE RICE, COOKED, FOR SERVING

PICADILLO DE RES

YIELD: 4 SERVINGS / **ACTIVE TIME:** 10 MINUTES / **TOTAL TIME:** 35 MINUTES

Picadillo is a great base that can be used as a filling for empanadas, tostadas, sopes, and gorditas, or enjoyed as this recipe suggests.

1. Place the olive oil in a large skillet and warm it over medium heat. Add the ground beef, season it with salt, and cook, breaking the meat up with a fork, until browned, about 6 minutes.

2. Stir in the cumin, oregano, and chili powder, cook for 1 minute, and then stir in the tomato paste, onion, and peppers. Cook until the onion is tender, about 5 minutes.

3. Add the bay leaves, potatoes, carrots, and tomatoes and cook until the potatoes are tender and the flavors have developed to your liking, about 20 minutes. If using peas in the dish, add them during the last 5 minutes of cooking the potatoes.

4. Serve with cilantro and sour cream.

INGREDIENTS:

2   TABLESPOONS EXTRA-VIRGIN OLIVE OIL

2   LBS. GROUND BEEF

    SALT, TO TASTE

1   TEASPOON CUMIN

1½ TEASPOONS DRIED MEXICAN OREGANO

1½ TEASPOONS CHILI POWDER

1   TABLESPOON TOMATO PASTE

1   ONION, FINELY DICED

2   SERRANO CHILE PEPPERS, STEMMED, SEEDED, AND CHOPPED

2   BAY LEAVES

1   LB. YUKON GOLD POTATOES, PEELED AND DICED

8   OZ. CARROTS, PEELED AND FINELY DICED

3   LARGE TOMATOES, FINELY DICED

½   CUP PEAS (OPTIONAL)

½   BUNCH OF FRESH CILANTRO, CHOPPED, FOR SERVING

1   CUP SOUR CREAM, FOR SERVING

PUERCO EN PIPIAN VERDE

Pipian verde is a complex and herbaceous sauce that features a nice blend of greens, chiles, and toasty goodness from the nuts.

1. Place the olive oil in a large saucepan and warm over medium heat. Add the peanuts and almonds and fry until fragrant and browned, about 4 minutes. Place the pumpkin seeds in the skillet and cook, stirring frequently to make sure that they don't burn, until golden brown. Place the nuts and pumpkin seeds in the blender. Set the pan aside and leave the olive oil in it.

2. Place the pork in a saucepan with three-quarters of the white onion and 3 garlic cloves. Cover with water, bring to a boil, and then reduce the heat so that it simmers gently. After 45 minutes, season generously with salt. Cook the pork until tender, about 1 hour.

3. Add the tomatillos, chile peppers, spinach, cilantro, lettuce, and epazote to the blender gradually and puree until smooth. When all of these have been incorporated, add the green onions, cumin seeds, sesame seeds, and remaining onion and garlic and puree until incorporated. If necessary, add some of the pork cooking liquid to the puree to get the desired consistency.

4. Warm the oil in the large saucepan and pour in the sauce. Season with salt, bring the sauce to a boil, and cook for 5 minutes. Reduce the heat so that the sauce simmers gently and cook for another 30 minutes.

5. Add the pork to the sauce and cook for 5 minutes. Serve with warm tortillas and garnish with additional sesame seeds.

INGREDIENTS:

¼ CUP EXTRA-VIRGIN OLIVE OIL

½ CUP RAW PEANUTS

½ CUP RAW ALMONDS

1 LB. GREEN PUMPKIN SEEDS

2 LBS. PORK SHOULDER, CUT INTO 3-INCH CUBES

1 WHITE ONION, QUARTERED

6 GARLIC CLOVES

SALT, TO TASTE

1 LB. TOMATILLOS, HUSKED, RINSED, AND QUARTERED

3 SERRANO CHILE PEPPERS, STEMMED, SEEDED, AND FINELY DICED

1 JALAPEÑO CHILE PEPPER, STEMMED, SEEDED, AND FINELY DICED

1 PASILLA CHILE PEPPER, STEMMED, SEEDED, AND CHOPPED

1 CUP PACKED FRESH SPINACH

½ BUNCH OF FRESH CILANTRO, CHOPPED

1 CUP CHOPPED ROMAINE LETTUCE

3 SPRIGS OF FRESH EPAZOTE

1 BUNCH OF GREEN ONIONS, TRIMMED AND CHOPPED

1 TABLESPOON CUMIN SEEDS

2 TABLESPOONS SESAME SEEDS, PLUS MORE FOR GARNISH

CORN TORTILLAS (SEE PAGE 352), WARM, FOR SERVING

LUIS'S CARNITAS

YIELD: 6 SERVINGS / **ACTIVE TIME:** 15 MINUTES / **TOTAL TIME:** 2 HOURS AND 15 MINUTES

Carnitas, or "little meats," is pork, usually from the shoulder or leg, that is braised in lard until the meat is tender and falling apart. This classic recipe has a blend of warm spices and sweetness that is excellent with tortillas, salsa verde, and pickled onion.

1. Season the pork with salt, pepper, and the cumin.

2. Place the lard in a Dutch oven and warm it over medium-high heat. Add the pork, onion, garlic, orange juice, and cinnamon stick and cook until the pork is very tender and well browned, about 1½ hours. Adjust the heat as necessary to ensure it doesn't brown too quickly.

3. Preheat the oven to 375°F and place a cooling rack in a rimmed baking sheet. When the pork is very tender, add the cola and cook for about 10 minutes.

4. Remove the pork from the pot and place it on the cooling rack. Place in the oven and roast until the outside is crispy, 10 to 20 minutes.

5. Serve with salsa and tortillas and garnish with pickled onion and cilantro.

INGREDIENTS:

4   LBS. PORK SHOULDER OR PORK BELLY, CUT INTO 3-INCH CUBES

      SALT AND PEPPER, TO TASTE

1   TABLESPOON CUMIN

4   CUPS LARD

1   ONION, QUARTERED

1   HEAD OF GARLIC, HALVED

      JUICE OF 2 ORANGES

1   CINNAMON STICK

1   (12 OZ.) CAN OF COLA

      SALSA VERDE TATEMADA (SEE PAGE 480), FOR SERVING

      CORN TORTILLAS (SEE PAGE 352), WARM, FOR SERVING

      PICKLED RED ONION (SEE PAGE 515), FOR GARNISH

      FRESH CILANTRO, CHOPPED, FOR GARNISH

GORDITAS DE PICADILLO DE RES

YIELD: 4 SERVINGS / **ACTIVE TIME:** 25 MINUTES / **TOTAL TIME:** 45 MINUTES

Gorditas are a thick tortilla—the word translates as "chubby"—that puffs up when cooked, either fried in oil or on a comal. They can be stuffed with nearly anything, but the picadillo is a great default option.

1. Place the cabbage in a bowl of ice water.

2. Working with 3 ounces of prepared masa at a time, form it into a ball with your hands, place it on a work surface, and press down until it is even. Place the pressed masa in a dry comal or cast-iron skillet and cook until lightly browned all over, about 3 minutes per side.

3. Add 1 tablespoon of the oil to a skillet and warm it over medium heat. Add the disks of masa one at a time and fry until golden brown on both sides, about 6 minutes. Transfer to a paper towel–lined plate and repeat with the remaining oil and disks of masa.

4. Drain the cabbage and pat it dry.

5. Cut a small slit in the edge of each gordita, taking care not to cut all of the way through. Stuff the gordita with the picadillo, garnish with the cabbage, cotija cheese, and sour cream, and serve with the salsa verde and pickled onion.

INGREDIENTS:

4 OZ. CABBAGE, SHREDDED

12 OZ. PREPARED MASA (SEE PAGE 352)

1 CUP EXTRA-VIRGIN OLIVE OIL

PICADILLO DE RES (SEE PAGE 73), WARMED

4 OZ. COTIJA CHEESE

½ CUP SOUR CREAM

SALSA CRUDA VERDE (SEE PAGE 525), FOR SERVING

PICKLED RED ONION (SEE PAGE 515), FOR SERVING

EMPANADAS DE PICADILLO

YIELD: 4 SERVINGS / **ACTIVE TIME:** 35 MINUTES / **TOTAL TIME:** 1 HOUR AND 40 MINUTES

These deep-fried pockets of masa be can filled with an array of ingredients. This preparation features picadillo, and is perfect as an appetizer, or as a quick and easy lunch.

1. Wet your hands. Working with 1 oz. of masa at a time, gently form it into a ball. Place the masa in a tortilla press lined with two sheets of plastic (two squares of 1-gallon plastic bag and a rolling pin can also be used).

2. Press the masa gently to form ⅛-inch-thick round.

3. Place 2 oz. of picadillo in the center of the round and use one sheet of plastic to fold the round over the picadillo, forming a half-moon. Press down on the edge to crimp and seal the empanada.

4. Repeat Steps 1–3 with the remaining masa and picadillo.

5. Place the olive oil in a deep skillet and warm over low heat until it is 310°F. Place one empanada in the oil at a time and fry until golden brown, about 5 minutes, adjusting the heat to make sure the temperature of the oil does not get too high. Drain the cooked empanadas on a paper towel–lined plate.

6. Serve with cabbage, cilantro, pickled onion, your preferred salsas, sour cream, and cotija cheese.

INGREDIENTS:

3 CUPS PREPARED MASA (SEE PAGE 352)

1 LB. PICADILLO DE RES (SEE PAGE 73)

8 OZ. COTIJA CHEESE, PLUS MORE FOR SERVING

2 CUPS EXTRA-VIRGIN OLIVE OIL

8 OZ. CABBAGE, FINELY SHREDDED, FOR SERVING

½ BUNCH OF FRESH CILANTRO, FOR SERVING

PICKLED RED ONION (SEE PAGE 515), FOR SERVING

SALSA, FOR SERVING

½ CUP SOUR CREAM, FOR SERVING

RABO DE RES EN SALSA ROJA

YIELD: 4 SERVINGS / **ACTIVE TIME:** 20 MINUTES / **TOTAL TIME:** 1 HOUR AND 20 MINUTES

This oxtail recipe utilizes low and slow cooking to achieve a wonderfully tender beef and a spicy and rich sauce.

1. Place the chiles in a bowl of hot water and soak them for 20 minutes.

2. Place water in a medium saucepan and bring it to a boil. Add the tomatoes and boil until tender, about 10 minutes. Drain and place them in a blender. Drain the chiles and add them to the blender along with the garlic and onion. Puree until smooth and set aside.

3. Place the olive oil in a Dutch oven and warm it over medium heat. Add the oxtail, season with salt and pepper, and sear until browned all over. Remove from the pot and set aside.

4. Strain the puree into the pot and warm over low heat for 5 minutes.

5. Return the oxtail to the pot, add 4 cups of water along with the marjoram, ginger, and bay leaves, and simmer over low heat until the oxtail is very tender, about 1½ hours.

6. Serve with rice or warm tortillas.

INGREDIENTS:

2 DRIED PUYA CHILE PEPPERS

6 LARGE TOMATOES

3 GARLIC CLOVES

¼ WHITE ONION

2 TABLESPOONS EXTRA-VIRGIN OLIVE OIL

2 LBS. OXTAIL

   SALT AND PEPPER, TO TASTE

1 TEASPOON DRIED MARJORAM

1 TABLESPOON GRATED FRESH GINGER

2 BAY LEAVES

   CORN TORTILLAS (SEE PAGE 352), WARM, FOR SERVING (OPTIONAL)

   WHITE RICE, COOKED, FOR SERVING (OPTIONAL)

CHILES EN NOGADA

YIELD: 4 SERVINGS / **ACTIVE TIME:** 45 MINUTES / **TOTAL TIME:** 1 HOUR AND 15 MINUTES

An iconic dish from Mexico City that features a stuffed poblano, a sweet and creamy sauce, and pomegranate seeds, managing to fly the colors of the Mexican flag and echo the country's rich history all at once.

1. If you do not have a gas stove, preheat a grill or an oven to 400°F. Roast the poblanos over an open flame, on the grill, or in the oven until the skin is blackened and blistered all over, turning occasionally. Place the poblanos in a heatproof bowl, cover with plastic wrap, and let sit for 10 minutes.

2. Remove the charred skins from the poblanos. Make a small slit in the peppers and remove the seeds.

3. Place the nuts, Queso Fresco, crema, and sugar in a blender and puree until smooth. If the sauce seems too thick, incorporate more crema until the sauce is the desired texture. Season the sauce with salt and set it aside.

4. Stuff the peppers with the picadillo.

5. To serve, spoon the sauce over the peppers and garnish with the pomegranate seeds and cilantro.

INGREDIENTS:

4   POBLANO CHILE PEPPERS

1   CUP ALMONDS OR WALNUTS

¼   CUP QUESO FRESCO (SEE PAGE 522)

2   CUPS CREMA OR SOUR CREAM, PLUS MORE AS NEEDED

½   TABLESPOON SUGAR

   SALT, TO TASTE

3   CUPS PICADILLO DE RES (SEE PAGE 73), AT ROOM TEMPERATURE

¼   CUP POMEGRANATE SEEDS, FOR GARNISH

   FRESH CILANTRO, CHOPPED, FOR GARNISH

CHILORIO

YIELD: 6 SERVINGS / **ACTIVE TIME:** 15 MINUTES / **TOTAL TIME:** 1 HOUR AND 35 MINUTES

A spicy and flavorful dish of tender pulled pork. This is perfect for serving family style with warm tortillas or Arroz a la Mexicana.

1. Season the pork with salt and let it sit at room temperature.

2. Place the olive oil in a Dutch oven and warm it over medium heat. Add the chiles and fry until fragrant.

3. Transfer the chiles to a blender, add the remaining ingredients, except for the tortillas or rice, and puree until smooth.

4. Working with one piece of pork at a time, place it in the Dutch oven and sear until browned on all sides.

5. Pour the puree over the pork. If the pork is not covered, add water until it is.

6. Cover the Dutch oven and cook the pork over low heat until tender and falling apart, about 2 hours.

7. Serve with the sauce and warm tortillas or rice.

INGREDIENTS:

- 4   **LBS. BONELESS PORK SHOULDER, CUT INTO 4 PIECES**
-     **SALT, TO TASTE**
- 2   **TABLESPOONS EXTRA-VIRGIN OLIVE OIL**
- 4   **GUAJILLO CHILE PEPPERS, STEMMED AND SEEDED**
- 2   **ANCHO CHILE PEPPERS, STEMMED AND SEEDED**
- 6   **GARLIC CLOVES**
- ¼   **WHITE ONION**
- 2   **CUPS ORANGE JUICE**
- ¼   **CUP WHITE VINEGAR**
- 1   **TABLESPOON DRIED MEXICAN OREGANO**
- ½   **TABLESPOON CUMIN**
- ½   **TABLESPOON BLACK PEPPER**
-     **CORN TORTILLAS (SEE PAGE 352), WARM, FOR SERVING (OPTIONAL)**
-     **ARROZ A LA MEXICANA (SEE PAGE 529), FOR SERVING (OPTIONAL)**

CARNE EN SU JUGO

YIELD: 4 SERVINGS / **ACTIVE TIME:** 15 MINUTES / **TOTAL TIME:** 50 MINUTES

This recipe from Jalisco utilizes the simple techniques the state is known for, taking a humble cut of meat and patiently drawing out the tenderness and flavor locked deep within.

1. In a small saucepan, add water, the tomatillos, garlic, and serrano chiles. Bring to a boil and cook until tender, about 10 minutes. Drain, transfer the vegetables to a blender, and puree until smooth. Season the puree with salt and set it aside.

2. Place the olive oil in a Dutch oven and warm it over medium-low heat. Add the bacon and cook until golden brown, about 10 minutes. Remove the bacon from the pot and set aside.

3. Drain excess fat from the pot, raise the heat to high, and add the beef, searing until browned all over. Remove the beef from the pot and set it aside.

4. Add the onion and cook until it starts to soften, about 5 minutes. Return the beef and the bacon to the pot, pour the puree over everything, and, if necessary, add water until the meat is covered.

5. Cook over low heat until the meat is very tender, about 40 minutes.

6. Stir in the cilantro and the pinto beans and cook until warmed through. Taste, adjust the seasoning as necessary, and serve with warm tortillas and lime wedges.

INGREDIENTS:

3	TOMATILLOS, HUSKED AND RINSED
4	GARLIC CLOVES
2	SERRANO CHILE PEPPERS, STEMMED, SEEDED, AND MINCED
	SALT, TO TASTE
¼	CUP EXTRA-VIRGIN OLIVE OIL
1	LB. BACON, CHOPPED
4	LBS. BEEF CHUCK, CUT INTO 2- TO 3-INCH-LONG STRIPS
1	ONION, FINELY DICED
1	BUNCH OF FRESH CILANTRO, CHOPPED
1	LB. COOKED OR CANNED PINTO BEANS
	CORN TORTILLAS (SEE PAGE 352), WARM, FOR SERVING
	LIME WEDGES, FOR SERVING

BEEF MACHACA WITH POTATOES & EGGS

YIELD: 4 SERVINGS / **ACTIVE TIME:** 15 MINUTES / **TOTAL TIME:** 45 MINUTES

Machaca is dried, shredded meat, and can be found at Latin markets. You may also use shredded beef or pork in this recipe if machaca proves tough to find.

1. Place the olive oil in a large saucepan and warm over medium heat. Add the onion and cook until translucent, about 3 minutes, stirring frequently. Add the machaca, potatoes, and tomatoes and 1 cup of water and cook until the machaca is rehydrated and the potatoes are tender, about 20 minutes.

2. Place the jalapeños in a dry skillet and cook over medium heat until the skins are charred and the chiles are aromatic, about 10 minutes, turning the peppers as needed. Remove from the pan and let cool slightly. Slice the chiles thin and stir them into the machaca mixture.

3. When the potatoes are tender, add the beaten eggs to the pan, season with salt, and cook until the eggs are set, about 4 minutes, stirring occasionally.

4. Serve with the Flour Tortillas and Frijoles de la Olla.

INGREDIENTS:

2 TABLESPOONS EXTRA-VIRGIN OLIVE OIL

1 TABLESPOON MINCED WHITE ONION

1 LB. BEEF MACHACA

8 OZ. RUSSET POTATOES, PEELED AND FINELY DICED

2 LARGE TOMATOES, FINELY DICED

2 JALAPEÑO CHILE PEPPERS, CHARRED

4 LARGE EGGS, BEATEN

   SALT, TO TASTE

4 FLOUR TORTILLAS (SEE PAGE 444), FOR SERVING

   FRIJOLES DE LA OLLA (SEE PAGE 257), FOR SERVING

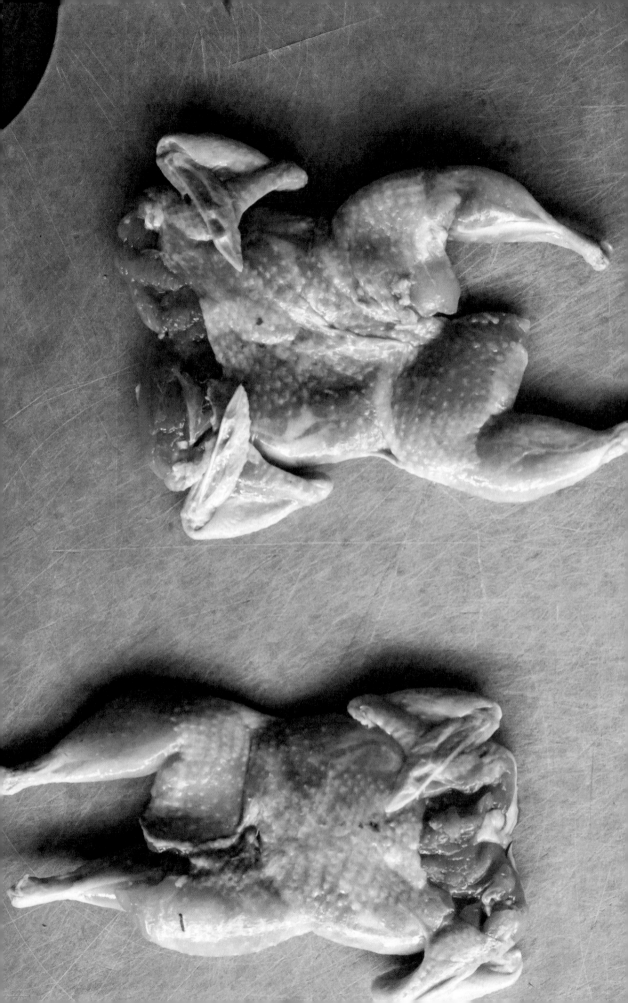

POULTRY

$\mathcal{M}$exico's reliance on sauces and bold flavors means that its cuisine is well set up to partner beautifully with the mild and malleable flavor of poultry, transforming its blank canvas into complex and endlessly intriguing works of art.

As you might expect, this concord is also capable of producing the occasional masterpiece, such as the decadent Muscovy Duck Breast Mole (see page 98) and the fiery Tinga de Pollo (see page 114). And for those who want poultry in its ultimate form, fried chicken, there is an offering featuring a masa-based batter on page 122 that may shift your approach for good.

MUSCOVY DUCK BREAST MOLE

YIELD: 4 SERVINGS / **ACTIVE TIME:** 1 HOUR / **TOTAL TIME:** 2 HOURS

This sweet and savory mole is also wonderful over chicken or a hearty vegetable like mushrooms.

1. Place the sesame seeds in a dry skillet and toast over medium heat until lightly browned, about 2 minutes, shaking the pan occasionally. Remove the sesame seeds from the pan and place them in a blender.

2. Add the cloves, cinnamon stick, anise seeds, and coriander seeds to the skillet and toast until fragrant, shaking the pan so that they do not burn. Transfer to the blender.

3. Place half of the lard in a skillet and warm over medium heat. Add the chiles and fry until fragrant and pliable. Transfer to a bowl of hot water and soak for 20 minutes.

4. Place the raisins, almonds, pumpkin seeds, and tortillas in the skillet and sauté until the seeds turn golden brown, about 3 minutes. Transfer the contents of the skillet to the blender, add the chiles and half of the stock, and puree until smooth.

5. Place the remaining lard in a stockpot and warm over medium heat. Add the puree, cook for 3 minutes, and then stir in the remaining stock and the chocolate. Reduce the heat and simmer for 30 minutes, stirring frequently.

6. Season the duck breast with salt and pepper.

7. Place the canola oil in a medium skillet and warm it over high heat. Place the duck breast in the pan, skin side down, and sear for 2 to 3 minutes. Turn the duck breast over and sear for 2 to 3 minutes. Turn the duck breast over and sear until the skin is crispy and golden brown, while basting the duck with the fat that has rendered.

8. Remove the duck from the pan and let it rest for 5 minutes.

9. To serve, slice the duck breast into medallions. Place the mole in the center of the plate, set the duck on top, and garnish with cilantro.

INGREDIENTS:

- ½ CUP SESAME SEEDS, TOASTED, PLUS MORE FOR GARNISH
- 5 WHOLE CLOVES
- 1 CINNAMON STICK
- ½ TEASPOON ANISE SEEDS
- ¼ TEASPOON CORIANDER SEEDS
- 6 TABLESPOONS LARD
- 6 GUAJILLO CHILE PEPPERS, STEMMED AND SEEDED
- 4 ANCHO CHILE PEPPERS, STEMMED AND SEEDED
- ¼ CUP RAISINS
- ¼ CUP BLANCHED ALMONDS
- ¼ CUP PUMPKIN SEEDS
- 2 CORN TORTILLAS (SEE PAGE 352), TORN INTO PIECES
- 4 CUPS CHICKEN OR VEGETABLE STOCK (SEE PAGE 341 OR 346)
- 1 TABLET OF ABUELITA CHOCOLATE
- 1 BONELESS, SKIN-ON DUCK BREAST
-   SALT AND PEPPER, TO TASTE
- 2 TABLESPOONS CANOLA OIL
-   FRESH CILANTRO, CHOPPED, FOR GARNISH

CODORNIZ A LA PARILLA

YIELD: 4 SERVINGS / ACTIVE TIME: 30 MINUTES / TOTAL TIME: 24 HOURS

Quail is a very common bird to eat in the Yucatan. It does not have to be cooked to an interior temperature of 165°F, despite what many recommend. A temperature of about 140°F ensures that it is still juicy and slightly pink in the center. Quail also makes for a delicious milanesa (see page 131).

1. Place the water and salt in a saucepan and warm over low heat, stirring until the salt has dissolved. Remove and let the brine cool completely. Place the quail in the brine for 12 to 24 hours.

2. Remove the quail from the brine and let them air-dry in the refrigerator for 1 to 2 hours.

3. Place the allspice berries, cinnamon stick, coriander seeds, cumin seeds, cloves, peppercorns, and bay leaves in a dry skillet and toast until fragrant, shaking the pan so that they do not burn. Grind into a fine powder with a mortar and pestle.

4. Place the toasted spice powder, oregano, marjoram, ancho chile powder, orange juice, and lime juice in a blender and puree until the mixture is a smooth paste. Rub the paste over the quail and marinate for at least 30 minutes.

5. Preheat a gas or charcoal grill to medium-high heat (about 450°F). Clean the grates and brush them with the olive oil.

6. Place the quail on the grill, breast side down, and cook until crispy and caramelized, 2 to 3 minutes. Turn them over and cook until the interior is about 140°F, 1 to 2 minutes. Remove the quail from heat and let them rest for 10 minutes.

7. Serve the quail with lime wedges, tortillas, and salsa quemada.

INGREDIENTS:

- 8   CUPS FILTERED WATER
- ¼   CUP KOSHER SALT, PLUS MORE TO TASTE
- 4   SEMI-BONELESS QUAIL
- 1   TABLESPOON ALLSPICE BERRIES
- 1   CINNAMON STICK
- 3   TABLESPOONS CORIANDER SEEDS
- 2   TABLESPOONS CUMIN SEEDS
- ½   TEASPOON WHOLE CLOVES
- 2   TABLESPOONS BLACK PEPPERCORNS
- 1½   TEASPOONS WHITE PEPPERCORNS
- 3   BAY LEAVES
- 1   TEASPOON DRIED MEXICAN OREGANO
- 1   TEASPOON DRIED MARJORAM
- 1   TABLESPOON ANCHO CHILE POWDER
- 3½   TABLESPOONS ORANGE JUICE
- 3½   TABLESPOONS FRESH LIME JUICE
- 2   TABLESPOONS EXTRA-VIRGIN OLIVE OIL
-    LIME WEDGES, FOR SERVING
-    CORN TORTILLAS (SEE PAGE 352), WARM, FOR SERVING
-    SALSA QUEMADA, FOR SERVING

CHICKEN EN SALSA CREMOSA
DE CHAMPIÑONES

YIELD: 4 SERVINGS / **ACTIVE TIME:** 10 MINUTES / **TOTAL TIME:** 40 MINUTES

This recipe is a classic way of preparing poultry for special occasions, like quinceañeras and holidays.

1. Place the olive oil in a skillet and warm over medium-high heat.

2. Season the chicken with salt and pepper, place it in the pan, and sear the chicken on both sides for about 1 minute per side.

3. Add the mushrooms and cook for about 30 seconds. Add the shallot and garlic and cook for another 30 seconds, stirring frequently.

4. Deglaze the pan with the white wine and cook until the liquid has reduced by half. Stir in the heavy cream, Oaxaca cheese, and cumin and cook until chicken is cooked through, about 6 minutes.

5. To serve, spoon the sauce over the chicken and vegetables and garnish with cilantro.

INGREDIENTS:

2 TABLESPOONS EXTRA-VIRGIN OLIVE OIL

1 LB. BONELESS, SKINLESS CHICKEN BREASTS

SALT AND PEPPER, TO TASTE

6 BUTTON MUSHROOMS, QUARTERED

1 SHALLOT, CHOPPED

1 GARLIC CLOVE, SLICED

¼ CUP WHITE WINE

½ CUP HEAVY CREAM

¼ CUP SHREDDED OAXACA CHEESE

1 TEASPOON CUMIN

FRESH CILANTRO, CHOPPED, FOR GARNISH

CHICKEN CHORIZO

YIELD: 4 SERVINGS / ACTIVE TIME: 45 MINUTES / TOTAL TIME: 24 HOURS

Chorizo is traditionally prepared with pork—this version provides a leaner option that sacrifices nothing in terms of flavor.

1. Place the chiles in a heatproof bowl, pour boiling water over them, and let them sit for 30 minutes. Drain and let cool. When cool enough to handle, remove the stems, seeds, and skins from the peppers.

2. Grind the chicken thighs in a meat grinder or food processor. Place the ground meat in a large mixing bowl, add the chiles, Recado Rojo, garlic, thyme, oregano, cumin, paprika, cayenne, ground cloves, onion powder, salt, and pepper and stir to combine. Cover with plastic wrap and let the mixture marinate in the refrigerator overnight.

3. Place the chorizo in a large skillet and cook over medium heat until cooked through, about 3 to 4 minutes, stirring occasionally. Add the tortilla chips and salsa verde and cook for another 2 minutes. Transfer the mixture to a serving bowl and tent it with aluminum foil.

4. Melt the butter in a separate skillet, add the eggs, and cook to desired level of doneness. Arrange the eggs over the chorizo-and-tortilla chip mixture and serve with the queso enchilada, pickled onion, avocado, chopped cilantro, lime wedges, and crema.

INGREDIENTS:

- 2 OZ. GUAJILLO CHILE PEPPERS
- 2 OZ. PASILLA CHILE PEPPERS
- 2 SKIN-ON, BONELESS CHICKEN THIGHS
- 1 TABLESPOON RECADO ROJO (SEE PAGE 497)
- 2 GARLIC CLOVES, CHOPPED
- 1 TABLESPOON DRIED THYME
- 1 TABLESPOON DRIED MEXICAN OREGANO
- 1 TABLESPOON CUMIN
- 2 TABLESPOONS SMOKED PAPRIKA
- 1 TEASPOON CAYENNE PEPPER
- 1 TEASPOON GROUND CLOVES
- 1 TEASPOON ONION POWDER
- SALT AND PEPPER, TO TASTE
- 2 CUPS TORTILLA CHIPS
- SALSA VERDE TATEMADA (SEE PAGE 480)
- 2 TABLESPOONS UNSALTED BUTTER
- 8 EGGS
- QUESO ENCHILADO, SHREDDED, FOR SERVING
- PICKLED RED ONION (SEE PAGE 515), FOR SERVING
- AVOCADO, SLICED, FOR SERVING
- FRESH CILANTRO, CHOPPED, FOR SERVING
- LIME WEDGES, FOR SERVING
- CREMA OR SOUR CREAM, FOR SERVING

MIXIOTES DE POLLO

YIELD: 4 SERVINGS / **ACTIVE TIME:** 30 MINUTES / **TOTAL TIME:** 2 HOURS

The origin of this dish dates back to the reign of the Aztecs in central Mexico, where various cuts of meat were wrapped in plants and cooked over an open fire. While the mixiote leaves are difficult to source in the States, banana leaves and parchment paper are good substitutes.

1. Warm a cast-iron pan or comal over medium heat. Add the chiles and toast until pliable and fragrant, about 30 seconds. Place in hot water and soak for 20 to 30 minutes.

2. Add the allspice berries, cloves, bay leaves, and cinnamon stick to the skillet and toast until fragrant, shaking the pan so that they do not burn. Grind into a fine powder with a mortar and pestle.

3. Place the chiles, ground spices, garlic, vinegar, orange juice, and lime juice in a blender and puree until smooth.

4. Rub the puree over the chicken and marinate for at least 30 minutes. If time allows, marinate for up to 24 hours.

5. Place the chicken in the center of the mixiote leaves and cover with the onion, cactus, and hoja santa. Season the mixture with salt. Fold the mixiote leaves over the chicken and use kitchen twine to hold the packet closed.

6. Bring water to a boil in a saucepan. Place a steaming basket over the water and place the mixiote packet in it. Steam until the chicken is cooked through and very tender, about 1 hour. Make sure to keep an eye on the water level in the pan so that it does not completely evaporate.

7. Remove the packet from the steaming basket and let it rest for 10 minutes. Serve with tortillas, lime wedges, and the Salsa Borracha.

INGREDIENTS:

4	ANCHO CHILE PEPPERS, STEMMED AND SEEDED
4	GUAJILLO CHILE PEPPERS, STEMMED AND SEEDED
½	TEASPOON ALLSPICE BERRIES, TOASTED AND GROUND
½	TEASPOON WHOLE CLOVES, TOASTED AND GROUND
2	BAY LEAVES
1	CINNAMON STICK
10	GARLIC CLOVES
7	TABLESPOONS APPLE CIDER VINEGAR
7	TABLESPOONS ORANGE JUICE
7	TABLESPOONS FRESH LIME JUICE
3-4	LB. WHOLE CHICKEN, SEPARATED INTO PIECES
	MIXIOTE LEAVES, AS NEEDED
1	SMALL WHITE ONION, JULIENNED
3½	OZ. CACTUS, SPINES REMOVED, BLANCHED, AND CUT INTO STRIPS
2	FRESH HOJA SANTA LEAVES
	SALT, TO TASTE
	CORN TORTILLAS (SEE PAGE 352), WARM, FOR SERVING
	LIME WEDGES, FOR SERVING
	SALSA BORRACHA (SEE PAGE 508), FOR SERVING

PAVO EN ESCABECHE

YIELD: 8 SERVINGS / ACTIVE TIME: 1 HOUR / TOTAL TIME: 24 HOURS

This dish is a great alternative to roasted or fried turkey for Thanksgiving. The brightness of the spice here complements a wide variety of sides, and eats well as leftovers.

1. Place the allspice berries, cloves, peppercorns, and cinnamon stick in a dry skillet and toast until fragrant, shaking the pan so that they do not burn. Grind into a fine powder with a mortar and pestle.

2. Place the spice powder, oregano, marjoram, garlic cloves, and three-quarters of the white vinegar in a blender and puree until the mixture is a thick paste. Add the remaining vinegar as needed to get the desired consistency. Season with salt.

3. Coat the turkey with the recado blanco paste and marinate overnight. If time is a factor, marinate for at least 1 to 2 hours.

4. Preheat a charcoal or gas grill to medium-high heat (about 450°F). Season the turkey with salt and grill it on all sides until deeply charred but not cooked all the way through. Take care not to move the turkey too much on the grill so that the skin stays intact. Remove the turkey from the grill and set it aside.

5. Place the chiles on the grill and cook, turning occasionally, until blistered and black on both sides. Place in a heatproof mixing bowl, cover with plastic, and steam for 5 to 10 minutes. Peel the skin off of the chiles, cut them into strips, and set aside.

6. Place the turkey in a stockpot or a saucepan that is deep enough to allow it to be covered with water by 2 to 3 inches. Add the head of garlic, bay leaves, and ½ cup of the recado blanco. Cover with water and bring to a simmer. Cook until the turkey is cooked through and just beginning to fall apart.

7. Add the Escabeche to the stew and season it with salt. Simmer an additional 10 minutes.

8. Serve the turkey in large bowls either on or off the bone with good amounts of the Escabeche, lime wedges, and the strips of roasted chile.

INGREDIENTS:

½	TEASPOON ALLSPICE BERRIES
½	TEASPOON WHOLE CLOVES
3½	OZ. BLACK PEPPERCORNS
1	CINNAMON STICK
1	TEASPOON DRIED MEXICAN OREGANO
1	TEASPOON DRIED MARJORAM
8	GARLIC CLOVES
14	TABLESPOONS WHITE VINEGAR
	SALT, TO TASTE
7-8	LB. WHOLE TURKEY
4-5	XCATIC OR ANAHEIM CHILE PEPPERS
1	HEAD OF GARLIC, HALVED
3	BAY LEAVES
	ESCABECHE (SEE PAGE 518)

TINGA DE POLLO

YIELD: 6 SERVINGS / **ACTIVE TIME:** 20 MINUTES / **TOTAL TIME:** 1 HOUR AND 20 MINUTES

Although the dish is traditionally made with pork or beef, this version of tinga includes chicken. Also, the flavor-packed cooking liquid can be cooled down, strained, and kept in the refrigerator up to 1 week, or frozen up to a month to be used in another dish.

1. Place the chicken in a large pot and cover with cold water by at least an inch. Add the salt and bay leaves and bring the water to a simmer. Cook the chicken until the meat pulls away from the bone, about 40 minutes.

2. While the chicken is simmering, place the olive oil in a large skillet and warm over medium heat. Add the onion and garlic and cook, stirring frequently, until the onion is translucent, about 3 minutes. Reduce the heat to low and cook until the onion has softened.

3. Add the diced tomatoes and cook for another 5 minutes.

4. Shred the chicken and reserve 2 cups of the cooking liquid. Place the chiles in a bowl with 1 cup of the cooking liquid and let them sit until tender, about 20 minutes.

5. Chop the chiles, add them to the skillet along with the shredded chicken, and cook, stirring occasionally, until the flavor has developed to your liking, about 8 minutes. Add the remaining cooking liquid to the pan if it becomes too dry.

6. Season with salt and serve over tostadas or tortillas with pickled onion, and Queso Fresco.

INGREDIENTS:

2 BONE-IN, SKIN-ON CHICKEN LEGS

2 BONE-IN, SKIN-ON CHICKEN THIGHS

2 TABLESPOONS KOSHER SALT, PLUS MORE TO TASTE

2 BAY LEAVES

1 TABLESPOON EXTRA-VIRGIN OLIVE OIL

1 WHITE ONION, SLICED THIN

1 GARLIC CLOVE, SLICED THIN

3 LARGE TOMATOES, DICED

2 CHIPOTLE CHILE PEPPERS, STEMMED AND SEEDED

TOSTADAS, FOR SERVING (OPTIONAL)

CORN TORTILLAS (SEE PAGE 352), WARM, FOR SERVING (OPTIONAL)

PICKLED RED ONION (SEE PAGE 515), FOR SERVING

QUESO FRESCO (SEE PAGE 522), FOR SERVING

MOLE POBLANO

YIELD: 4 SERVINGS / **ACTIVE TIME:** 1 HOUR / **TOTAL TIME:** 3 HOURS

One of the most iconic dishes of Mexico, a pre-Hispanic recipe that is revered across the country and traditionally served to honor loved ones that have passed away during Day of the Dead celebrations. This version is Chef Luis Robles's grandmother's recipe, simplified slightly so that everyone can make it at home.

1. Place the chicken in a large stockpot, cover it with cold water, and add the white onion, garlic, and cinnamon sticks, along with a pinch of salt. Bring to a boil, lower the heat, and simmer the chicken until the meat pulls away from the bones, about 40 minutes.

2. Carefully remove the chicken and let it cool. When it is cool enough to handle, shred the chicken with a fork and set it aside. Keep the broth simmering while you work on the sauce. Remove the garlic cloves and peel them when cool enough to handle.

3. Place the lard in a large skillet and warm over medium heat. Add the chiles and fry until fragrant and pliable, about 2 minutes. Transfer them to a blender, place the sesame seeds, almonds, and bread in the pan and fry until just browned, about 2 minutes. Transfer the mixture to the blender.

4. Add the banana and chocolate to the blender. Add 1 cup of the broth and the garlic cloves and blend until the mixture is smooth.

5. Place the puree in a saucepan and warm it over medium-low heat. Taste, season with salt or sugar if necessary, and add the shredded chicken. Warm the chicken through, serve with tortillas and pickled onion, and garnish each portion with cilantro and additional sesame seeds.

INGREDIENTS:

3-4 LB. WHOLE CHICKEN

½ WHITE ONION

4 GARLIC CLOVES, UNPEELED

1-2 CINNAMON STICKS

SALT, TO TASTE

1 CUP LARD

4 DRIED CALIFORNIA OR GUAJILLO CHILE PEPPERS, STEMMED AND SEEDED

3 CHIPOTLE MECO CHILE PEPPERS, STEMMED AND SEEDED

3 PASILLA CHILE PEPPERS, STEMMED AND SEEDED

2 CHIPOTLE MORITA CHILE PEPPERS, STEMMED AND SEEDED

2 MULATO OR NEGRO CHILE PEPPERS, STEMMED AND SEEDED

½ CUP SESAME SEEDS, PLUS MORE FOR GARNISH

½ CUP WHOLE ALMONDS

3 SLICES OF BREAD

1 RIPE BANANA

4 OZ. MEXICAN OR DARK CHOCOLATE

SUGAR, TO TASTE

CORN TORTILLAS (SEE PAGE 352), WARM, FOR SERVING

PICKLED RED ONION (SEE PAGE 515), FOR SERVING

FRESH CILANTRO, CHOPPED, FOR GARNISH

MASA-BATTERED FRIED CHICKEN

YIELD: 4 SERVINGS / **ACTIVE TIME:** 45 MINUTES / **TOTAL TIME:** 1 HOUR AND 15 MINUTES

A wonderfully crispy fried chicken can result when you use masa harina in place of all-purpose flour or bread crumbs. For fans of sweet and spicy foods, top this with some Habanero Honey (see page 533).

1. Season the chicken thighs with salt and pepper.

2. Place the masa in a baking dish, add the salt, and then add the water. Stir to combine. Stick a spoon into the batter; you want it to coat the spoon and drip slowly off. Depending on the masa used, you may need to add more water.

3. Dredge the chicken in the masa mixture until it is evenly coated.

4. Add canola oil to a Dutch oven until it is 2 inches deep and warm to 375°F.

5. Gently slip the chicken into the warm oil, making sure not to crowd the pot, which will lower the temperature of the oil. Cook until cooked through, golden brown, and crispy, 15 to 18 minutes. Remove and transfer to a paper towel–lined plate to drain.

INGREDIENTS:

2	LBS. CHICKEN THIGHS
½	TEASPOON KOSHER SALT, PLUS MORE TO TASTE
	BLACK PEPPER, TO TASTE
1	LB. MASA HARINA
¾	CUP WATER, PLUS MORE AS NEEDED
	CANOLA OIL, AS NEEDED

POLLO VERACRUZANO

YIELD: 4 SERVINGS / ACTIVE TIME: 15 MINUTES / TOTAL TIME: 45 MINUTES

Traditionally, seafood would serve as the protein here, but taking the dish's classic flavors of onion, peppers, and olives and pairing them with whole chicken legs and thighs makes for a hearty, family-style dinner.

1. Season the chicken with salt and pepper. Place the olive oil in a Dutch oven and warm it over medium heat. Add the chicken and sear until golden brown on both sides, about 5 minutes per side. Remove the chicken from the pan and set it aside.

2. Add the peppers, onion, and garlic, reduce the heat to low, and cook until the peppers have softened, about 8 minutes, stirring occasionally.

3. Return the chicken to the pan and deglaze the pan with the white wine, stock, and caper brine, scraping up any browned bits from the bottom of the pot. Add the capers, olives, tomatoes, and oregano (if using), bring to a simmer, and cook until the chicken is cooked through, about 15 minutes.

4. To serve, arrange the chicken on a plate, place some of the vegetables on top, and spoon some of the cooking liquid over everything.

INGREDIENTS:

4   BONE-IN, SKIN-ON CHICKEN LEGS

4   BONE-IN, SKIN-ON CHICKEN THIGHS

    SALT AND PEPPER, TO TASTE

3   TABLESPOONS EXTRA-VIRGIN OLIVE OIL

2   RED BELL PEPPERS, STEMMED, SEEDED, AND SLICED THIN

1   WHITE ONION, SLICED THIN

2   GARLIC CLOVES, MINCED

½   CUP WHITE WINE

2   CUPS CHICKEN STOCK (SEE PAGE 341)

2   TABLESPOONS CAPER BRINE

2   TABLESPOONS CAPERS, CHOPPED

½   CUP CHOPPED GREEN OLIVES

4   CUPS CHOPPED CANNED TOMATOES

¼   CUP DRIED MEXICAN OREGANO (OPTIONAL)

VALET
PARKING AMP

ENCHILADAS DE MOLE

YIELD: 4 SERVINGS / **ACTIVE TIME:** 10 MINUTES / **TOTAL TIME:** 35 MINUTES

Enchiladas in the US are typically made with a store-bought red or green sauce. Employing the richness of Mole Negro allows the dish to fulfill its potential.

1. Preheat the oven to 350°F. Place the mole in a small saucepan and warm it over low heat.

2. Place some of the olive oil in a skillet and warm it over low heat. Warm the tortillas one at a time and set them aside. Replenish the oil in the pan as needed.

3. Dip the warmed tortillas in the mole until completely coated and transfer them to a plate.

4. Fill the tortillas with the shredded chicken and roll them up. Place them in a baking dish, seam side down, and pour more mole over the top.

5. Place the dish in the oven and bake until warmed through. Remove from the oven and serve with pickled onion, Queso Fresco, and cilantro.

INGREDIENTS:

2   CUPS MOLE NEGRO (SEE PAGES 440–441)

2   TABLESPOONS EXTRA-VIRGIN OLIVE OIL

8   CORN TORTILLAS (SEE PAGE 352)

1   LB. LEFTOVER CHICKEN, SHREDDED

1   CUP PICKLED RED ONION ONION (SEE PAGE 515), FOR SERVING

8   OZ. QUESO FRESCO (SEE PAGE 522), FOR SERVING

½   BUNCH OF FRESH CILANTRO, FOR SERVING

MILANESA DE POLLO

YIELD: 4 SERVINGS / **ACTIVE TIME:** 10 MINUTES / **TOTAL TIME:** 30 MINUTES

A quick, light, and delicious dinner. The same method may be used with a fish fillet or beef.

1. Ask your butcher to pound the chicken breasts until they are no more than ¼ inch thick. You can also do this at home, placing the chicken between pieces of plastic wrap and using a cast-iron skillet or mallet.

2. Place the bread crumbs in a shallow bowl. Place the eggs in a separate bowl and beat until scrambled.

3. Place the olive oil in a deep skillet and warm it over medium-heat until it is hot enough that a bread crumb sizzles gently when added.

4. Season the chicken breasts with salt, dip them in the beaten eggs, and then into the bread crumbs until coated all over. Gently press on the bread crumbs so that they adhere to the chicken.

5. Working with one breast at a time, add the chicken to the oil, and fry until golden brown on both sides and cooked through, about 10 minutes. Transfer the cooked chicken breasts to a paper towel–lined plate to drain.

6. When all of the chicken has been cooked, serve with the Ensalada de Nopales, tortillas, and rice.

INGREDIENTS:

2   LBS. CHICKEN BREASTS

2   CUPS BREAD CRUMBS

4   LARGE EGGS

    SALT, TO TASTE

1   CUP EXTRA-VIRGIN OLIVE OIL

    ENSALADA DE NOPALES (SEE PAGE 272), FOR SERVING

    CORN TORTILLAS (SEE PAGE 352), FOR SERVING

    WHITE RICE, COOKED, FOR SERVING

SEAFOOD

*M*exico's construction, with ample coastline on both sides, means that its cuisine, rightly, places a powerful emphasis upon utilizing the bountiful fruits of the sea that are so readily available.

This warm acceptance of the environment has led to the incorporation of a dish that might be better than any other at preserving the unparalleled freshness the sea is famed for: ceviche. That simple dish, where seafood is sliced thin and cured in lime juice and salt, appears here in two unique forms (see pages 146–147 and 195). Lobster fans will find a few preparations to add to their summer itinerary (see page 136 and 143), and the adventurous set will do well to consider the Pulpo al Pastor (see page 155), an uncommonly beautiful and delicious preparation.

LANGOSTA AL MOJO DE AJO

YIELD: 4 SERVINGS / ACTIVE TIME: 30 MINUTES / TOTAL TIME: 30 MINUTES

This recipe is probably the most simple and delicious way to cook lobster. It is recommended that you make extra mojo de ajo, the sauce, to freeze for later.

1. Place the garlic cloves in a dry skillet and toast them over medium heat until lightly charred in spots, about 10 minutes, turning occasionally. Remove from the pan and peel the garlic.

2. Place the butter in a skillet and melt it over medium heat. Add the garlic and continue cooking until the butter begins to foam and brown slightly. Remove the pan from heat and let the mixture cool to room temperature.

3. Place the butter, garlic, guajillo powder, and epazote in a blender and puree until smooth. Transfer three-quarters of the mojo de ajo to a large mixing bowl. Place the remaining mojo de ajo in a small bowl and set it aside. Let cool completely.

4. Add the lobster tails to the mojo in the large mixing bowl and let them marinate for at least 15 to 20 minutes.

5. Preheat a grill to medium-high heat (about 450°F). Place a small bowl containing the reserved mojo de ajo beside the grill. Place the lobster tails on the grill, flesh side down, and grill until caramelized and almost cooked through, 3 to 4 minutes.

6. Flip the tails over and brush with some of the reserved mojo de ajo. Grill until completely cooked through, 1 to 2 minutes. Serve with lime wedges and any remaining mojo de ajo.

INGREDIENTS:

10 OZ. GARLIC CLOVES, UNPEELED

1 CUP UNSALTED BUTTER, PLUS 2 TABLESPOONS

2 TABLESPOONS GUAJILLO CHILE POWDER

2 TABLESPOONS FRESH EPAZOTE LEAVES

SALT, TO TASTE

4 LOBSTER TAILS, SPLIT IN HALF LENGTHWISE SO THAT THE FLESH IS EXPOSED

LIME WEDGES, FOR SERVING

136 | MEXICAN FOOD

GULF ROCK SHRIMP AGUACHILE
WITH AVOCADO PANNA COTTA

YIELD: 4 SERVINGS / **ACTIVE TIME:** 15 MINUTES / **TOTAL TIME:** 1 HOUR

Aguachile involves curing fresh shrimp in the acid of lime juice, similar to the method used to make ceviche. The variation below, served beside an avocado custard, is an elevated version of the popular dish.

1. Place the cucumber, garlic, cilantro, jalapeño, lime juice, salt, and pepper in a blender and puree until smooth.

2. Strain the puree into a bowl, pressing down to push as much of it through as possible.

3. Add the shrimp to the bowl, cover it with plastic wrap, and chill in the refrigerator until the shrimp turns pink, 40 to 50 minutes.

4. Serve alongside the Avocado Panna Cotta.

AVOCADO PANNA COTTA

1. Place the sheets of gelatin in a bowl of ice water and let them sit until softened, about 20 minutes.

2. Combine the milk, heavy cream, and lemon zest in a medium saucepan and bring to a simmer. Remove the pan from heat and let the mixture steep for 10 minutes.

3. Remove the gelatin from the ice bath and squeeze to remove excess water. Add to the cream and stir until they have been incorporated and the mixture is smooth.

4. Place the avocado in a blender and add half of the milk mixture. Puree until smooth.

5. Stir the puree back into the saucepan. Pour the mixture into the wells of a muffin tin and refrigerate overnight before serving.

INGREDIENTS:

½	ENGLISH CUCUMBER
1	GARLIC CLOVE
½	CUP FRESH CILANTRO, CHOPPED
½	JALAPEÑO CHILE PEPPER, STEMMED, SEEDED, AND SLICED
¾	CUP FRESH LIME JUICE
	SALT AND PEPPER, TO TASTE
8	OZ. MEXICAN GULF ROCK SHRIMP, SHELLED AND DEVEINED
	AVOCADO PANNA COTTA (SEE RECIPE), FOR SERVING

AVOCADO PANNA COTTA

2	SHEETS OF GELATIN
1	CUP WHOLE MILK
1	CUP HEAVY CREAM
	ZEST OF ½ LEMON
	FLESH OF 1 AVOCADO
	SALT, TO TASTE

BAJA LOBSTER & STREET CORN SALAD

YIELD: 4 SERVINGS / ACTIVE TIME: 25 MINUTES / TOTAL TIME: 50 MINUTES

Street corn salad is as common as tacos in Mexico. However, slight regional variations do exist that highlight ingredients specific to a particular area. This variation is a marriage between a traditional esquites and the famed Puerto Nuevo lobster.

1. To begin preparations for the salad, preheat the oven to 375°F. Combine the mayonnaise, crema, lime juice, Tapatio, queso enchilado, salt, and pepper in a salad bowl, stir to combine, and set it aside.

2. Place the corn kernels in small mixing bowl with the butter and toss to combine. Place them on a baking sheet and roast until golden brown, 15 to 20 minutes.

3. Stir the corn kernels into the salad bowl and let cool. Chill the salad in the refrigerator.

4. To begin preparations for the lobster, place the butter in a skillet and warm over medium-low heat.

5. Remove the meat from the lobster tail using kitchen scissors. Add the meat to the pan and poach until it turns a reddish orange, 4 to 5 minutes. Remove the lobster meat from the pan with a slotted spoon and let it cool.

6. Slice the lobster into small medallions. To serve, spoon the corn salad onto each plate and arrange a few lobster medallions on top of each portion. Sprinkle the Tajín over the dishes and garnish with cilantro.

INGREDIENTS:

FOR THE SALAD

¼ CUP MAYONNAISE

¼ CUP CREMA OR SOUR CREAM

1 TEASPOON FRESH LIME JUICE

¼ TEASPOON TAPATIO HOT SAUCE

½ CUP GRATED QUESO ENCHILADO

SALT AND PEPPER, TO TASTE

KERNELS FROM 2 EARS OF CORN

2 TABLESPOONS UNSALTED BUTTER, MELTED

FOR THE LOBSTER

½ CUP UNSALTED BUTTER

5-6 OZ. LOBSTER TAIL (BAJA PREFERRED)

2 TABLESPOONS TAJÍN

FRESH CILANTRO, FINELY CHOPPED, FOR GARNISH

STRIPED SEA BASS CEVICHE

YIELD: 4 SERVINGS / **ACTIVE TIME:** 1 HOUR AND 15 MINUTES / **TOTAL TIME:** 24 HOURS

Ceviche is a quintessential dish in any coastal Mexican town. This version is inspired by the tropical climate of Tulum, as it incorporates coconut, lime, and chiles.

1. Preheat a gas or charcoal grill to medium-high heat (450°F). Place the tomatillos on the grill and grill until charred all over, about 6 minutes, turning occasionally. Remove the tomatillos from the grill and set them aside. When the tomatillos are cool enough to handle, chop them.

2. Place the coconut oil in a skillet and warm it over medium heat. Add the ginger, shallots, and garlic and cook until the onion is translucent, about 3 minutes, stirring frequently.

3. Add the tomatillos to the skillet and cook until all of the liquid has evaporated. Deglaze the pan with the soy sauce and fish sauce, scraping up any browned bits from the bottom of the pan.

4. Add the coconut milk and lemongrass and bring the mixture to a boil. Remove the pan from heat and let the mixture cool. Store in the refrigerator overnight.

5. Remove the lemongrass and add the scallions, cilantro, and lemon juice to the mixture. Place it in a blender and puree until smooth.

6. Place the serrano peppers in a mixing bowl and season with salt, lime juice, and lime zest. Strain the puree into the bowl, add the sea bass, and chill in the refrigerator for 40 to 50 minutes.

7. Drain the sea bass and season it with lime juice, lime zest, and salt.

8. Combine the shallots, coconut, and toasted peanuts in a mixing bowl and season with the Coconut Dressing. Arrange the salad as a line in the middle of a plate.

9. Place the sea bass in a line next to the salad, garnish with additional cilantro and serrano, and serve.

INGREDIENTS:

5	OZ. TOMATILLOS, HUSKED AND RINSED
1	TABLESPOON COCONUT OIL
	5-INCH PIECE OF FRESH GINGER, PEELED AND DICED
2½	SHALLOTS, DICED
6	GARLIC CLOVES, DICED
5	TABLESPOONS SOY SAUCE
1½	TABLESPOONS FISH SAUCE
3½	CUPS COCONUT MILK
1	LEMONGRASS STALK, PEELED AND BRUISED
1	BUNCH OF SCALLIONS, TRIMMED AND SLICED
1	LARGE BUNCH OF FRESH CILANTRO, CHOPPED, PLUS MORE FOR GARNISH
7	TABLESPOONS FRESH LEMON JUICE
2	SERRANO CHILE PEPPERS, STEMMED, SEEDED, AND SLICED, PLUS MORE FOR GARNISH
	SALT, TO TASTE
	LIME JUICE, TO TASTE
	LIME ZEST, TO TASTE
¼	LB. SEA BASS, SLICED
2	TABLESPOONS SHAVED FRESH COCONUT
2	SHALLOTS, JULIENNED
	COCONUT DRESSING (SEE RECIPE)
¼	CUP TOASTED PEANUTS

COCONUT DRESSING

1. Combine all of the ingredients in a mixing bowl and chill in the refrigerator for 30 minutes.

2. Place the mixture in a blender and puree until emulsified, making sure the mixture does not get hot at all.

3. Strain the dressing through a fine-mesh sieve.

INGREDIENTS:

COCONUT DRESSING

1	1 (14 OZ.) CAN OF COCONUT MILK
3½	OZ. GINGER, PEELED AND GRATED
14	TABLESPOONS FRESH LEMON JUICE
1⅓	TEASPOONS KOSHER SALT
5	TEASPOONS SUGAR
1½	CUPS FRESH CILANTRO, CHOPPED
1½	TABLESPOONS CORIANDER SEEDS

VUELVA LA VIDA COCTEL DE CAMARONES

YIELD: 4 SERVINGS / **ACTIVE TIME:** 30 MINUTES / **TOTAL TIME:** 30 MINUTES

This Veracruz classic is a great start to a dinner, or served for brunch after a long night with friends and family. This revitalizing feature is where the name vuelva la vida or "return to life" comes from. If you prefer a milder flavor, swap in tomato juice for the clamato.

1. Place water in a medium saucepan, add the shrimp shells, lemon, salt, oregano, and bay leaves, and bring to a boil. Reduce the heat and simmer for 10 minutes.

2. Add the shrimp and turn off the burner. Let the shrimp poach in the hot broth for 1 minute. Remove the shrimp and let it cool.

3. Place the juices, horseradish, ketchup, fish sauce, hot sauce, clamato, and Worcestershire sauce in a mixing bowl and stir to combine.

4. Add the onion, garlic, avocado, jalapeño, tomatoes, and shrimp and fold to incorporate them. Garnish with cilantro and serve with lime wedges and tostadas.

INGREDIENTS:

1	LB. SHRIMP, SHELLED AND DEVEINED, SHELLS RESERVED
1	LEMON, HALVED
¼	CUP KOSHER SALT, PLUS MORE TO TASTE
1	TABLESPOON DRIED MEXICAN OREGANO
2	BAY LEAVES
7	TABLESPOONS FRESH LIME JUICE
1½	TABLESPOONS FRESH LEMON JUICE
5	TABLESPOONS ORANGE JUICE
1	TABLESPOON HORSERADISH
14	TABLESPOONS KETCHUP
1¼	TABLESPOONS FISH SAUCE
7	TABLESPOONS VALENTINA MEXICAN HOT SAUCE
7	TABLESPOONS SPICY CLAMATO
2⅔	TABLESPOONS WORCESTERSHIRE SAUCE
1	SMALL RED ONION, JULIENNED
5	GARLIC CLOVES, GRATED
	FLESH OF 1 AVOCADO, DICED
2	JALAPEÑO CHILE PEPPERS, BRUNOISED
2	ROMA TOMATOES, DICED
	FRESH CILANTRO, FOR GARNISH
	LIME WEDGES, FOR SERVING
	TOSTADAS, FOR SERVING

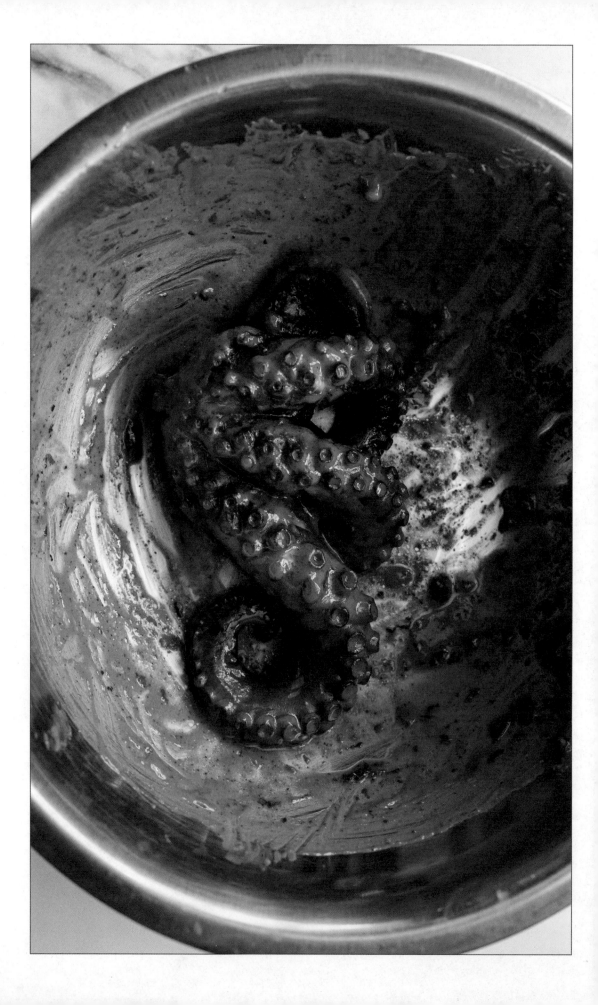

PULPO AL PASTOR

YIELD: 4 TO 6 SERVINGS / **ACTIVE TIME:** 30 MINUTES / **TOTAL TIME:** 3 HOURS

The classic al pastor marinade is as good for octopus as it is for pork.

1. Place the allspice, cloves, and cinnamon stick in a dry skillet and toast until fragrant, shaking the pan frequently. Grind to a powder using a mortar and pestle or a spice grinder.

2. Place the chiles in the skillet and toast over medium heat until they darken and become fragrant and pliable. Submerge them in a bowl of hot water and let them soak for 30 minutes.

3. Drain the chiles and reserve the liquid. Add the chiles, toasted spice powder, juices, Recado Rojo, garlic cloves, and oregano to a blender and puree until smooth. Season the al pastor marinade with salt and set it aside.

4. Bring water to a boil in a large saucepan. Place the octopus in the boiling water and poach for 3 minutes. Remove the octopus and let it cool.

5. Preheat the oven to 300°F. Place the octopus, epazote, bay leaves, head of garlic, and onion in a Dutch oven and add stock until half of the octopus is covered. Cover the Dutch oven, place it in the oven, and braise for 2 to 3 hours, until the thickest part of the tentacles are very tender. Remove the octopus from the braising liquid and let it cool.

6. Place the octopus in the al pastor marinade and marinate for a minimum of 30 minutes.

7. Preheat a gas or charcoal grill to high heat (about 500°F). Clean the grates, remove the octopus from the marinade, and shake to remove any excess. Place the octopus on the grill and grill until it is caramelized and crispy on all sides, 5 to 7 minutes, taking care not to let the octopus burn.

8. Serve with tortillas, lime wedges, Salsa de Aguacate, and cilantro

INGREDIENTS:

3	ALLSPICE BERRIES
2	WHOLE CLOVES
½	CINNAMON STICK
3	CHIPOTLE MORITA CHILE PEPPERS
2	DRIED CHILES DE ARBOL
7	GUAJILLO CHILE PEPPERS
2	TABLESPOONS FRESH LIME JUICE
2	TABLESPOONS ORANGE JUICE
2	TABLESPOONS GRAPEFRUIT JUICE
7	TABLESPOONS PINEAPPLE JUICE
½	CUP RECADO ROJO (SEE PAGE 497)
5	GARLIC CLOVES
⅛	TEASPOON DRIED MEXICAN OREGANO
	SALT, TO TASTE
6-8	LB. OCTOPUS, BEAK REMOVED AND HEAD CLEANED
1	SMALL BUNCH OF FRESH EPAZOTE
3	BAY LEAVES
1	HEAD OF GARLIC, HALVED AND GENTLY CHARRED
1	WHITE ONION, QUARTERED AND CHARRED
8	CUPS CHICKEN STOCK (SEE PAGE 341)
	CORN TORTILLAS (SEE PAGE 352), FOR SERVING
	LIME WEDGES, FOR SERVING
	SALSA DE AGUACATE (SEE PAGE 503), FOR SERVING
	FRESH CILANTRO, CHOPPED, FOR SERVING

CAMARONES EN ADOBO

This recipe is great for tacos, over vegetables, or in a torta.

1. Place the dried chiles in a dry skillet and toast over medium heat until they darken and become fragrant and pliable. Submerge them in a bowl of hot water and let them soak for 15 to 20 minutes.

2. Drain the chiles and reserve the soaking liquid. Add the chiles to a blender along with the garlic, tomatoes, chipotles, and a small amount of the soaking liquid and puree until the mixture is a smooth paste. Season the adobo marinade with salt and let it cool completely.

3. Place the shrimp in the adobo and marinate for at least 20 to 30 minutes.

4. Place some of the lard in a large skillet and warm it over medium-high heat. Working in batches if needed to avoid crowding the pan, add the shrimp and cook until they are just firm and turn pink, 2 to 3 minutes. Add more lard to the pan if it starts to look dry.

5. Serve in tortillas with chopped onion, cilantro, and lime wedges.

INGREDIENTS:

4	GUAJILLO CHILLE PEPPERS, STEMMED AND SEEDED
6	GARLIC CLOVES
2	SMALL ROMA TOMATOES
3	TABLESPOONS CHIPOTLES EN ADOBO
	SALT, TO TASTE
1	LB. LARGE SHRIMP, SHELLED AND DEVEINED
¼	CUP LARD
	CORN TORTILLAS (SEE PAGE 352), FOR SERVING
	WHITE ONION, CHOPPED, FOR SERVING
	FRESH CILANTRO, CHOPPED, FOR SERVING
	LIME WEDGES, FOR SERVING

OSTIONES AL TAPESCO

YIELD: 4 SERVINGS / **ACTIVE TIME:** 30 MINUTES / **TOTAL TIME:** 45 MINUTES

Chef Gabe Erales: "I first had this dish in Tabasco when I was visiting an oyster farm. The cooking procedure imparts a beautiful smoky flavor." In order to obtain that aforementioned beautiful flavor, a charcoal grill is necessary.

1. Preheat a charcoal grill to medium-high heat (about 450°F). When the grill is hot and the coals are glowing and covered with a thin layer of ash, place a grill rack on top of the coals and cover with the allspice leaves.

2. Place the closed oysters on top and cover with the banana leaves. The leaves will begin to smolder and then catch fire. After 3 to 4 minutes, the oysters will begin to open and absorb the smoke. Using tongs, carefully remove the oysters and arrange them on a plate to serve.

3. Place the olive oil, lime juice, chiles, and cilantro in a bowl and stir until thoroughly combined. Serve this sauce and the saltines alongside the oysters.

INGREDIENTS:

1 BUNCH OF GREEN ALLSPICE LEAVES OR BAY LEAVES

12 OYSTERS, RINSED AND SCRUBBED

1 SMALL BUNCH OF BANANA LEAVES

7 TABLESPOONS EXTRA-VIRGIN OLIVE OIL

7 TABLESPOONS FRESH LIME JUICE

3 SERRANO CHILE PEPPERS, STEMMED, SEEDED, AND MINCED

1 CUP FRESH CILANTRO STEMS, CHOPPED

SALTINES, FOR SERVING

MEXTLAPIQUE DE CALLO DE HACHA

YIELD: 4 SERVINGS / **ACTIVE TIME:** 40 MINUTES / **TOTAL TIME:** 40 MINUTES

This dish is typically prepared with fish, but this variation includes scallops because of their unique sweet flavor, which goes well with the corn.

1. Season the scallops with the salt and ground chiles.

2. Place the tomatoes, onion, and jalapeños in a mixing bowl and stir to combine. Season the mixture with salt.

3. Place three scallops in each corn husk and cover with some of the vegetable mixture and epazote. Drizzle olive oil over the top.

4. Tie the corn husks at both ends by using a piece of torn corn husk. Add more corn husk as need to fully enclose the scallops.

5. Preheat a grill to medium heat (400°F) or warm a cast-iron skillet over medium heat. Place the packets of scallops on the cooking surface and cook until the husks begin to char, 3 to 4 minutes. The scallops should be cooked through.

6. Serve with lime wedges.

INGREDIENTS:

12	SCALLOPS, FEET REMOVED AND RINSED
	SALT, TO TASTE
2	PASILLA CHILE PEPPERS, GROUND
2	ANCHO CHILE PEPPERS, GROUND
3	ROMA TOMATOES, DICED
¾	SMALL YELLOW ONION, DICED
3	JALAPEÑO PEPPERS, DICED
8-12	CORN HUSKS, DRIED AND REHYDRATED
6	FRESH EPAZOTE LEAVES
	EXTRA-VIRGIN OLIVE OIL, TO TASTE
	LIME WEDGES, FOR SERVING

PAN DE CAZON

YIELD: 4 SERVINGS / **ACTIVE TIME:** 40 MINUTES / **TOTAL TIME:** 40 MINUTES

This Yucatean classic is a great alternative to a traditional enchilada.

1. Place the habaneros in a dry skillet and cook over medium heat until charred, turning frequently. Set the charred habanero aside and let cool. When cool enough to handle, remove the stems and seeds from the peppers and chop the remaining flesh. Gloves are recommended for handling the habanero, as its liquid can prove severely irritating to skin.

2. Bring a saucepan of water to a boil. Season very generously with salt and add a few sprigs of epazote.

3. Add the fish and poach until just cooked through, 2 to 3 minutes. Remove the fish, let it cool, and shred with a fork once it is cool enough to handle.

4. Place some of the lard in a large skillet and warm it over medium-high heat. Add half of the onion and garlic and cook until the onion is translucent, about 3 minutes. Season the mixture with salt and oregano, add the fish and the citrus juices to the pan, and cook until the flavors are combined, 1 to 2 minutes. Remove the pan from heat and set it aside.

5. In a separate skillet, add the remaining lard and warm it over medium-high heat. Add the remaining onion and garlic along with a few sprigs of epazote and cook until the onion is translucent, about 3 minutes. Add to a blender along with the tomatoes and black beans and puree until smooth.

6. Place the black bean puree in a saucepan and bring it to a boil. Reduce the heat and simmer until it has reduced by one-quarter, about 15 minutes.

7. Working quickly, dip the tortillas one at a time into the black bean puree until coated lightly on both sides. Place in the center of a plate. Top with about 2 oz. of the fish mixture. Repeat with three more tortillas. For the fourth tortilla, spread the black bean puree only on one side and place it, coated side down, on top of the stack.

8. Cover the stack with about ¼ cup of the puree and garnish with some of the charred habanero and cilantro. Repeat with the remaining tortillas, fish mixture, puree, habanero, and cilantro.

INGREDIENTS:

4	HABANERO CHILE PEPPERS
	SALT, TO TASTE
1	SMALL BUNCH OF FRESH EPAZOTE
1	LB. DOGFISH, COD, OR MONKFISH, BONED
¼	CUP LARD
1	WHITE ONION, CHOPPED
5	GARLIC CLOVES, MINCED
1	TEASPOON DRIED MEXICAN OREGANO
	ZEST AND JUICE OF 1 LIME
	ZEST AND JUICE OF 1 ORANGE
4	ROMA TOMATOES, QUARTERED
1	CUP CANNED OR COOKED BLACK BEANS
16	CORN TORTILLAS (SEE PAGE 352), WARMED AND WRAPPED IN FOIL
	FRESH CILANTRO, CHOPPED, FOR SERVING

Ceviche, see pages 146–147, 195

CARNITAS DE ATUN

YIELD: 4 SERVINGS / **ACTIVE TIME:** 40 MINUTES / **TOTAL TIME:** 40 MINUTES

This preparation is a healthier alternative to fish tacos that still has a nice level of fat and flavor.

1. Season the tuna with salt and the guajillo powder. Combine the juices in a mixing bowl, add the tuna and bay leaf, and marinate for 15 minutes.

2. Place the lard in a skillet and warm over high heat. Add the tuna and panfry until the outside is crispy and caramelized and the inside rare, 3 to 4 minutes.

3. Serve in tortillas with cabbage, lime wedges, and pico de gallo.

INGREDIENTS:

1   LB. TUNA LOIN, SLICED

    SALT, TO TASTE

3   TABLESPOONS GUAJILLO CHILE POWDER

¼   CUP FRESH LIME JUICE

¼   CUP ORANGE JUICE

1   BAY LEAF

¼   CUP LARD OR EXTRA-VIRGIN OLIVE OIL

    CORN TORTILLAS (SEE PAGE 352), WARM, FOR SERVING

    CABBAGE, FINELY SHREDDED, FOR SERVING

    LIME WEDGES, FOR SERVING

    PICO DE GALLO (SEE PAGE 281), FOR SERVING

AGUACHILE VERDE DE CAMARÓN

YIELD: 4 SERVINGS / **ACTIVE TIME:** 20 MINUTES / **TOTAL TIME:** 20 MINUTES

There are many variations of aguachile, and you will learn to adjust the recipe to your acidity and heat preferences accordingly. If you prefer a less raw shrimp, simply let it cure longer.

1. Place the lime juice, serrano peppers, cilantro, olive oil, apple juice, and honey in a blender and puree until smooth. Season the aguachile with salt and set it aside.

2. Slice the shrimp in half lengthwise and place them in a shallow bowl. Cover with the red onion, cucumber, and avocado.

3. Pour the aguachile over the shrimp and let it cure for 5 to 10 minutes before enjoying. Serve with tostadas or saltines.

INGREDIENTS:

1¾ CUPS FRESH LIME JUICE

3 SERRANO CHILE PEPPERS, STEMMED AND SEEDED

1 CUP FRESH CILANTRO, CHOPPED, PLUS MORE FOR GARNISH

3 TABLESPOONS EXTRA-VIRGIN OLIVE OIL

2 TABLESPOONS APPLE JUICE

1 TEASPOON HONEY

SALT, TO TASTE

1 LB. SHRIMP, SHELLED AND DEVEINED

¼ RED ONION, JULIENNED

1 CUCUMBER, SLICED

FLESH OF 1 AVOCADO, DICED

TOSTADAS OR SALTINES, FOR SERVING

TIKIN XIC

YIELD: 2 TO 4 SERVINGS / ACTIVE TIME: 30 MINUTES / TOTAL TIME: 1 HOUR

This Yucatan classic makes use of recado rojo, which provides a unique flavor to the fish, similar to that of cochinita pibil (see page 28). Chef Gabe Erales also recommends cooking this fish over an open flame whenever possible; however, you have to take care not to burn the banana leaves when you do.

1. Preheat the oven to 450°F. Rub the inside and outside of the snapper with the Recado Rojo. Let the fish marinate for at least 30 minutes. If time allows, marinate the snapper for up to 24 hours.

2. Remove any stiff spines from the banana leaves and cut the leaves into pieces large enough to wrap up the fish completely. Toast the banana leaves over an open flame or in a dry cast-iron skillet until bright green and very pliable.

3. Place the fish in the banana leaves and top with the sliced habanero and cilantro. Season with salt, fold the banana leaves over so that they completely cover the fish, and tie the packet closed with kitchen twine.

4. Place the packet on a baking sheet, place it in the oven, and roast until just cooked through, 15 to 20 minutes depending on the thickness of the fish. Remove from the oven and let the fish rest in the packet for 5 minutes.

5. Open the packet, divide the snapper between the serving plates, and serve with tortillas, lime wedges, and Salsa de Chiltomate.

INGREDIENTS:

1   WHOLE RED SNAPPER, SCALED AND CLEANED

1½   CUPS RECADO ROJO (SEE PAGE 497)

BANANA LEAVES, AS NEEDED

2   HABANERO CHILE PEPPERS, STEMMED, SEEDED, AND SLICED

1   BUNCH OF FRESH CILANTRO

SALT, TO TASTE

CORN TORTILLAS (SEE PAGE 352), WARM, FOR SERVING

LIME WEDGES, FOR SERVING

SALSA DE CHILTOMATE (SEE PAGE 477), FOR SERVING

MASA-BATTERED FISH TACOS

YIELD: 4 SERVINGS / **ACTIVE TIME:** 30 MINUTES / **TOTAL TIME:** 1 HOUR

Baja California, the Mexican state neighboring California, is the birthplace of the battered fish taco. There's plenty of sides that pair well with these tacos, but a simple slaw dressed with lime juice is particularly wonderful.

1. Season the tilapia with salt and pepper.

2. Place the masa in a baking dish, add the salt, and then add the water. Stir to combine. Stick a spoon into the batter; you want it to coat the spoon and drip slowly off. Depending on the masa used, you may need to add more water.

3. Dredge the tilapia in the masa mixture until it is evenly coated.

4. Add canola oil to a Dutch oven until it is 2 inches deep and warm to 375°F.

5. Gently slip the tilapia into the warm oil, making sure not to crowd the pot, which will lower the temperature of the oil. Fry until cooked through, golden brown, and crispy, 8 to 10 minutes. Remove and transfer to a paper towel–lined plate to drain.

6. Chop the fish into bite-size pieces and serve in tortillas along with cabbage, crema, beans, and pico de gallo.

INGREDIENTS:

2   LBS. TILAPIA, CUT INTO SMALLER PIECES

½   TEASPOON KOSHER SALT, PLUS MORE TO TASTE

     BLACK PEPPER, TO TASTE

1   LB. MASA HARINA

¾   CUP WATER, PLUS MORE AS NEEDED

     CANOLA OIL, AS NEEDED

     CORN TORTILLAS (SEE PAGE 352), WARM, FOR SERVING

     CABBAGE, FINELY SHREDDED, FOR SERVING

     CREMA OR SOUR CREAM, FOR SERVING

     FRIJOLES DE LA OLLA (SEE PAGE 257), FOR SERVING

     PICO DE GALLO (SEE PAGE 281), FOR SERVING

SMOKED TROUT TOSTADAS

YIELD: 4 SERVINGS / ACTIVE TIME: 10 MINUTES / TOTAL TIME: 15 MINUTES

Cuisine in Baja California primarily consists of seafood, ranging from fresh clams and sea urchin tostadas to dishes that rely on smoked fish, such as this one. Smoked trout has a more subtle flavor than smoked tuna, another beloved delicacy in the region.

1. Coat a large skillet with olive oil and warm over medium heat. Add the onion and garlic and cook until the onion is translucent, about 3 minutes, stirring frequently.

2. Stir the trout and achiote into the pan and cook, stirring to break up the trout, until warmed through, about 3 minutes.

3. Turn off the heat, stir in the remaining ingredients, and let the mixture sit for a minute or two before serving with tortillas.

INGREDIENTS:

½ CUP EXTRA-VIRGIN OLIVE OIL, PLUS MORE AS NEEDED

1 LARGE WHITE ONION, SLICED THIN

4 GARLIC CLOVES, SLICED

1 LB. SMOKED TROUT, SHREDDED

2 TEASPOONS ACHIOTE POWDER

8 OZ. CARROTS, PEELED AND GRATED

½ CUP SAUERKRAUT

2 TABLESPOONS CHOPPED CASTELVETRANO OLIVES

2 TABLESPOONS FRESH LEMON JUICE

2 TABLESPOONS KOSHER SALT

CORN OR FLOUR TORTILLAS (PAGE 352 OR 444), WARM, FOR SERVING

COCKTAIL DE MARISCO

YIELD: 4 SERVINGS / **ACTIVE TIME:** 5 MINUTES / **TOTAL TIME:** 1 HOUR

Seafood cocktails are a quintessential dish in all coastal towns, each with their own variation based on local customs. This recipe is typical of Baja California.

1. Place all of the ingredients, except the tortillas and lime wedges, in a large mixing bowl and gently stir until combined.

2. Cover the bowl with plastic wrap and chill in the refrigerator for 1 hour.

3. Garnish with additional cilantro and serve with tortillas and lime wedges.

INGREDIENTS:

- 1 CUP SHELLED AND DEVEINED SHRIMP
- 1 CUP CRAB KNUCKLE MEAT
- 1 CUP OCTOPUS, COOKED AND DICED
- 1½ CUPS CLAMATO
- 1 CUP KETCHUP
- 1 TABLESPOON FRESH LEMON JUICE
- 1 CUCUMBER, DICED
- FLESH OF 2 AVOCADOS, DICED
- 2 TOMATOES, DICED
- 1 RED ONION, DICED
- 1 CUP FRESH CILANTRO, CHOPPED, PLUS MORE FOR GARNISH
- 2 JALAPEÑO CHILE PEPPERS, STEMMED, SEEDED, AND DICED
- 1 TEASPOON TAJÍN
- SALT AND PEPPER, TO TASTE
- CORN TORTILLAS (SEE PAGE 352), FOR SERVING
- LIME WEDGES, FOR SERVING

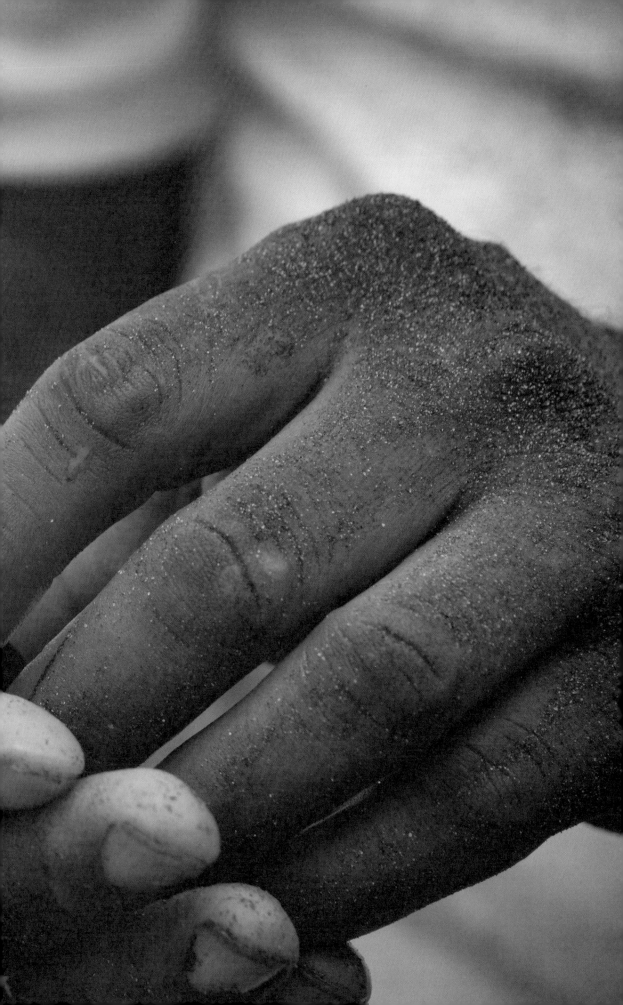

PESCADO VERACRUZ

YIELD: 2 SERVINGS / **ACTIVE TIME:** 15 MINUTES / **TOTAL TIME:** 45 MINUTES

Pescado veracruzano is a traditional recipe from, well, Veracruz. It can be made with any light fish you choose, and grilled or sautéed. Ask your local fish market to clean and gut the fish for you, leaving the head and tail on.

1. Using a sharp knife, score the fish three to four times on each side, about a ¼ inch deep. Lightly season the snapper with salt and pepper and set aside.

2. Combine the tomatoes, olives, and capers in a mixing bowl.

3. Place the olive oil in a large skillet and warm over medium-high heat. Add the onion, bell pepper, and garlic and cook until they have softened, about 7 minutes, stirring frequently.

4. Stir in the tomato mixture. Place the fish on top of the vegetables, add the caper brine, and cover the pan. Cook over low heat until the fish is fully cooked through, about 20 minutes.

5. To serve, divide the vegetables between the serving plates and top each one with a piece of the red snapper.

INGREDIENTS:

1-2 LBS. RED SNAPPER, SCALED, CLEANED, AND GUTTED, HEAD AND TAIL LEFT ON

SALT AND PEPPER, TO TASTE

4 LARGE TOMATOES, SEEDED AND FINELY DICED

4 OZ. GREEN OLIVES, PITTED AND QUARTERED

¼ CUP CAPERS

2 TABLESPOONS EXTRA-VIRGIN OLIVE OIL

1 WHITE ONION, SLICED THIN

1 RED BELL PEPPER, STEMMED, SEEDED, AND SLICED THIN

5 GARLIC CLOVES, SLICED THIN

1 TABLESPOON CAPER BRINE

COCTEL DE CAMARON

YIELD: 4 SERVINGS / **ACTIVE TIME:** 35 MINUTES / TOTAL TIME 1 HOUR AND 35 MINUTES

This shrimp cocktail recipe is perfect for the hot weather, as it is refreshing and light, the perfect blend of ingredients for a revitalizing appetizer or lunch.

1. Prepare an ice bath and bring water to a boil in a medium saucepan. Add salt and the shrimp and poach until the shrimp turn bright pink. Plunge them into the ice bath and then peel them. Let the poaching liquid cool and place the shrimp in the refrigerator.

2. When the poaching liquid is cool, place half of it in a bowl. Add the tomatoes, onion, cucumber, and ketchup and stir to combine.

3. Cut the shrimp into ½-inch pieces and add them to the vegetable mixture. Stir in the lime juice, serrano peppers, and cilantro, taste, and season with salt if necessary.

4. Chill in the refrigerator for 1 hour before serving with tostadas and lime wedges.

INGREDIENTS:

SALT, TO TASTE

1 LB. SHRIMP, DEVEINED, SHELLS ON

2 LARGE TOMATOES, SEEDED AND FINELY DICED

¼ WHITE ONION, FINELY DIVED

1 CUCUMBER, PEELED, SEEDED, AND FINELY DICED

½ CUP KETCHUP OR CLAMATO

JUICE OF 3 LIMES

2 SERRANO CHILE PEPPERS, STEMMED, SEEDED, AND FINELY CHOPPED

1 BUNCH OF FRESH CILANTRO, FINELY CHOPPED

TOSTADAS OR SALTINES, FOR SERVING

LIME WEDGES, FOR SERVING

PESCADO ADOBADO EN HOJA DE PLATANO

YIELD: 4 SERVINGS / **ACTIVE TIME:** 20 MINUTES / **TOTAL TIME:** 1 HOUR AND 10 MINUTES

A dobo appears in various recipes throughout Mexico, and this one uses an achiote-based paste, which will lend deep, earthy, and complex flavor to any whole fish. The banana leaves add a bit more flavor, and an aroma that makes this dish perfect for entertaining.

1. Place the guajillo peppers in a bowl of hot water and soak for 15 minutes.

2. Drain the peppers and place them in a blender. Add the serrano peppers, garlic, Recado Rojo, vinegar, and oil and puree until smooth. Season the adobo marinade with salt, reserve a ¼ cup for serving, and set the rest aside.

3. Remove any stiff spines from the banana leaves and cut the leaves into pieces large enough to wrap up the fish completely. Toast the banana leaves over an open flame or in a dry cast-iron skillet until bright green and very pliable.

4. Season the fish with salt and pepper and place it in the banana leaves. Pour the adobo over the fish and place the bay leaves on top. Fold the banana leaves over so that they completely cover the fish and tie the packet closed with kitchen twine.

5. Transfer the fish to the refrigerator and marinate for at least an hour. If time allows, you can marinate the fish overnight.

6. Preheat the oven to 375°F. Place the packet containing the fish in a roasting pan, place in the oven, and roast until cooked through, about 12 minutes. Remove from the oven and let the fish rest for 5 minutes.

7. Cut open the banana leaves and brush the fish with the reserved adobo. Garnish with pickled onion and cilantro and serve with warm tortillas.

INGREDIENTS:

6   GUAJILLO CHILE PEPPERS, STEMMED AND SEEDED

2   SERRANO CHILE PEPPERS

3   GARLIC CLOVES

2   TABLESPOONS RECADO ROJO (SEE PAGE 497)

2   TABLESPOONS WHITE VINEGAR

¼   CUP EXTRA-VIRGIN OLIVE OIL

    SALT AND PEPPER, TO TASTE

2   BANANA LEAVES

2   LBS. SEA BASS OR RED SNAPPER

3   BAY LEAVES

    PICKLED RED ONION (SEE PAGE 515), FOR GARNISH

1   BUNCH OF FRESH CILANTRO, CHOPPED, FOR GARNISH

    CORN TORTILLAS (SEE PAGE 352), WARM, FOR SERVING

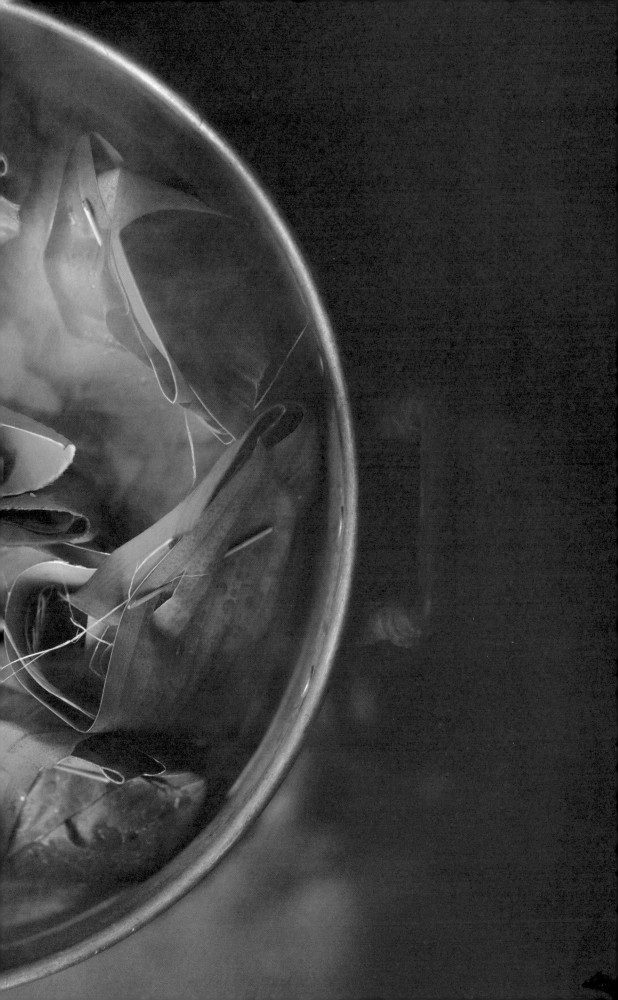

CEVICHE DE PESCADO

YIELD: 6 SERVINGS / **ACTIVE TIME:** 25 MINUTES / **TOTAL TIME:** 2 HOURS

Ceviche can be made with a variety of seafood and other ingredients, producing an almost endless amount of possible combinations.

1. Place the fish in a bowl and season with salt. Add the peppers, cilantro, and lime juice, stir to combine, and chill in the refrigerator for 2 hours, allowing the fish to cure.

2. Pile the ceviche on top of tostadas and serve with the onion, tomatoes, avocado, cucumber, hot sauce, and additional cilantro.

INGREDIENTS:

2   LBS. HALIBUT OR RED SNAPPER FILLETS, BONED AND DICED

     SALT, TO TASTE

1   JALAPEÑO CHILE PEPPER, STEMMED, SEEDED, AND FINELY DICED

2   SERRANO CHILE PEPPERS, STEMMED, SEEDED, AND FINELY DICED

½   BUNCH OF FRESH CILANTRO, FINELY CHOPPED, PLUS MORE FOR SERVING

     JUICE OF 6 LARGE LIMES

     TOSTADAS OR SALTINES, FOR SERVING

¼   RED ONION, SLICED THIN, FOR SERVING

8   OZ. CHERRY TOMATOES, PEELED AND DICED, FOR SERVING

     FLESH OF 1 AVOCADO, DICED, FOR SERVING

1   CUCUMBER, PEELED AND FINELY DICED, FOR SERVING

     HOT SAUCE, FOR SERVING

PESCADO ZARANDEADO

YIELD: 4 SERVINGS / **ACTIVE TIME:** 10 MINUTES / **TOTAL TIME:** 40 MINUTES

Colorful and light, this is the perfect seafood dish for grilling season, providing the big flavors the family wants.

1. Using a sharp knife, score each side of the fish four times. Season them with salt, the oregano, and cumin and place them in a large roasting pan.

2. Place the chile peppers in a bowl of boiling water and soak for 10 minutes. Drain the peppers, reserve the soaking liquid, and place the chiles in a blender.

3. Add the garlic and Maggi sauce and puree until smooth, adding the reserved liquid as needed to get the desired texture.

4. Pour the puree over the fish and marinate for 20 minutes.

5. Preheat a grill to medium-high heat (about 450°F) and coat the grates with nonstick cooking spray.

6. Place the fish on the grill and grill for 4 minutes. Turn the fish over and grill until cooked through, another 4 minutes.

7. Remove from the grill and pour the lime juice over it. Serve immediately with warm tortillas.

INGREDIENTS:

2	WHOLE RED SNAPPER, SCALED, CLEANED, GUTTED, AND BUTTERFLIED
	SALT, TO TASTE
½	TEASPOON DRIED MEXICAN OREGANO
1	TEASPOON CUMIN
3	GUAJILLO CHILE PEPPERS, STEMMED AND SEEDED
2	ANCHO CHILE PEPPERS, STEMMED AND SEEDED
3	GARLIC CLOVES
2	TABLESPOONS MAGGI SEASONING OR WORCESTERSHIRE SAUCE
¼	CUP FRESH LIME JUICE
	CORN TORTILLAS (SEE PAGE 352), WARM, FOR SERVING

CAMARONES A LA DIABLA

YIELD: 4 SERVINGS / **ACTIVE TIME:** 20 MINUTES / **TOTAL TIME:** 35 MINUTES

This shrimp dish brings a lot of heat and spiciness, as the name diabla, or "deviled," suggests. Perfect with rice, it is quick and easy to prepare and serve with a refreshing drink (like the Tepache de Piña on page 791). Another way to cook the shrimp is grilling it lightly for 4 minutes, and then adding it to the sauce on the stove.

1. Place the chile peppers in a bowl of boiling water and soak for 10 minutes. Drain, reserve the soaking liquid, and place the chiles in a blender.

2. Add the garlic, tomatoes, and onion to the blender and puree until smooth, adding the reserved liquid as needed. Season the puree with the salt.

3. Place the olive oil in a large skillet and warm over medium-high heat. Add the puree and cook for 5 minutes, stirring occasionally.

4. Add the shrimp, lower the heat, and cook until the shrimp turn pink and curl up slightly.

5. To serve, ladle the sauce and shrimp over white rice.

INGREDIENTS:

10 GUAJILLO CHILE PEPPERS

4 DRIED CHILES DE ARBOL

3 GARLIC CLOVES, CHOPPED

4 LARGE TOMATOES, QUARTERED

½ WHITE ONION, CHOPPED

1 TABLESPOON KOSHER SALT

2 TABLESPOONS EXTRA-VIRGIN OLIVE OIL

1 LB. SHRIMP, SHELLED AND DEVEINED

WHITE RICE, COOKED, FOR SERVING

MASA-CRUSTED SARDINES
WITH PICKLED MANZANO

YIELD: 2 SERVINGS / **ACTIVE TIME:** 10 MINUTES / **TOTAL TIME:** 30 MINUTES

This unexpected appetizer is quick and delicious, made to share with friends while drinking a cold beverage, whether it be a beer or one of the many options in the Cocktails & Beverages chapter.

1. Rinse the sardines and pat them dry with a paper towel. Season lightly with salt.

2. Place the masa harina, flour, half of the Mole Spice, the cumin, and paprika in a mixing bowl and stir to combine.

3. Dredge the sardines in the masa mixture until completely coated. Set them on paper towels and let them rest for 5 minutes.

4. After 5 minutes, dredge the sardines in the masa mixture again until coated. The resting period allows the sardines to release a bit of moisture, which will help more of the masa stick to them, producing a lighter and crispier result.

5. Place the olive oil in a deep skillet and warm it to 325°F. Working in batches, gently slip the sardines into the oil and fry them until crispy and golden brown, about 4 minutes, turning them over once. Place the fried sardines on a paper towel–lined plate to drain and sprinkle the remaining Mole Spice over them.

6. To serve, spread some of the chile mayo on each serving plate, arrange a few sardines and pickled peppers on top, and serve with lime wedges.

MOLE SPICE

1. Place all of the ingredients in a mixing bowl and stir to combine.

INGREDIENTS:

8   OZ. SARDINES, CLEANED AND HEADS REMOVED

    SALT, TO TASTE

1   CUP MASA HARINA

¼   CUP ALL-PURPOSE FLOUR

1   TABLESPOON MOLE SPICE (SEE RECIPE)

½   TEASPOON CUMIN

1   TEASPOON PAPRIKA

2   CUPS EXTRA-VIRGIN OLIVE OIL

¼   CUP CHILE TOREADO MAYO (SEE PAGE 226)

¼   CUP PICKLED MANZANO PEPPER (SEE PAGE 528)

    LIME WEDGES, FOR SERVING

MOLE SPICE

1   TEASPOON ALLSPICE

½   TEASPOON GROUND CLOVES

½   TEASPOON CINNAMON

½   TEASPOON CUMIN

1   TEASPOON CORIANDER

1   TEASPOON GROUND GINGER

VEGETABLES

As a spin through the produce section at any grocery store in the US will tell you, the climate in Mexico is extremely conducive to fostering a wide array of vegetables and fruits.

That surfeit obscures the uncommon offerings that are enjoyed within Mexico's borders, like the crunchy and fresh-tasting chayote, which goes beautifully with the famed pipian rojo sauce (see page 244). The uniquely bitter huauzontle is also featured, providing gravitas to an otherwise airy fritter (see page 223). And the guest at most every meal in Mexico, beans, get dressed up in their most traditional guises (see page 254 and 257).

GUANAJUATO STRAWBERRY & BEET SALAD

YIELD: 4 SERVINGS / **ACTIVE TIME:** 20 MINUTES / **TOTAL TIME:** 2 HOURS

The state of Guanajuato is one of the principal producers of strawberries in Mexico. Consequently, the region offers variations of tropical salads like this iteration with queso fresco, wild baby arugula, and a cilantro-and-sunflower seed pesto.

1. Preheat the oven to 375°F. Rinse the beets under cold water and scrub them to remove any excess dirt. Pat dry and place them in a baking dish.

2. Drizzle the olive oil over the beets and season them generously with salt and pepper. Place them in the oven and roast until tender, about 1 hour.

3. Remove from the oven and let the beets cool.

4. When the beets are cool enough to handle, peel and dice them. Place them in a bowl with the pesto and toss to coat. Add the strawberries, cheese, arugula, and annatto oil, toss until evenly distributed, and serve.

CILANTRO PESTO

1. Place all of the ingredients in a food processor and blitz until emulsified and smooth. Place in the refrigerator and chill until ready to serve.

INGREDIENTS:

3	LARGE GOLDEN BEETS
½	CUP EXTRA-VIRGIN OLIVE OIL
	SALT AND PEPPER, TO TASTE
	CILANTRO PESTO (SEE RECIPE)
12	GUANAJUATO STRAWBERRIES, HULLED AND HALVED
2	CUPS SHREDDED QUESO FRESCO (SEE PAGE 522)
4	OZ. WILD BABY ARUGULA
2	TABLESPOONS ANNATTO OIL

CILANTRO PESTO

1	CUP FRESH CILANTRO
1	GARLIC CLOVE
¼	CUP ROASTED AND SHELLED SUNFLOWER SEEDS
¼	CUP SHREDDED QUESO ENCHILADA
¼	CUP EXTRA-VIRGIN OLIVE OIL
1	TEASPOON FRESH LEMON JUICE
	SALT AND PEPPER, TO TASTE

KOJI-MARINATED SWEET POTATOES
WITH SALSA MACHA

YIELD: 4 SERVINGS / **ACTIVE TIME:** 5 MINUTES / **TOTAL TIME:** 1 HOUR AND 45 MINUTES

The use of koji is most typical in Asian foods, however it is a treasured ingredient in kitchens worldwide, used to intensify the flavors in countless dishes.

1. Preheat the oven to 275°F. Wash the sweet potatoes, pat them dry, and poke a few holes in them.

2. Place the sweet potatoes in a baking dish, pour the shio koji over them, and turn the potatoes so that they are completely covered.

3. Place in the oven and roast until the sweet potatoes are very tender, about 1½ hours.

4. Remove from the oven, slice, and serve with the Salsa Macha.

INGREDIENTS:

4   SATSUMA SWEET POTATOES

¼   CUP SHIO KOJI

     SALSA MACHA (SEE PAGE 521)

FRIED BRUSSELS SPROUTS

YIELD: 4 SERVINGS / **ACTIVE TIME:** 30 MINUTES / **TOTAL TIME:** 30 MINUTES

This Mexican-inspired side beautifully balances spice with sweetness and creamy cheese, and has plenty of texture thanks to the sunflower seeds and fried Brussels sprouts.

1. Add canola oil to a Dutch oven until it is about 2 inches deep and warm to 350°F over medium heat.

2. Working in batches so as not to crowd the pot, gently slip the Brussels sprouts into the oil and fry until crispy and golden brown, 2 to 3 minutes. Transfer to a paper towel–lined plate and let the Brussels sprouts drain.

3. Place the Brussels sprouts in a bowl, add the Habanero Agave, and stir until the Brussels sprouts are coated. Season with salt and pepper, transfer to a serving dish, and garnish with the sunflower seeds and queso enchilada.

HABANERO AGAVE

1. Place all of the ingredients in a small saucepan and cook over medium heat until reduced by half, 15 to 20 minutes. Remove from heat, strain through a coffee filter, and use as desired.

INGREDIENTS:

	CANOLA OIL, AS NEEDED
3	CUPS BRUSSELS SPROUTS, TRIMMED AND HALVED
¼	CUP HABANERO AGAVE (SEE RECIPE)
	SALT AND PEPPER, TO TASTE
	SUNFLOWER SEEDS, ROASTED AND SHELLED, FOR GARNISH
	QUESO ENCHILADO, SHREDDED, FOR GARNISH

HABANERO AGAVE

1	CUP AGAVE NECTAR
2	TEASPOONS FRESH LIME JUICE
1	TEASPOON HABANERO POWDER

PURITOS DE PLATANO MACHO RELLENO DE FRIJOLES NEGROS Y MOLE NEGRO

YIELD: 4 SERVINGS / **ACTIVE TIME:** 45 MINUTES / **TOTAL TIME:** 1 HOUR AND 45 MINUTES

Chef Gabe Erales: "I first ate this dish in Tabasco at one of the most magical restaurants, Cocina Chontal, where Chef Nelly creates some of the most incredible food. This recipe can be challenging if the plantains aren't perfect. So be sure to choose some that are ripe, but not overripe."

1. Place the plantains, stock, bay leaves, and chile peppers in a large saucepan and bring to a simmer. Cook for 15 minutes, until the plantains start to open and are very soft.

2. Remove the plantains from the pan and let them cool. When cool enough to handle, remove them from their peels, place them in a bowl, and discard the peels. Mash the plantains until smooth and season them with salt.

3. Place one-quarter of the plantains in the center of each banana leaf and form each portion into a ¼-inch-thick rectangle. Leave enough room on each side of the plantain mash so that the banana leaves can be rolled up.

4. Place ¼ cup of the beans in the center of the plantains. Using the banana leaf to guide, roll the plantains over the black beans so that the mash completely encases the beans. Roll the banana leaf around the filling so that it completely encases the mixture. Twist the ends of the roll in opposite directions until very tight and tie each end with kitchen twine. Place the packets in the refrigerator and chill for 30 minutes.

5. Place the olive oil in a large cast-iron skillet and warm over medium heat. Add the packets and cook for approximately 1 minute on each side. Remove them from the pan and then remove the banana leaves.

6. Return the puritos to the pan and cook until caramelized on both sides, 3 to 4 minutes.

7. To serve, ladle ¼ cup of the mole onto each plate and top with the purito, either left whole or sliced. Serve with Queso Fresco and onion.

INGREDIENTS:

4   PLANTAINS, RIPE AND MOSTLY BLACK, UNPEELED

12 CUPS CHICKEN STOCK (SEE PAGE 341)

2   BAY LEAVES

2   PASILLA CHILE PEPPERS, STEMMED AND SEEDED

    SALT, TO TASTE

4   PIECES OF BANANA LEAVES, CUT INTO 12 x 6-INCH RECTANGLES, RIBS AND SPINES REMOVED, TOASTED

    FRIJOLES NEGROS REFRITOS (SEE PAGE 254)

3   TABLESPOONS EXTRA-VIRGIN OLIVE OIL

2   CUPS MOLE NEGRO (SEE PAGES 440–441), FOR SERVING

1   CUP SHREDDED QUESO FRESCO (SEE PAGE 522), FOR SERVING

    RED ONION, JULIENNED, FOR SERVING

CAMOTE CON MOLE BLANCO

YIELD: 4 SERVINGS / ACTIVE TIME: 45 MINUTES / TOTAL TIME: 1 HOUR AND 45 MINUTES

Mole blanco (white mole) is one of the rarest in Mexico, and its subtlety and lightness honor the rich flavors of the roasted sweet potato.

1. Preheat the oven to 450°F. Wash the sweet potatoes, pat them dry, and poke a few holes in each one.

2. Place them in a baking dish, drizzle the olive oil over the potatoes, and season with salt. Stir until the potatoes are covered, place them in the oven, and roast until so tender that a knife can easily be pushed into their centers, about 1 hour.

3. Remove the sweet potatoes from the oven and let them cool slightly. Slice the potatoes once they are cool enough to handle.

4. Ladle about ¼ cup of the mole onto each plate and top with the sweet potato. Garnish with some purslane and enjoy.

INGREDIENTS:

4   LARGE SWEET POTATOES

¼   CUP EXTRA-VIRGIN OLIVE OIL

     SALT, TO TASTE

     MOLE BLANCO (SEE PAGE 458), WARM

     PURSLANE, RINSED WELL AND STEMMED, FOR GARNISH

HUAUZONTLES RELLENO
DE QUESO CON CHILTOMATE

YIELD: 4 SERVINGS / **ACTIVE TIME:** 30 MINUTES / **TOTAL TIME:** 30 MINUTES

Huauzontles are a delicious superfood related to quinoa, amaranth, and epazote. They are delicious, but be sure to remove all the tough stems or eating them will be quite unpleasant.

1. Prepare an ice bath and bring water to a boil in a medium saucepan. Add salt and the huauzontles and boil for 2 minutes. Remove the greens from the water and shock them in the ice bath.

2. Place the huauzontles in a kitchen towel and gently wring it to remove as much water as possible.

3. Place the huauzontles, salt, cheese, cornstarch, masa, vodka, baking powder, and baking soda in the work bowl of a stand mixer fitted with the paddle attachment and beat until combined. Slowly add the Topo Chico and beat until the mixture is the consistency of a thick pancake batter. It should not be runny at all. Let the mixture rest for 20 minutes.

4. If the batter looks too dry after resting, incorporate more Topo Chico until the consistency is right.

5. Place the egg whites in a separate bowl and whip them until they are stiff peaks. Add them to the batter and gently beat until incorporated. The mixture should hold its shape when portioned out.

6. Add canola oil to a Dutch oven until it is 2 inches deep and warm to 350°F over medium heat. Gently drop ¼-cup portions of the batter into the oil and fry until golden brown and cooked all the way through, 4 to 5 minutes, turning the fritters as necessary. Transfer the cooked fritters to a paper towel–lined plate to drain.

7. Ladle about a ¼ cup of salsa onto each plate, top with the fritters, and serve with lime wedges.

INGREDIENTS:

SALT, TO TASTE

3½ OZ. HUAUZONTLES, STEMMED

1 TABLESPOON KOSHER SALT, PLUS MORE TO TASTE

3½ OZ. OAXACA CHEESE, SHREDDED

¾ CUP CORNSTARCH

3½ CUPS MASA HARINA

⅓ CUP VODKA

¼ TEASPOON BAKING POWDER

¼ TEASPOON BAKING SODA

⅔ CUP TOPO CHICO, PLUS MORE AS NEEDED

¼ CUP EGG WHITES

CANOLA OIL, AS NEEDED

SALSA DE CHILTOMATE (SEE PAGE 477), FOR SERVING

LIME WEDGES, FOR SERVING

HUAUZONTLE

Pronounced correctly by few (it's wah-zont-lay), and experienced by even fewer, the huauzontle has a storied history in Mexico. This nutritious, high-protein heirloom was the fourth most important crop in pre-Hispanic Mexico (after maize, beans, and chia), and so prized by the Aztecs that it was used as a tribute in religious ceremonies. The Spanish sensed its power and banned it soon after their conquest of Mexico, a move that removed it from the country's diet in all but a few outposts. As Mexican cuisine has risen in esteem, huauzontle's slightly bitter, earthy taste has also grown in popularity. It is still difficult to find, even in Mexico, but, as it's a hardy crop that thrives in adverse conditions, is a threat to spread the world over.

COFFEE & ANCHO ROASTED CARROTS
WITH CHILE TOREADO MAYO

YIELD: 4 SERVINGS / **ACTIVE TIME:** 45 MINUTES / **TOTAL TIME:** 45 MINUTES

The dark flavors of coffee and ancho chile work well with sweet, charred carrots. The chile-spiked mayo is a delicious amalgam of acid, fat, and heat. Try to track down a younger bunch of rainbow carrots, as they are sweeter.

1. Preheat the oven to 420°F. Place the carrots in a mixing bowl, add the olive oil, and toss to coat.

2. Combine the coffee, ancho chile powder, toasted coriander, and sumac in a small bowl and then sprinkle the mixture over the carrots. Season with salt and toss until the carrots are evenly coated.

3. Place the carrots in a baking dish, place it in the oven, and roast the carrots until they are charred, cooked through, and al dente, 15 to 20 minutes. Remove from the oven and let the carrots cool.

4. Warm a large cast-iron pan or comal over high heat. Add the serrano peppers and cook until charred all over, turning occasionally. Transfer the charred peppers to a bowl and add the soy sauce and lime juice. Let the peppers macerate for 15 minutes.

5. Place the peppers in a bowl and mash them into a paste. Stir it into the mayonnaise, and then incorporate the soy-and-lime mixture a bit at a time until the taste is to your liking.

6. Spread the mayonnaise on a serving plate, arrange the carrots on top, and garnish with the leafy carrot greens.

INGREDIENTS:

- 1   BUNCH OF ORGANIC RAINBOW CARROTS, LEAFY GREENS RESERVED FOR GARNISH
- 2   TABLESPOONS EXTRA-VIRGIN OLIVE OIL
- 2   TABLESPOONS INSTANT COFFEE
- 2   TABLESPOONS ANCHO CHILE POWDER
- ⅛   TEASPOON CORIANDER SEEDS, TOASTED AND GROUND
- 1   TABLESPOON SUMAC POWDER
-     SALT, TO TASTE
- 2   SERRANO CHILE PEPPERS
- 2   TABLESPOONS SOY SAUCE
- 2   TABLESPOONS FRESH LIME JUICE
- 1   CUP MAYONNAISE

TOMATO AGUACHILE

YIELD: 4 SERVINGS / ACTIVE TIME: 20 MINUTES / TOTAL TIME: 12 HOURS

This dish is a light and beautiful way to start a meal, especially during the summertime, when perfectly ripe tomatoes should be available locally. If you are feeling extra ambitious, ferment the tomato puree for a couple days before straining to add a nice, natural acidity.

1. Place the Roma tomatoes and dried chiles in a blender and pulse until the mixture is a coarse puree. Line a fine-mesh sieve or colander with cheesecloth, place it over a bowl, and pour the puree into the cheesecloth. Let the "tomato water" drip through for a minimum of 8 hours.

2. Season the tomato water with salt, stir in the lime juice, and set it aside. The pulp can be reserved, dehydrated, and turned into a flavorful seasoning powder.

3. Form the masa into small, crouton-sized balls. Add olive oil to a skillet until it is about 1 inch deep and warm it to 350°F. Working in batches, add the balls of masa to the oil and fry until they are very crispy. Transfer to a paper towel–lined plate to drain.

4. In a mixing bowl, combine the cherry tomatoes, cucumber, and aguachile and drizzle a bit of olive oil over the mixture.

5. Transfer the mixture to a shallow bowl and top with the Queso Fresco, red onion, serrano pepper, fried masa, and cilantro. Sprinkle a flaky sea salt over the dish, preferably Maldon.

INGREDIENTS:

2   LBS. ROMA TOMATOES

1   GUAJILLO CHILE PEPPER, STEMMED AND SEEDED

4   DRIED CHILES DE ARBOL

    SALT, TO TASTE

1   CUP FRESH LIME JUICE

½   CUP PREPARED MASA (SEE PAGE 352)

    EXTRA-VIRGIN OLIVE OIL, AS NEEDED

1   LB. CHERRY TOMATOES, HALVED

1   CUP PEELED AND DICED CUCUMBER

2   CUPS SHREDDED QUESO FRESCO (SEE PAGE 522)

1   SMALL RED ONION, JULIENNED

1   SERRANO CHILE PEPPER, STEMMED, SEEDED, AND SLICED VERY THIN

1   SMALL BUNCH OF FRESH CILANTRO

BETABEL WITH SALSA
MACHA Y QUESO FRESCO

YIELD: 4 SERVINGS / **ACTIVE TIME:** 15 MINUTES / **TOTAL TIME:** 1 HOUR

This recipe is a great way to serve beets to people that typically don't like them. Also, the nuttiness and spice of the Salsa Macha balances well against the earthy and salty Queso Fresco.

1. Preheat the oven to 420°F. If the beets are not similar in size, cut them so that they are. This will help them cook at the same rate. Place them on a large sheet of aluminum foil, drizzle the olive oil over the top, and season with salt.

2. Close the foil up so that it is a packet, with the seam on top. Place the packet on a parchment-lined baking sheet and roast in the oven until the beets are tender and just cooked through, about 45 minutes. A knife or a cake tester should be able to puncture the beet with minimal effort when they are done.

3. Remove from the oven and let the beets cool slightly. Peel and dice the beets. To avoid staining your hands when peeling the beets, gloves are recommended.

4. Place the beets in a serving dish and dress with the Salsa Macha. Garnish with the Queso Fresco and sorrel and serve.

INGREDIENTS:

1	LB. RED AND GOLDEN BEETS, RINSED WELL AND PATTED DRY
3	TABLESPOONS EXTRA-VIRGIN OLIVE OIL
	SALT, TO TASTE
¼	CUP SALSA MACHA (SEE PAGE 521)
2	CUPS SHREDDED QUESO FRESCO (SEE PAGE 522)
2	OZ. SORREL OR OTHER GREENS, FOR GARNISH

MUSHROOM BARBACOA

YIELD: 4 SERVINGS / **ACTIVE TIME:** 1 HOUR / **TOTAL TIME:** 8 HOURS

Gabe Erales: "Barbacoa is often made with goat, lamb, or the head of a cow. Over the years I have learned that cooking mushrooms often parallel that of a protein."

1. Place the coriander, cloves, allspice, cumin, and peppercorns in a dry skillet and toast until fragrant, shaking the pan frequently. Use a mortar and pestle or a spice grinder to grind the mixture into a powder.

2. Place the chiles in the skillet and toast until they are fragrant and pliable. Transfer the chiles to a bowl of hot water and soak for 20 minutes.

3. Drain the chiles and reserve the soaking liquid. Place the chiles, one of the onions, two of the garlic cloves, and some of the soaking liquid in a blender and puree until smooth. Add the toasted spice powder, orange and lime juice, and pulse until incorporated.

4. Season the mixture with salt and place it in a mixing bowl. Add the mushrooms and let them marinate for at least 6 hours.

5. Preheat the oven to 420°F. Remove the mushrooms from the marinade and place them in the banana leaves. Layer the remaining onion and garlic, bay leaves, and avocado leaves (if using) on top, fold the banana leaves to form a packet, and tie it closed with kitchen twine.

6. Place the packet on a parchment-lined baking sheet, place it in the oven, and roast for 20 minutes.

7. Remove from the oven and open the parcel up. Return to the oven and roast for an additional 10 to 15 minutes to caramelize the mushrooms.

8. Remove from the oven and serve with tortillas, Salsa Borracha, additional onion, cilantro, and lime wedges.

INGREDIENTS:

- 1 TABLESPOON CORIANDER SEEDS
- ½ TEASPOON WHOLE CLOVES
- ½ TEASPOON ALLSPICE BERRIES
- ½ TEASPOON CUMIN SEEDS
- 1½ TABLESPOONS BLACK PEPPERCORNS
- 1 ANCHO CHILE PEPPER, STEMMED AND SEEDED
- 1 GUAJILLO CHILE PEPPER, STEMMED AND SEEDED
- 1 CHIPOTLE CHILE PEPPER, STEMMED AND SEEDED
- 1 PASILLA CHILE PEPPER, STEMMED AND SEEDED
- 2 SMALL ONIONS, SLICED, PLUS MORE FOR SERVING
- 5 GARLIC CLOVES
- 1 CUP ORANGE JUICE
- 1 CUP FRESH LIME JUICE
- SALT, TO TASTE
- 2¼ LBS. MUSHROOMS, JULIENNED
- BANANA LEAVES, SPINES REMOVED AND TOASTED, AS NEEDED
- 2 BAY LEAVES
- 2 AVOCADO LEAVES (OPTIONAL)
- CORN TORTILLAS (SEE PAGE 352), FOR SERVING
- SALSA BORRACHA (SEE PAGE 508), FOR SERVING
- FRESH CILANTRO, CHOPPED, FOR SERVING
- LIME WEDGES, FOR SERVING

VERDOLAGAS EN SALSA VERDE

YIELD: 4 SERVINGS / **ACTIVE TIME:** 30 MINUTES / **TOTAL TIME:** 30 MINUTES

Verdolagas, or purslane, is a healthy, delicious, and succulent quelite that holds up well to stewing. The salsa verde in this recipe provides a delicious brightness to balance the flavor of the purslane.

1. Place the lard in a saucepan and warm it over medium heat. Add the onion and cook until it is translucent, about 3 minutes, stirring occasionally.

2. Add the garlic and cook for about 1 minute. Add the purslane and cook for 20 to 30 seconds, stirring to coat. Add the chile, epazote, and salsa verde, reduce the heat, and simmer the mixture for 15 minutes.

3. Season the mixture with salt and serve with Queso Fresco, tortillas, and lime wedges.

INGREDIENTS:

2   TABLESPOONS LARD

1   SMALL WHITE ONION, BRUNOISED

10 GARLIC CLOVES, MINCED

1   LB. PURSLANE, RINSED WELL AND STEMMED

3-4 FRESH EPAZOTE LEAVES

1   CHIPOTLE MORITA CHILE PEPPER, STEMMED, SEEDED, AND MINCED

2   CUPS SALSA CRUDA VERDE (SEE PAGE 525)

    SALT, TO TASTE

    QUESO FRESCO (SEE PAGE 522), SHREDDED, FOR SERVING

    CORN TORTILLAS (SEE PAGE 352), WARM, FOR SERVING

    LIME WEDGES, FOR SERVING

CHAYOTE EN PIPIAN ROJO

YIELD: 4 SERVINGS / **ACTIVE TIME:** 30 MINUTES / **TOTAL TIME:** 45 MINUTES

Pipian is a seed-based sauce, and here we see it paired with chayote, a vegetable whose flavor is something like what the offspring of a cucumber and squash would taste like.

1. Cut the chayote in quarters and remove the pits.

2. Place the chayote in a saucepan and cover with stock by 1 or 2 inches. Season the stock generously with salt and bring it to a simmer. Cook the chayote until it is al dente. Remove and let cool in the refrigerator.

3. Place the lard in a large cast-iron skillet and warm over medium-high heat. Place the chayote in the pan, cut side down, and sear until caramelized. Repeat with the other cut sides.

4. Ladle about a ¼ cup of the Pipian Rojo onto each serving plate, top with some of the chayote, and sprinkle flaky sea salt over the top, preferably Maldon. Garnish with the cilantro, parsley, and toasted pumpkin seeds and enjoy.

INGREDIENTS:

2-3   LARGE CHAYOTES

CHICKEN STOCK (SEE PAGE 341), AS NEEDED

SALT, TO TASTE

2   TABLESPOONS LARD

1½   CUPS PIPIAN ROJO (SEE PAGE 484), WARM

FRESH CILANTRO, CHOPPED, FOR GARNISH

FRESH PARSLEY, CHOPPED, FOR GARNISH

PUMPKIN SEEDS, TOASTED, FOR GARNISH

FRIJOL AYOCOTE WITH PASILLA YOGURT

YIELD: 8 SERVINGS / **ACTIVE TIME:** 30 MINUTES / **TOTAL TIME:** 1 HOUR

Ayocotes are thick-skinned runner beans that are full of starch, a quality that helps them transform into a meaty and creamy wonder when cooked perfectly. Pair these beans with spicy yogurt for heat, creaminess, and acidity.

1. Discard any floating beans. Drain the beans and remove any small pebbles from them.

2. Place the cumin seeds, peppercorns, and allspice in a dry skillet and toast until fragrant, shaking the pan frequently. Remove the pan from heat.

3. Place the oil in a large saucepan and warm over medium heat. Add the onion and cook until it is translucent, about 3 minutes. Add the garlic, cinnamon, and toasted spices and cook, stirring frequently, for 1 minute. Turn off the heat and add the bay leaf and epazote (if desired).

4. Add the beans and cover by 2 inches with the unsalted stock. Bring to a simmer over medium heat, reduce the heat, and cover the pan. Gently simmer the beans until they are very tender, about 2 hours. A good test for when the beans are done is to remove spoonful containing five beans and blow on them—if the skin peels back on all of the beans, they are ready.

5. Place the chiles in a dry skillet and toast them over medium heat until fragrant and pliable. Remove from the pan and let them cool. Using a mortar and pestle or a spice grinder, grind the chiles into a powder.

6. Fold the pasilla powder into the yogurt. Stir in the lime juice and season with salt.

7. Drain the beans and reserve the broth. Ladle the beans into bowls, spoon a bit of the broth over them, and top each portion with a dollop of the pasilla yogurt. Serve with cilantro, tortillas, and diced avocado.

INGREDIENTS:

1   LB. RANCHO GORDO AYOCOTE BEANS, SOAKED OVERNIGHT

1   TABLESPOON CUMIN SEEDS

1   TABLESPOON BLACK PEPPERCORNS

2   ALLSPICE BERRIES

2   TABLESPOONS EXTRA-VIRGIN OLIVE OIL

1   SMALL YELLOW ONION, BRUNOISED

10 GARLIC CLOVES

¼   CINNAMON STICK, GRATED

1   BAY LEAF

3-6 FRESH EPAZOTE LEAVES (OPTIONAL)

    UNSALTED CHICKEN OR VEGETABLE STOCK (SEE PAGE 341 OR 346), AS NEEDED

4   PASILLA CHILE PEPPERS, STEMMED AND SEEDED

2   CUPS YOGURT

    JUICE OF 1 LIME

    SALT, TO TASTE

    FRESH CILANTRO, CHOPPED, FOR SERVING

    CORN TORTILLAS (SEE PAGE 352), WARM, FOR SERVING

    AVOCADO, DICED, FOR SERVING

QUESADILLAS DE CHAMPIÑONES

YIELD: 6 SERVINGS / **ACTIVE TIME:** 20 MINUTES / **TOTAL TIME:** 45 MINUTES

Quesadillas are a great way to use freshly made masa tortillas, and can support a wide array of fillings. Serve as an appetizer, or a light yet luscious main course.

1. Place the chiles in a bowl of warm water and soak for 20 minutes. Drain and chop the chiles.

2. Place the olive oil in a large skillet and warm it over medium heat. Add the onion, garlic, and chiles and cook until the onion has softened, about 5 minutes, stirring frequently.

3. Add the chopped tomato and epazote leaves, season the mixture with salt, and cook, stirring occasionally, for another 5 minutes. Remove the pan from heat and set the salsa aside.

4. Working with moist hands and 4 ounces of masa at a time, form the masa into a golf ball–sized sphere. Line a tortilla press with squares of resealable plastic bag. Place the ball on the press and gently press down. Rotate the masa and plastic 180° and press down again. Repeat until you have used all of the masa.

5. Warm a comal or a cast-iron skillet over medium-high heat. Place a freshly made tortilla on the pan and spoon some of the Mushroom Barbacoa over it. Cover with some of the cheese, place another tortilla on top, and add some cheese on top. Lay another tortilla on top and press down to seal the filling. Cook until the quesadillas are golden brown on both sides and the cheese is melted, about 6 minutes.

6. Repeat until all of the barbacoa has been used and serve with the salsa.

INGREDIENTS:

3   DRIED CHILES DE ARBOL, STEMMED AND SEEDED

1   TABLESPOON EXTRA-VIRGIN OLIVE OIL

½   WHITE ONION, SLICED THIN

2   GARLIC CLOVES

2   LARGE TOMATOES, FINELY DICED

6   FRESH EPAZOTE LEAVES

      SALT, TO TASTE

1   LB. PREPARED MASA (SEE PAGE 352)

3   CUPS MUSHROOM BARBACOA (SEE PAGE 239)

2   CUPS SHREDDED QUESO FRESCO (SEE PAGE 522)

2   CUPS SHREDDED OAXACA CHEESE (OPTIONAL)

FRIJOLES NEGROS REFRITOS

YIELD: 6 SERVINGS / **ACTIVE TIME:** 15 MINUTES / **TOTAL TIME:** 15 MINUTES

The simplicity and nutrients beans carry make them a pillar of Mexican cuisine. If you prefer a smooth texture in your refried beans, simply add them to a blender or food processor instead of mashing them.

1. Place the lard in a large skillet and warm over medium heat. Add the chiles and garlic to the pan and cook until fragrant, about 1 minute. Remove them from the pan and set them aside. When cool enough to handle, finely chop the chiles and garlic.

2. Add the black beans and fry for 2 minutes, stirring frequently.

3. Using a fork or wooden spoon, smash the beans to create an uneven mixture of mashed and whole beans. Stir the chiles and garlic back into the pan and season the beans with salt. Top with the epazote and serve.

INGREDIENTS:

½ CUP LARD

4 DRIED CHILES DE ARBOL, STEMMED AND SEEDED

3 GARLIC CLOVES

4 CUPS COOKED OR CANNED BLACK BEANS

SALT, TO TASTE

LEAVES FROM 3 SPRIGS OF FRESH EPAZOTE

FRIJOLES DE LA OLLA

YIELD: 6 SERVINGS / **ACTIVE TIME:** 10 MINUTES / **TOTAL TIME:** 24 HOURS

This classic dish is an excellent accompaniment to any of the recipes featured in this book. Also, you'll want to get in the habit of saving the broth that results from cooking the beans, as it is loaded with rich flavor.

1. Place 8 cups of water in a medium saucepan and bring it to a boil.

2. Add the beans, onion, garlic, and vinegar and cook until the beans are tender, about 1½ hours.

3. Remove a spoonful containing five beans from the pan and blow on them—if their skins peel back, they're ready.

4. Season with salt and the epazote and drain, making sure to reserve the broth.

INGREDIENTS:

1   CUP DRIED BLACK BEANS, SORTED, RINSED, AND SOAKED OVERNIGHT

1   WHITE ONION, QUARTERED

3   GARLIC CLOVES

1   TABLESPOON WHITE VINEGAR

    SALT, TO TASTE

5   SPRIGS OF FRESH EPAZOTE

FLOR DE CALABAZA CON QUESO
FRESCO Y HIERBABUENA

YIELD: 4 SERVINGS / **ACTIVE TIME:** 20 MINUTES / **TOTAL TIME:** 50 MINUTES

The mint and lemon in the recipe add bright and herbaceous notes in this quick and delicious appetizer.

1. Place the squash blossoms on a paper towel–lined baking sheet.

2. Finely chop the hierbabuena and combine it with the Queso Fresco. Add the lemon zest and juice, season the mixture with salt, and stir to combine.

3. Stuff the squash blossoms with the mixture, taking care not to tear the flowers.

4. In a small bowl, combine the flour, baking powder, egg yolks, and seltzer water and work the mixture with a whisk until it is a smooth batter. Let the batter rest for 20 minutes.

5. Place the canola oil in a deep skillet and warm to 350°F over medium heat.

6. Fold the tips of the squash blossoms closed and dip them into the batter until completely coated. Gently slip them into the oil and fry until crispy and golden brown all over, about 2 minutes, making sure you only turn the squash blossoms once.

7. Drain the fried squash blossoms on the baking sheet. Season them lightly with salt and, if desired, drizzle honey over them before serving.

INGREDIENTS:

10	SQUASH BLOSSOMS, STAMENS REMOVED
1	BUNCH OF FRESH HIERBABUENA OR SPEARMINT
2	CUPS SHREDDED QUESO FRESCO (SEE PAGE 522)
	ZEST AND JUICE OF 1 LEMON
	SALT, TO TASTE
1	CUP ALL-PURPOSE FLOUR
1	TEASPOON BAKING POWDER
2	EGG YOLKS
1	CUP SELTZER WATER
2	CUPS CANOLA OIL
2	TABLESPOONS HONEY (OPTIONAL)

CALABACITAS CON ELOTE Y QUESO FRESCO

YIELD: 4 SERVINGS / **ACTIVE TIME:** 15 MINUTES / **TOTAL TIME:** 35 MINUTES

A simple and delicious dish that may be made with whatever squash is in season. It's a rustic dish that will be served family style in households across Mexico.

1. Place the oil in a skillet and warm over low heat. Add the chiles and toast lightly until fragrant, taking care not to burn them. Remove the chiles from the pan and set them aside. When cool enough to handle, chop the chiles.

2. Add the onion and garlic to the pan and cook until the onion is translucent, about 3 minutes, stirring frequently.

3. Add the corn and cook for 2 minutes, stirring occasionally. Add the tomatoes and cook until they begin to release their juices.

4. Add the squash, season the mixture with salt, and cook until the vegetables are tender, about 10 minutes.

5. Add the epazote to the pan and cook for 1 minute. Remove them from the pan, add the chiles, and stir until evenly distributed.

6. To serve, top the calabacitas with the shredded cheese.

INGREDIENTS:

2   TABLESPOONS EXTRA-VIRGIN OLIVE OIL

3   DRIED CHILES DE ARBOL, STEMMED AND SEEDED

½   WHITE ONION, DICED

3   GARLIC CLOVES, SLICED THIN

     KERNELS FROM 2 EARS OF CORN

2   LARGE TOMATOES, SEEDED AND DICED

4   MEXICAN SQUASH, DICED

     SALT, TO TASTE

3   SPRIGS OF FRESH EPAZOTE

1   CUP SHREDDED QUESO FRESCO (SEE PAGE 522)

TORTITAS DE COLIFLOR

YIELD: 4 SERVINGS / **ACTIVE TIME:** 25 MINUTES / **TOTAL TIME:** 45 MINUTES

This light yet filling recipe is one that can be made with whichever vegetable you have on hand, and what is in season.

1. Bring water to a boil in a medium saucepan and prepare an ice bath.

2. Cut the cauliflower into 3-inch-wide florets. Add these and salt to the water and boil for 5 minutes. Remove the cauliflower from the water and shock it in the ice bath. Drain and place the cauliflower on paper towels to dry.

3. In the work bowl of a stand mixer fitted with the whisk attachment, add the egg whites and whip on high until they hold stiff peaks. Add the egg yolks one at a time, reduce the speed to low, and beat until just incorporated, about 2 minutes. Add 2 tablespoons of the flour and again beat until just incorporated, as you do not want to overwork the batter.

4. Place the oil in a deep skillet and warm it to 310°F.

5. Bring water to a boil in a medium saucepan. Add the tomatoes, garlic, and onion and cook until tender, about 7 minutes. Drain, place the vegetables in a blender, and puree until smooth. Season the sauce with salt, stir in the oregano, and set it aside.

6. Place the remaining flour in a shallow bowl and dredge the cauliflower in it until coated.

7. Gently slip the cauliflower into the oil and fry until it is crispy and golden brown, turning just once. If necessary, work in batches to avoid overcrowding the pan. Place the cauliflower fritters on a paper towel–lined plate and season them with salt.

8. Serve the sauce alongside the fritters.

INGREDIENTS:

1	LARGE HEAD OF CAULIFLOWER
	SALT, TO TASTE
4	EGG WHITES
4	EGG YOLKS
1	CUP ALL-PURPOSE FLOUR
2	CUPS EXTRA-VIRGIN OLIVE OIL
2	LARGE TOMATOES
2	GARLIC CLOVES
¼	WHITE ONION
1	TEASPOON DRIED MEXICAN OREGANO

CHILES RELLENOS

YIELD: 6 SERVINGS / **ACTIVE TIME:** 1 HOUR / **TOTAL TIME:** 2 HOURS

Chiles rellenos, or "stuffed chiles," may take some practice to get perfect, but the result is worth it—a crispy exterior and an interior that melts in your mouth.

1. Roast the poblanos over an open flame, on the grill, or in the oven until charred all over. Place them in a bowl, cover it with plastic wrap, and let them sit for 5 minutes.

2. Remove the chiles from the bowl and remove the charred skin with your hands.

3. Using a sharp paring knife, make a cut close to the stems of the peppers. Remove the seed pod, but leave the stems attached.

4. Stuff the chiles with 1 to 2 ounces of cheese (the amount depends on the size of the chile) and use toothpicks to seal the small cuts you've made.

5. In the work bowl of a stand mixer fitted with the whisk attachment, add the egg whites and whip on high until they hold stiff peaks.

6. Add the egg yolks, reduce the speed to low, and beat until just incorporated, about 30 seconds. Add ½ cup of flour and again beat until just incorporated, as you do not want to overwork the batter.

7. Place the oil in a large, deep skillet and warm it to 325°F.

8. Bring water to a boil in a medium saucepan. Add the tomatoes, garlic, and onion and cook until tender, about 7 minutes. Drain, place the vegetables in a blender, and puree until smooth. Season the sauce with salt, stir in the oregano, and set it aside.

9. Place the remaining flour on a baking sheet. Dredge the chiles in the flour until coated on all sides. Dip the chiles into the batter and gently slip them into the oil.

10. Fry the chiles until crispy and golden brown, about 5 minutes, making sure you turn them just once. Drain on a paper towel–lined plate.

11. When all of the chiles have been cooked, serve them alongside the tomato sauce.

INGREDIENTS:

6	LARGE POBLANO CHILE PEPPERS
1	LB. OAXACA OR MONTEREY JACK CHEESE
4	EGG WHITES
4	EGG YOLKS
2	CUPS ALL-PURPOSE FLOUR
2	CUPS CANOLA OIL
2	LARGE TOMATOES
2	GARLIC CLOVES
¼	WHITE ONION
	SALT, TO TASTE
1	TEASPOON DRIED MEXICAN OREGANO

ENSALADA DE NOPALES

YIELD: 4 SERVINGS / ACTIVE TIME: 30 MINUTES / TOTAL TIME: 45 MINUTES

This simple salad is a versatile accompaniment to many of the dishes in this book and may be served cold or warm, and at any time of the day.

1. Place the nopales in a small bowl and season all over with the salt. Let rest for 15 minutes.

2. Combine the onion, tomatoes, and cilantro in a separate bowl.

3. Place the nopales and 1 tablespoon of water in a large skillet, cover it, and cook over medium heat until the nopales is tender, about 12 minutes. Remove from the pan and let cool. When cool enough to handle, cut the nopales into ¼-inch strips.

4. Stir the nopales into the tomato mixture, add the lemon juice, and season the salad with salt. If desired, serve with Queso Fresco or cotija cheese.

INGREDIENTS:

- 3   LARGE NOPALES, SPINES REMOVED
- 1   TABLESPOON KOSHER SALT, PLUS MORE TO TASTE
- ½   WHITE ONION, FINELY DICED
- 2   LARGE TOMATOES, FINELY DICED
- ½   BUNCH OF FRESH CILANTRO, CHOPPED

JUICE OF 1 LEMON

QUESO FRESCO (SEE PAGE 522), FOR SERVING (OPTIONAL)

COTIJA CHEESE, FOR SERVING (OPTIONAL)

CHILAQUILES ROJOS

YIELD: 4 SERVINGS / **ACTIVE TIME:** 30 MINUTES / **TOTAL TIME:** 35 MINUTES

A traditional breakfast recipe composed of fried and torn tortillas, eggs, sliced onion, and queso fresco. In the state of Sinaloa the dish is often made with cream, whereas in Guadalajara, the dish is often cooked in small pots known as cazuelas until the tortillas are cooked down to thicken the sauce. In the northeast part of Mexico, this red sauce is traditionally used.

1. Bring water to a boil in a medium saucepan. Add the tomatoes, garlic, and half of the onion and cook until tender, about 7 minutes.

2. Place the chiles in a bowl and pour some of the hot water over them. Drain the remaining water, place the vegetables in a blender, and puree until smooth. Leave the puree in the blender. Let the chiles soak for 15 minutes.

3. Place the canola oil in a deep skillet and warm it to 350°F. Add the tortillas and fry until crispy, about 3 minutes. Place the fried tortillas on a paper towel–lined plate and let them drain.

4. Preheat the oven to 350°F. Add the chiles to the puree and blitz until smooth. Season the puree generously with salt and set it aside.

5. Place the olive oil in a large cast-iron skillet and warm over medium heat. Add the remaining onion and cook until translucent, about 3 minutes.

6. Add the sauce and the tortillas to the skillet and stir until everything is coated in the sauce. Crack the eggs on top, crumble the Queso Fresco over everything, and place the skillet in the oven.

7. Bake until the eggs are cooked as desired and the cheese is slightly melted. Serve with additional cheese and ciltantro.

INGREDIENTS:

4	LARGE TOMATOES
2	GARLIC CLOVES
½	WHITE ONION, SLICED THIN
2	GUAJILLO CHILE PEPPERS, STEMMED AND SEEDED
2	DRIED CHILES DE ARBOL, STEMMED AND SEEDED
2	CUPS CANOLA OIL
1	LB. CORN TORTILLAS (SEE PAGE 352), CUT INTO TRIANGLES
	SALT, TO TASTE
2	TABLESPOONS EXTRA-VIRGIN OLIVE OIL
4	LARGE EGGS
2	CUPS QUESO FRESCO (SEE PAGE 522), PLUS MORE FOR SERVING
	FRESH CILANTRO, CHOPPED, FOR SERVING)

TAQUITOS DE REQUESÓN CON RAJAS

YIELD: 4 SERVINGS / **ACTIVE TIME:** 20 MINUTES / **TOTAL TIME:** 35 MINUTES

Mexican requesón and roasted poblano peppers are the perfect filling for these crispy rolled tacos, which will be hard to resist just out of the pan.

1. Roast the poblano chiles over an open flame, on the grill, or in the oven until charred all over. Place the poblanos in a bowl, cover it with plastic wrap, and let them steam for 10 minutes. When cool enough to handle, remove the skins, seeds, and stems from the poblanos and slice the remaining flesh thin.

2. Stir the poblanos into the requesón, season with salt, and set the mixture aside.

3. Place the tortillas in a dry skillet and warm for 1 minute on each side. Fill the tortillas with the cheese-and-poblano mixture and roll them up tight.

4. Place the oil in a skillet and warm over medium heat. Place the tortillas in the pan, seam side down, and cook for 1 minute before turning them over. Cook the taquitos until brown on all sides and place on a paper towel–lined plate to drain.

5. Serve the taquitos with Guacamole and salsa.

INGREDIENTS:

2	POBLANO CHILE PEPPERS
2	CUPS REQUESÓN OR FRESH RICOTTA CHEESE
	SALT, TO TASTE
8	CORN TORTILLAS (SEE PAGE 352)
¼	CUP EXTRA-VIRGIN OLIVE OIL
	GUACAMOLE (SEE PAGE 432), FOR SERVING
	SALSA, FOR SERVING

TAQUITOS DE PAPA

YIELD: 4 SERVINGS / **ACTIVE TIME:** 30 MINUTES / **TOTAL TIME:** 45 MINUTES

Simple and classic homestyle cooking, taquitos are a perfect way to add an intriguing, light, and delicious appetizer to your next gathering.

1. Place the potatoes in a small saucepan and cover with cold water. Bring it to a boil, season the water with salt, and reduce the heat so that the potatoes simmer. Cook until tender, about 18 minutes.

2. Drain the potatoes, place them in a mixing bowl, and mash until smooth. Season with salt.

3. Fill the tortillas with the potatoes and either roll them up tight or fold over to form half-moons.

4. Place the oil in a deep skillet and warm over medium heat. Add the filled tortillas to the oil and fry until browned and crispy. Place the taquitos on a paper towel–lined plate to drain.

5. Combine the tomatoes, onion, and chiles in a small mixing bowl. Season the pico de gallo with salt and stir in the cilantro.

6. Top the taquitos with the cabbage and serve with the pico de gallo and cotija cheese.

INGREDIENTS:

2   RUSSET POTATOES, PEELED AND QUARTERED

    SALT, TO TASTE

6   CORN TORTILLAS (SEE PAGE 352)

1   CUP EXTRA-VIRGIN OLIVE OIL

2   LARGE TOMATOES, FINELY DICED

½   ONION, FINELY DICED

2   JALAPEÑO CHILE PEPPERS, STEMMED, SEEDED, AND FINELY DICED

1   CUP FRESH CILANTRO, CHOPPED

2   CUPS FINELY SHREDDED GREEN CABBAGE

2   CUPS CRUMBLED COTIJA CHEESE, FOR SERVING

SOUPS

With all its wonderful sauces and condiments, Mexican cuisine inclines toward soupy, a wonderful attribute, considering what a pleasant utensil the tortilla makes for scooping up the rich remnants.

That facility for composing comforting bowls extends, despite the warm temperatures that reign throughout the country, into soup. From the pozole (see page 288 and 304) that frequently serves as the centerpiece of a celebration and the menudo that provides a soft landing spot after a long, hard night (see page 293), to simple seafood- and vegetable-enriched broths that make the most of readily available ingredients, you'll soon see that Mexican cuisine maintains its momentum when confronted with the stockpot.

POZOLE BLANCO

YIELD: 10 SERVINGS / **ACTIVE TIME:** 1 HOUR / **TOTAL TIME:** 3 HOURS

Pozole is a traditional soup that may have origins in the state of Jalisco, but variations are seen throughout the country, including versions with ground shrimp, green or red broths, and any number of meats. You may forgo using calcium oxide by cooking the hominy over low heat for 2 hours.

1. Drain the hominy and place it in a large saucepan. Add the water, calcium oxide, and salt and bring to a boil. Cook for 30 minutes.

2. Drain the hominy and run it under cold water, rubbing the hominy between your hands to remove the loosened husks. Set the hominy aside.

3. Place the pork and chicken in a large saucepan. Fill the pan with water until it is no less than 2 inches from the top. Add the onion and garlic, season with salt, and bring to a simmer. Reduce the heat to low and cook until the pork and chicken are tender and falling apart, about 2 hours.

4. Remove the chicken from the pot. Remove the bones and skin and save the bones for another preparation.

5. Use a strainer to remove the garlic skins from the broth. Return the chicken to the pot, add the hominy, and cook for another 30 minutes.

6. Ladle the pozole into warmed bowls and serve with radish, cabbage, lime wedges, and salsa.

INGREDIENTS:

1½   LBS. DRIED HOMINY, SOAKED OVERNIGHT

16   CUPS WATER, PLUS MORE AS NEEDED

½   OZ. CALCIUM OXIDE

1   TABLESPOON KOSHER SALT, PLUS MORE TO TASTE

2   LB. PORK BUTT, CUT INTO 2-INCH CUBES

2   LBS. BONE-IN, SKIN-ON CHICKEN

1   ONION, HALVED

1   HEAD OF GARLIC

RADISHES, SLICED THIN, FOR SERVING

GREEN CABBAGE, FINELY SHREDDED, FOR SERVING

LIME WEDGES, FOR SERVING

SALSA OR HOT SAUCE, FOR SERVING

MENUDO

YIELD: 10 SERVINGS / **ACTIVE TIME:** 30 MINUTES / **TOTAL TIME:** 3 HOURS

This spicy soup is served on weekends in homes across the country, and is particularly great the morning after a night on the town. Also, a butcher will be willing to cut the marrow bones for you if you're nervous about doing so at home.

1. Place the tripe and marrow bones in a large saucepan and fill it with water. Bring to a boil, season generously with salt, and reduce the heat to low. Cook for 2½ hours.

2. Place the chiles in a bowl. Pour 2 cups of the warm broth over the chiles and let them soak for 20 minutes.

3. Place the chilies, soaking liquid, tomato, and garlic in a blender and puree until smooth. Strain the sauce into the saucepan, stir in the oregano and cumin, and add the hominy, if using. Continue to cook over low heat.

4. When the flavor has developed to your liking and the tripe is very tender, ladle the soup into warmed bowls and garnish with the chopped onion, cilantro, and additional arbol chile and oregano. Serve with warm tortillas and lime wedges.

INGREDIENTS:

- 3 LB. HONEYCOMB TRIPE, CUT INTO 2- TO 3-INCH PIECES
- 1 LB. MARROW BONES, CUT INTO 3-INCH PIECES
- SALT, TO TASTE
- 6 GUAJILLO CHILE PEPPERS, STEMMED AND SEEDED
- 2 DRIED CHILES DE ARBOL, STEMMED AND SEEDED, PLUS MORE FOR GARNISH
- 1 LARGE TOMATO
- 3 GARLIC CLOVES
- 1 TABLESPOON DRIED MEXICAN OREGANO, PLUS MORE FOR GARNISH
- 1 TEASPOON CUMIN
- 5 CUPS HOMINY (OPTIONAL, SEE PAGE 288 FOR HOMEMADE)
- WHITE ONION, CHOPPED, FOR GARNISH
- ½ CUP CHOPPED FRESH CILANTRO, FOR GARNISH
- CORN TORTILLAS (SEE PAGE 352), WARM, FOR SERVING
- LIME WEDGES, FOR SERVING

MOMMA'S SOPA DE CONCHITAS

YIELD: 4 SERVINGS / ACTIVE TIME: 20 MINUTES / TOTAL TIME: 35 MINUTES

This classic noodle soup is served throughout the year in Mexico, but becomes a national treasure during the winter.

1. Place the oil, pasta, onion, and garlic in a medium saucepan and cook, stirring occasionally, until the shells are golden brown, 4 to 5 minutes.

2. Place the tomatoes in a blender and add 1 cup of the stock. Puree until smooth, add the puree to the pan, and stir in the remaining stock, cumin, salt, and pepper. Simmer the soup until the shells are tender, 10 to 12 minutes.

3. Ladle the soup into warm bowls and garnish with cilantro. Spoon the roasted marrow out of the bones and onto the soup and serve with the Lime Crema.

BONE MARROW

1. Preheat the oven to 450°F. Place the marrow bones upright on a baking sheet, place them in the oven, and roast for 15 minutes. Remove from the oven and use immediately.

LIME CREMA

1. Place the ingredients in a small bowl, stir to combine, and use as desired.

INGREDIENTS:

¼	CUP EXTRA-VIRGIN OLIVE OIL
8	OZ. SMALL SHELL PASTA
½	WHITE ONION, DICED
2	GARLIC CLOVES, DICED
2	MEDIUM HEIRLOOM TOMATOES
6	CUPS CHICKEN STOCK (SEE PAGE 341)
2⅓	TABLESPOONS CUMIN
	SALT AND PEPPER, TO TASTE
	FRESH CILANTRO, CHOPPED, FOR GARNISH
	BONE MARROW (SEE RECIPE), FOR GARNISH
	LIME CREMA (SEE RECIPE), FOR SERVING

BONE MARROW

4	MARROW BONES

LIME CREMA

3	OZ. CREMA (MEXICAN SOUR CREAM)
1	TABLESPOON FRESH LIME JUICE
	SALT, TO TASTE

SOPA DE HONGOS

YIELD: 4 SERVINGS / **ACTIVE TIME:** 30 MINUTES / **TOTAL TIME:** 1 HOUR AND 15 MINUTES

Mushrooms play an important role in the Maya and other indigenous cultures, as the fungi is mentioned in various codices, primarily for spiritual and medicinal practices. This soup pays homage to those deep traditions.

1. Place the water in a medium saucepan and bring it to a simmer. Add the mushroom stems and simmer for 10 to 15 minutes to create a flavorful broth. Strain the broth and set it aside.

2. Place the chiles in a dry skillet and toast them for 30 seconds. Remove the chiles from the pan and chiffonade them.

3. Place the butter in a clean medium saucepan and melt over medium-high heat. Add the mushrooms and cook until they are well browned, about 15 minutes, stirring occasionally.

4. Add the onion and cook until translucent, about 3 minutes, stirring occasionally. Add the garlic and chiles and cook until fragrant, about 1 minute. Add the mushroom broth and bring to a gentle simmer.

5. Place the epazote, thyme, and bay leaf in a sachet of cheesecloth and add it to the soup. Simmer the soup until the flavor has developed to your liking, 20 to 30 minutes.

6. Season the soup with salt and ladle it into warmed bowls.

INGREDIENTS:

8   CUPS WATER

1   LB. SHIITAKE MUSHROOMS, STEMS RESERVED, CAPS QUARTERED

3-4   PASILLA CHILE PEPPERS, STEMMED AND SEEDED

3   TABLESPOONS UNSALTED BUTTER

1   SMALL WHITE ONION, BRUNOISED

7   GARLIC CLOVES, MINCED

3-4   FRESH EPAZOTE LEAVES

1   SMALL BUNCH OF THYME

1   BAY LEAF

    SALT, TO TASTE

SOPA DE CHORIZO, AYOCOTES Y ACELGAS

YIELD: 4 SERVINGS / **ACTIVE TIME:** 30 MINUTES / **TOTAL TIME:** 24 HOURS

This dish is reminiscent of cassoulet in some ways with strong flavors from the chorizo, earthiness from the chard, and creaminess from the ayocote beans.

1. Drain the beans and set them aside.

2. Place the chorizo in a large saucepan and cook it over medium-low heat until the fat has rendered, 2 to 3 minutes.

3. Add the onion and chard stems and cook until the onion is translucent, about 3 minutes. Add the garlic, bay leaf, and chiles and cook for 1 minute, until fragrant, stirring frequently.

4. Add the chard leaves and cook, stirring frequently, until they start to wilt, about 2 minutes.

5. Add the stock, epazote, and the beans and bring the soup to a gentle simmer. Cook until the beans are tender, about 45 minutes to 1 hour. Season with salt and serve with the lime wedges and toasted bread.

INGREDIENTS:

1   LB. DRIED AYOCOTE BEANS (RANCHO GORDO PREFERRED), SOAKED OVERNIGHT

8   OZ. MEXICAN CHORIZO, CASING REMOVED

1   LARGE WHITE ONION, BRUNOISED

1   LB. SWISS CHARD, CLEANED, LEAVES TORN, STEMS DICED

10 GARLIC CLOVES, MINCED

1   BAY LEAF

1   CHIPOTLE MORITA CHILE PEPPER, STEMMED, SEEDED, AND HALVED

1   GUAJILLO CHILE PEPPER, STEMMED, SEEDED, AND CHIFFONADE

8   CUPS CHICKEN OR VEGETABLE STOCK (SEE PAGE 341 OR 346)

1   SMALL BUNCH OF FRESH EPAZOTE

    SALT, TO TASTE

    LIME WEDGES, FOR SERVING

    BUTTERED AND TOASTED BOLILLO OR TELERA, FOR SERVING

SERE DE PESCADO

YIELD: 4 SERVINGS / **ACTIVE TIME:** 30 MINUTES / **TOTAL TIME:** 1 HOUR

This dish is a great demonstration of the global influences that Mexican cuisine has effortlessly incorporated.

1. Preheat a grill to medium heat (about 400°F) or warm a cast-iron skillet over medium heat. Place the tomatoes on the cooking surface and cook until charred all over, turning frequently. Remove the tomatoes and let them cool briefly. When cool enough to handle, chop the tomatoes and set them aside.

2. Place half of the olive oil in a large skillet and warm over medium heat. Add the onion, garlic, serrano peppers, chile de arbol, and oregano and cook until the onion turns translucent, about 3 minutes, stirring frequently.

3. Add the tomatoes and cook and they start to collapse, about 10 minutes, stirring occasionally.

4. Add the coconut milk, stock, and bay leaf and simmer for 20 minutes, stirring occasionally.

5. Stir in the lime zest, lime juice, and the honey. Season the broth with salt and remove it from heat.

6. Warm the remaining olive oil in a cast-iron skillet over medium-high heat. Pat the halibut fillets dry with a paper towel and season generously with salt.

7. Place the halibut in the pan, skin side down, and cook until caramelized and crispy, 2 to 3 minutes. Turn the halibut over and cook until just cooked through and opaque. Remove from the pan and let the halibut rest for 3 minutes.

8. Ladle ¼ cup of the broth into each bowl and top with a fillet. Serve with lime wedges, radishes, scallions, and cilantro.

INGREDIENTS:

3	SMALL ROMA TOMATOES
¼	CUP EXTRA-VIRGIN OLIVE OIL
¾	SMALL WHITE ONION, CHOPPED
10	GARLIC CLOVES, MINCED
2	SERRANO CHILE PEPPERS, STEMMED, SEEDED, AND MINCED
1	DRIED CHILE DE ARBOL, STEMMED, SEEDED, AND MINCED
⅛	TEASPOON DRIED MEXICAN OREGANO
2	CUPS COCONUT MILK
6	CUPS FISH STOCK (SEE PAGE 345)
1	BAY LEAF
	ZEST AND JUICE OF 1 LIME
2	TEASPOONS HONEY
	SALT, TO TASTE
1½	LBS. HALIBUT FILLETS, BONED
	LIME WEDGES, FOR SERVING
	RADISHES, SLICED THIN, FOR SERVING
	SCALLIONS, TRIMMED AND SLICED, FOR SERVING
	FRESH CILANTRO, CHOPPED, FOR SERVING

BAJA TORTILLA SOUP

YIELD: 4 SERVINGS / **ACTIVE TIME:** 25 MINUTES / **TOTAL TIME:** 1 HOUR

There are numerous variations of tortilla soup in Mexico, like the Sopa Azteca, Mexico City's version. As you might expect, the versions in coastal towns center around seafood, like the hearty blue crab in this Baja-inspired dish.

1. Preheat the oven to 375°F. In a mixing bowl, combine the tomatillos, tomatoes, onion, garlic, and jalapeño. Add the oil, smoked paprika, chili powder, cumin, salt, and pepper and stir until the vegetables are coated.

2. Transfer the mixture to a baking sheet. Place the tortillas on a separate baking sheet. Place the pans in the oven and roast until the tomatillos and tomatoes are charred and starting to collapse, and the tortillas are toasted and crisp, about 20 minutes. Remove from the oven and let the vegetables cool slightly. When cool enough to handle, chop the vegetables roughly, making sure to peel the garlic cloves and remove the stem and seeds from the jalapeño before chopping them.

3. Place the stock in a medium saucepan and bring it to a boil. Add the vegetables and any juices to the pan. Add the tortillas and simmer the soup until the flavors are combined, about 5 minutes.

4. Transfer the soup to a blender and puree until smooth. Ladle the soup into warm bowls and garnish each portion with some crabmeat, crema, and avocado oil. Serve with cilantro and fried tortilla strips.

INGREDIENTS:

- 6   TOMATILLOS, HUSKED AND RINSED WELL
- 3   MEDIUM HEIRLOOM TOMATOES
- ½   WHITE ONION, CHOPPED
- 2   GARLIC CLOVES, UNPEELED
- 1   JALAPEÑO CHILE PEPPER
- 2   TEASPOONS EXTRA-VIRGIN OLIVE OIL
- 1   TEASPOON SMOKED PAPRIKA
- 1   TEASPOON CHILI POWDER
- 1   TEASPOON CUMIN
-    SALT AND PEPPER, TO TASTE
- 6   CORN TORTILLAS (SEE PAGE 352)
- 4   CUPS VEGETABLE STOCK (SEE PAGE 346)
-    MARYLAND BLUE CRAB KNUCKLE MEAT, FOR GARNISH
-    LIME CREMA (SEE PAGE 294), FOR GARNISH
-    AVOCADO OIL, FOR GARNISH
-    FRESH CILANTRO, CHOPPED, FOR SERVING
-    FRIED TORTILLA STRIPS, FOR SERVING

POZOLE

YIELD: 8 SERVINGS / **ACTIVE TIME:** 30 MINUTES / **TOTAL TIME:** 14 HOURS AND 15 MINUTES

This traditional Mexican soup once had ritual significance, in part because it is divine.

1. Coat the bottom of a Dutch oven with the olive oil and warm it over medium-high heat. Add the pork and onion, season with salt and pepper, and cook, stirring occasionally, until pork and onion are well browned, about 10 minutes.

2. Add the chipotles and hominy, cover the mixture with water, and add the thyme and cumin. Bring the soup to a boil, reduce the heat so that it simmers, and cook until the pork and hominy are very tender, about 1½ hours, stirring occasionally.

3. Add the garlic, cook for 5 minutes, and taste the soup. Adjust the seasoning as necessary, ladle the soup into warmed bowls, garnish with cilantro, and serve with lime wedges.

INGREDIENTS:

2 TABLESPOONS EXTRA-VIRGIN OLIVE OIL

2 LBS. BONELESS PORK SHOULDER, CUBED

1 LARGE YELLOW ONION, CHOPPED

SALT AND PEPPER, TO TASTE

4 DRIED CHIPOTLE PEPPERS, STEMMED, SEEDED, AND CHOPPED

2 CUPS HOMINY (SEE PAGE 288 FOR HOMEMADE)

1 TABLESPOON FRESH THYME

2 TABLESPOONS CUMIN

3 GARLIC CLOVES, MINCED

FRESH CILANTRO, CHOPPED, FOR GARNISH

LIME WEDGES, FOR SERVING

BUTTERNUT SQUASH & CHORIZO BISQUE

YIELD: 4 SERVINGS / **ACTIVE TIME:** 15 MINUTES / **TOTAL TIME:** 1 HOUR AND 30 MINUTES

This toothsome bisque is the result of pitting sweet against spicy, producing stunning results.

1. Preheat the oven to 400°F. Place the squash, onion, 2 tablespoons of the olive oil, and a pinch of salt in a bowl and toss to combine. Place the mixture in a baking dish and roast until the onion is browned, about 15 to 25 minutes. Transfer the onion to a bowl, return the squash to the oven, and roast for another 20 to 30 minutes, until the squash is fork tender. Remove from the oven and transfer to the bowl containing the onion.

2. Place the remaining olive oil in a skillet and warm it over medium-high heat. When the oil starts to shimmer, add the chorizo and cook, turning occasionally, until it is browned all over, about 5 minutes. Transfer the chorizo to a paper towel–lined plate to drain. When cool enough to handle, chop the chorizo into bite-sized pieces.

3. Place the squash, onion, bay leaves, cream, stock, and milk in a large saucepan and bring to a boil over medium-high heat, while stirring often. Reduce heat so that the soup simmers and cook until the flavor is to your liking, about 20 minutes.

4. Remove the bay leaves, transfer the soup to a food processor or blender, and puree until smooth. Return the soup to the saucepan, stir in the chorizo, and bring to a simmer. Add the butter, stir until it has melted, and serve.

INGREDIENTS:

1	LARGE BUTTERNUT SQUASH, PEELED AND SLICED
1	ONION, SLICED
3	TABLESPOONS EXTRA-VIRGIN OLIVE OIL
	SALT AND PEPPER, TO TASTE
8	OZ. MEXICAN CHORIZO, CASING REMOVED
2	BAY LEAVES
1	CUP HEAVY CREAM
1	CUP VEGETABLE STOCK (SEE PAGE 346)
1	CUP WHOLE MILK
4	TABLESPOONS UNSALTED BUTTER

SOPA DE CHILE POBLANO

YIELD: 2 SERVINGS / **ACTIVE TIME:** 20 MINUTES / **TOTAL TIME:** 30 MINUTES

This soup can be served both warm and chilled, depending on the time of the year. If you want more charred flavor here, simply don't remove the skins from the poblanos after roasting them.

1. Place the poblanos in a dry comal or cast-iron skillet and toast them until charred all over. You can also do this under the broiler or over an open flame. Place the charred chiles in a heatproof bowl and cover with plastic wrap. Let them sit for 10 minutes.

2. Remove the skins, stems, and seeds from the chiles and discard. Roughly chop the remaining flesh and set it aside.

3. Place the butter in a large saucepan and melt over medium-high heat. Add the onion and cook until it starts to soften, about 5 minutes, stirring occasionally. Add the garlic and cook for 1 minute.

4. Add the poblanos, serrano peppers, jalapeño, and kale and cook for 2 to 3 minutes, stirring occasionally. Add the stock and bring the soup to a boil. Reduce the heat to medium-low, add the cream, and simmer until the broth has reduced slightly, about 30 minutes.

5. Transfer the soup to a blender, add the tortillas, and puree until smooth, at least 1 minute.

6. Ladle the soup into warm bowls and top each one with a generous dollop of yogurt. Garnish with cilantro and additional serrano pepper and serve with lime wedges and tortilla strips.

INGREDIENTS:

- 1   LB. POBLANO CHILE PEPPERS
- 3   TABLESPOONS UNSALTED BUTTER
- 1   SMALL WHITE ONION
- 7   GARLIC CLOVES, MINCED
- 2   SERRANO CHILE PEPPERS, STEMMED, SEEDED, AND DICED, PLUS MORE FOR GARNISH
- 1   JALAPEÑO CHILE PEPPER, STEMMED, SEEDED, AND DICED
- 3½   OZ. KALE OR SPINACH, STEMS REMOVED
- 4   CUPS CHICKEN OR VEGETABLE STOCK (SEE PAGE 341 OR 346)
- ½   CUP HEAVY CREAM
- 2   CORN TORTILLAS (SEE PAGE 352), TOASTED
- ½   CUP YOGURT
- ½   BUNCH OF FRESH CILANTRO, CHOPPED, FOR GARNISH
-   LIME WEDGES, FOR SERVING
-   FRIED TORTILLA STRIPS, FOR SERVING

CARNE ADOBADA

YIELD: 6 SERVINGS / ACTIVE TIME: 30 MINUTES / TOTAL TIME: 24 HOURS

A rich, chili-like stew that benefits greatly from sitting in the refrigerator overnight.

1. Place the oil in a large saucepan and warm it over medium heat. Add the flour and cook, stirring, until it is a light golden brown, about 5 minutes.

2. Stir in the chile powder and then slowly add the stock, stirring to prevent any lumps from forming. Add the garlic, marjoram, cumin, salt, and pepper and cook for 2 minutes. Remove from heat and let cool.

3. Place the pork in a large casserole pan. Pour the contents of the saucepan over it and stir until combined. Place in refrigerator to marinate overnight.

4. Preheat the oven to 300°F. Place the stew in the oven and cook for at least 4 hours, removing to stir occasionally.

5. When the sauce has thickened and the meat is very tender, ladle into warmed bowls, and serve with tortillas.

HAM STOCK

1. Place all of the ingredients in a stockpot and bring to a boil. Reduce the heat so that the stock simmers and cook for 1 hour.

2. Strain through a fine sieve and chill in the refrigerator. Remove the fat layer and use as desired.

INGREDIENTS:

2	TABLESPOONS EXTRA-VIRGIN OLIVE OIL
3	TABLESPOONS ALL-PURPOSE FLOUR
¼	CUP NEW MEXICO CHILE POWDER
6	CUPS HAM STOCK (SEE RECIPE)
4	GARLIC CLOVES, MINCED
1	TABLESPOON CHOPPED FRESH MARJORAM
½	TEASPOON CUMIN
	SALT AND PEPPER, TO TASTE
2½	LBS. PORK SHOULDER, CUBED
	CORN TORTILLAS (SEE PAGE 352), WARM, FOR SERVING

HAM STOCK

12	OZ. HAM
8	CUPS WATER
2	GARLIC CLOVES
1	ONION, CHOPPED
1	BAY LEAF
1	SPRIG OF FRESH THYME

SOPA DE FLOR DE CALABAZA

YIELD: 4 SERVINGS / **ACTIVE TIME:** 30 MINUTES / **TOTAL TIME:** 30 MINUTES

The squash blossom is widely used in Mexico's southern states. They can be tough to find outside of that region, so when in season it pays to purchase as many as you can and pickle them.

1. Place the olive oil in a saucepan and warm it over medium heat. Add the onion, garlic, and chiles and cook until the onion is translucent, about 3 minutes, stirring frequently.

2. Add the squash and half of the squash blossoms and cook for 1 to 2 minutes, stirring frequently. Season the mixture with salt, add the epazote and stock, and simmer the soup until the squash is tender, about 20 minutes.

3. Transfer the soup to a blender and puree until smooth, about 1 minute. Return the soup to the saucepan and stir in the remaining squash blossoms.

4. Ladle the soup into warm bowls, drizzle some olive oil over each portion, and serve with the cheese and lime wedges.

INGREDIENTS:

2   TABLESPOONS EXTRA-VIRGIN OLIVE OIL, PLUS MORE FOR GARNISH

1   MEDIUM YELLOW ONION, BRUNOISED

7   GARLIC CLOVES, MINCED

2   OZ. GUERO OR MANZANA CHILE PEPPERS, STEMMED AND SEEDED

8   OZ. SQUASH, PEELED AND SEEDED

1   LB. SQUASH BLOSSOMS, RINSED WELL, STAMENS REMOVED

    SALT, TO TASTE

3   SPRIGS OF FRESH EPAZOTE

8   CUPS CHICKEN OR VEGETABLE STOCK (SEE PAGE 341 OR 346)

1   CUP SHREDDED QUESO FRESCO (SEE PAGE 522), FOR SERVING

    LIME WEDGES, FOR SERVING

SOPA DE FRIJOL COLADO

YIELD: 4 SERVINGS / **ACTIVE TIME:** 30 MINUTES / **TOTAL TIME:** 2 HOURS

This is a wonderful soup, as it can easily be adapted into many things, such as a sauce for enfrijoladas or chilaquiles.

1. Drain the beans and remove any small pebbles or debris.

2. Place the coriander and cumin seeds in a dry skillet and toast over medium heat until fragrant, shaking the pan to keep them from burning. Use a mortar and pestle or a spice grinder to grind them to a fine powder.

3. Place the lard in a large saucepan and warm over medium heat. Add the onion, garlic, bay leaf, toasted spice powder, chile powders, thyme, oregano, and marjoram and cook, stirring frequently, until the onion is translucent, about 3 minutes.

4. Add the beans and cover with cold water by 4 inches. Add the epazote, bring to a simmer, and cook the beans until very tender, about 1 hour and 30 minutes. Drain the beans and reserve the cooking liquid for another preparation.

5. Remove the bay leaf and epazote from the mixture, place it in a blender, and puree until smooth.

6. Place the puree in a clean saucepan, add the stock, and simmer until the flavor has developed to your liking.

7. Season the soup with salt, ladle it into warmed bowls, and serve with the tortillas, lime wedges, and cheese.

INGREDIENTS:

- 1   LB. BLACK BEANS, SOAKED OVERNIGHT
- ½   TEASPOON CORIANDER SEEDS
- ½   TEASPOON CUMIN SEEDS
- 2   TABLESPOONS LARD
- 1   SMALL YELLOW ONION, BRUNOISED
- 7   GARLIC CLOVES, MINCED
- 1   BAY LEAF
- ½   TEASPOON GUAJILLO CHILE POWDER
- ½   TEASPOON CHIPOTLE CHILE POWDER
- ½   TEASPOON DRIED THYME
- ½   TEASPOON DRIED MEXICAN OREGANO
- ½   TEASPOON DRIED MARJORAM
- 1   SMALL BUNCH OF FRESH EPAZOTE, STEMMED, PLUS MORE FOR SERVING
- 8   CUPS CHICKEN OR VEGETABLE STOCK (SEE PAGE 341 OR 346)
-     SALT, TO TASTE
-     CORN TORTILLAS (SEE PAGE 352), WARM, FOR SERVING
-     LIME WEDGES, FOR SERVING
-     COTIJA CHEESE, FOR SERVING

PUCHERO DE TRES CARNES

YIELD: 4 SERVINGS / **ACTIVE TIME**: 1 HOUR / **TOTAL TIME**: 1 HOUR AND 30 MINUTES

The hearty, comforting three-meat stew is characteristic of Yucatecan gastronomy. The vegetables in the dish are also representative of the region.

1. Place the garlic cloves in a dry skillet and toast them over medium heat until lightly charred in spots, about 10 minutes, turning occasionally. Remove from the pan and let the garlic cool slightly. When the garlic is cool enough to handle, peel and finely dice it.

2. Place the coriander seeds, cumin seeds, peppercorns, star anise, and cloves in the skillet and toast until fragrant, shaking the pan to keep them from burning. Use a mortar and pestle or a spice grinder to grind them to a fine powder.

3. Place some lard in a large saucepan and melt it over medium heat. Working with one protein at a time, add them to the pan and sear until browned all over. Remove the browned meats and set them aside. Add some of the remaining lard to the pan if it starts to look dry while searing the meat. When the chicken is cool enough to handle, chop it into cubes.

4. Add the onion, garlic, toasted spice powder, oregano, achiote powder, cinnamon, and bay leaves to the pan and cook until the onion is translucent, about 3 minutes. Return the meat to the pan along with any juices. Cover the mixture with stock and bring the soup to a simmer. Cook until the meat is very tender, about 1 hour.

5. Remove the proteins and strain the broth. Return the broth to the pan and bring it to a simmer. Working with one at a time, add the sweet potato, carrots, potatoes, squash, cabbage, and plantain to the pan and simmer until tender. Set the vegetables aside with the meat.

6. Season the broth with salt and add the chickpeas. Cook until warmed through.

7. Divide the meats and vegetables between the serving bowls. Ladle some broth into each and serve with tortillas and Salpicon de Rabano y Chile Habanero.

INGREDIENTS:

14	GARLIC UNPEELED
½	TEASPOON CORIANDER SEEDS
½	TEASPOON CUMIN SEEDS
½	TEASPOON BLACK PEPPERCORNS
1	STAR ANISE POD
2	WHOLE CLOVES
¼	CUP LARD
1	LB. BONELESS, SKINLESS CHICKEN THIGHS
1	LB. BEEF CHUCK, CUBED
1	LB. PORK SHOULDER, CUBED
1	MEDIUM WHITE ONION, HALVED AND CHARRED
¼	TEASPOON DRIED MEXICAN OREGANO
½	TEASPOON ACHIOTE POWDER
¼	TEASPOON CINNAMON
2	BAY LEAVES
4	CUPS CHICKEN STOCK (SEE PAGE 341) OR WATER
¾	CUP SWEET POTATO, LARGE DICE
¾	CUP DICED CARROTS
¾	CUP DICED POTATO
¾	DICED SQUASH
8	OZ. CABBAGE, QUARTERED
8	OZ. RIPENED PLANTAIN, SLICED ½-INCH THICK
½	CUP COOKED CHICKPEAS
	CORN TORTILLAS (SEE PAGE 352), WARM, FOR SERVING
	SALPICON DE RABANO Y CHILE HABANERO (SEE PAGE 486), FOR SERVING

SOPA DE CAMARÓN SECO

YIELD: 4 SERVINGS / **ACTIVE TIME:** 30 MINUTES / **TOTAL TIME:** 1 HOUR

Sopa de camarón seco can be found all over Mexico, but is more common along the coasts. The preservation of shrimp allowed this dish to be enjoyed in the landlocked areas of Mexico, as it suddenly enabled seafood to be easily transported.

1. Place the chiles in a dry skillet and toast until fragrant and pliable. Remove the chiles from the pan and chop them.

2. Place water in a medium saucepan and bring it to a simmer. Add the dried shrimp and epazote and simmer for 10 minutes. Remove the pan from heat and let the mixture steep for 10 minutes. Strain and reserve the shrimp and the broth.

3. Place the lard in a medium saucepan and warm over medium heat. Add the onion, garlic, chiles, and half of the shrimp and cook, stirring, for 1 to 2 minutes. Add the oregano, shrimp broth, bay leaf, and tortilla and simmer for 5 to 10 minutes.

4. Remove the bay leaf and discard it. Place the soup in a blender and puree until smooth, 2 to 3 minutes. Return the mixture to the pan and simmer for 5 minutes.

5. Season the soup with salt. Divide the remaining shrimp between the serving bowls and ladle the soup into each one. Serve with lime wedges.

INGREDIENTS:

4	GUAJILLO CHILE PEPPERS, STEMMED AND SEEDED
2-3	DRIED CHILES DE ARBOL, STEMMED AND SEEDED
8	OZ. DRIED SHRIMP, WITH HEADS AND TAILS
2-3	FRESH EPAZOTE LEAVES
2	TABLESPOONS LARD
1	SMALL WHITE ONION, JULIENNED
4	GARLIC CLOVES, SLICED THIN
⅛	TEASPOON DRIED MEXICAN OREGANO
1	BAY LEAF
1	CORN TORTILLA (SEE PAGE 352), TOASTED
	SALT, TO TASTE
	LIME WEDGES, FOR SERVING

CALDO DE ESPINAZO DE PUERCO

YIELD: 4 SERVINGS / **ACTIVE TIME:** 15 MINUTES / **TOTAL TIME:** 1 HOUR AND 15 MINUTES

S tews such as this pork neck soup are a perfect example of how well Mexican cuisine uses all of the animal, leaving nothing to waste. Ask your local butcher to give you the bones, as they still have a significant amount of meat.

1. Rinse the pork bones under cold water. Place them in a large saucepan and cover with water. Bring to a simmer.

2. Bring water to a boil in a small saucepan. Place the chiles in a bowl and cover with the boiling water. Soak for 15 minutes. Drain the chiles and reserve the soaking liquid.

3. Place the chiles and garlic in a blender, add a little of the soaking liquid, and puree until smooth. Stir the puree into the simmering broth.

4. Add the onion and chickpeas to the pan and cook until the meat on the pork neck bones and the chickpeas are very tender, about 50 minutes.

5. Season the soup with salt. Remove the chickpeas from the soup and place them in a blender. Add 2 cups of the broth and puree until smooth. Stir the puree back into the soup and cook until it thickens slightly.

6. Stir in the watercress and ladle the soup into warmed bowls.

INGREDIENTS:

4   LBS. PORK NECK BONES

10   DRIED CALIFORNIA OR
     NEW MEXICO CHILE
     PEPPERS, STEMMED AND
     SEEDED

2   GARLIC CLOVES

½   WHITE ONION

½   CUP DRIED CHICKPEAS,
     SOAKED OVERNIGHT

     SALT, TO TASTE

1   BUNCH OF WATERCRESS,
     CHOPPED

SOPA DE PAPA

YIELD: 4 SERVINGS / **ACTIVE TIME:** 10 MINUTES / **TOTAL TIME:** 35 MINUTES

A classic, comforting recipe that is great for kids just home from school. This quick and easy preparation can easily be adjusted to incorporate vegetables other than those listed here.

1. Bring water to a boil in a small saucepan. Add the tomatoes, garlic, and onion and cook until softened, about 10 minutes. Drain, place the vegetables in a blender, and puree until smooth.

2. Place the olive oil in a medium saucepan and warm over medium heat. Strain the puree into the pan and add the oregano, potatoes, and 2 cups of water. Bring to a simmer and cook until the potatoes are tender but not falling apart, about 15 minutes.

3. Season the soup with salt, ladle it into warmed bowls, and garnish each portion with Queso Fresco and sprigs of cilantro.

INGREDIENTS:

- 4 LARGE TOMATOES
- 2 GARLIC CLOVES
- ¼ WHITE ONION
- 1 TABLESPOON EXTRA-VIRGIN OLIVE OIL
- 1 TEASPOON DRIED MEXICAN OREGANO
- 4 YUKON GOLD POTATOES, PEELED AND DICED
-   SALT, TO TASTE
- 1 CUP SHREDDED QUESO FRESCO (SEE PAGE 522)
- ½ BUNCH OF FRESH CILANTRO

Menudo
See page 293

SOPA DE FIDEO

YIELD: 6 SERVINGS / **ACTIVE TIME:** 10 MINUTES / **TOTAL TIME:** 25 MINUTES

The simplicity is what makes this soup so special. If you're looking to make it more substantial, top it with cheese or a grilled chicken leg.

1. Place the tomatoes, onion, and garlic in a blender and puree until smooth.

2. Place the oil in a medium saucepan and warm over medium-high heat. Add the pasta and cook until lightly browned, stirring occasionally.

3. Reduce the heat to low and carefully strain the puree into the pan. Cook for 2 minutes and then add 2 cups of water. Bring the soup to a simmer and cook until the pasta has expanded and is tender, approximately 15 minutes.

4. Season the soup with salt and ladle it into warmed bowls.

INGREDIENTS:

4	LARGE TOMATOES
½	ONION
2	GARLIC CLOVES
1	TABLESPOON EXTRA-VIRGIN OLIVE OIL
8	OZ. DRIED FIDEO OR ANGEL HAIR PASTA
	SALT, TO TASTE

CALDO DE PESCADO

YIELD: 6 SERVINGS / **ACTIVE TIME:** 10 MINUTES / **TOTAL TIME:** 1 HOUR

Good for cold or hot weather, full of nutrients, and flexible, this is a classic in every Mexican home.

1. Cut the fillets into 3-inch pieces. Place the head and the tail of the fish in a saucepan, add 8 to 10 cups of water, and bring to a simmer over medium heat. Cook for 20 minutes and drain the stock into a large bowl. Reserve the fish head.

2. Place the chiles in a bowl of hot water and let them soak for 20 minutes.

3. Place the tomatoes in a small saucepan, add water, and simmer over medium heat until tender. Drain the tomatoes and place them in a blender. Add the onion, garlic, and chiles and puree until smooth.

4. Place the olive oil in a large saucepan and warm over medium heat. Strain the puree into the pan and cook for 5 minutes.

5. Add the pepper, salt, stock, bay leaves, carrots, celery, potatoes, and oregano and cook until the vegetables start to soften, about 20 minutes.

6. Add the fish and shrimp and simmer until they are cooked through, about 7 minutes.

7. Taste, adjust the seasoning, and add the fish head to the soup. Ladle into warmed bowls and garnish each portion with some of the cilantro.

INGREDIENTS:

- 2 LBS. RED SNAPPER, FILLETED AND BONED, HEAD AND TAIL RESERVED
- 2 DRIED CALIFORNIA CHILE PEPPERS, STEMMED AND SEEDED
- 4 LARGE TOMATOES
- ¼ WHITE ONION
- 2 GARLIC CLOVES
- 2 TABLESPOONS EXTRA-VIRGIN OLIVE OIL
- 1 TEASPOON BLACK PEPPER
- 2 TABLESPOONS KOSHER SALT
- 2 BAY LEAVES
- 3 LARGE CARROTS, PEELED AND CUT ON A BIAS
- 4 CELERY STALKS, PEELED AND DICED
- 2 RUSSET POTATOES, PEELED AND DICED
- 1 TEASPOON DRIED MEXICAN OREGANO
- 1 LB. SHRIMP, SHELL ON, CLEANED AND DEVEINED
- ½ BUNCH OF FRESH CILANTRO

ALBONDIGAS SOUP

YIELD: 6 SERVINGS / **ACTIVE TIME:** 25 MINUTES / **TOTAL TIME:** 50 MINUTES

The humble meatball has not just survived, it thrives in all environments because it is a guaranteed source of comfort. If you cannot track down hierbabuena, substitute spearmint.

1. In a large mixing bowl, combine the ground beef, egg, rice, hierbabuena, oregano, and parsley and season the mixture with salt. Form the mixture into meatballs that weigh about 1 ounce a piece.

2. Place the tomatoes, onion, and garlic in a small saucepan, add water, and boil until the vegetables are tender. Drain, add the vegetables to a blender with the cumin and tomato paste, and puree until smooth.

3. Place the oil in a large saucepan and warm over medium heat. Add the puree and cook for 2 minutes.

4. Add 4 cups of water and season with salt. If desired, add more sprigs of hierbabuena to the broth. Bring to a simmer.

5. Add the carrots and meatballs and cook over low heat until the meatballs are completely cooked through, about 20 minutes.

6. Add the zucchini and cook until tender, about 5 minutes.

7. Ladle the soup into warmed bowls and serve with warm tortillas and roasted chiles.

INGREDIENTS:

2	LBS. GROUND BEEF
1	EGG
2	TABLESPOONS COOKED RICE
3	SPRIGS OF FRESH HIERBABUENA, FINELY CHOPPED, PLUS MORE TO TASTE
2	SPRIGS OF FRESH OREGANO, FINELY CHOPPED
½	BUNCH OF FRESH PARSLEY, FINELY CHOPPED
4	LARGE TOMATOES
¼	ONION
2	GARLIC CLOVES
1	TEASPOON CUMIN
½	TEASPOON TOMATO PASTE
2	TABLESPOONS EXTRA-VIRGIN OLIVE OIL
	SALT, TO TASTE
3	CARROTS, PEELED AND SLICED
3	ZUCCHINI, SLICED
	CORN TORTILLAS (SEE PAGE 352), WARM, FOR SERVING
	ROASTED SERRANO OR JALAPEÑO CHILE PEPPERS, FOR SERVING

CALDO DE RES

YIELD: 10 SERVINGS / **ACTIVE TIME:** 20 MINUTES / **TOTAL TIME:** 1 HOUR AND 10 MINUTES

Braising the beef produces a flavorful broth that is great on a cold, rainy day. If you're a fan of chayote squash, swap them in for the Mexican squash here.

1. Place the beef in a large saucepan and fill the pan with water. Bring to a boil, season with salt, reduce the heat to medium, and simmer until the meat is tender, approximately 1 hour.

2. Add the carrots, onion, and cabbage and cook for 20 minutes.

3. Add the potatoes and squash and cook until tender, about 20 minutes.

4. Ladle the soup into warmed bowls and serve with lemon wedges, salsa (a red salsa is recommended), and warm tortillas.

INGREDIENTS:

5   LBS. BONELESS BEEF CHUCK, CUT INTO 4-INCH CUBES

    SALT, TO TASTE

3   CARROTS

1   WHITE ONION, HALVED

1   GREEN CABBAGE, QUARTERED

5   YUKON GOLD POTATOES, QUARTERED

4   MEXICAN SQUASH, SLICED

    LEMON WEDGES, FOR SERVING

    SALSA, FOR SERVING

    CORN TORTILLAS (SEE PAGE 352), WARM, FOR SERVING

SOPA DE LENTEJAS

YIELD: 4 SERVINGS / **ACTIVE TIME:** 10 MINUTES / **TOTAL TIME:** 1 HOUR AND 30 MINUTES

A slight twist on the bean-centric soups that are so popular in Mexican cuisine.

1. Place the lentils in a bowl of cold water and soak for 1 hour. Drain the lentils, rinse them thoroughly, and discard any small pebbles or debris.

2. Place the olive oil in a medium saucepan and warm over medium heat. Add the carrots, onion, celery, and garlic and cook until the onion is translucent, about 3 minutes, stirring frequently.

3. Add the lentils and cook for 2 minutes, stirring constantly.

4. Add the stock, tomatoes, and bay leaves and bring the soup to a boil. Reduce the heat and simmer until the lentils are tender, about 25 minutes.

5. If desired, add the spinach and cook until wilted, about 2 minutes. Season the soup with salt, ladle it into warm bowls, and garnish with cilantro.

INGREDIENTS:

1	CUP GREEN LENTILS
1	TABLESPOON EXTRA-VIRGIN OLIVE OIL
2	CARROTS, PEELED AND FINELY DICED
1	ONION, FINELY DICED
2	CELERY STALKS, PEELED AND FINELY DICED
2	GARLIC CLOVES, SLICED THIN
5	CUPS CHICKEN STOCK (SEE PAGE 341) OR WATER
1	CUP CHOPPED CANNED TOMATOES
2	BAY LEAVES
1	CUP SPINACH (OPTIONAL)
	SALT, TO TASTE
1	BUNCH OF FRESH CILANTRO, CHOPPED, FOR GARNISH

CHICKEN STOCK

YIELD: 8 CUPS / **ACTIVE TIME:** 20 MINUTES / **TOTAL TIME:** 6 HOURS

Shifting from store-bought to homemade stock is the easiest way to lift what comes out of your kitchen.

1. Place the chicken bones in a stockpot and cover with cold water. Bring to a simmer over medium-high heat and use a ladle to skim off any impurities that rise to the surface.

2. Add the vegetables, thyme, peppercorns, and bay leaf, reduce the heat to low, and simmer for 5 hours, while skimming to remove any impurities that rise to the surface.

3. Strain, allow to cool slightly, and transfer to the refrigerator. Leave uncovered and let the stock cool completely. Remove layer of fat and cover. The stock will keep in the refrigerator for 3 to 5 days, and in the freezer for up to 3 months.

INGREDIENTS:

7	LBS. CHICKEN BONES, RINSED
4	CUPS CHOPPED YELLOW ONIONS
2	CUPS CHOPPED CARROTS
2	CUPS CHOPPED CELERY
3	GARLIC CLOVES, CRUSHED
3	SPRIGS OF FRESH THYME
1	TEASPOON BLACK PEPPERCORNS
1	BAY LEAF

BEEF STOCK

YIELD: 8 CUPS / **ACTIVE TIME:** 20 MINUTES / **TOTAL TIME:** 6 HOURS

If you want an extra-smooth stock, try using veal bones instead of beef bones. Lamb bones can also be used, but we recommend that you pair them with beef bones to balance the flavor.

1. Place the beef bones in a stockpot and cover with cold water. Bring to a simmer over medium-high heat and use a ladle to skim off any impurities that rise to the surface.

2. Add the vegetables, thyme, peppercorns, and bay leaf, reduce the heat to low, and simmer for 5 hours, while skimming to remove any impurities that rise to the surface.

3. Strain, let the stock cool slightly, and transfer to the refrigerator. Leave uncovered and let cool completely. Remove layer of fat and cover. The stock will keep in the refrigerator for 3 to 5 days, and in the freezer for up to 3 months.

INGREDIENTS:

7	LBS. BEEF BONES, RINSED
4	CUPS CHOPPED YELLOW ONIONS
2	CUPS CHOPPED CARROTS
2	CUPS CHOPPED CELERY
3	GARLIC CLOVES, CRUSHED
3	SPRIGS OF FRESH THYME
1	TEASPOON BLACK PEPPERCORNS
1	BAY LEAF

FISH STOCK

YIELD: 6 CUPS / **ACTIVE TIME:** 20 MINUTES / **TOTAL TIME:** 4 HOURS

Y ou want to avoid using fish such as salmon or tuna in this stock, as their bold flavors will overwhelm it.

1. Place the olive oil in a stockpot and warm it over low heat. Add the vegetables and cook until the liquid they release has evaporated.

2. Add the whitefish bodies, the aromatics, the salt, and the water to the pot, raise the heat to high, and bring to a boil. Reduce heat so that the stock simmers and cook for 3 hours, while skimming to remove any impurities that float to the surface.

3. Strain the stock through a fine sieve, let it cool slightly, and place in the refrigerator, uncovered, to chill. When the stock is completely cool, remove the fat layer from the top and cover. The stock will keep in the refrigerator for 3 to 5 days, and in the freezer for up to 3 months.

INGREDIENTS:

¼ CUP EXTRA-VIRGIN OLIVE OIL

1 LEEK, TRIMMED, RINSED WELL, AND CHOPPED

1 LARGE YELLOW ONION, UNPEELED, ROOT CLEANED, CHOPPED

2 LARGE CARROTS, CHOPPED

1 CELERY STALK, CHOPPED

¾ LB. WHITEFISH BODIES

4 SPRIGS OF FRESH PARSLEY

3 SPRIGS OF FRESH THYME

2 BAY LEAVES

1 TEASPOON BLACK PEPPERCORNS

1 TEASPOON KOSHER SALT

8 CUPS WATER

VEGETABLE STOCK

YIELD: 6 CUPS / **ACTIVE TIME:** 20 MINUTES / **TOTAL TIME:** 3 HOURS

A great way to make use of your vegetable trimmings. Just void starchy vegetables such as potatoes, as they will make the stock cloudy.

1. Place the olive oil and the vegetables in a large stockpot and cook over low heat until the liquid they release has evaporated. This will allow the flavor of the vegetables to become concentrated.

2. Add the garlic, parsley, thyme, bay leaf, water, peppercorns, and salt. Raise the heat to high and bring to a boil. Reduce heat so that the stock simmers and cook for 2 hours, while skimming to remove any impurities that float to the top.

3. Strain through a fine sieve, let the stock cool slightly, and place in the refrigerator, uncovered, to chill. Remove the fat layer and cover. The stock will keep in the refrigerator for 3 to 5 days, and in the freezer for up to 3 months.

INGREDIENTS:

2   TABLESPOONS EXTRA-VIRGIN OLIVE OIL

2   LARGE LEEKS, TRIMMED AND RINSED WELL

2   LARGE CARROTS, PEELED AND SLICED

2   CELERY STALKS, SLICED

2   LARGE YELLOW ONIONS, SLICED

3   GARLIC CLOVES, UNPEELED BUT SMASHED

2   SPRIGS OF FRESH PARSLEY

2   SPRIGS OF FRESH THYME

1   BAY LEAF

8   CUPS WATER

½   TEASPOON BLACK PEPPERCORNS

    SALT, TO TASTE

MASA

*M*aize, with its wide cultivation and endless uses, has been a cornerstone of Mexico since the civilization began.

Yes, you'll gain the ability to turn out corn tortillas (see page 352) that exceed anything available at the store. But you'll also learn how to turn the simple mixture of masa harina, warm water, and salt into a number of dishes that will reveal how this humble grain came to form a foundation that allows Mexican cuisine to stand so tall.

TORTILLAS DE MASA HARINA

YIELD: 32 TORTILLAS / **ACTIVE TIME:** 30 MINUTES / **TOTAL TIME:** 30 MINUTES

Making tortillas takes practice, but once you learn to make them correctly, you will never want to eat a store-bought one again. The key is getting a feel for the proper level of hydration in the masa so that the tortillas will puff up when cooked. Masienda or Bob's Red Mill are both good choices when looking for a quality masa harina.

1. In the work bowl of stand mixer fitted with the paddle attachment, combine the masa harina and salt. With the mixer on low speed, slowly begin to add the water. The mixture should come together as a soft, smooth dough. This is the prepared masa that is mentioned in a number of recipes in this book. You want the masa to be moist enough so that when a small ball of it is pressed flat in your hands the edges do not crack. Also, the masa should not stick to your hands when you peel it off your palm.

2. Let the masa rest for 10 minutes and check the hydration again. You may need to add more water depending on environmental conditions.

3. Warm a comal or cast-iron skillet over high heat. Portion the masa into 1-ounce balls and cover them with a damp linen towel.

4. Line the tortilla press with two 8-inch circles of plastic. You can use a grocery store bag, a resealable bag, or even a standard kitchen trash bag as a source for the plastic. Place the masa balls in the center of a circle and gently push down on it with the palm of one hand to flatten. Place the other plastic circle on top and then close the tortilla press, applying firm, even pressure to flatten the masa into a round tortilla.

5. Open the tortilla press and remove the top layer of plastic. Carefully pick up the tortilla and carefully remove the bottom piece of plastic.

6. Gently lay the tortilla flat in the pan, taking care to not wrinkle it. Cook for 15 to 30 seconds, until the edges begin to lift up slightly. Turn the tortilla over and let it cook for 30 to 45 seconds before turning it over one last time. If the hydration of the masa was correct and the heat is high enough, the tortilla should puff up and inflate. Remove the tortilla from the pan and store in a tortilla warmer lined with a linen towel. Repeat until all of the prepared masa has been made into tortillas.

INGREDIENTS:

- 1 LB. MASA HARINA
- 1½ TABLESPOONS KOSHER SALT
- 3 CUPS WARM FILTERED WATER, PLUS MORE AS NEEDED

HUARACHES WITH WILD MUSHROOMS & EPAZOTE

YIELD: 4 SERVINGS / **ACTIVE TIME:** 45 MINUTES / **TOTAL TIME:** 1 HOUR

A preparation that is the perfect way to start or conclude an evening. Maitake, oyster, and hen of the woods are all good options for the mushrooms here.

1. Place the olive oil in a skillet and warm it over medium-high heat. Add the chiles and fry until fragrant and pliable. Remove the chiles from the pan and let them cool slightly. When cool enough to handle, finely dice the chiles.

2. Add the mushrooms to the pan and cook, stirring occasionally, until well browned, about 12 minutes. Transfer the mushrooms to a bowl.

3. Add the onion to the pan and cook, stirring frequently, until well browned, about 10 minutes. Add the garlic, cook for 1 minute, and then stir in the mushrooms and chiles. Add the epazote, season the mixture with salt, and transfer it to a bowl.

4. Working with 2 oz. of masa at a time, form it into a cup that fits into the palm of your hand. Place some of the refried beans in the center and close the cup of masa, sealing the beans. Gently form the masa into a flat patty and then shape it into an oval.

5. Line a tortilla press with plastic. Place one of the ovals in the press and place another piece of plastic on top. Apply firm, even pressure and press the oval until flat and about ¼ inch thick. Repeat with the remaining masa.

6. Warm the pan over medium heat. Add the huaraches one at a time and cook until golden brown on both sides, about 2 minutes per side.

7. Place a layer of the mushroom mixture on top of the huaraches and top with the cheese, salsa, cilantro, and pickled onion.

INGREDIENTS:

¼   CUP EXTRA-VIRGIN OLIVE OIL

2   DRIED CHILES DE ARBOL, STEMMED AND SEEDED

1   LB. WILD MUSHROOMS, CHOPPED

½   WHITE ONION, SLICED THIN

3   GARLIC CLOVES, SLICED THIN

1   SMALL BUNCH OF FRESH EPAZOTE, TORN

     SALT, TO TASTE

2   LBS. PREPARED MASA (SEE PAGE 352)

2   CUPS FRIJOLES NEGROS REFRITOS (SEE PAGE 254)

2   CUPS SHREDDED QUESO FRESCO (SEE PAGE 522)

½   CUP SALSA

     FRESH CILANTRO, CHOPPED, FOR GARNISH

     PICKLED RED ONION (SEE PAGE 515), FOR SERVING

ABUELA'S SOPES

YIELD: 1 SERVING / **ACTIVE TIME:** 20 MINUTES / **TOTAL TIME:** 20 MINUTES

This recipe is a specialty of Chef Augie Saucedo's grandmother. Sopes prepared in this manner revive memories of his abuela selling sopes at their local church.

1. Place the masa and water in a mixing bowl and work the mixture until it is soft and pliable. Form into a small ball and gently flatten until it resembles a thick tortilla. Pinch the edge to raise it slightly, so that the masa becomes a shallow bowl.

2. Place the oil in a small saucepan and warm it to 375°F. Place the masa bowl in the oil and fry until golden brown, about 3 minutes. Transfer to a paper towel–lined plate and let it drain.

3. Layer the beans, chorizo, lettuce, tomatoes, and avocado atop the bowl and serve with the cheese and salsa.

INGREDIENTS:

3   OZ. PREPARED MASA (SEE PAGE 352)

½   TEASPOON WATER

1   CUP CANOLA OIL

3   TABLESPOONS FRIJOLES NEGROS REFRITOS (SEE PAGE 254)

3   TABLESPOONS CHICKEN CHORIZO (SEE PAGE 109)

2   TABLESPOONS FINELY SHREDDED ICEBERG LETTUCE

2   CHERRY TOMATOES, HALVED

  AVOCADO, SLICED

  QUESO ENCHILADO, SHREDDED FOR SERVING

  SALSA QUEMADA, FOR SERVING

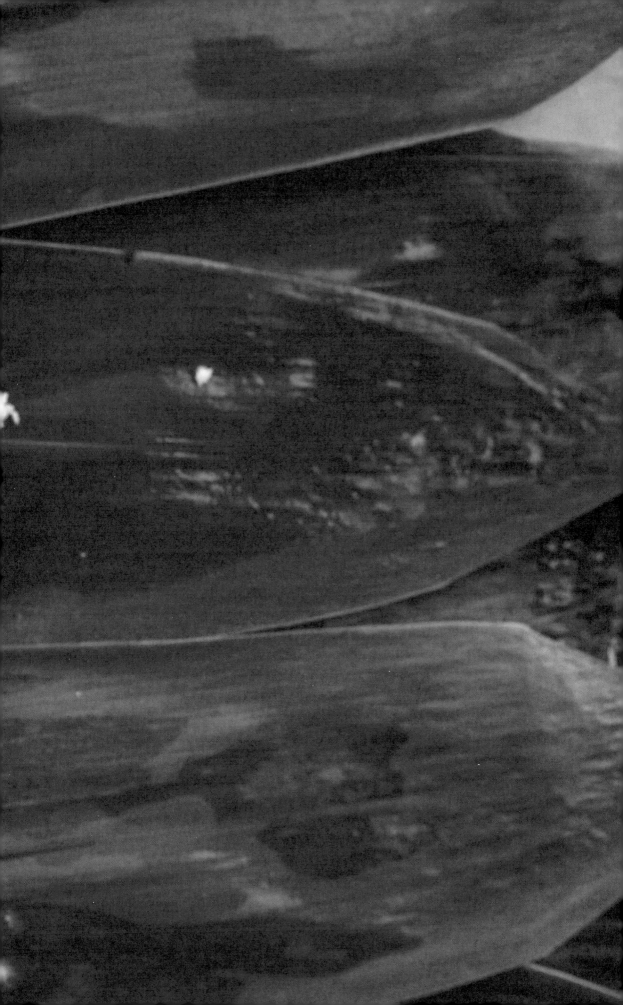

MOLOTES DE FRIJOL Y QUESO

YIELD: 4 SERVINGS / **ACTIVE TIME:** 20 MINUTES / **TOTAL TIME:** 20 MINUTES

Molotes are commonly found in the state of Oaxaca, but, as with many masa preparations in Mexican cuisine, you will see similar iterations of this dish throughout Mexico, bearing different names. Numerous fillings can be used, but frijoles and queso are the most popular.

1. Add oil to a Dutch oven until it is 2 inches deep and warm it to 350°F.

2. Divide the masa into four balls and line a tortilla press with plastic. Working with one ball at a time, place it in the center of the plastic and gently push down with the palm of one hand to flatten it. Cover with another piece of plastic and then close the tortilla press. Apply firm, even pressure to flatten the masa to about ¼ inch thick. Open the tortilla press and remove the top piece of plastic. Carefully remove the other piece of plastic.

3. Place some of the beans and cheese in the center of the round and add 1 to 2 leaves of epazote. Fold the round in half and press down on the edge of the masa to seal. Cover with a damp linen towel and make the rest of the molotes.

4. Working in batches of one or two, slip the molotes the oil and fry until golden brown and crispy, about 4 minutes. Transfer to a paper towel–lined plate to drain. When all of the molotes have been fried, serve with cilantro, crema, salsa verde, and lime wedges.

INGREDIENTS:

CANOLA OIL, AS NEEDED

8 OZ. PREPARED MASA (SEE PAGE 352)

½ CUP FRIJOLES NEGROS REFRITOS (SEE PAGE 254)

1 CUP OAXACA OR CHIHUAHUA CHEESE

1 SMALL BUNCH OF FRESH EPAZOTE

FRESH CILANTRO, CHOPPED, FOR SERVING

CREMA OR SOUR CREAM, FOR SERVING

SALSA CRUDA VERDE (SEE PAGE 525), FOR SERVING

LIME WEDGES, FOR SERVING

COMAL

The comal is a smooth, flat griddle commonly found in kitchens throughout Mexico, Central America, and parts of South America. For centuries, the comal was made of untreated clay and placed over a fire, balanced on top of three to four large stones. Today, a comal is commonly made of cast iron or stainless steel, and sized to fit over a burner on a stove. Whatever the composition, a comal is similar to a cast-iron skillet in that it becomes seasoned with frequent use, imparting more and more flavor to whatever touches it. This flavoring aspect, along with the comal's flat surface and slow distribution and rentention of heat, makes it the overwhelming favorite for cooking tortillas and other masa-based preparations, though roasting vegetables, chiles, and aromatics are other common uses. As with other seasoned cookware, comals are a popular heirloom, improving as they pass through and connect generations.

MASA FOR TAMALES

YIELD: 3 LBS. / **ACTIVE TIME:** 30 MINUTES / **TOTAL TIME:** 30 MINUTES

Making prepared masa for tamales requires patience in order to properly hydrate the corn flour, otherwise the masa will be dry and crumbly after being cooked. Always make sure to add cold stock so that you don't melt the whipped lard, which will result in a less desirable texture.

1. Place the lard in the work bowl of a stand mixer fitted with the paddle attachment. Add the baking powder and salt and beat until the mixture is light and fluffy, about 3 minutes.

2. Slowly add the masa and beat until it is thoroughly incorporated. Beat for another 2 to 3 minutes, adding the stock a little at a time until the mixture is the consistency of a very thick pancake batter. Cover with plastic wrap and chill in the refrigerator for 1 hour.

3. Remove the masa from the refrigerator and check its consistency. If the masa is too thick, incorporate additional stock until the masa is the correct consistency.

4. Form a teaspoon of the masa into a ball and drop it into a cup of cold water. The ball should float. If it doesn't float, beat the masa for another 5 to 10 minutes. Do not allow the masa to get warm, as the lard will melt and make the tamales too dense. Cover with plastic wrap and chill in the refrigerator until ready to use.

INGREDIENTS:

1   CUP LARD, CHILLED

2   TABLESPOONS BAKING POWDER

1½ TABLESPOONS KOSHER SALT

2   LBS. PREPARED MASA (SEE PAGE 352)

2   CUPS CHICKEN OR VEGETABLE STOCK (SEE PAGE 341 OR 346), CHILLED, PLUS MORE AS NEEDED

TAMALES DE CHULIBU'UL

YIELD: 12 TAMALES / **ACTIVE TIME:** 30 MINUTES / **TOTAL TIME:** 1 HOUR AND 30 MINUTES

Chef Gabe Erales: "I first had Chulibu'ul at a restaurant in Merida that serves numerous guisados for breakfast, and quickly realized that its contrasting textures would make it a perfect filling for tamales."

1. Remove the spines from the banana leaves, taking care not to crack the leaves. Place the banana leaves in a dry skillet and toast them briefly so that they become pliable.

2. Cut the banana leaves into 8 x 10–inch rectangles.

3. Take a leaf and lay it, shiny side down, on a flat surface with the short side parallel to you. Place 3½ ounces of the masa in the center of the leaf and form it into a rectangle.

4. Place about ¼ cup of Chulibu'ul in the center of the masa. Fold the banana leaf over itself in thirds so that the masa encloses the filling. Fold the banana leaf over again in the same manner, creating a long packet. Fold the two open edges of the banana leaf toward the center. Press down on the edges of the masa until compact.

5. Bring water to a simmer in a saucepan and place a steaming basket over it. Place the tamales in the basket, seam side down, and steam for 1 hour.

6. To test if the tamales are done, remove one and unwrap it. If the banana leaf easily comes away from the masa, they are ready. If the masa is still sticking to the leaf, steam for another 10 to 20 minutes.

7. When the tamales are done, remove them from the steamer and let them cool for 5 minutes before enjoying. To reheat after cooling completely, steam them, or place them in a banana leaf and toast in a hot cast-iron skillet.

INGREDIENTS:

1 PACKAGE OF BANANA LEAVES

MASA FOR TAMALES (SEE PAGE 365)

4 CUPS CHULIBU'UL (SEE PAGE 534)

SALSA DE CHILTOMATE (SEE PAGE 477), FOR SERVING

JOROCHES DE CHORIZO Y FRIJOLES COLADOS

YIELD: 12 DUMPLINGS / ACTIVE TIME: 30 MINUTES / TOTAL TIME: 30 MINUTES

These masa dumplings are commonly found in the Yucatan and bear some resemblance to molotes, only they are smaller, and usually paired with different sauces.

1. Place the masa, lard, and salt in a mixing bowl and work the mixture until it is homogeneous and thoroughly kneaded.

2. Divide the masa into 1½-oz. balls. Place them on a baking sheet lined with parchment paper.

3. Using a finger, press a hole into the center of each masa ball. Place some of the chorizo in the indentation and then form the dough over it. Cover the joroches with plastic wrap.

4. Place the soup and stock in a saucepan and bring to a simmer.

5. Add the joroches and cook until they are firm and set, about 15 to 20 minutes. Remove the joroches from the pot and cook the soup until it has reduced slightly and thickened.

6. Divide the joroches between the serving bowls, ladle the soup over the top, and serve with cheese, X'nipek, and cilantro.

INGREDIENTS:

2   LBS. PREPARED MASA (SEE PAGE 352)

3½   TABLESPOONS LARD

2   TEASPOONS KOSHER SALT

8   OZ. MEXICAN CHORIZO, COOKED

     SOPA DE FRIJOL COLADO (SEE PAGE 317)

4   CUPS CHICKEN STOCK (SEE PAGE 341)

     COTIJA CHEESE, FOR SERVING

     X'NIPEK (SEE PAGE 487), FOR SERVING

     FRESH CILANTRO, CHOPPED, FOR SERVING

TORTILLA GRUESA DE HOJA SANTA Y QUESO

YIELD: 4 SERVINGS / ACTIVE TIME: 30 MINUTES / TOTAL TIME: 30 MINUTES

Tortillas gruesa can be found throughout Tabasco and made with a variety of ingredients from asiento and chile amashito to garlic. A tablespoon of lard or another cooking fat can be added to the pan to give the flatbreads an extra crispy texture.

1. Place the masa, hoja santa, cheese, and salt in a mixing bowl and work the mixture until it is smooth and homogenous. Form the masa into four balls.

2. Line a tortilla press with plastic, place one of the balls in the press, and place another piece of plastic on top. Apply firm, even pressure and press the masa into a ½-inch-thick tortilla. Cover with a moist linen towel and repeat with the remaining balls.

3. Warm a comal or cast-iron skillet over medium-high heat. Working with one tortilla at a time, place it in the skillet and cook for 2 minutes. Turn it over and cook for another 2 minutes. Turn the tortilla over one last time and cook until it starts to char, about 2 minutes.

4. Remove from the pan and let the tortillas cool slightly. When all of the tortillas have been cooked, serve with lime wedges and salsa.

INGREDIENTS:

2 LBS. PREPARED MASA (SEE PAGE 352)

3 TABLESPOONS FRESH HOJA SANTA, FINELY CHOPPED

1 CUP SHREDDED OAXACA CHEESE (CAN SUBSTITUTE MUENSTER OR SIMILAR CHEESE)

2 TEASPOONS KOSHER SALT

   LIME WEDGES, FOR SERVING

   SALSA DE ARBOL (SEE PAGE 498), FOR SERVING

TLACOYOS DE HONGOS

YIELD: 4 SERVINGS / **ACTIVE TIME:** 45 MINUTES / **TOTAL TIME:** 45 MINUTES

Tlacoyos can be filled with innumerable ingredients, but mushrooms are among the very best. If you have access to fava beans, and the patience to shell them, they can also make for a wonderful filling.

1. Form the masa into 4-oz. balls and cover them with a damp linen towel.

2. Place the olive oil in a skillet and warm it over medium-high heat. Add the mushrooms and cook, stirring occasionally, until they are well browned, about 12 minutes.

3. Add the onion, season the mixture with salt, and cook until the onion is translucent. Remove the pan from heat and set the mixture aside.

4. Line a tortilla press with plastic, place one of the balls in the press, and place another piece of plastic on top. Apply firm, even pressure and press the masa into a ¼-inch-thick round. Cover with a damp linen towel and repeat with the remaining balls.

5. Place the mushroom mixture in the center of each round and fold the masa over it to form a half-moon. Pinch the edges to seal and flatten the tlacoyos.

6. Place the lard in a comal or cast-iron skillet and warm over medium-high heat. Add the tlacoyos and cook until browned on both sides, about 2 minutes.

7. Serve the tlacoyos with salsa, onion, crema, and cilantro.

INGREDIENTS:

1   LB. PREPARED MASA (SEE PAGE 352)

1   TABLESPOON EXTRA-VIRGIN OLIVE OIL

8   OZ. MUSHROOMS, JULIENNED

1   SMALL WHITE ONION, BRUNOISED

   SALT, TO TASTE

2   TABLESPOONS LARD

   SALSA DE AGUACATE (SEE PAGE 503), FOR SERVING

   RED ONION, JULIENNED, FOR SERVING

   CREMA, FOR SERVING

   FRESH CILANTRO, CHOPPED, FOR SERVING

TETELAS DE AGUACATE
CON REQUESÓN Y NOPALES

YIELD: 4 SERVINGS / **ACTIVE TIME:** 20 MINUTES / **TOTAL TIME:** 20 MINUTES

Making tetelas is another preparation that requires considerable practice to find the proper technique when handling the delicate masa.

1. Place the nopales in a saucepan and cover with water by 2 inches. Season generously with salt, add the baking soda, and bring the water to a simmer. Cook until the cactus is tender, 3 to 5 minutes. Drain, rinse the cactus under cold water, and place it in a mixing bowl.

2. Place the vinegar and sugar in a small saucepan and bring it to a boil. Pour the brine over the cactus, add the oregano, garlic, serrano, and bay leaves and let the mixture cool to room temperature.

3. Divide the masa into 2-oz. balls. Line a tortilla press with plastic, place one of the balls in the press, and place another piece of plastic on top. Apply firm, even pressure and press the masa into a ¼-inch-thick round.

4. Place 2 tablespoons of the cheese in the center of each tortilla along with a couple slices of avocado. Fold one-third of the tortilla over the cheese and avocado. Repeat with two other sides of the tortilla to form a triangle.

5. Place the lard in a comal or cast-iron skillet and warm over medium-high heat. Add the tetalas and cook until browned on both sides, about 2 minutes. Serve with salsa and cilantro.

INGREDIENTS:

8	OZ. NOPALES, SPINES REMOVED, CLEANED, AND JULIENNED
	SALT, TO TASTE
½	TEASPOON BAKING SODA
1	CUP DISTILLED WHITE VINEGAR
1	TABLESPOON CANE SUGAR
1	TEASPOON DRIED MEXICAN OREGANO
2	GARLIC CLOVES
1	SERRANO CHILE PEPPER, STEMMED, SEEDED, AND SLICED
2	BAY LEAVES
8	OZ. PREPARED MASA (SEE PAGE 352)
1	CUP REQUESÓN OR RICOTTA CHEESE
	FLESH OF 1 LARGE AVOCADO, SLICED
2	TABLESPOONS LARD
	SALSA VERDE TATEMADA (SEE PAGE 480), FOR SERVING
	FRESH CILANTRO, CHOPPED, FOR SERVING

TACOS DORADOS DE FRIJOL, CHORIZO Y CAMOTE

YIELD: 12 TACOS / **ACTIVE TIME:** 45 MINUTES / **TOTAL TIME:** 45 MINUTES

A great preparation to turn to throughout the week, as it is a wonderful landing spot for leftovers.

1. Preheat the oven to 400°F. Place the sweet potatoes in a mixing bowl, add the lard, and toss until the potatoes are coated. Season with salt and the chile powder, spread the potatoes in an even layer on a baking sheet, and place in the oven. Roast until cooked through and crispy, about 30 minutes. Remove and season with the oregano.

2. Divide the masa into 1-oz. balls. Line a tortilla press with plastic, place one of the balls in the press, and place another piece of plastic on top. Apply firm, even pressure and press the masa into a ¼-inch-thick tortilla. Repeat with the remaining balls of masa.

3. Warm a comal or cast-iron skillet over medium-high heat. Working with one tortilla at a time, gently lay it in the pan, taking care to not wrinkle it. Cook for 15 to 30 seconds, until the edges begin to lift up slightly. Turn the tortilla over and let it cook for 30 to 45 seconds before turning it over one last time. If the hydration of the masa was correct and the heat is high enough, the tortilla should puff up and inflate. Remove the tortilla from the pan and store in a tortilla warmer lined with a linen towel.

4. Place the oil in a skillet and warm it over medium heat. Fill the tortillas with beans, chorizo, and sweet potatoes, taking care not to overfill.

5. Place the tacos in the skillet and fry on each side until golden brown and crispy. Serve with the onion, salsa, cilantro, and cheese.

INGREDIENTS:

- 1 LB. SWEET POTATOES, PEELED AND DICED
- 2 TABLESPOONS LARD
- SALT, TO TASTE
- 2 TEASPOONS GUAJILLO CHILE POWDER
- 2 TEASPOONS DRIED MEXICAN OREGANO
- 1 LB. PREPARED MASA (SEE PAGE 352)
- 3 TABLESPOONS EXTRA-VIRGIN OLIVE OIL
- 1 CUP FRIJOLES NEGROS REFRITOS (SEE PAGE 254)
- 4 OZ. CHORIZO ROJO, COOKED
- 1 SMALL RED ONION, JULIENNED
- MORITA SALSA (SEE PAGE 505), FOR SERVING
- FRESH CILANTRO, CHOPPED, FOR SERVING
- COTIJA CHEESE, CRUMBLED, FOR SERVING

HUEVOS RANCHEROS

YIELD: 4 SERVINGS / **ACTIVE TIME:** 15 MINUTES / **TOTAL TIME:** 20 MINUTES

A delicious alternative to straightforward eggs in the morning, these "ranch-style" eggs have the perfect balance of brightness and heft.

1. Place half of the olive oil in a large skillet and warm over medium-high heat. Add the tortillas and fry for about 1 minute on each side. Transfer to a paper towel–lined plate and let them drain.

2. Place the tomatoes, onion, and chiles in a blender and puree until smooth.

3. Place 2 tablespoons of the remaining olive oil in a small skillet and warm over medium heat. Carefully add the puree, reduce the heat to low, and cook the salsa for 5 minutes. Season with salt and then set the salsa aside.

4. Place the remaining oil in a skillet, add the eggs, season the yolks generously with salt, and cook as desired.

5. To assemble, place an egg on top of a fried tortilla, spoon the salsa on top, and garnish with the cheese and cilantro. Serve with the Frijoles de la Olla.

INGREDIENTS:

- ¾ CUP EXTRA-VIRGIN OLIVE OIL
- 4 CORN TORTILLAS (SEE PAGE 352)
- 3 LARGE TOMATOES
- ¼ ONION
- 2 SERRANO CHILE PEPPERS, STEMMED, SEEDED, AND SLICED

  SALT, TO TASTE
- 4 EGGS
- ½ CUP CHOPPED FRESH CILANTRO
- 8 OZ. QUESO FRESCO (SEE PAGE 522), FOR GARNISH

  FRIJOLES DE LA OLLA (SEE PAGE 257), FOR SERVING

MEMELAS DE CHICHARRON

YIELD: 4 SERVINGS / ACTIVE TIME: 1 HOUR / TOTAL TIME: 2 HOURS

Memelas are open-faced tacos that, as you might imagine, can accommodate a number of fillings. This particular preparation benefits greatly from the slight heat provided by the salsa, which can be red, green, or a combination of both.

1. Form the masa into 2-oz. balls. Gently press the balls into an oblong shape and line a tortilla press with plastic. Place one of the ovals in the press and place another piece of plastic on top. Apply firm, even pressure and press the oval until flat and about ¼ inch thick. Repeat with the remaining masa.

2. Warm a comal or cast-iron skillet over medium-high heat. Working with one memela at a time, place it in the pan and cook until golden and crispy on each side, about 6 minutes.

3. Spread the beans over the masa, top with the chicarron, and sprinkle cheese over everything. Garnish with the pickled onion and cilantro and serve with your favorite salsa.

INGREDIENTS:

3   CUPS PREPARED MASA (SEE PAGE 352)

1   CUP FRIJOLES NEGROS REFRITOS (SEE PAGE 254)

CHICHARRON EN SALSA ROJA (SEE PAGE 62)

8   OZ OAXACA CHEESE, SHREDDED

PICKLED RED ONION (SEE PAGE 515), FOR GARNISH

1   BUNCH OF FRESH CILANTRO, CHOPPED, FOR GARNISH

SALSA, FOR SERVING

CHICKEN TINGA SOPES

YIELD: 6 SERVINGS / **ACTIVE TIME:** 35 MINUTES / **TOTAL TIME:** 45 MINUTES

This versatile recipe also works well with Carne Asada (see page 58), al pastor pork (see page 155 for the marinade), and numerous vegetarian options.

1. Form the masa into 2-oz. balls and flatten them between your hands until each one is a disk. Pinch the edge of each disk to form a raised edge, shaping the masa into a shallow bowl.

2. Place the oil in a cast-iron skillet and warm to 350°F. Working with one sope at a time, gently slip it into the oil and fry until golden brown and crispy. Transfer to a paper towel–lined baking sheet to drain.

3. Spoon some beans into each sope and top with the Tinga de Pollo, cheese, cabbage, and radishes. Serve with salsa.

INGREDIENTS:

- 3 CUPS PREPARED MASA (SEE PAGE 352)
- 1 CUP EXTRA-VIRGIN OLIVE OIL
- 1 CUP FRIJOLES NEGROS REFRITOS (SEE PAGE 254)
- TINGA DE POLLO (SEE PAGE 114)
- 3 OZ. QUESO FRESCO (SEE PAGE 522), SHREDDED
- 1 CUP SHREDDED GREEN CABBAGE OR ICEBERG LETTUCE
- 1 BUNCH OF RADISHES, TRIMMED AND SLICED THIN
- SALSA, FOR SERVING

HUEVOS MOTULEÑOS

YIELD: 4 SERVINGS / **ACTIVE TIME:** 20 MINUTES / **TOTAL TIME:** 30 MINUTES

This recipe is unique and full of contrasting flavors, with sweetness from plantains, smoke from the chorizo, and a decadent creaminess from the eggs. If desired, this recipe is also commonly served with peas, and diced ham frequently stands in for the chorizo.

1. Place the tomatoes, onion, garlic, and 1 of the habanero peppers in a blender and puree until smooth. Season the salsa with salt.

2. Place 2 tablespoons of the oil in a small saucepan and warm it over medium-high heat. Carefully add the salsa and cook for 2 minutes. Reduce the heat to low, cook for another 5 minutes, and remove the pan from heat.

3. Place the remaining oil in a skillet and warm it over medium heat. Add the plantains and cook until golden brown on both sides, about 5 minutes. Transfer to a paper towel–lined plate to drain.

4. If using chorizo, add it to the pan and cook until crispy and cooked through, about 5 minutes.

5. Working with one tortilla at a time, place them in the pan and fry until golden brown on both sides, about 1 minute per side. Transfer to a paper towel–lined plate to drain.

6. Remove excess oil from the pan, add the eggs, generously season the yolks with salt, and cook the eggs as desired.

7. To assemble, spread the beans over the tortillas, top with two eggs, and spoon the salsa over the eggs. Sprinkle the cheese and chorizo over everything and serve with the fried plantains.

INGREDIENTS:

3	LARGE TOMATOES
¼	WHITE ONION
1	GARLIC CLOVE
2	HABANERO CHILE PEPPERS, STEMMED, SEEDED, AND SLICED
	SALT, TO TASTE
¾	CUP EXTRA-VIRGIN OLIVE OIL
2	PLANTAINS, PEELED AND SLICED INTO ¼ INCH ROUNDS
4	OZ. CHORIZO, CHOPPED (OPTIONAL)
6	CORN TORTILLAS (SEE PAGE 352)
8	WHOLE EGGS
2	CUPS FRIJOLES NEGROS REFRITOS (SEE PAGE 254)
1	CUP SHREDDED QUESO FRESCO (SEE PAGE 522)

ANTOJITOS

O r, "little cravings." These small bites fuel a street food scene that is one of the most extensive in the world. Less formal and filling than a standard meal, these quickly consumable preparations do not lag behind in terms of providing satisfaction and enjoyment, to the point that they have become some of Mexico's most beloved exports.

Featuring a pair of decadent tortas (see page 418 and 423), an esquites bulked up with the rich longaniza sausage (see page 424), guacamole, the rare preparation that is good beside just about everything, at just about any time of day (see page 432), and a host of other flavor-packed recipes, you'll soon be welcoming the magic of Mexico's streets into your home.

CHARRED PEPPER TARTARE

YIELD: 6 SERVINGS / ACTIVE TIME: 1 HOUR / TOTAL TIME: 8 HOURS

Tartare typically is a dish of raw meat with egg; however, in this meatless iteration, charred and smoked chiles are the accompaniment to the egg.

1. Preheat a gas or charcoal grill to medium-high heat (about 450°F). Place the poblanos and infused oil in a mixing bowl and toss until the peppers are coated.

2. Place the peppers on the grill and cook until charred all over, turning them as needed. Place the peppers in a heatproof bowl, cover it with plastic wrap, and let them steam for 15 minutes.

3. Remove most of the charred skin from the peppers, leaving about one-quarter of it on. Remove the stems and seeds from the peppers, place them on dehydrator racks, and dehydrate for 6 hours at 140°F. They should still be chewy, rather than crispy.

4. Chop the dehydrated peppers and place them in a bowl.

5. Add all of the remaining ingredients, except for the egg yolks and Morita Oil, and stir to combine. Set the mixture aside.

6. Place the egg yolks in a vacuum bag, seal it, and sous vide at 140°F for 40 minutes. Remove the egg yolks from the water bath and let them cool completely.

7. Prepare a smoker (using local wood whenever possible), place the egg yolks in the smoking tray, and smoke for 4 hours.

8. Top the dehydrated poblano mixture with the smoked egg yolks and serve with the Morita Oil.

CHARRED PEPPER EMULSION

1. Preheat the oven to 400°F. Cut off the top of the head of garlic, drizzle some olive oil over the cloves, and sprinkle salt on top. Place the top back on the garlic, place the entire head in a piece of foil, and seal. Place in the oven and roast until the garlic is extremely tender. Remove from the oven and let cool.

2. Preheat a gas or charcoal grill to medium-high heat (about 450°F). Place the poblanos and some olive oil in a mixing bowl and toss until the peppers are coated.

3. Place the peppers on the grill and cook until charred all over,

INGREDIENTS:

1¼	LBS. POBLANO CHILE PEPPERS
3	TABLESPOONS GARLIC-INFUSED OIL
1	CUP TOASTED ALMONDS
1	TEASPOON CAPERS
1	HEAD OF GARLIC
1	TABLESPOON KOSHER SALT
3	TABLESPOONS SHERRY VINEGAR
1	CHIPOTLE MORITA CHILE PEPPER, STEMMED AND SEEDED
3	TABLESPOONS FRESH LEMON JUICE
	CHARRED PEPPER EMULSION (SEE RECIPE)
6	LARGE EGG YOLKS
	MORITA OIL (SEE RECIPE), FOR SERVING

CHARRED PEPPER EMULSION

1	HEAD OF GARLIC
	EXTRA-VIRGIN OLIVE OIL, TO TASTE
2	TABLESPOONS KOSHER SALT, PLUS MORE TO TASTE
1¼	LBS. POBLANO CHILE PEPPERS
1	CUP ALMONDS, TOASTED
1	TEASPOON CAPERS
½	CUP SHERRY VINEGAR
2	TABLESPOONS PAPRIKA
3	TABLESPOONS FRESH LEMON JUICE
1¼	CUPS GARLIC-INFUSED OLIVE OIL

turning them as needed. Place the peppers in a heatproof bowl, cover it with plastic wrap, and let them steam for 15 minutes.

4. Remove most of the charred skin from the peppers, leaving about one-quarter of it on. Remove the stems and seeds from the peppers, place the remaining flesh in a blender, and squeeze the roasted garlic cloves into the blender.

5. Add the remaining ingredients, except for the infused oil, and puree until smooth. Slowly stream in the oil and puree until it has been emulsified.

MORITA OIL

1. Place the chiles and oil in a blender and puree for 7 minutes. Let the mixture sit at room temperature for 24 hours.

2. Strain before using or storing.

INGREDIENTS:

MORITA OIL

7   OZ. CHIPOTLE MORITA
      CHILE PEPPERS, STEMMED
      AND SEEDED

4½ CUPS CANOLA OIL

COLECTIVO ADN

LA CATRINA FEST MX

Adry del Rocio
Carlosalberto GH
Ruben Poncia

PIG EAR SALAD

YIELD: 4 SERVINGS / **ACTIVE TIME:** 30 MINUTES / **TOTAL TIME:** 1 HOUR AND 30 MINUTES

The toasted rice powder called for here is very easy to make at home—simply place a few tablespoons of jasmine rice in a dry skillet, toast it over medium heat, and then grind it into a fine powder with a mortar and pestle.

1. Place the stock in a medium saucepan and add the chiles, white onion, whole cloves of garlic, and bay leaf. Bring to a simmer, add the pig ears, and gently simmer until they are very tender. You want to be able to pass a knife through the pig ears with ease. Drain the pig ears and let them cool. When cool, slice them into ½-inch-thick pieces.

2. Add canola oil to a Dutch oven until it is about 2 inches deep and warm it to 350°F.

3. Place the rice flour in a bowl, dredge the pig ears in the flour until coated, and then place them in the oil. Fry until crispy on the outside, about 45 seconds. Transfer to a paper towel–lined plate to drain and season the pig ears with salt.

4. Place all of the remaining ingredients, except for the epazote powder, in a mixing bowl, add the fried pig ears, and toss to combine. Top with the epazote powder and serve.

INGREDIENTS:

4	CUPS CHICKEN STOCK (SEE PAGE 341)
2	CHIPOTLE MORITA CHILE PEPPERS, STEMMED AND SEEDED
½	WHITE ONION, SLICED
4	GARLIC CLOVES, 2 LEFT WHOLE, 2 DICED
1	BAY LEAF
1½	LBS. PIG EARS, TRIMMED
	CANOLA OIL, AS NEEDED
2	CUPS RICE FLOUR
	SALT AND PEPPER, TO TASTE
¼	RED ONION, SLICED
2	TABLESPOONS TOASTED RICE POWDER
15	CURRY LEAVES
10	CHERRY TOMATOES, HALVED
2	TABLESPOONS TOASTED RICE POWDER
	JUICE OF 3 LIMES
2	TABLESPOONS EXTRA-VIRGIN OLIVE OIL
1	TABLESPOON GINGER JUICE
1	TABLESPOON EPAZOTE POWDER

CURED SARDINES

YIELD: 4 SERVINGS / **ACTIVE TIME:** 15 MINUTES / **TOTAL TIME:** 24 HOURS

Cured sardines are common appetizers in coastal regions, especially Baja California. If fresh sardines are difficult to come by, canned sardines can be used.

1. Remove the spines from the sardines and butterfly them. Place them on a silpat-lined baking sheet, skin side down.

2. Combine the salt and sugar in a mixing bowl and sprinkle some of the mixture over the sardines. Turn the sardines over and sprinkle this side with the salt-and-sugar mixture.

3. Cover the pan with plastic wrap and chill in the refrigerator for 1 day.

4. Transfer the sardines to a fresh silpat-lined baking sheet and pat them dry with paper towels. You don't want to rinse the sardines.

5. Place the sardines in a container, cover with olive oil, and store in the refrigerator. Enjoy with tostadas or sardines.

INGREDIENTS:

1	LB. FRESH SARDINES
¾	CUP KOSHER SALT
¼	CUP SUGAR
	EXTRA-VIRGIN OLIVE OIL, AS NEEDED
	TOSTADAS OR SALTINES, FOR SERVING

KOJI-FRIED SARDINES

YIELD: 4 SERVINGS / **TOTAL TIME:** 15 MINUTES / **ACTIVE TIME:** 25 MINUTES

Koji is a fungus that grows on grains such as rice and barley, and it is one of the easiest and trendiest ways to turn a dish into an umami bomb.

1. Add canola oil to a Dutch oven until it is about 2 inches deep and warm it to 350°F.

2. Combine the flour, koji, salt, and pepper in a mixing bowl and stir to combine. Dredge the sardines in the mixture, gently slip them into the oil, and fry until golden brown, about 1 minute. Drain on a paper towel–lined plate and enjoy.

INGREDIENTS:

	CANOLA OIL, AS NEEDED
2	CUPS ALL-PURPOSE FLOUR, PLUS 1½ TABLESPOONS
¾	OZ. KOJI, FINELY GROUND
1	TEASPOON KOSHER SALT
½	TEASPOON BLACK PEPPER
3½	OZ. FRESH SARDINES, CLEANED

BEEF BARBACOA TACOS

YIELD: 4 SERVINGS / **ACTIVE TIME:** 30 MINUTES / **TOTAL TIME:** 24 HOURS

Barbacoa is traditionally prepared over an open flame or in a pit that has been dug in the ground, but this inventive preparation allows you to approximate that unique flavor in your home oven.

---

1. Place the beef in a large mixing bowl and season it with salt and pepper.

2. Place the ginger, cloves, allspice, red wine vinegar, garlic, pickling spices, chiles, sesame seeds, water, flour, and chili powder in a blender and puree until smooth.

3. Pour the puree over the beef and stir until it is coated. Cover the bowl with plastic wrap and let it marinate in the refrigerator overnight.

4. Preheat the oven to 350°F. Place the beef in a large roasting pan and add the bay leaves and about 6 cups water. Cover the pan with aluminum foil, place in the oven, and braise until the meat is falling apart, about 4 hours.

5. Remove from the oven, use two forks to shred the meat, and serve with the cheese, onion, cilantro, tortillas, and pickled onion.

INGREDIENTS:

5   LBS. BEEF SHOULDER, TRIMMED AND CUBED

     SALT AND PEPPER, TO TASTE

1   TEASPOON GRATED FRESH GINGER

2   WHOLE CLOVES

1   TEASPOON ALLSPICE

¼   CUP RED WINE VINEGAR

2   GARLIC CLOVES

½   (4 OZ.) BAG OF PICKLING SPICES

4   DRIED NEW MEXICO CHILE PEPPERS, STEMMED AND SEEDED

1   TEASPOON SESAME SEEDS

¾   CUP WATER

¼   CUP ALL-PURPOSE FLOUR

⅓   CUP CHILI POWDER

6   BAY LEAVES

     OAXACA CHEESE, SHREDDED, FOR SERVING

     ONION, CHOPPED, FOR SERVING

     FRESH CILANTRO, CHOPPED, FOR SERVING

12   CORN TORTILLAS (SEE PAGE 352), WARM, FOR SERVING

     PICKLED RED ONION (SEE PAGE 515), FOR SERVING

CHILAQUILES VERDES

YIELD: 4 SERVINGS / **ACTIVE TIME:** 15 MINUTES / **TOTAL TIME:** 30 MINUTES

The word *chilaquiles* has origins in the indigenous language, Nahuatl, meaning "chiles and greens." This dish is a typical breakfast dish in many households and is best with refried beans, either pinto or black, and fried eggs.

1. Place the tomatillos, pequin chile, onion, garlic, jalapeños, stock, and cumin in a medium saucepan and bring to a simmer over medium heat. Cook until the tomatillos have collapsed, about 20 minutes.

2. Stir the cilantro into the mixture, season it with salt and pepper, and set it aside.

3. Place the butter in a skillet and medium it over medium heat. Add the eggs, salt the yolks generously, and cook as desired. Remove the eggs from the pan.

4. Add the tortilla chips and chorizo to the pan and cook until warmed through.

5. To serve, layer the tortilla chips, chorizo, and beans on the serving plates, top with the eggs, and ladle the sauce over everything.

INGREDIENTS:

4   CUPS HUSKED, RINSED, AND CHOPPED TOMATILLOS

1   TABLESPOON CHOPPED PEQUIN CHILE PEPPER

1   ONION, CHOPPED

4   CUPS GARLIC CLOVES

2   JALAPEÑO CHILE PEPPERS, STEMMED, SEEDED, AND MINCED

4   CUPS CHICKEN STOCK (SEE PAGE 341)

1   TEASPOON CUMIN

2   CUPS FRESH CILANTRO, CHOPPED

    SALT AND PEPPER, TO TASTE

2   TABLESPOONS UNSALTED BUTTER

8   EGGS

2   CUPS TORTILLA CHIPS

1   CUP CHICKEN CHORIZO (SEE PAGE 109)

    FRIJOLES NEGROS REFRITOS (SEE PAGE 254), FOR SERVING

TORTAS DE LOMO

YIELD: 4 SERVINGS / **ACTIVE TIME:** 10 MINUTES / **TOTAL TIME:** 1 HOUR AND 25 MINUTES

Tortas can be filled with just about everything. This particular variation is born out of a favorite dish from Chef Luis Robles's childhood. The pork loin may also be shredded and then fried in a moderate amount of lard until very crispy.

1. Bring water to a boil in a medium saucepan. Add the pork, onion, and garlic, season generously with salt, and reduce the heat to low. Cook until the pork is tender, about 45 minutes.

2. Remove the pork from the pan and let it rest for 10 minutes.

3. Spread mayonnaise on each side of the bread.

4. Place the olive oil in a skillet and warm it over medium-high heat. Slice the pork thin, add it to the pan, and sear until crispy and golden brown on both sides, about 4 minutes. Remove the pork from the pan and set it aside.

5. Drain excess oil from the pan, place the bread in the pan, mayo side down, and cook until it is golden brown. Remove from the pan and assemble the tortas, layering the pork, Escabeche, and cheese. Cut the sandwiches in half and enjoy.

INGREDIENTS:

1	LB. PORK TENDERLOIN
½	WHITE ONION, CHOPPED
3	GARLIC CLOVES
	SALT, TO TASTE
½	CUP MAYONNAISE
4	BOLILLO, HALVED LENGTHWISE
2	TABLESPOONS EXTRA-VIRGIN OLIVE OIL
1	CUP ESCABECHE (SEE PAGE 518)
8	OZ. QUESO PANELA, SLICED

TORTAS AHOGADAS

YIELD: 4 SERVINGS / **ACTIVE TIME:** 15 MINUTES / **TOTAL TIME:** 25 MINUTES

Ahogada translates to "drowned," referring to the entire sandwich being dipped in a hot chili sauce. It is a street food staple across Guadalajara and Jalisco.

1. Bring water to a boil in a medium saucepan. Add the pork, season generously with salt, and reduce the heat to low. Cook until the pork is tender, about 45 minutes.

2. Bring water to a boil in a medium saucepan and add the tomatoes, chiles, and garlic. Cook until tender, about 10 minutes. Drain, place the mixture in a blender, and puree until smooth. Strain the sauce into a bowl and season with salt. Stir in the oregano and white vinegar.

3. Place the olive oil in a skillet and warm it over medium-high heat. Slice the pork thin, add it to the pan, and sear until crispy and golden brown on both sides, about 4 minutes. Remove the pork from the pan and set it aside.

4. Slice the bread in half lengthwise and fill with the pork loin.

5. Place the sauce in a pan large enough that a torta can easily be dipped into it. Bring to a simmer and dip the tortas in the sauce until they are smothered. Serve with pickled onion.

INGREDIENTS:

1 LB. PORK TENDERLOIN

SALT, TO TASTE

5 LARGE TOMATOES, CHOPPED

10 DRIED CHILES DE ARBOL, STEMMED AND SEEDED

2 GARLIC CLOVES, MINCED

1 TABLESPOON DRIED MEXICAN OREGANO

2 TABLESPOONS WHITE VINEGAR

2 TABLESPOONS EXTRA-VIRGIN OLIVE OIL

4 BOLILLO, BIROTE, OR BAGUETTES

PICKLED RED ONION (SEE PAGE 515), FOR SERVING

ESQUITES CON LONGANIZA

YIELD: 4 SERVINGS / **ACTIVE TIME:** 15 MINUTES / **TOTAL TIME:** 35 MINUTES

A slight refinement of a street food classic. This dish can be made vegetarian by swapping in chopped poblanos for the sausages, and adding them to the pan along with the onion.

1. Dice the onion so that the pieces are about the same size as the corn kernels.

2. Place the olive oil in the pan and warm it over medium heat. Add the longaniza and cook, breaking it up with a fork, until it is lightly browned and cooked through, about 7 minutes.

3. Drain any excess fat from the pan, add the onion, and cook until translucent, about 3 minutes. Add the chiles, cook for 2 minutes, and then add the corn. Cook until the corn is tender, about 10 minutes.

4. Return the longaniza to the pan and cook for 2 minutes. Taste, season with salt, and remove the pan from heat.

5. Divide between the serving bowls, top each portion with some of the cheese, chili powder, and mayonnaise. Serve with the lime wedges.

INGREDIENTS:

1	WHITE ONION
	KERNELS FROM 4 EARS OF CORN
1	TABLESPOON EXTRA-VIRGIN OLIVE OIL
1	LB. LONGANIZA SAUSAGES, CASING REMOVED
3	DRIED CHILES DE ARBOL, STEMMED, SEEDED, AND CHOPPED
	SALT, TO TASTE
1	CUP COTIJA CHEESE
2	TABLESPOONS CHILI POWDER
¼	CUP MAYONNAISE
	LIME WEDGES, FOR SERVING

PORK TORO WITH ARBOL MACHA

YIELD: 4 SERVINGS / **ACTIVE TIME:** 20 MINUTES / **TOTAL TIME:** 4 HOURS AND 30 MINUTES

There's plenty of Asian influence in this preparation, which is inspired in part by the jerky-and-salsa dishes that frequently serve as snacks at sporting events in the northern states of Mexico.

1. Place all of the ingredients, except for the Arbol Macha, in a mixing bowl and stir until the pork neck is coated. Place the bowl in the refrigerator and let the pork neck marinate for 4 hours.

2. Preheat a gas or charcoal grill to high heat (about 500°F). Place the pork neck on the grill and grill until the interior is 145°F.

3. Remove the pork from the grill and let it rest for 10 minutes before serving with the Arbol Macha.

ARBOL MACHA

1. Place all of the ingredients in a mortar and use a pestle to work the mixture until it comes together as a chunky paste.

INGREDIENTS:

1	LB. PORK NECK, CUT INTO ½-INCH-THICK SLICES
4	TEASPOONS THIN SOY SAUCE
2	TABLESPOONS THICK SOY SAUCE
1	TABLESPOON BROWN SUGAR
1	TEASPOON FINE SEA SALT
	CILANTRO, CHOPPED, TO TASTE
3	DRIED CHILES DE ARBOL
	ARBOL MACHA (SEE RECIPE), FOR SERVING

ARBOL MACHA

¼	CUP LIGHTLY SALTED PEANUTS, CRUSHED
2	TEASPOONS FISH SAUCE
6-8	CHILES DE ARBOL, STEMMED AND SEEDED
3	TOMATILLOS, HUSKED AND RINSED WELL CHARRED AND CRUSHED
⅓	CUP FRESH LIME JUICE
¼	CUP CHOPPED FRESH CILANTRO

QUESO FUNDIDO

YIELD: 4 SERVINGS / **ACTIVE TIME:** 15 MINUTES / **TOTAL TIME:** 35 MINUTES

Afun and delicious appetizer that will set any gathering off on the right foot.

1. Preheat the oven to 375°F. Place the olive oil in a medium cast-iron skillet and warm it over medium-low heat. Add the chorizo and cook, breaking it up with a fork, until browned and cooked through. Transfer the chorizo to a bowl and drain all but 1 tablespoon of fat from the pan.

2. Place the onion in the pan and cook until it is translucent, about 3 minutes. Remove the pan from heat.

3. Combine the cheeses and spread half of the mixture over the bottom of the pan. Layer half of the chorizo on top, and then repeat with the remaining cheese and chorizo.

4. Place the skillet in the oven and bake until the cheese is golden brown and bubbling, about 10 minutes. Garnish with cilantro and serve with warm tortillas.

INGREDIENTS:

1   TABLESPOON EXTRA-VIRGIN OLIVE OIL

8   OZ. MEXICAN CHORIZO, CASING REMOVED

¼   WHITE ONION, FINELY DICED

1   CUP GRATED OAXACAN CHEESE

½   CUP GRATED MONTEREY JACK CHEESE

FRESH CILANTRO, CHOPPED, FOR GARNISH

CORN TORTILLAS (SEE PAGE 352), WARM, FOR SERVING

GUACAMOLE

YIELD: 4 SERVINGS / **ACTIVE TIME:** 15 MINUTES / **TOTAL TIME:** 25 MINUTES

A pretty close to perfect dish: easy to prepare, freighted with big flavor, and able to fit in at breakfast, lunch, or dinner.

1. Combine the tomato, onion, and serrano peppers in a small bowl. Place the garlic clove in a medium bowl.

2. Add the avocados to the bowl containing the garlic and stir until well combined. Stir in the lime juice and season with salt.

3. Add the tomato mixture and stir until it has been incorporated. Add the cilantro and stir to combine. Taste and adjust the seasoning if necessary.

4. Enjoy with anything you please, at any time of day.

INGREDIENTS:

1	LARGE TOMATO, FINELY DICED
½	ONION, FINELY DICED
2	SERRANO CHILE PEPPERS, FINELY DICED
1	GARLIC CLOVE, MASHED
4	LARGE AVOCADOS, PITTED AND DICED
6	TABLESPOONS FRESH LIME JUICE
	SALT, TO TASTE
½	CUP FRESH CILANTRO, CHOPPED

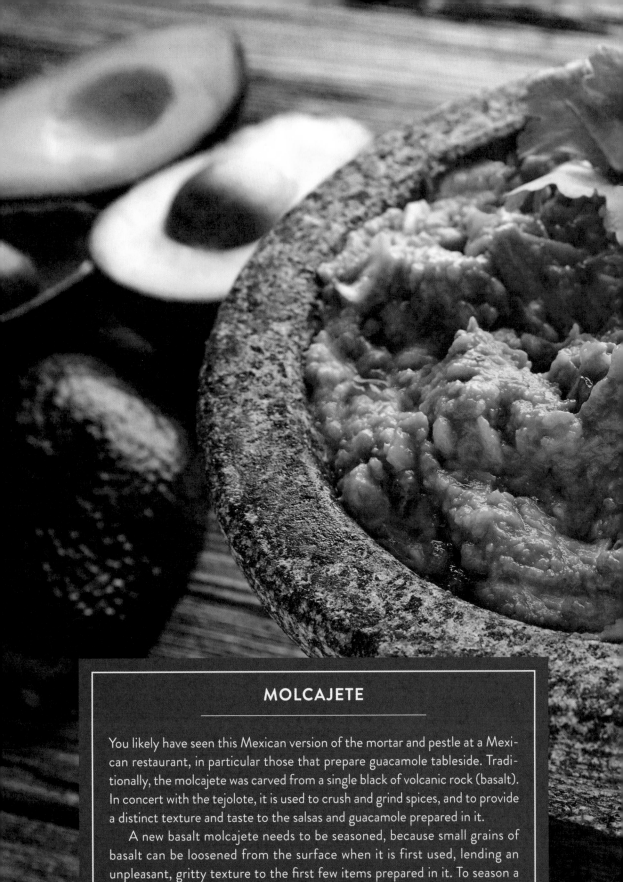

MOLCAJETE

You likely have seen this Mexican version of the mortar and pestle at a Mexican restaurant, in particular those that prepare guacamole tableside. Traditionally, the molcajete was carved from a single black of volcanic rock (basalt). In concert with the tejolote, it is used to crush and grind spices, and to provide a distinct texture and taste to the salsas and guacamole prepared in it.

A new basalt molcajete needs to be seasoned, because small grains of basalt can be loosened from the surface when it is first used, lending an unpleasant, gritty texture to the first few items prepared in it. To season a molcajete, grind uncooked white rice a handful at a time until it has no visible grains of basalt in it.

SAUCES, SALSAS & SIDES

*I*f one was looking to find a fourth piece to form a square out of the elemental items of Mexican cuisine, it would have to be mole, a sauce with depths and twists that beguile even the most subtle of palates, featuring a method that is similarly steeped in mystery, a dark art handed down through the generations. Some of the shadows surrounding this preparation are cleared away in this chapter. Perhaps not enough to make you a revered master, but more than enough to get you on track toward turning out your own heirloom-worthy version.

On top of a quartet of moles, there are numerous salsas and sides that will fit beautifully beside the preparations that have preceded this chapter, and are also capable of making a memorable meal out little more than a few tortillas and a protein or vegetable.

MOLE NEGRO

YIELD: 2 CUPS / **ACTIVE TIME:** 1 HOUR / **TOTAL TIME:** 4 HOURS

The most famous sauce in all of Mexico. This particular recipe was inspired by a Chef Susana Trilling preparation. If you cannot find the chihuacle chile pepper, substitute additional pasilla and/or ancho chiles.

1. Place 2 quarts of water in a saucepan and bring it to a simmer. Turn off the heat.

2. Warm a comal or cast-iron skillet over medium-high heat. Place all of the chiles in the pan and toast until they are charred all over. Using a spatula to press down on the chiles as they toast works nicely.

3. Place the chiles in the hot water and soak for 30 minutes. Preheat the oven to 350°F.

4. Drain the chiles and reserve the soaking liquid. Place the chiles in a blender and puree until smooth, adding the reserved liquid as needed. Strain the puree into a bowl, pressing down to extract as much liquid as possible, and discard the solids, or dehydrate and use as a spice powder.

5. Place the sesame seeds, almonds, and pecans on a parchment-lined baking sheet and toast them until they are dark brown, 10 to 12 minutes. Remove from the oven and let cool.

6. Place the onions, garlic, tomatoes, and tomatillos in the dry comal or skillet and toast until charred all over, turning them occasionally. Peel the garlic cloves, place the charred vegetables in a blender, and puree until smooth. Strain the puree into a bowl, pressing down to extract as much liquid as possible, and discard the solids.

7. Place the cinnamon sticks, peppercorns, cloves, avocado leaf, hoja santa leaf, and bay leaf in a dry skillet and toast them until fragrant, shaking the pan to prevent them from burning. Remove from the pan and let cool. When the mixture has cooled, use a mortar and pestle or a spice grinder to grind it into a fine powder.

8. Place all of the chile seeds in a dry skillet and toast over medium-high heat until thoroughly blackened. Make sure to open windows, turn on the kitchen fan, and wear a mask, as the toasted seeds will produce noxious fumes.

9. Use a long match or a kitchen torch to light the seeds on fire. When they burn out, place them in a bowl of cold water. Soak the

INGREDIENTS:

2-3	DRIED CHIHUACLE NEGRO CHILE PEPPERS, STEMMED AND SEEDED, SEEDS RESERVED
1	CHIPOTLE MECO CHILE PEPPER, STEMMED AND SEEDED, SEEDS RESERVED
2	ANCHO CHILE PEPPERS, STEMMED AND SEEDED, SEEDS RESERVED
2	PASILLA CHILE PEPPERS, STEMMED AND SEEDED, SEEDS RESERVED
3	GUAJILLO CHILE PEPPERS, STEMMED AND SEEDED, SEEDS RESERVED
3	TABLESPOONS SESAME SEEDS
¼	CUP BLANCHED ALMONDS
3	TABLESPOONS PECANS
1½	SMALL WHITE ONIONS, CUT INTO 12 PIECES
10	GARLIC CLOVES, UNPEELED
5	ROMA TOMATOES, HALVED
4	OZ. TOMATILLOS, HUSKED AND RINSED
2	STICKS OF MEXICAN CINNAMON
¼	TEASPOON BLACK PEPPERCORNS
¼	TEASPOON WHOLE CLOVES
1	AVOCADO LEAF
1	HOJA SANTA LEAF
1	BAY LEAF
16	CUPS CHICKEN STOCK (SEE PAGE 341)

seeds in cold water, and change the water every 10 minutes for a total of three changes. After the final soak, drain the seeds, place them in the blender with 1 cup of stock, and puree until smooth. Strain the liquid into a bowl through a fine-mesh sieve.

10. Place half of the lard in a skillet and warm it over medium heat. Add the bread and fry until it is dark brown. Remove it from the pan and set it aside.

11. Add the plantain and fry until it is dark brown and caramelized, about 4 minutes. Remove it from the pan and set it aside.

12. Add the raisins and fry them until plump and caramelized, about 3 minutes. Remove from the pan and set them aside.

13. Add the toasted nuts and sesame seeds and fry for about 1 minute. Place the nuts and seeds in the blender with a small amount of stock and puree until the mixture is a smooth paste.

14. Add the vegetable puree, toasted chile puree, chile seed puree, spice powder, raisins, plantains, and bread and puree until smooth. Strain the puree into a bowl through a fine-mesh sieve, again pressing down to get as much liquid as possible.

15. Place the remaining lard in a large saucepan and warm it over medium-high heat. Add the chile puree and cook until it bubbles vigorously, stirring with a whisk to prevent the mixture from scorching. Reduce the heat to a simmer and cook for 30 minutes.

16. Add the thyme and oregano and cook for 1 to 2 hours, adding the stock as needed.

17. When the rawness of the ingredients has been completely cooked out, add the chocolate and stir to incorporate. Season with salt and let the mole cool, then taste and adjust the seasoning as necessary. As it sits, the mole will take on stronger, increasingly delicious flavors.

INGREDIENTS:

½ CUP LARD

1¾ OZ. BRIOCHE BREAD

½ CUP CHOPPED OVERRIPE PLANTAIN

2 TABLESPOONS RAISINS

½ TEASPOON DRIED THYME

½ TEASPOON DRIED MEXICAN OREGANO

5⅓ OZ. MEXICAN CHOCOLATE

SALT, TO TASTE

TORTILLAS DE HARINA DE TRIGO

YIELD: 18 TORTILLAS / **ACTIVE TIME:** 45 MINUTES / **TOTAL TIME:** 1 HOUR AND 30 MINUTES

Flour tortillas play an important role in northern Mexico due to the abundance of Sonoran wheat. If you are able to source this type of wheat, we recommend doing so, as the flavor is incredible.

1. In the work bowl of a stand mixer fitted with the paddle attachment, combine the flour, salt, and baking powder and beat on low speed for 30 seconds.

2. Gradually add the lard and beat until the mixture resembles coarse bread crumbs.

3. Fit the mixer with the dough hook and set it to low speed. Add the water in a slow stream until the dough begins to come together, 2 to 3 minutes. The dough should begin to pull away from the sides of the mixing bowl, leaving no residue behind. Increase the speed to medium and continue mixing until the dough becomes very soft, shiny, and elastic. Please note that more or less of the water may be required due to environmental conditions and/or variations in the flour.

4. Remove the dough from the work bowl and place it in a mixing bowl. Cover with plastic wrap or a damp kitchen towel and let it rest at room temperature for 30 to 45 minutes.

5. Portion the dough into rounds the size of golf balls, approximately 1½ oz. each. Using the palms of your hands, roll the rounds in a circular motion until they are seamless balls. Place on a parchment-lined baking sheet and cover with plastic wrap. Let them rest at room temperature for 20 minutes.

6. Working on a very smooth and flour-dusted work surface, roll out the balls of dough until they are between ⅛ and ¼ inch thick and about 8 inches in diameter. Stack the tortillas, separating each one with pieces of parchment paper that have been cut to size.

7. Warm a comal or a cast-iron skillet over medium-high heat. Gently place a tortilla on the cooking surface. It should immediately sizzle and begin to puff up. Do not puncture it. Cook, turning frequently, for 20 to 30 seconds per side, until lightly golden brown in spots. Stack in a linen towel, a tortilla warmer, or a plastic resealable bag so it continues to steam and repeat with the remaining tortillas.

INGREDIENTS:

- 1   LB. ALL-PURPOSE FLOUR, PLUS MORE AS NEEDED

- 1   TABLESPOON KOSHER SALT

- 1   TABLESPOON BAKING POWDER

- 2½   OZ. LARD OR UNSALTED BUTTER, MELTED

- 8-10   OZ. WARM, FILTERED WATER (105°F)

SWEET CORN & PEPITA GUACAMOLE

YIELD: 4 SERVINGS / **ACTIVE TIME:** 15 MINUTES / **TOTAL TIME:** 30 MINUTES

The addition of grilled corn adds smoke to this classic, creamy dip, and the pumpkin seeds add a little nuttiness and texture.

1. Preheat a gas or charcoal grill to medium-high heat (about 450°F). Place the corn on the grill and cook until it is charred all over and the kernels have softened enough that there is considerable give in them.

2. Remove the corn from the grill and let it cool. When cool enough to handle, husk the corn and cut off the kernels.

3. Combine the corn, pumpkin seeds, and pomegranate seeds in a small bowl. Place the avocados in a separate bowl and mash until just slightly chunky. Stir in the corn mixture, the onion, cilantro, and lime juice, season the mixture with salt and pepper, and work the mixture until the guacamole is the desired texture.

INGREDIENTS:

1   EAR OF YELLOW CORN, WITH HUSK ON

1   OZ. PUMPKIN SEEDS

1   OZ. POMEGRANATE SEEDS

FLESH OF 3 AVOCADOS

½   RED ONION, CHOPPED

½   CUP FRESH CILANTRO, CHOPPED

1   TEASPOON FRESH LIME JUICE

SALT AND PEPPER, TO TASTE

CHILE COLORADO

YIELD: 4 CUPS / **ACTIVE TIME:** 30 MINUTES / **TOTAL TIME:** 1 HOUR AND 30 MINUTES

This chile sauce can be used to add complexity and spice to any dish.

1. Place the chiles in a dry skillet and toast until they are pliable and fragrant. Place them in a bowl of hot water and soak for 30 minutes.

2. Place the coriander seeds, allspice berries, and cumin seeds in the skillet and toast until fragrant, shaking the pan frequently to keep them from burning. Grind the toasted seeds to a fine powder with a mortar and pestle or a spice grinder.

3. Place the olive oil in the skillet and warm it over medium heat. Add the onion, garlic, toasted spice powder, marjoram, oregano, and thyme and cook, stirring frequently, until the onion is translucent, about 3 minutes.

4. Drain the chiles and reserve the soaking liquid. Place the chiles and onion mixture in a blender and puree until smooth, adding the reserved liquid as necessary.

5. Place the lard in a Dutch oven and warm it over high heat. Carefully add the puree (it will splatter) and the bay leaves, reduce the heat to low, and simmer for 1 hour, adding stock as necessary to get the flavor and texture to your liking. Season with salt before using or storing.

INGREDIENTS:

7   OZ. GUAJILLO CHILE PEPPERS, STEMMED AND SEEDED

1¾   OZ. ANCHO CHILE PEPPERS, STEMMED AND SEEDED

⅓   OZ. DRIED CHILES DE ARBOL, STEMMED AND SEEDED

1   TABLESPOON CORIANDER SEEDS

1½   TEASPOONS ALLSPICE BERRIES

1¼   TABLESPOONS CUMIN SEEDS

1   TABLESPOON EXTRA-VIRGIN OLIVE OIL

1   WHITE ONION, SLICED

10   GARLIC CLOVES

1   TABLESPOON DRIED MARJORAM

1   TABLESPOON DRIED MEXICAN OREGANO

1   TABLESPOON DRIED THYME

3   TABLESPOONS LARD

2   BAY LEAVES

     CHICKEN OR VEGETABLE STOCK (SEE PAGE 341 OR 346), AS NEEDED

     SALT, TO TASTE

MOLE MANCHAMANTELES

YIELD: 6 TO 8 SERVINGS / **ACTIVE TIME:** 30 MINUTES / **TOTAL TIME:** 2 HOURS AND 30 MINUTES

Make sure to have extra napkins at the ready when serving this mole. Manchamanteles translates to "tablecloth stainer"—so it can be messy.

1. Preheat the oven to 400°F. Place the piloncillo and water in a saucepan and bring to a boil, stirring to dissolve the piloncillo. Toss the apple, pear, and peach in the syrup, place them in a baking dish, and roast until caramelized, about 20 minutes.

2. Place the sesame seeds in a dry skillet and toast until lightly browned, shaking the pan frequently to keep them from burning. Add the cinnamon, coriander seeds, allspice berries, cumin seeds, and star anise to the skillet and toast until fragrant, shaking the pan frequently to keep them from burning. Grind the mixture to a fine powder with a mortar and pestle or a spice grinder.

3. Place the onion and garlic in the skillet and toast over medium heat until charred, about 10 minutes, turning occasionally. Remove from the pan and let them cool. When cool enough to handle, peel the garlic cloves.

4. Place the lard in a Dutch oven and warm over medium heat. Add the chiles and fry until pliable and fragrant. Remove the chiles and soak in hot water for 20 minutes.

5. Place the raisins and plantain in the lard and fry until the raisins are puffy and the plantain has caramelized. Add all of the ingredients to the Dutch oven and cook for 1 to 2 hours, adding stock as needed.

6. Place the mixture in a blender and puree until smooth. Strain, season with salt, and use as desired.

INGREDIENTS:

- 8 OZ. PILONCILLO
- 1 CUP WATER
- 1 APPLE, PEELED, CORED, AND SLICED
- 1 PEAR, PEELED, CORED, AND SLICED
- 1 PEACH, HALVED, PITTED, AND SLICED
- ¾ CUP SESAME SEEDS
- ½ MEXICAN CINNAMON STICK
- 1¼ TABLESPOONS CORIANDER SEEDS
- 1½ TEASPOONS ALLSPICE BERRIES
- 1 TABLESPOON CUMIN SEEDS
- 2 STAR ANISE PODS
- 1 WHITE ONION, QUARTERED
- 5 GARLIC CLOVES, UNPEELED
- 7 TABLESPOONS LARD
- 6 ANCHO CHILE PEPPERS, STEMMED AND SEEDED
- 5 GUAJILLO CHILE PEPPERS, STEMMED AND SEEDED
- 2 CHIPOTLE MECO CHILE PEPPERS, STEMMED AND SEEDED
- ½ CUP GOLDEN RAISINS
- 1 RIPE PLANTAIN, PEELED AND SLICED
- 10½ OZ. ROMA TOMATOES, HALVED
- CHICKEN STOCK (SEE PAGE 341), AS NEEDED
- SALT, TO TASTE

MOLE BLANCO

YIELD: 4 CUPS / **ACTIVE TIME:** 30 MINUTES / **TOTAL TIME:** 1 HOUR

Mole Blanco is one of the less common moles in Mexico, but also a very versatile one that can work with vegetables and proteins. Take care not to add too much color to any of the ingredients or you won't end up with a beautiful, white mole.

1. Use a mortar and pestle or a spice grinder to turn the pine nuts, sunflower seeds, and sesame seeds into a paste, adding stock as needed.

2. Place the olive oil in a Dutch oven and warm over medium heat. Add the tomatillos, garlic, onion, habanero, turnip, fennel, apple, bread crumbs, raisins, and plantain and cook until the onion is translucent, about 3 minutes, stirring so that the contents of the pan do not take on any color.

3. Add the seed paste, masa harina, white pepper, allspice, fennel, and coriander and stir to incorporate. Add the milk and stock and simmer until the fruits and vegetables are tender.

4. Stir in the white chocolate. Taste and adjust the seasoning as necessary. Place the mixture in a blender and puree until smooth. Strain before using or storing.

INGREDIENTS:

1	TABLESPOON PINE NUTS, LIGHTLY TOASTED
1	TABLESPOON SUNFLOWER SEEDS, LIGHTLY TOASTED
1	TABLESPOON SESAME SEEDS, LIGHTLY TOASTED
3½	TABLESPOONS CHICKEN STOCK (SEE PAGE 341), PLUS MORE AS NEEDED
2	TABLESPOONS EXTRA-VIRGIN OLIVE OIL
1½	TOMATILLOS, HUSKED AND RINSED
1	GARLIC CLOVE
¼	WHITE ONION
1	TABLESPOON CHOPPED HABANERO CHILE PEPPER
2	TABLESPOONS CHOPPED TURNIP
1	TABLESPOON CHOPPED FENNEL
1	TABLESPOON PEELED AND CHOPPED GREEN APPLE
1	TABLESPOON SOURDOUGH BREAD CRUMBS
1	TABLESPOON GOLDEN RAISINS
1	TABLESPOON MINCED PLANTAIN
3	TABLESPOONS MASA HARINA
⅛	TEASPOON WHITE PEPPER
⅛	TEASPOON ALLSPICE
	PINCH OF GROUND FENNEL SEEDS
1	CORIANDER SEED, TOASTED AND GROUND
3½	TABLESPOONS MILK
1	TEASPOON GRATED WHITE CHOCOLATE
	SALT, TO TASTE

PRESERVED LIMES
WITH CHILE DE ARBOL & SPICES

YIELD: 8 SERVINGS / **ACTIVE TIME:** 15 MINUTES / **TOTAL TIME:** 2 TO 4 WEEKS

Pureeing the ingredients listed below will make for a wonderful sauce that can also be used as a Michelada mix.

1. Juice the limes into a large bowl and save the spent halves. Add all of the remaining ingredients and stir until the mixture is a paste.

2. Put on gloves, add the spent halves, and work the mixture until well combined.

3. Transfer the mixture to an airtight container and gently press down on it to make sure there are no pockets that air can get into. Seal the container and store at room temperature or chill in the refrigerator until the lime halves are tender. This will take about 2 weeks at room temperature, and a month in the refrigerator. Mince the limes and use as desired.

INGREDIENTS:

7	LIMES
2	TABLESPOONS CARDAMOM SEEDS, GROUND
2	TABLESPOONS SMOKED SPANISH PAPRIKA
2	TABLESPOONS TURMERIC
1½	TEASPOONS CUMIN SEEDS, TOASTED AND GROUND
3	TABLESPOONS KOSHER SALT
5	CHILES DE ARBOL, STEMMED, SEEDED, AND GROUND

STRAWBERRY HOT SAUCE

YIELD: 4 CUPS / **ACTIVE TIME:** 30 MINUTES / **TOTAL TIME:** 2 HOURS

The utility of this hot sauce changes according to how thick or thin you want it. When the consistency is thinner, it should be used to season and glaze meats. If you want it thicker, use it as a spread or topping.

1. Place the strawberries and salt in a blender and puree until smooth. Let the mixture sit at room temperature for 1 hour.

2. Place the chiles, strawberry puree, and water in a saucepan and bring to a boil, making sure to stir and scrape the bottom of the pan frequently to keep a skin from forming.

3. Add the cumin and coriander and cook another 20 minutes, stirring and scraping frequently.

4. Working in batches, transfer the mixture to the blender and puree for about 3 minutes. The strawberry seeds should break down, as they have been cooking for a while.

5. Strain the mixture through a fine-mesh sieve into a clean saucepan. Add the vinegars and cook over medium-high heat until the sauce has reduced by half.

6. Season the sauce generously with salt and store it in mason jars.

INGREDIENTS:

1	LB. STRAWBERRIES, RINSED AND HULLED
2	TEASPOONS KOSHER SALT, PLUS MORE TO TASTE
3½	OZ. CHILES DE ARBOL
4	CUPS WATER
1½	TEASPOONS CUMIN
1	TABLESPOON CORIANDER
1¼	CUPS APPLE CIDER VINEGAR, PLUS 1 TABLESPOON
1¾	CUPS DISTILLED WHITE VINEGAR

PICKLED PINEAPPLE

YIELD: 4 SERVINGS / **ACTIVE TIME:** 40 MINUTES / **TOTAL TIME:** 2 DAYS

The acidity and sweetness of this pickled fruit pairs well with pork dishes. Green hot peppers can be added during the fermentation process to add some spice.

1. Preheat a gas or charcoal grill to medium heat (400°F).

2. Place the star anise, cinnamon stick, and chiles in a saucepan and toast until fragrant, about 2 minutes, shaking the pan frequently. Add the vinegars and sugar, generously season with salt, and bring to a boil, stirring to dissolve the sugar.

3. Pour the brine into a sterilized mason jar.

4. Place the pineapple on the grill and grill until charred on both sides, about 8 minutes. Add to the brine while it is warm and let the mixture cool to room temperature. Cover and refrigerate for 2 days before using.

INGREDIENTS:

2	STAR ANISE PODS
½	CINNAMON STICK
2	DRIED CHILES DE ARBOL
2¼	CUPS APPLE CIDER VINEGAR
7	TABLESPOONS WHITE VINEGAR
3	TABLESPOONS SUGAR
	SALT, TO TASTE
1	PINEAPPLE, PEELED, CORED, AND SLICED

EPAZOTE OIL

YIELD: 1 CUP / **ACTIVE TIME:** 5 MINUTES / **TOTAL TIME:** 5 MINUTES

Epazote is most commonly found in dishes from Puebla, and its taste is similar to cilantro, only more bitter. This oil is best as a dressing on tomatoes or in cocktails.

1. Place the ingredients in a blender and puree until combined, making sure it takes no longer than 40 seconds.

2. Strain through a coffee filter. To preserve the oil for as long as possible, and to maintain the color, store it in the freezer.

INGREDIENTS:

3½ OZ. FRESH EPAZOTE

14 TABLESPOONS EXTRA-VIRGIN OLIVE OIL

EPAZOTE

This herb, used medicinally to treat intestinal parasites for centuries, carries a powerful taste that takes some folks a bit of time to get used to. But it is an everyday part of cooking in Mexico, prized for the rustic quality it adds to a dish. Epazote is a weed that grows quickly and has spread through the Americas. It carries notes of oregano, anise, citrus, and mint, as well as an element some feel is similar to tar or creosote. One thing to keep in mind when cooking with epazote: the flavor compounds in it do not stand up to heating for a long time, so add it to dishes near the end of cooking.

CHARRED ESCABECHE

YIELD: 6 SERVINGS / **ACTIVE TIME:** 30 MINUTES / **TOTAL TIME:** 1 DAY

Escabeche in Mexico most commonly refers to spicy pickled vegetables. In other countries, escabeche usually includes meat or fish.

1. Place the water, vinegars, sugar, and salt in a saucepan and bring to a boil, stirring to dissolve the sugar and salt. Pour the mixture into a large, sterilized mason jar and add the thyme, garlic, and bay leaves.

2. Warm a large cast-iron skillet over high heat for 5 minutes.

3. Spray the skillet with nonstick cooking spray and add the jalapeños. Weight them down with a smaller pan and cook until charred, about 5 minutes.

4. Place the jalapeños in the brine, add the carrots to the skillet, and weight them down with the smaller pan. Cook until charred, add them to the brine, and let the mixture cool to room temperature before covering and storing in the refrigerator. Let sit for at least 1 day before using.

INGREDIENTS:

3½   TABLESPOONS WATER

2⅓   TABLESPOONS APPLE CIDER VINEGAR

¼   CUP WHITE VINEGAR

1   TABLESPOON SUGAR

1   TABLESPOON KOSHER SALT

2   SPRIGS OF FRESH THYME

2   GARLIC CLOVES

2   BAY LEAVES

5   OZ. JALAPEÑO CHILE PEPPERS, HALVED

1⅓   LBS. CARROTS, PEELED AND SLICED ON A BIAS

CUMIN & CILANTRO VINAIGRETTE

YIELD: 2 CUPS / **ACTIVE TIME:** 10 MINUTES / **TOTAL TIME:** 10 MINUTES

The nutty, earthy, and bitter tones present in cumin complement the strong, citrusy flavor of cilantro. This vinaigrette is ideal for simple salads and seafood.

1. Add the cumin seeds in a dry skillet and toast over low heat until fragrant, shaking the pan to keep them from burning. Remove the seeds from the pan and place them in a blender.

2. Place all of the remaining ingredients, except for the olive oil, in the blender and puree until smooth. With the blender running, slowly add the olive oil until it has been emulsified.

INGREDIENTS:

- ¼ CUP CUMIN SEEDS
- ¼ CUP BROWN SUGAR
- 3 EGG YOLKS
- ⅓ CUP RED WINE VINEGAR
- ½ CUP WATER
- 2 CUPS FRESH CILANTRO, CHOPPED

  SALT AND PEPPER, TO TASTE
- 1½ CUPS EXTRA-VIRGIN OLIVE OIL

SALSA DE CHILTOMATE

YIELD: 1½ CUPS / **ACTIVE TIME:** 20 MINUTES / **TOTAL TIME:** 1 HOUR

This recipe is inspired by the cuisine in the Yucatan, where there is a deep tradition of roasting chiles until well charred.

1. Preheat the oven to 450°F. Line a baking sheet with parchment paper, place the tomatoes, chiles, onion, and garlic on it, and place in the oven.

2. Roast until the vegetables are charred all over, checking every 5 minutes or so and removing them as they become ready.

3. Peel the garlic cloves, remove the stem and seeds from the habanero (gloves are strongly recommended while handling habaneros), and place the roasted vegetables in a blender. Puree until smooth.

4. Place the olive oil in a medium saucepan and warm it over medium-high heat. Carefully pour the puree into the pan, reduce the heat, and simmer until it has reduced slightly and the flavor is to your liking, 15 to 20 minutes.

5. Season with salt, stir in the lime juice, and let the salsa cool. Taste, adjust the seasoning if necessary, and use as desired.

INGREDIENTS:

8½ OZ. ROMA TOMATOES, HALVED

2 HABANERO CHILE PEPPERS

1 SMALL WHITE ONION, QUARTERED

4 GARLIC CLOVES, UNPEELED

2 TABLESPOONS EXTRA-VIRGIN OLIVE OIL

SALT, TO TASTE

JUICE OF 1 LIME

SALSA VERDE TATEMADA

YIELD: 1½ CUPS / **ACTIVE TIME:** 20 MINUTES / **TOTAL TIME:** 30 MINUTES

This salsa is common in the Yucatean town of Quintana Roo. To prepare this salsa in the traditional way, mix the ingredients together using a molcajete and a tejolote.

1. Warm a comal or cast-iron skillet over high heat. Place the tomatillos, garlic, onion, and chiles in the pan and cook until charred all over, turning them occasionally.

2. Remove the vegetables from the pan and let them cool slightly.

3. Peel the garlic cloves and remove the stems and seeds from the chiles. Place the charred vegetables in a blender, add the cilantro, and puree until smooth.

4. Season the salsa with salt and use as desired.

INGREDIENTS:

1   LB. TOMATILLOS, HUSKED AND RINSED

5   GARLIC CLOVES, UNPEELED

1   SMALL WHITE ONION, QUARTERED

10   SERRANO CHILE PEPPERS

2   BUNCHES OF FRESH CILANTRO, LEAVES AND STEMS

  SALT, TO TASTE

BARBACOA ADOBO

YIELD: 1½ CUPS / **ACTIVE TIME:** 20 MINUTES / **TOTAL TIME:** 45 MINUTES

Adobo is used in various dishes throughout Mexico, including in the famed slow-cooked beef, where the roasted chiles enhance the smoky flavor.

1. Place the coriander, cloves, allspice, cumin, and peppercorns in a dry skillet and toast until fragrant, shaking the pan to keep them from burning. Using a mortar and pestle or a spice grinder, grind the mixture into a fine powder.

2. Place the chiles in the pan and toast until fragrant and pliable. Place the toasted chiles in a bowl of hot water and soak for 20 minutes.

3. Drain the chiles and reserve the soaking liquid. Place the chiles in a blender, add the juices, onions, garlic, and avocado leaves (if using), and puree until smooth, adding the reserved liquid as needed.

4. Stir in the juices, season the adobo with salt, and use as desired.

INGREDIENTS:

- 1 TABLESPOON CORIANDER SEEDS
- 1½ TEASPOONS WHOLE CLOVES
- 1½ TEASPOONS ALLSPICE BERRIES
- 1 TABLESPOON CUMIN SEEDS
- 1½ TABLESPOONS BLACK PEPPERCORNS
- 1 ANCHO CHILE PEPPER, STEMMED AND SEEDED
- 1 GUAJILLO CHILE PEPPER, STEMMED AND SEEDED
- 1 CHIPOTLE CHILE PEPPER, STEMMED AND SEEDED
- 1 PASILLA CHILE PEPPER, STEMMED AND SEEDED
- 14 TABLESPOONS ORANGE JUICE
- 14 TABLESPOONS FRESH LIME JUICE
- 2 SMALL ONIONS, SLICED
- 5 GARLIC CLOVES
- 2 AVOCADO LEAVES (OPTIONAL)
- SALT, TO TASTE

PIPIAN ROJO

YIELD: 2 CUPS / **ACTIVE TIME:** 30 MINUTES / **TOTAL TIME:** 45 MINUTES

This is considered a native dish of Mexico, however there are similar seed-based sauces in South and Central America. After straining the chile puree, dehydrate the pulp to make a seasoning powder.

1. Warm a dry comal or cast-iron skillet over medium heat. Place the chiles in the pan and toast until fragrant and pliable. Place the toasted chiles in a bowl of hot water and soak for 20 minutes.

2. Drain the chiles and reserve the soaking liquid. Place the chiles in a blender and puree, adding the reserved liquid as needed. Strain into a bowl and reserve the pulp for another preparation.

3. Place the strained liquid in the blender, add all of the remaining ingredients, except for the lard, and puree until smooth.

4. Place the lard in a medium saucepan and warm it over medium-high heat. Carefully add the puree and stir for 1 minute. Reduce the heat and simmer until the mixture is the desired texture. Season with salt and use as desired.

INGREDIENTS:

4   GUAJILLO CHILE PEPPERS, STEMMED AND SEEDED

1   ANCHO CHILE PEPPER, STEMMED AND SEEDED

2   DRIED CHILES DE ARBOL, STEMMED AND SEEDED

3½   OZ. PUMPKIN SEEDS, HULLED

⅔   CUP SESAME SEEDS

2½   ROMA TOMATOES

¾   SMALL WHITE ONION

4   GARLIC CLOVES

2   ALLSPICE BERRIES

1   WHOLE CLOVE

4   CINNAMON STICKS

2   CORN TORTILLAS (SEE PAGE 352), TOASTED

4   CUPS CHICKEN OR VEGETABLE STOCK (SEE PAGE 341 OR 346)

2-3   LARGE CHAYOTES, PITTED

2   TABLESPOONS LARD

    SALT, TO TASTE

SALPICON DE RABANO Y CHILE HABANERO

YIELD: 1½ CUPS / **ACTIVE TIME:** 20 MINUTES / **TOTAL TIME:** 1 HOUR AND 30 MINUTES

The addition of citrus to this salsa adds another layer of complexity and balances out the strong flavors of the charred chiles.

1. Roast the habanero over an open flame, in the oven, or on the grill until it is charred all over. Let it cool briefly, remove the stem and seeds (wearing gloves is strongly recommended when handling habaneros), and mince the remaining flesh.

2. Place the habaneros in a bowl, add the remaining ingredients, and let the mixture macerate for at least 1 hour before serving.

INGREDIENTS:

2   HABANERO CHILE PEPPERS

4-5   RADISHES, TRIMMED AND JULIENNED

1   BAY LEAF

⅛   TEASPOON DRIED MEXICAN OREGANO

½   CUP FRESH LIME JUICE

½   CUP ORANGE JUICE

1   TABLESPOON EXTRA-VIRGIN OLIVE OIL

     SALT, TO TASTE

X'NIPEK

YIELD: 1 CUP / **ACTIVE TIME:** 10 MINUTES / **TOTAL TIME:** 20 MINUTES

The texture of salsas in Mexico varies depending on the region, with some smooth and creamy while others carry a chunky texture. X'nipek comes from the Yucatan, and is similar to pico de gallo.

1. Place all of the ingredients, except for the salt, in a bowl and stir until combined. Let the mixture macerate for 10 minutes.

2. Season with salt and use as desired.

INGREDIENTS:

4   ROMA TOMATOES, SEEDED AND DICED

2-3   HABANERO PEPPERS, STEMMED, SEEDED, AND MINCED

1½   SMALL RED ONIONS, JULIENNED

1¼   CUPS FRESH CILANTRO, CHOPPED

1¾   OZ. FRESH LIME JUICE

10   TABLESPOONS ORANGE JUICE

1½   TEASPOONS DRIED MEXICAN OREGANO

SALT, TO TASTE

CHILES TOREADOS

YIELD: 1 CUP / **ACTIVE TIME:** 20 MINUTES / **TOTAL TIME:** 1 HOUR

f you cannot find Maggi seasoning sauce at the nearby grocery store, Worcestershire sauce can be substituted.

1. Warm a comal or cast-iron skillet over high heat. Place the chiles in the pan and toast until they are very charred all over, turning occasionally. Remove the chiles from the pan and let them cool.

2. Place the onion and garlic cloves in the pan and toast until lightly charred, turning them occasionally. Remove them from the pan and let cool.

3. Peel the garlic cloves and mince them. Julienne the onion and place it and the garlic in a mixing bowl.

4. Remove all but one-quarter of the charred skin from the chiles. Remove the stems and seeds and finely chop the remaining flesh. Add it to the garlic mixture along with the remaining ingredients and stir until combined.

5. Let the mixture macerate for at least 30 minutes before serving.

INGREDIENTS:

8-10	SERRANO OR JALAPEÑO CHILE PEPPERS
1	SMALL WHITE ONION, QUARTERED
2-3	GARLIC CLOVES, UNPEELED
½	CUP SOY SAUCE
½	CUP FRESH LIME JUICE
2	TABLESPOONS MAGGI SEASONING SAUCE

MOLE VERDE

YIELD: 2 CUPS / **ACTIVE TIME:** 20 MINUTES / **TOTAL TIME:** 40 MINUTES

Blanching the kale and herbs allows the sauce to retain a vibrant green color, but this step can be omitted if the mole will be used to braise proteins or vegetables.

1. Preheat the oven to 325°F. Place the cloves, allspice, cumin, and coriander in a dry skillet and toast until fragrant, shaking the pan to keep them from burning. Use a mortar and pestle or a spice grinder to grind the mixture into a fine powder.

2. Place the sesame and pumpkin seeds on a parchment-lined baking sheet, place it in the oven, and toast until just golden brown, about 7 minutes. Remove from the oven and let the seeds cool.

3. Prepare an ice bath and bring generously salted water to a simmer in a large saucepan. Add the fresh herbs and the kale and cook for 30 to 45 seconds. Drain and shock them in the ice bath. Place the mixture in a linen towel and wring it to extract as much water as possible. Transfer the mixture to a blender.

4. Place the tomatillos, serrano peppers, garlic, and onion in a saucepan and cover by 1 inch with water. Season the water with salt and bring to a simmer. Cook until the vegetables are tender, about 15 minutes. Drain and add them to the blender.

5. Add the toasted seeds and the fine spice powder to the blender and puree until smooth. Season the mole with salt and gently warm it before serving.

INGREDIENTS:

¼	TEASPOON WHOLE CLOVES
¼	TEASPOON ALLSPICE BERRIES
¼	TEASPOON CUMIN SEEDS
½	TEASPOON CORIANDER SEEDS
⅓	CUP SESAME SEEDS
3	TABLESPOONS PUMPKIN SEEDS, TOASTED
	SALT, TO TASTE
1½	CUPS FRESH EPAZOTE LEAVES
½	CUP FRESH MINT LEAVES
½	CUP FRESH PARSLEY LEAVES
1	CUP FRESH HOJA SANTA LEAVES
2	CUPS FRESH CILANTRO LEAVES
2	OZ. KALE, STEMS AND RIBS REMOVED
½	LB. TOMATILLOS, HUSKED AND RINSED
3	SERRANO CHILE PEPPERS
10	GARLIC CLOVES
1	SMALL WHITE ONION, QUARTERED

RECADO ROJO

YIELD: 3 CUPS / **ACTIVE TIME:** 20 MINUTES / **TOTAL TIME:** 20 MINUTES

This paste of annatto, garlic, citrus, spices, and salt has become one of the signature flavors of both Yucatean and Oaxacan cuisines.

1. Place the achiote paste and juices in a bowl and let the mixture sit for 15 minutes.

2. Place the mixture and the remaining ingredients in a blender and puree until smooth.

3. Taste, adjust the seasoning as needed, and use as desired.

INGREDIENTS:

- 3½ OZ. YUCATECA ACHIOTE PASTE
- 14 TABLESPOONS FRESH LIME JUICE
- 14 TABLESPOONS ORANGE JUICE
- 7 TABLESPOONS GRAPEFRUIT JUICE
- 1 TEASPOON DRIED MEXICAN OREGANO
- 1 TEASPOON DRIED MARJORAM
- 1 HABANERO CHILE PEPPER, STEMMED AND SEEDED
- 5 GARLIC CLOVES
- 1 CINNAMON STICK, GRATED
- SALT, TO TASTE

SALSA DE ARBOL

YIELD: ½ CUP / **ACTIVE TIME:** 10 MINUTES / **TOTAL TIME:** 10 MINUTES

This salsa is ubiquitous in people's homes and at street food stalls in Mexico, as it pairs well with many dishes.

1. Place the lard in a cast-iron skillet and warm it over medium heat. Add the chiles and fry until fragrant and pliable. Place the chiles in a bowl of warm water and let them soak for 20 minutes.

2. Place the garlic cloves in the skillet and fry until fragrant, about 1 minute. Place them in a blender.

3. Drain the chiles and reserve the soaking liquid. Add the chiles to the blender and puree until the mixture is smooth, adding the reserved liquid as needed to get the desired texture.

4. Season the salsa with salt and use as desired.

INGREDIENTS:

¼   CUP LARD

3½   OZ. DRIED CHILES DE ARBOL, STEMMED AND SEEDED

1   OZ. GUAJILLO CHILE PEPPERS, STEMMED AND SEEDED

10   GARLIC CLOVES

     SALT, TO TASTE

SALSA DE AGUACATE

YIELD: 2 CUPS / ACTIVE TIME: 10 MINUTES / TOTAL TIME: 10 MINUTES

A bright green salsa that is a great option for topping vegetarian tacos.

1. Place the tomatillos, onion, garlic, and avocado in a blender and puree until smooth.

2. Add the cilantro and pulse until incorporate. Taste, season the salsa with lime juice and salt, and use as desired.

INGREDIENTS:

½ LB. TOMATILLOS, HUSKED AND RINSED

½ WHITE ONION

4 GARLIC CLOVES

⅔ CUP DICED AVOCADO

4 CUPS FRESH CILANTRO LEAVES

FRESH LIME JUICE, TO TASTE

SALT, TO TASTE

FERMENTED CHILE ADOBO

YIELD: 2 CUPS / **ACTIVE TIME:** 10 MINUTES / **TOTAL TIME:** 3 DAYS

A great pantry item because it's so versatile. It's useful as a quick fish or chicken marinade, but also very delicious on skirt steak.

1. Place the water and salt in a saucepan and bring it to a simmer, stirring to dissolve the salt. Turn off the heat and let the brine cool slightly.

2. Place the chiles, bay leaves, and garlic in a fermentation crock or large, food-grade storage container. Cover with the brine and place some plastic wrap on the surface. Let the mixture sit at room temperature for 3 to 5 days.

3. Place the cinnamon stick, cloves, and bay leaves in a dry skillet and toast until fragrant, shaking the pan to prevent them from burning. Use a mortar and pestle or a spice grinder to grind the mixture into a fine powder.

4. Strain the liquid from the fermented mixture and reserve it.

5. Place the chiles and garlic in a blender, add the toasted spices, vinegar, and oregano, and puree until the mixture is a smooth paste, adding the reserved liquid as needed to get the desired texture. Store in the refrigerator.

INGREDIENTS:

13¼   CUPS WATER

⅓   CUP KOSHER SALT

2¼   LBS. CHIPOTLE MORITA CHILE PEPPERS, STEMMED AND SEEDED

2   BAY LEAVES

10   GARLIC CLOVES, SMASHED

1   CINNAMON STICK

⅛   TEASPOON WHOLE CLOVES

½   CUP APPLE CIDER VINEGAR

1   TEASPOON DRIED MEXICAN OREGANO

MORITA SALSA

YIELD: 2 CUPS / **ACTIVE TIME:** 15 MINUTES / **TOTAL TIME:** 45 MINUTES

Chipotle morita chiles tend to be harder than many other chiles so it's important to hydrate them properly before using. They are also an excellent chile to ferment, so consider using them in the chile adobo recipe on the opposite page.

1. Place the chiles in a skillet and gently toast until fragrant and pliable. Place the chiles in a bowl of hot water and let them soak for 30 minutes.

2. Drain the chiles, place them in a blender, and add the tomatoes, onion, and garlic. Puree until smooth.

3. Season the salsa with salt and use as desired.

INGREDIENTS:

- 3½ OZ. CHIPOTLE MORITA CHILE PEPPERS, STEMMED AND SEEDED
- 5 ROMA TOMATOES, HALVED
- 1 SMALL WHITE ONION, QUARTERED
- 5 GARLIC CLOVES
- SALT, TO TASTE

SALSA BORRACHA

YIELD: 1½ CUPS / **ACTIVE TIME:** 20 MINUTES / **TOTAL TIME:** 30 MINUTES

The beer adds a very unique flavor that goes wonderfully with braised and smoked meats. Substituting half the amount of mezcal for the beer will also produce an amazing result.

1. Preheat a comal or cast-iron skillet over medium-high heat. Add the tomatillos, onion, and garlic and toast until charred all over, turning them as needed. Remove the vegetables from the pan and let them cool. When cool enough to handle, peel the garlic cloves and place the mixture in a blender.

2. Place half of the lard in the skillet and warm it over medium heat. Add the chiles and fry until fragrant and pliable. Place the chiles in the blender.

3. Add the beer, mezcal, and Maggi and puree until smooth.

4. Place the remaining lard in a saucepan and warm it over medium heat. Add the puree and fry it for 5 minutes. Season the salsa with salt and use as desired.

INGREDIENTS:

8	OZ. TOMATILLOS, HUSKED AND RINSED
¾	SMALL WHITE ONION
5	GARLIC CLOVES, UNPEELED
2	TABLESPOONS LARD
3	PASILLA CHILE PEPPERS, STEMMED AND SEEDED
2	CHIPOTLE MORITA CHILE PEPPERS, STEMMED AND SEEDED
3½	OZ. MEXICAN LAGER
1	TEASPOON MEZCAL OR TEQUILA
1	TEASPOON MAGGI SEASONING SAUCE
	SALT, TO TASTE

DZIKIL P'AAK

YIELD: 1½ CUPS / **ACTIVE TIME:** 30 MINUTES / **TOTAL TIME:** 30 MINUTES

Traditionally, dzikil p'aak is loose like a salsa; however, contemporary restaurants tend to prefer the hummus-like texture here. To achieve the traditional texture, add more tomatoes to the preparation, and remember to adjust the seasoning before serving.

1. Preheat a comal or cast-iron skillet over medium-high heat. Add the tomatoes, tomatillos, onion, garlic, and habanero and toast until charred all over, turning them as needed.

2. Remove the vegetables from the pan and let them cool. When cool enough to handle, peel the garlic cloves, remove the stems and seeds from the habaneros (it is strongly recommended that you wear gloves while handling the habaneros), and place the mixture in a food processor.

3. Place the pumpkin seeds in the food processor and pulse until the mixture is a thick paste. Add the juices, cilantro, and Maggi and pulse until the mixture is a hummus-like consistency.

4. Season with salt and use as desired.

INGREDIENTS:

3	ROMA TOMATOES
4	OZ. TOMATILLOS, HUSKED AND RINSED
¾	SMALL WHITE ONION
4	GARLIC CLOVES, UNPEELED
2	HABANERO CHILE PEPPERS
7	OZ. PUMPKIN SEEDS, HULLED AND ROASTED
7	TABLESPOONS FRESH LIME JUICE
7	TABLESPOONS ORANGE JUICE
1½	CUPS FRESH CILANTRO
1	TEASPOON MAGGI SEASONING SAUCE
	SALT, TO TASTE

CHILEATOLE VERDE

YIELD: 2 CUPS / **ACTIVE TIME:** 30 MINUTES / **TOTAL TIME:** 30 MINUTES

Chileatole verde has strong roots in Puebla, Mexico, but is found all over the country, particularly in Oaxaca, Veracruz, and Tlaxcala. If freshly ground nixtamal masa can be sourced, then the dish will be significantly more delicious than when it is made with masa harina.

1. Place 2 tablespoons of the lard in a large skillet and warm over medium heat. Add half of the corn, the onion, and the garlic and cook until the onion is translucent, about 3 minutes, stirring frequently. Remove the mixture from the pan, season it with salt, and let it cool.

2. Place half of the stock and the masa in a blender and puree until thoroughly combined. Place the masa mixture in a saucepan and warm over low heat.

3. Place the vegetable mixture in the blender, add the epazote, hoja santa, cilantro, serrano chiles, honey, and bay leaf, and puree until smooth.

4. Stir the puree into the simmering masa. Simmer until the chileatole is the consistency of a thick soup, adding the remaining stock as needed.

5. Place the remaining lard in a skillet and warm it over medium heat. Add the remaining corn and cook until just tender, about 4 minutes, stirring occasionally. Remove the pan from heat and divide the corn between the serving bowls.

6. Season the chileatole with salt. Ladle the chileatole over the corn. Garnish with additional epazote and serve with lime wedges and warm tortillas.

INGREDIENTS:

3	TABLESPOONS LARD
1	LB. FRESH CORN KERNELS
½	SMALL WHITE ONION, JULIENNED
3	GARLIC CLOVES, SLICED
	SALT, TO TASTE
4	CUPS CHICKEN STOCK (SEE PAGE 341)
4	OZ. FRESH MASA OR 2½ OZ. MASA HARINA
2-3	FRESH EPAZOTE LEAVES, PLUS MORE FOR GARNISH
1	FRESH HOJA SANTA LEAF (OPTIONAL)
1½	CUPS FRESH CILANTRO
3	SERRANO CHILE PEPPERS, STEMMED AND SEEDED
1	TABLESPOON HONEY
1	BAY LEAF
	LIME WEDGES, FOR SERVING
	CORN TORTILLAS (SEE PAGE 352), WARM, FOR SERVING

PICKLED RED ONION

YIELD: 2 CUPS / **ACTIVE TIME:** 10 MINUTES / **TOTAL TIME:** 2 HOURS

A great topping for tacos, and really almost any dish in this book. This pickling brine can be used with whatever vegetable you have on hand.

1. Place the vinegar, water, salt, and sugar in a saucepan and bring to a boil, stirring to dissolve the salt and sugar.

2. Place the onion in a bowl, pour the brine over it, and let cool completely.

3. Transfer the onion and brine to a sterilized mason jar and store in the refrigerator for up to 2 weeks.

INGREDIENTS:

½ CUP APPLE CIDER VINEGAR

½ CUP WATER

2 TABLESPOONS KOSHER SALT

2 TABLESPOONS SUGAR

1 RED ONION, SLICED THIN

ESCABECHE

YIELD: 4 CUPS / **ACTIVE TIME:** 10 MINUTES / **TOTAL TIME:** 2 HOURS

A great addition to tacos or tostadas, and equally valuable as a side dish or snack.

1. Place the jalapeños, carrot, onion, garlic, and cauliflower in a bowl and toss to combine.

2. Place the marjoram, oregano, bay leaf, salt, and sugar in a bowl and stir to combine.

3. Place the spice mixture in a small saucepan along with the vinegar. Bring the mixture to a boil.

4. Pour the hot brine over the vegetables and let cool completely.

5. Transfer the vegetables and brine to a sterilized mason jar and store it in the refrigerator for up to 1 month.

INGREDIENTS:

3   JALAPEÑO CHILE PEPPERS, STEMMED, SEEDED, AND SLICED

1   CARROT, PEELED AND SLICED

½   WHITE ONION, SLICED THIN

2   GARLIC CLOVES

    FLORETS FROM ½ HEAD OF CAULIFLOWER

1   TEASPOON DRIED MARJORAM

1   TEASPOON DRIED MEXICAN OREGANO

1   BAY LEAF

2   TABLESPOONS KOSHER SALT

½   TEASPOON SUGAR

1½   CUPS WHITE VINEGAR

SALSA MACHA

A versatile and delicious base that can be altered to incorporate various chiles and made with or without nuts.

1. Place the sesame seeds in a large skillet and toast over low heat until browned, shaking the pan as needed to keep them from burning. Remove from the pan and place them in a mortar.

2. Place the lard in the large skillet and warm over medium heat. Add the almonds and fry until golden brown, shaking the pan to prevent them from burning. Remove the almonds and place them in the mortar.

3. Reduce the heat to low, add the chiles, and fry them until fragrant and lightly toasted, turning them as needed to keep them from burning. Transfer them to the mortar.

4. Add the garlic, vinegar, and sugar to the mortar and use a pestle to work the mixture until it is a slightly chunky paste. Use immediately or store in the refrigerator, where it will keep for up to 2 weeks.

INGREDIENTS:

1	OZ. WHITE SESAME SEEDS
¼	CUP LARD
¼	CUP UNSALTED ALMONDS
10	DRIED CHILES DE ARBOL, STEMMED AND SEEDED
1	ANCHO CHILE PEPPER, STEMMED AND SEEDED
2	GARLIC CLOVES, SLICED THIN
2	TABLESPOONS WHITE VINEGAR
1	TEASPOON SUGAR

QUESO FRESCO

YIELD: 3 CUPS / **ACTIVE TIME:** 30 MINUTES / **TOTAL TIME:** 24 HOURS

A key to tempering the heat of the chiles that so often appear in Mexican dishes, queso fresco is similar to a farmer's cheese, and adds a refreshing element whenever it appears.

1. Place the milk and salt in a medium saucepan and bring to a gentle simmer over medium-low heat.

2. When the mixture reaches 180°F, remove the pan from heat, add the vinegar, and gently stir the mixture with a wooden spoon. You should see small curds begin to form. Cover the pot and let it rest for 45 minutes.

3. Strain the curds into a chinois lined with cheesecloth. Let the curds release all of their liquid, using a small plate to weight down the curds.

4. Form the cheesecloth containing the curds into a bundle and let the cheese cool overnight.

5. The cheese will be ready to crumble, shred, or break into chunks once fully cooled. Store in the refrigerator for up to 1 week.

INGREDIENTS:

8   CUPS WHOLE MILK

2   TABLESPOONS KOSHER SALT

1⅓ CUPS WHITE VINEGAR

SALSA CRUDA VERDE

YIELD: 2 CUPS / **ACTIVE TIME:** 5 MINUTES / **TOTAL TIME:** 15 MINUTES

A bright and flavorful sauce that can feature more or less chiles depending on what accent needs to be provided in a particular preparation.

1. Place the tomatillos, serrano peppers, and garlic in a blender and puree until combined but still chunky, about 1 minute.

2. Add the avocado and pulse until incorporated.

3. Season the salsa with salt and use as desired.

INGREDIENTS:

4 TOMATILLOS, HUSKED AND RINSED, AND QUARTERED

5 SERRANO CHILE PEPPERS, STEMMED AND SEEDED

1 GARLIC CLOVE

FLESH OF ½ AVOCADO

SALT, TO TASTE

BAY LEAF OIL

YIELD: ½ CUP / **ACTIVE TIME:** 20 MINUTES / **TOTAL TIME:** 24 HOURS

Don't hesitate to make other herb-infused oils in this manner. Cilantro is an especially good option.

1. Place the bay leaves and olive oil in a blender and puree until smooth, about 5 minutes.

2. Strain the oil into a bowl through a coffee filter and season it with salt.

3. Prepare an ice bath and place the bowl containing the oil in it. Transfer to the refrigerator and let it sit overnight.

4. Pour the mixture through a cheesecloth-lined sieve and let it sit until the oil is free of any debris. Use immediately or store in the refrigerator, where it will keep for up to 2 weeks.

INGREDIENTS:

1   OZ. BAY LEAVES

10   TABLESPOONS EXTRA-VIRGIN OLIVE OIL

      SALT, TO TASTE

PICKLED MANZANO PEPPER

YIELD: 2 CUPS / **ACTIVE TIME:** 5 MINUTES / **TOTAL TIME:** 2 HOURS

You can substitute these pickled peppers in any recipe that calls for pickled onion.

1. Place the manzano peppers in a small mixing bowl.

2. Place the remaining ingredients in a small saucepan and bring to a boil, stirring to dissolve the sugar.

3. Pour the brine over the peppers and let them cool completely.

4. Place the peppers and brine in a sterilized mason jar and store in the refrigerator for up to 1 week.

INGREDIENTS:

4 WHOLE MANZANO CHILE PEPPERS, STEMMED, SEEDED, AND SLICED THIN

¼ CUP APPLE CIDER VINEGAR

¼ CUP WATER

1 TABLESPOON SUGAR

1 TABLESPOON KOSHER SALT

ARROZ A LA MEXICANA

YIELD: 4 SERVINGS / **ACTIVE TIME**: 5 MINUTES / **TOTAL TIME**: 35 MINUTES

A quick and easy dish that always seems to pop up when one's in need of something comforting.

1. Preheat the oven to 375°F. Place the rice in a sieve or colander and run it under cold water until the water runs clear. Drain the rice well and set it aside.

2. Place the olive oil in a Dutch oven and warm it over medium heat. Add the onion, garlic, and carrot and cook until the onion is translucent, about 3 minutes, stirring frequently.

3. Add the rice and cook for 2 minutes, stirring continuously so that it gets covered by the oil.

4. Add the tomato puree and cook for 1 minute. Add the stock, bring the mixture to a boil, and add the bay leaf.

5. Reduce the heat and add the peas (if desired). Cover the pot and place it in the oven. Bake for 20 minutes.

6. Remove the rice from the oven and let it rest for 10 minutes.

7. Uncover the pot. The bay leaf should be on top of the rice. Remove the bay leaf and discard it. Fluff the rice with a fork and serve.

INGREDIENTS:

8	OZ. LONG-GRAIN RICE
1	ONION, FINELY DICED
1	GARLIC CLOVE
1	CARROT, PEELED AND FINELY DICED
½	CUP TOMATO PUREE OR TOMATO PASTE
2¼	CUPS CHICKEN STOCK (SEE PAGE 341) OR WATER
1	BAY LEAF
1	CUP PEAS (OPTIONAL)
1	TABLESPOON EXTRA-VIRGIN OLIVE OIL
	SALT, TO TASTE

HABANERO HONEY

YIELD: 1 CUP / **ACTIVE TIME:** 10 MINUTES / **TOTAL TIME:** 2 HOURS

The touch of heat amidst all that sweet is a surprise that goes down well every time. This is good with just about anything, whether it be over fish tacos or in your morning coffee.

1. Place the chili peppers and honey in a saucepan and bring to a very gentle simmer over medium-low heat. Reduce heat to lowest possible setting and cook for 1 hour.

2. Remove the saucepan from heat and let the mixture infuse for another hour.

3. Remove the peppers. Transfer the honey to a container, cover, and store in the refrigerator.

INGREDIENTS:

4   HABANERO CHILE PEPPERS, PIERCED

1   CUP HONEY

CHULIBU'UL

YIELD: 4 SERVINGS / **ACTIVE TIME:** 20 MINUTES / **TOTAL TIME:** 30 MINUTES

This is something of a Mexican succotash, with the black-eyed peas standing in for the lima beans. It's a wonderful side with spicy and smoky dishes, and also works well as a filling for a few of the preparations in the Masa chapter.

1. Place the lard in a large skillet and warm it over medium-high heat. Add the corn and cook until it begins to brown, 3 to 5 minutes, stirring occasionally.

2. Add the bell pepper and onion and cook until they begin to soften, 3 to 5 minutes, again stirring occasionally.

3. Add the tomatoes and cook until they collapse, about 7 minutes.

4. Stir in the black-eyed peas, oregano, salt, savory, and black pepper, cook until warmed through, and enjoy.

INGREDIENTS:

2   TABLESPOONS LARD

3   CUPS CORN KERNELS

1   GREEN BELL PEPPER, STEMMED, SEEDED, AND FINELY DICED

1   SMALL WHITE ONION, FINELY DICED

2   TOMATOES, CHOPPED

1   (14 OZ.) CAN OF BLACK-EYED PEAS, DRAINED AND RINSED

2   TEASPOONS DRIED MEXICAN OREGANO

1   TEASPOON KOSHER SALT

½   TEASPOON DRIED SAVORY

¼   TEASPOON BLACK PEPPER

DESSERTS

*I*n Mexican cuisine, sweets take a back seat to the other preparations. There are plenty of delicious options though, and innovative chefs are exploring the space more and more every day, finding new and illuminating uses for Mexico's beloved flavors. Some of these experiments, such as using a sweet mole as the base for brownies (see page 623), incorporating horchata's uniquely luscious spice in an ice cream (see page 542), and turning the crunch of a concha into a strawberry shortcake and bread pudding (see page 606 and 555).

It's not all innovation, however. Bulletproof recipes for the classics that have slowly but surely conquered the globe, like the churro and Mexican wedding cookies (see page 581 and 619), can also be found within.

HORCHATA ICE CREAM

YIELD: 2 QUARTS / **ACTIVE TIME:** 45 MINUTES / **TOTAL TIME:** 5 HOURS

Y ou could just make this ice cream with prepared horchata, eggs, vanilla, salt, and sugar, but it is nowhere near as luscious as the cream turned out in this preparation.

1. Prepare an ice bath. Place the rice, cinnamon, cream, and milk in a medium saucepan and bring it to a simmer.

2. Place the yolks and sugar in the work bowl of a stand mixer and whip until the mixture is pale and thick.

3. Add the milk mixture a little bit at a time, whisking constantly. When all of them milk mixture has been incorporated, return the tempered mixture back to the pan and cook over low heat until the mixture is thick enough to coat the back of a wooden spoon.

4. Remove the pan from heat, stir in the vanilla and salt, and strain the mixture into a bowl, pressing down on the solids to extract as much liquid them as possible.

5. Place the bowl in the ice bath until the custard is cool.

6. Churn the custard in an ice cream maker until it reaches the desired consistency. Transfer to an airtight container and freeze for 4 hours before topping with the Blue Corn Crunchies and enjoying.

INGREDIENTS:

4	CUPS COOKED WHITE RICE
1	TABLESPOON CINNAMON
4	CUPS HEAVY CREAM
6	CUPS MILK
1½	CUPS EGG YOLKS
2	CUPS SUGAR
2	TEASPOONS MEXICAN VANILLA EXTRACT
⅛	TEASPOON FINE SEA SALT
	BLUE CORN CRUNCHIES (SEE PAGE 607)

LECHE QUEMADA

YIELD: 36 SERVINGS / **ACTIVE TIME:** 40 MINUTES / **TOTAL TIME:** 1 HOUR AND 30 MINUTES

This recipe is based on an iteration from Monterrey in Central Mexico. It can be a tricky preparation, but wow is it worth it.

1. Grease a loaf pan with nonstick cooking spray. Place the sugar, evaporated milk, butter, salt, and vanilla in a large saucepan and bring to a boil. Add the brown sugar and stir until dissolved.

2. Cook over medium heat until the mixture comes together as a soft ball, stirring constantly.

3. Remove the pan from heat and stir vigorously until the mixture thickens.

4. Pour the mixture in the loaf pan and let it cool completely. Cut into squares and enjoy.

INGREDIENTS:

5½	CUPS SUGAR
2	(12 OZ.) CANS OF EVAPORATED MILK
5½	TABLESPOONS UNSALTED BUTTER
1	TEASPOON KOSHER SALT
1	TEASPOON MEXICAN VANILLA EXTRACT
½	CUP BROWN SUGAR

SWEET EMPANADAS

YIELD: 12 EMPANADAS / **ACTIVE TIME:** 30 MINUTES / **TOTAL TIME:** 2 HOURS

Sweet empanadas are found in panaderias all over Mexico, but the most commonly found flavor is pumpkin. That's the preparation here, but feel free to fill them with dulce de leche, Cajeta (see page 639), apple pie filling, pineapple, or any of your favorite flavors.

1. To begin preparations for the dough, place the flour in a large mixing bowl, add the sugar, salt, shortening, and butter. Work the mixture with a pastry blender until it resembles coarse bread crumbs.

2. Combine the egg yolks and water in a separate mixing bowl and add to the flour mixture a little at a time until it comes together as a dough, whisking to incorporate. Knead the dough until it is smooth but slightly shaggy, adding more water or flour as needed. Cover the dough in plastic wrap and chill in the refrigerator for about 1 hour.

3. Preheat the oven to 350°F and line a baking sheet with parchment paper. Roll out the dough on a floured surface to about ¼ inch thick. Cut it into 5-inch circles.

4. To prepare the filling, place the pumpkin, sugar, and cinnamon in a mixing bowl and stir until combined.

5. Place about 2 tablespoons of the filling in the bottom-middle half of each circle, fold into a half-moon, and crimp the edges to seal.

6. Place the empanadas on the baking sheet, brush the tops with the egg white, and place in the oven. Bake until golden brown, 20 to 25 minutes. Remove from the oven and briefly cool on wire racks before serving.

INGREDIENTS:

FOR THE DOUGH

4	CUPS SIFTED ALL-PURPOSE FLOUR, PLUS MORE AS NEEDED
3	TABLESPOONS SUGAR, PLUS 1 TEASPOON
1	TEASPOON KOSHER SALT
¾	CUP SHORTENING
2	TABLESPOONS UNSALTED BUTTER, CHILLED
2	EGG YOLKS
1	CUP COLD WATER, PLUS MORE AS NEEDED

FOR THE FILLING

1	(14 OZ.) CAN OF PUMPKIN PUREE
½	CUP SUGAR
1	TEASPOON CINNAMON
1	EGG WHITE, BEATEN

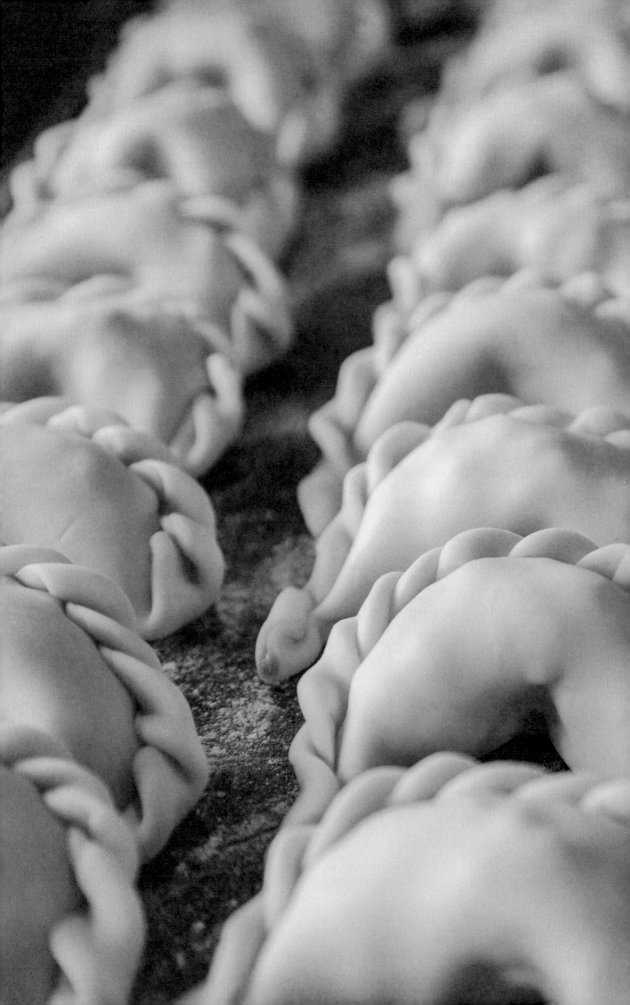

OREJAS

YIELD: 12 OREJAS / **ACTIVE TIME:** 15 MINUTES / **TOTAL TIME:** 1 HOUR

These crispy, sugary pastries treats are known worldwide by many different names. Orejas, which means "ears," is the Mexican version.

1. Preheat the oven to 425°F and line a baking sheet with parchment paper. Brush the puff pastry with some of the egg white.

2. Combine the cinnamon and sugar in a bowl and then sprinkle the mixture all over the puff pastry. Fold the short edges of the pastry inward until they meet in the middle. Brush lightly with the egg white and fold in half again until sealed together. Chill in the refrigerator for 15 to 20 minutes.

3. Cut the pastry into ½-inch-thick slices. Place the slices on the baking sheet, cut side up so you can see the folds.

4. Place in the oven and bake until golden brown, 8 to 12 minutes. Remove from oven and let cool on wire racks before enjoying.

INGREDIENTS:

- 1 SHEET OF FROZEN PUFF PASTRY, THAWED
- 1 EGG WHITE, BEATEN
- 1 TEASPOON CINNAMON
- ½ CUP SUGAR

ABUELITA'S CHOCOLATE POTS DE CRÈME

YIELD: 8 SERVINGS / **ACTIVE TIME:** 30 MINUTES / **TOTAL TIME:** 1 HOUR AND 30 MINUTES

This take on hot chocolate allows it a place at the dinner table year-round.

1. Preheat the oven to 325°F. Place the heavy cream and half & half in a medium saucepan and bring to a simmer over medium heat.

2. Remove the pan from heat, add the chocolate, and whisk until smooth.

3. Place the egg yolks, sugar, vanilla, and salt in a heatproof mixing bowl and slowly stream in the cream mixture, whisking continually to incorporate.

4. Strain the mixture through a fine sieve and then pour it into eight ramekins.

5. Place the ramekins in a large baking pan and fill the baking pan with water until it reaches halfway up the ramekins.

6. Place in the oven and bake until set, about 40 minutes. Remove from the oven and let cool before topping with whipped cream and enjoying.

INGREDIENTS:

6   CUPS HEAVY CREAM

1½   CUPS HALF & HALF

1   LB. ABUELITA CHOCOLATE, CHOPPED

18   EGG YOLKS

1   CUP SUGAR

1   TEASPOON PURE VANILLA EXTRACT

   PINCH OF KOSHER SALT

   WHIPPED CREAM, FOR SERVING

ARROZ CON LECHE

YIELD: 12 SERVINGS / **ACTIVE TIME:** 1 HOUR / **TOTAL TIME:** 1 HOUR AND 30 MINUTES

Arroz con leche, "rice with milk", is a sweet, slow-cooked rice pudding with cinnamon that is typical of Mexico. This dish was introduced to Mexico by the Spanish and is believed to have Moorish roots.

1. Prepare an ice bath. To prepare the base, combine the milk and vanilla bean in a saucepan and bring to a boil. Add the rice and cook over low heat, stirring frequently until the mixture has the consistency of creamy oatmeal. Transfer to a mixing bowl and set it in the ice bath to cool.

2. To begin preparations for the pastry cream, place the milk, half of the sugar, and the vanilla in a saucepan and warm over medium-low heat until the mixture starts to steam, stirring to dissolve the sugar.

3. Place the remaining sugar, cornstarch, and egg yolks in a mixing bowl and whip until the mixture is pale and fluffy. Incorporate the warm milk mixture a little bit at a time, whisking continually.

4. Add the tempered egg yolks to the saucepan and cook over medium-low heat until the mixture has thickened and is just about to come to a simmer.

5. Place the butter in the work bowl of a stand mixer fitted with the paddle attachment. Strain the warm mixture into the work bowl and beat until it has cooled. Transfer the pastry cream into a container and place plastic wrap directly on the surface to prevent a skin from forming. Chill in the refrigerator.

6. To prepare the meringue, place the powdered egg whites, water, and sugar in the work bowl of a stand mixer fitted with the whisk attachment. Whip until the mixture is voluminous and can hold stiff peaks. Chill the mixture in the refrigerator.

7. Combine the base and the pastry cream in a bowl. Add the meringue and fold to incorporate. Scoop into bowls, drizzle a little syrup over each portion, and sprinkle cinnamon on top.

INGREDIENTS:

FOR THE BASE

7	CUPS MILK
	SEEDS AND POD OF 1 VANILLA BEAN
4	CUPS COOKED RICE

FOR THE PASTRY CREAM

8	CUPS MILK
1	LB. SUGAR
2½	TEASPOONS PURE VANILLA EXTRACT
5½	OZ. CORNSTARCH
1½	CUPS EGG YOLKS
¼	CUP UNSALTED BUTTER

FOR THE MERINGUE

6.6	OZ. POWDERED EGG WHITES
3.3	OZ. WATER
1	TABLESPOON SUGAR

FOR TOPPING

	PILONCILLO SYRUP (SEE PAGE 557)
	CINNAMON, TO TASTE

CONCHA BREAD PUDDING

YIELD: 12 SERVINGS / *ACTIVE TIME:* 15 MINUTES / *TOTAL TIME:* 1 HOUR

When you're stuck with too many conchas, this crazy delicious bread pudding is a wonderful solution.

1. Preheat the oven to 325°F. Line an 18 x 13–inch baking sheet with parchment paper and coat with nonstick cooking spray.

2. Place all of the ingredients, except for the Conchas, in a large bowl and whisk until combined.

3. Add the Conchas, gently toss, and push them down so they are covered in the custard. Let the mixture sit for 15 minutes, tossing and pressing down on the bread a few times.

4. Spread the bread pudding in an even layer in the pan.

5. Place in the oven and bake until puffed up, golden brown, and bubbling along edges, about 30 minutes, making sure to rotate the pan halfway through. Remove from the oven and let cool slightly before enjoying.

INGREDIENTS:

4   EGGS

4   EGG YOLKS

4   CUPS HALF & HALF

¼   CUP SUGAR

1   TABLESPOON PURE VANILLA EXTRACT

½   TEASPOON FINE SEA SALT

2   LBS. STALE CONCHAS (SEE PAGES 602–603), CHOPPED

PILONCILLO SYRUP

YIELD: 3 CUPS / **ACTIVE TIME:** 10 MINUTES / **TOTAL TIME:** 1 HOUR

An unprocessed sugar with a rich flavor that rivals molasses, piloncillo is a natural to be reduced into a decadent syrup that should be used liberally in everything from desserts to cocktails.

1. Place all of the ingredients in a saucepan and bring to a boil, stirring to dissolve the piloncillo and sugar.

2. Remove the pan from heat and let it cool completely. Strain before using or storing.

INGREDIENTS:

8   OZ. PILONCILLO

2   CUPS WATER

2   TABLESPOONS ANCHO
     CHILE POWDER

½   CUP SUGAR

     SEEDS FROM ¼ VANILLA
     BEAN

MEXICAN VANILLA

Vanilla is typically categorized according to where the orchid that produces the bean is grown. Mexican vanilla adds a bit of nutmeg-y spice to vanilla's famously sweet and creamy quality, which makes it a wonderful addition to cinnamon- and nutmeg-heavy desserts, and it can also be used to dress up a piquant sauce.

BONBONAISE

YIELD: 30 TO 40 MARSHMALLOWS / **ACTIVE TIME:** 45 MINUTES / **TOTAL TIME:** 9 HOURS

Feel free to add any extract or compound to these marshmallows. Strawberry and vanilla are the most common offerings in Mexico.

1. Coat an 18 x 13–inch baking sheet with nonstick cooking spray, dust it with confectioners' sugar, and knock out any excess.

2. In the work bowl of a stand mixer fitted with the whisk attachment, add ½ cup of the cold water and sprinkle the gelatin over it.

3. Place the remaining water, the sugar, corn syrup, and salt in a saucepan and cook over medium heat until it is 240°F, 12 to 15 minutes.

4. Pour the hot syrup into the mixing bowl and whip on high until the bowl is just warm to the touch.

5. Stir in the vanilla and spread the mixture in the pan, working quickly. Dust the mixture generously with confectioners' sugar.

6. Let the mixture sit at room temperature, uncovered, for at least 8 hours, and up to 24.

7. Cut into the desired shapes. Place the coconut in a shallow bowl and toss the bonbonaise in the coconut until coated.

INGREDIENTS:

	CONFECTIONERS' SUGAR, AS NEEDED
1	CUP COLD WATER
3	TABLESPOONS GELATIN
1¼	CUPS SUGAR
1¼	CUPS CORN SYRUP
¼	TEASPOON FINE SEA SALT
2	TEASPOONS MEXICAN VANILLA EXTRACT
1	CUP SHREDDED COCONUT

COFFEE FLAN WITH BUÑUELOS

YIELD: 12 SERVINGS / **ACTIVE TIME:** 45 MINUTES / **TOTAL TIME:** 4 HOURS

F lan and buñuelos are extremely popular Mexican desserts, so combining them is sure to satisfy.

1. Preheat the oven to 350°F. Place the sugar and water in a saucepan and warm over medium heat until the mixture is caramelized. Do not stir the mixture, but gently swirl the pan once or twice. Pour the caramel into a square, 9-inch cake pan and let it cool.

2. In the work bowl of a stand mixer fitted with the paddle attachment, beat the cream cheese until light and fluffy. Incorporate the eggs one at a time, scraping down the work bowl as needed. Add the condensed milk and beat until incorporated.

3. Add the evaporated milk, vanilla, espresso, and salt and beat until the mixture is well combined. Strain through a chinois to remove excess liquid.

4. Pour the strained mixture evenly over the caramel. Cover the pan with aluminum foil and place it in a roasting pan. Fill the roasting pan with water until it comes halfway up the side of the cake pan.

5. Place the cake in the oven and bake until set, about 45 minutes. Remove from the oven and let cool.

6. Chill the flan in the refrigerator for 2 hours. Unmold, cut into 12 pieces, and place them on a plate. Drizzle some caramel over the flan and top each portion with a buñuelo.

INGREDIENTS:

1	CUP SUGAR
½	CUP WATER
12	OZ. CREAM CHEESE, SOFTENED
6	EGGS
1	(14 OZ.) CAN OF SWEETENED CONDENSED MILK
1	(12 OZ.) CAN OF EVAPORATED MILK
¼	TEASPOON PURE VANILLA EXTRACT
1	TABLESPOON FINELY GROUND ESPRESSO
¼	TEASPOON KOSHER SALT
	PERFECT CARAMEL (SEE PAGE 601), FOR SERVING
	BUÑUELOS (SEE PAGE 598), FOR SERVING

CHOCOFLAN

YIELD: 8 SERVINGS / **ACTIVE TIME**: 1 HOUR / **TOTAL TIME**: 3 HOURS

This dessert is fun to make, eat, and share as it combines two popular favorites, flan and chocolate cake. This uses a very basic caramel, but you can always use Cajeta (see page 639) or the Perfect Caramel (see page 601) if you'd rather.

1. To begin preparations for the caramel, place the sugar in a small saucepan and warm over medium heat, stirring constantly.

2. When all of the sugar has melted and turned amber, remove the pan from heat and pour into a greased Bundt pan, making sure the entire bottom of the pan is covered. Let cool for 10 minutes.

3. To prepare the flan, place all of the ingredients in a blender and puree until smooth. Set the mixture aside.

4. To begin preparations for the cake, preheat the oven to 350°F. In the work bowl of a stand mixer fitted with the paddle attachment, combine the butter and brown sugar and cream on medium speed until light and fluffy, about 5 minutes. Add the egg and vanilla and beat until incorporated.

5. Sift the flour, cocoa powder, baking soda, and baking powder together in a separate mixing bowl.

6. Place the instant coffee in a small bowl and add some of the milk. Heat the mixture in the microwave for a few seconds, until the instant coffee has dissolved. Stir the remaining milk into the coffee milk.

7. Alternating between the flour mixture and the milk mixture, add each one to the work bowl in three increments and beat until both mixtures have been incorporated and the overall mixture is a smooth batter.

8. Pour the batter into the Bundt pan, on top of the hardened caramel. Smooth the surface and gently tap the pan on the counter a couple of times to remove any air bubbles and ensure the top is level.

9. Slowly pour the flan over the back of the spoon so that it sits on top of the cake batter in an even layer.

10. Place the Bundt pan in a roasting pan. Pour hot water into the roasting pan until it goes at least 2 inches up the side of the Bundt pan. Place in the oven and bake until set, about 1 hour.

11. Remove from the oven and let the flan cool for at least 1 hour before turning out onto a serving dish.

INGREDIENTS:

FOR THE CARAMEL

1½	CUPS SUGAR

FOR THE FLAN

4	EGGS
1	(14 OZ.) CAN OF SWEETENED CONDENSED MILK
2½	CUPS EVAPORATED MILK
	PINCH OF KOSHER SALT
1	TEASPOON MEXICAN VANILLA EXTRACT

FOR THE CAKE

5.3	OZ. UNSALTED BUTTER
6.7	OZ. BROWN SUGAR
1	EGG
1	TABLESPOON MEXICAN VANILLA EXTRACT
7	OZ. ALL-PURPOSE FLOUR
1	OZ. COCOA POWDER
1	TEASPOON BAKING SODA
1	TEASPOON BAKING POWDER
¼	CUP INSTANT COFFEE
1	CUP MILK

CHOCOLATE-COVERED CHICHARRON

YIELD: 12 SERVINGS / **ACTIVE TIME:** 20 MINUTES / **TOTAL TIME:** 45 MINUTES

The rich, savory, and crunchy chicharron cries out for something sweet. Chocolate answers the call, and lifts the humble ingredient to startling heights.

1. Fill a small saucepan halfway with water and bring it to a simmer. Place the chocolate in a heatproof bowl, place it over the simmering water, and stir until is melted and smooth. Remove the bowl from heat and let it cool to 90°F.

2. Dip each chicharron into the melted chocolate to cover as much of it as desired.

3. Place on a parchment-lined baking sheet and let the chocolate set for 10 to 20 minutes before enjoying.

INGREDIENTS:

2 CUPS CHOPPED DARK CHOCOLATE, PLUS MORE FOR SERVING

½ (7 OZ.) BAG OF CHICHARRON

CHOCOLATE MOLE PROFITEROLES

YIELD: 50 PROFITEROLES / **ACTIVE TIME:** 20 MINUTES / **TOTAL TIME:** 1 HOUR

This is a dish that could be served family style, or a couple to a plate. If you have extra pastries, just freeze and thaw for 15 minutes before serving.

1. Preheat the oven to 375°F and line two baking sheets with parchment paper. Place the water, butter, salt, and sugar in a saucepan and bring it to a boil.

2. Add the flour and cook, stirring constantly, until the mixture pulls away from the side of the pan.

3. Place the mixture in the work bowl of a stand mixer fitted with the paddle attachment and beat until the dough is almost cool. Incorporate the eggs one at a time, scraping down the work bowl as needed.

4. Place the dough in a piping bag fitted with a round tip and pipe mounds of dough onto the baking sheets, making sure to leave enough space between them.

5. Place in the oven and bake until set and golden brown, 8 to 12 minutes. Remove from the oven and let the profiteroles cool completely.

6. Cut the profiteroles in half and fill each one with a scoop of ice cream. Drizzle the Chocolate Mole over the top and enjoy.

INGREDIENTS:

2 CUPS WATER

8 OZ. UNSALTED BUTTER

PINCH OF FINE SEA SALT

PINCH OF SUGAR

11 OZ. ALL-PURPOSE FLOUR

8 EGGS

CHOCOLATE ICE CREAM (SEE PAGE 572)

CHOCOLATE MOLE (SEE PAGE 575)

CHOCOLATE ICE CREAM

YIELD: 4 QUARTS / **ACTIVE TIME:** 30 MINUTES / **TOTAL TIME:** 8 HOURS

Whaṭ may well be the best delivery system for the miraculous and beloved flavor of chocolate.

1. Place the cocoa powder and 4 cups of the cream in a medium saucepan and warm over medium heat, whisking until the mixture is smooth and free of lumps.

2. Stir in the sugar, 4 cups of the half & half, and the remaining cream. Cook, stirring continually, until all of the sugar has dissolved.

3. Place the remaining half & half and the egg yolks in a deep hotel pan and stir to combine. Set the hotel pan in an ice bath.

4. Strain the hot cream mixture into the hotel pan and stir until the mixture is thoroughly combined. Place the hotel pan in the refrigerator and chill for 3 hours.

5. Place the chilled custard in an ice cream maker and churn until the desired consistency has been achieved. Transfer the ice cream to an airtight container and freeze for 4 hours before serving.

INGREDIENTS:

2½ CUPS COCOA POWDER

5 CUPS HEAVY CREAM

2½ LBS. SUGAR

15 CUPS HALF & HALF

40 EGG YOLKS

CHOCOLATE MOLE

YIELD: 8 CUPS / **ACTIVE TIME:** 30 MINUTES / **TOTAL TIME:** 1 HOUR

Here, the techniques that provide Mexico's moles their world-renowned flavors are used to transform what would otherwise be a ho-hum chocolate sauce.

1. Prepare an ice bath. Place the water, butter, and sugars in a large saucepan and bring to a boil.

2. Add the cream, salt, and cocoa powder and whisk until the mixture is smooth.

3. Strain the mixture into a heatproof bowl. Add the remaining ingredients and stir until thoroughly incorporated. Place the bowl in an ice bath and stir until completely cool. Puree and strain before enjoying.

INGREDIENTS:

6	CUPS WATER
1	LB. UNSALTED BUTTER
1½	LBS. SUGAR
1⅔	LBS. BROWN SUGAR
66⅓	OZ. HEAVY CREAM
½	TEASPOON FINE SEA SALT
2.2	LBS. COCOA POWDER
1	CUP SESAME SEEDS, TOASTED
¼	CUP PEANUT BUTTER
1	TABLESPOON MEXICAN VANILLA EXTRACT
2	TEASPOONS CAYENNE PEPPER
1	TEASPOON CINNAMON
1	TEASPOON ORANGE ZEST

CHOCOLATE TAMARIND TRUFFLES

YIELD: 40 TRUFFLES / **ACTIVE TIME:** 40 MINUTES / **TOTAL TIME:** 2 HOURS

Super delicious little bits of heaven with tangy tamarind. If you want these to be extra tangy, try doubling the amount.

1. Fill a small saucepan halfway with water and bring it to a simmer.

2. Place the cream, chocolates, and tamarind in a heatproof mixing bowl and place it over the simmering water. Stir until the mixture is smooth.

3. Remove from heat, stir in the vanilla, and strain the mixture into a hotel pan. Place in the refrigerator and let it cool completely.

4. Scoop the desired size for your truffles onto parchment-lined baking sheets. Return to the refrigerator and chill for 10 to 15 minutes.

5. Roll the scoops into balls using your hands. Place them back on the baking sheets and chill in the refrigerator.

6. Fill a small saucepan halfway with water and bring it to a simmer. Place additional chocolate in a heatproof bowl, place it over the simmering water, and stir until melted and smooth. Let cool for 5 minutes.

7. Dip the balls into the melted chocolate twice, so that they are completely coated. Place them back on the baking sheets and chill in the refrigerator until set.

8. When set, roll the truffles in cocoa powder until completely covered and enjoy.

INGREDIENTS:

2 CUPS HEAVY CREAM

1 LB. DARK CHOCOLATE, CHOPPED, PLUS MORE AS NEEDED

3 OZ. MILK CHOCOLATE, CHOPPED

5 OZ. TAMARIND PASTE

¼ CUP MEXICAN VANILLA EXTRACT

COCOA POWDER, FOR DUSTING

SPICY CHOCOLATE TRUFFLES

YIELD: 40 TRUFFLES / **ACTIVE TIME:** 40 MINUTES / **TOTAL TIME:** 1 HOUR AND 30 MINUTES

The addition of guajillo chiles to this truffle base really brings out their fruity, green tea–like flavor. You can also substitute ancho chiles here—the flavor will be darker and earthier.

1. Fill a small saucepan halfway with water and bring it to a simmer.

2. Place the cream, chocolates, and chiles in a heatproof mixing bowl and place it over the simmering water. Stir until the mixture is smooth.

3. Remove the pan from heat, stir in the vanilla, and strain the mixture into a hotel pan. Place in the refrigerator and let it cool completely.

4. Scoop the desired size for your truffles onto parchment-lined baking sheets. Return to the refrigerator and chill for 10 to 15 minutes.

5. Roll the scoops into balls using your hands. Place them back on the baking sheets and chill in the refrigerator.

6. Fill a small saucepan halfway with water and bring it to a simmer. Place additional chocolate in a heatproof bowl, place it over the simmering water, and stir until melted and smooth. Let the chocolate cool for 5 minutes.

7. Dip the balls into the melted chocolate twice, so that they are completely coated. Place them back on the baking sheets and chill in the refrigerator until set.

8. When set, roll the truffles in the cocoa powder until completely covered and enjoy.

INGREDIENTS:

2	CUPS HEAVY CREAM
1	LB. DARK CHOCOLATE, CHOPPED, PLUS MORE AS NEEDED
3	OZ. MILK CHOCOLATE, CHOPPED
5	OZ. GUAJILLO CHILE PEPPERS, STEMMED, SEEDED, AND GROUND
½	CUP MEXICAN VANILLA EXTRACT
¼	CUP COCOA POWDER

CHURROS

YIELD: 75 CHURROS / **ACTIVE TIME:** 25 MINUTES / **TOTAL TIME:** 30 MINUTES

Churros are the most popular Mexican sweet, no doubt because they are completely irresistible. This preparation is for a big batch, most of which you will have to freeze, but you can also enjoy a few straight out of the fryer.

1. Add canola oil to a Dutch oven until it is about 2 inches deep and warm to 350°F. Place the milk, water, sugar, and salt in a large saucepan and bring it to a boil.

2. Gradually add the flours and cook, stirring constantly, until the mixture pulls away from the sides of the pan.

3. Place the mixture in the work bowl of a stand mixer fitted with the paddle attachment and beat until the dough is almost cool. Incorporate the eggs one at a time, scraping down the work bowl as needed.

4. Place the dough in a piping bag fitted with a star tip. Pipe 6-inch lengths of dough into the oil and fry until golden brown. Place on paper towel–lined plates to drain and cool slightly. Toss in cinnamon sugar and enjoy, or store the churros in the freezer.

5. To serve frozen churros, preheat the oven to 450°F. Remove the churros from the freezer and toss in cinnamon sugar until coated. Place in the oven and bake for 5 minutes. Remove, toss in cinnamon sugar again, and serve with the chocolate sauce.

INGREDIENTS:

CANOLA OIL, AS NEEDED

35¼ OZ. MILK

81.1 OZ. WATER

2.8 OZ. SUGAR, PLUS MORE TO TASTE

1.4 OZ. SALT

38.8 OZ. "00" FLOUR

38.8 OZ. ALL-PURPOSE FLOUR

32 EGGS

CINNAMON, TO TASTE

MEXICAN CHOCOLATE SAUCE (SEE PAGE 584), FOR SERVING

MEXICAN CHOCOLATE SAUCE

YIELD: 6 QUARTS / **ACTIVE TIME:** 40 MINUTES / **TOTAL TIME:** 40 MINUTES

Similar to the Chocolate Mole on page 575, but the almonds add a bit of texture and sweetness, and ramp up the nuttiness significantly.

1. Place the sesame seeds in a dry skillet and toast over low heat until just browned. Remove from the pan and set aside.

2. Place the water, butter, sugars, cream, salt, vanilla, cinnamon, cayenne, sesame seeds, and peanut butter in a large saucepan and bring to a simmer, stirring frequently.

3. Remove the pan from heat, add the cocoa powder, and whisk until combined.

4. Place the almonds in a dry skillet and toast over low heat until just browned. Remove from the pan and set aside.

5. Strain the chocolate-and-cream mixture and reserve ¾ cup of the sesame seeds. Add these, 1 to 2 cups of the strained chocolate sauce, and the almonds to a blender and pulse until the almonds are finely ground.

6. Add the blended mixture to the strained chocolate sauce and cool the mixture in an ice bath. Store in the refrigerator until ready to use.

INGREDIENTS:

1	CUP SESAME SEEDS
4¾	CUPS WATER
1	LB. UNSALTED BUTTER
25	OZ. SUGAR
56	OZ. BROWN SUGAR
8	CUPS HEAVY CREAM
1½	TEASPOONS FINE SEA SALT
	SEEDS AND POD OF ½ VANILLA BEAN
1½	TEASPOONS CINNAMON
1	TEASPOON CAYENNE PEPPER
2	TABLESPOONS PEANUT BUTTER
2.2	LBS. COCOA POWDER
¾	CUP ALMONDS

CINNAMON & CHOCOLATE CAKE

YIELD: 1 CAKE / **ACTIVE TIME:** 1 HOUR / **TOTAL TIME:** 6 HOURS

If you are a cinnamon and chocolate lover this indulgent cake is for you. This cake can also be made ahead of time and frozen. If that's the route you take, pull it out 30 minutes before serving.

1. Preheat the oven to 300°F. Line two round, 9-inch cake pans with parchment paper and coat them with nonstick cooking spray.

2. Fill a small saucepan halfway with water and bring it to a simmer. Place the chocolate and butter in a heatproof bowl, place it over the simmering water, and stir until the mixture is melted and smooth. Remove from heat and let cool.

3. Stir the cinnamon into the cooled chocolate mixture.

4. Place the egg yolks and half of the sugar in the work bowl of a stand mixer fitted with the whisk attachment and whip until the mixture has tripled in volume.

5. Place the egg whites and remaining sugar in a separate mixing bowl and whip until the mixture holds medium peaks.

6. Fold the whipped egg yolks into the chocolate mixture. Fold the whipped egg whites in.

7. Pour 10 oz. of batter into each cake pan, place them in the oven, and bake until a knife inserted into their centers comes out clean, about 15 minutes.

8. Remove from the oven, set the pans on wire racks, and let the cakes cool completely.

9. Refrigerate for 4 hours. Cut the top ½ inch off of one of the cakes and spread some of the ganache over it. Place the other cake on top, spread the ganache over the entire cake, and enjoy.

INGREDIENTS:

14	OZ. DARK CHOCOLATE (64 PERCENT)
6½	OZ. UNSALTED BUTTER
2	TABLESPOONS CINNAMON
7	EGGS, SEPARATED
6	OZ. SUGAR
¼	TEASPOON FINE SEA SALT
	DARK CHOCOLATE GANACHE (SEE PAGE 590)

DARK CHOCOLATE GANACHE

YIELD: 1½ CUPS / **ACTIVE TIME:** 10 MINUTES / **TOTAL TIME:** 15 MINUTES

The key to adding a bit of chocolate and beauty to your cakes and pies. This preparation will work with any chocolate—dark, milk, or white.

1. Place the chocolate in a heatproof mixing bowl and set aside.

2. Place the heavy cream in a small saucepan and bring to a simmer over medium heat.

3. Pour the cream over the chocolate and let the mixture rest for 1 minute.

4. Gently whisk the mixture until thoroughly combined. Use immediately if drizzling over a cake or serving with fruit. Let the ganache cool for 2 hours if piping. The ganache will keep in the refrigerator for up to 5 days.

INGREDIENTS:

8   OZ. DARK CHOCOLATE

1   CUP HEAVY CREAM

COCONUT TRES LECHES

YIELD: 1 CAKE / **ACTIVE TIME:** 1 HOUR / **TOTAL TIME:** 4 HOURS

Lori Sauer: "This recipe was adapted years ago from a friend in Tijuana. His original recipe was strictly tres leches, but I wanted to put my own spin on it with coconut, and create a fluffier texture for the sponge."

1. Preheat the oven to 325°F. Coat a baking pan with nonstick cooking spray. To begin preparations for the sponge cake, place the egg whites and sugar in the work bowl of a stand mixer fitted with the whisk attachment and whip to full volume.

2. Combine the flour, sea salt, and baking powder in a separate bowl.

3. Incorporate the egg yolks into the meringue one at a time. Add one-third of the meringue into the dry mixture along with the water and vanilla and beat until incorporated. Add another one-third of the meringue and fold to combine. Add the remaining one-third and carefully fold until incorporated.

4. Transfer the batter into the baking pan and gently spread until it is even. Place in the oven and bake until a knife inserted into the center comes out clean, about 40 minutes.

5. While the cake is in the oven, prepare the soaking liquid. Place all of the ingredients in a saucepan and warm it over medium heat, stirring to combine. When the mixture starts to steam and all of the sugar has dissolved, remove the pan from heat.

6. Pour the soaking liquid over the cake and chill it in the refrigerator for 2 hours.

7. To serve, top slices with the berries, drizzle some of the liquid from macerating the berries over everything, and enjoy.

INGREDIENTS:

FOR THE SPONGE CAKE

16   EGGS, SEPARATED

28.2 OZ. SUGAR

28.9 OZ. ALL-PURPOSE FLOUR, SIFTED

⅔   TEASPOON FINE SEA SALT

¼   CUP BAKING POWDER

4.6 OZ. WATER

5   TEASPOONS MEXICAN VANILLA EXTRACT

    RAICILLA-SOAKED BERRIES (SEE PAGE 594)

FOR THE SOAKING LIQUID

2   (14 OZ.) CANS OF SWEETENED CONDENSED MILK

2   (12 OZ.) CANS OF EVAPORATED MILK

½   CUP HEAVY CREAM

1¾ CUPS COCONUT MILK

½   CUP SUGAR

RAICILLA-SOAKED BERRIES

YIELD: 6 SERVINGS / **ACTIVE TIME:** 5 MINUTES / **TOTAL TIME:** 1 HOUR

If you cannot find Raicilla, a spirit from southwest of Jalisco, you can try macerating the berries in mezcal or tequila.

1. Place all of the ingredients in a mixing bowl and stir gently to combine.

2. Let the berries macerate for at least 1 hour before enjoying.

INGREDIENTS:

2   CUPS FRESH BERRIES

½   CUP CONFECTIONERS' SUGAR

¼   CUP RAICILLA

BUÑUELOS

YIELD: 12 PASTRIES / **ACTIVE TIME:** 20 MINUTES / **TOTAL TIME:** 1 HOUR

This take on fried dough came to Mexico via the Spanish. It can be topped with almost anything you like, but the Piloncillo Syrup on page 557 is the traditional choice.

1. In a large mixing bowl, combine the flour, baking powder, sugar, and salt. Add the egg, melted butter, and vanilla and work the mixture until it resembles coarse bread crumbs.

2. Incorporate water 1 tablespoon at a time until the mixture comes together as a soft, smooth dough. Cover the mixing bowl with plastic wrap and let it rest for 30 minutes.

3. Divide the dough into 12 portions and roll them out as thin as possible, without breaking them, on a flour-dusted work surface.

4. Add canola oil to a Dutch oven until it is about 2 inches deep and warm it to 350°F. Working in batches to avoid crowding the pot, gently slip the buñuelos into the oil and fry until crispy and golden brown, about 2 minutes. Transfer to a paper towel–lined plate and let them drain before enjoying.

INGREDIENTS:

2 CUPS ALL-PURPOSE FLOUR, PLUS MORE AS NEEDED

1 TEASPOON BAKING POWDER

1 TABLESPOON SUGAR

½ TEASPOON KOSHER SALT

1 EGG

1 TABLESPOON UNSALTED BUTTER, MELTED AND COOLED

1 TEASPOON MEXICAN VANILLA EXTRACT

WATER, AS NEEDED

CANOLA OIL, AS NEEDED

PERFECT CARAMEL

YIELD: 3 CUPS / **ACTIVE TIME:** 15 MINUTES / **TOTAL TIME:** 30 MINUTES

Adding the water in two steps slows the speed at which the sugar cooks and greatly reduces the chances that it will burn, meaning that you can count on your desserts receiving the rich aromas and deep flavors that quality caramel supplies.

1. Prepare an ice bath. Place the sugar and 1½ cups of the water in a saucepan and bring to a boil. Cook until the mixture is amber.

2. Remove the pan from heat and carefully deglaze the mixture with the remaining water. The mixture will splatter, so use a good deal of caution here.

3. Return the pan to the stove and melt any residual caramelized sugar over low heat.

4. Place the caramel in the ice bath and let it cool completely before using or storing.

INGREDIENTS:

3	CUPS SUGAR
3¾	CUPS WATER

CONCHAS

YIELD: 42 CONCHAS / **ACTIVE TIME:** 1 HOUR AND 30 MINUTES / **TOTAL TIME:** 13 HOURS

Conchas are a traditional Mexican sweet bread that get their name from the striped shell "pasta" or crunchy topping.

1. To begin preparations for the dough, place the milk, sugar, and yeast in the work bowl of a stand mixer fitted with the dough hook attachment and stir gently to combine. Let the mixture sit until it is foamy, about 10 minutes.

2. Add the eggs and stir gently to incorporate. Add the vanilla, flour, salt, and cardamom and work the mixture until it comes together as a scraggly dough.

3. Knead the dough on medium speed for about 3 minutes. Add the butter in four increments and work the mixture for 2 minutes after each addition, scraping down the work bowl as needed.

4. Increase the mixer's speed and knead the dough until it can be lifted cleanly out of the bowl, about 10 minutes.

5. Place the dough on a flour-dusted work surface and lightly flour your hands and the top of the dough. Fold the edges of the dough toward the middle and gently press them into the dough. Carefully turn the dough over and use your palms to shape the dough to form a tight ball. Carefully pick up the dough and place it in a mixing bowl. Let it rise in a naturally warm place until it has doubled in size, about 1 hour.

6. Place the dough on a flour-dusted work surface and press down gently to deflate the dough with your hands. Fold in the edges toward the middle and press them in. Carefully flip the dough over and tighten the dough into a ball with a smooth, taut surface.

7. Place the dough back in the mixing bowl, cover it with plastic wrap, and chill in the refrigerator for 8 hours.

8. Divide the dough into 2.6-oz. portions and form them into balls. Place the balls on parchment-lined baking sheets, cover with kitchen towels, and let them rise at room temperature for 2 hours.

9. To begin preparations for the topping, place all of the ingredients in the work bowl of a stand mixer fitted with the paddle attachment and beat until the mixture comes together as a smooth dough.

INGREDIENTS:

FOR THE DOUGH

2	CUPS WARMED MILK (90°F)
2	CUPS SUGAR
2	OZ. ACTIVE DRY YEAST
18	OZ. EGGS
	SEEDS OF 1 VANILLA BEAN
45	OZ. ALL-PURPOSE FLOUR, PLUS MORE AS NEEDED
½	OZ. FINE SEA SALT
⅛	TEASPOON (SCANT) CARDAMOM
1	LB. UNSALTED BUTTER, SOFTENED

FOR THE TOPPING

6	OZ. ALL-PURPOSE FLOUR
6	OZ. CONFECTIONERS' SUGAR
4.8	OZ. UNSALTED BUTTER, SOFTENED

10. Divide the topping into ⅓-oz. portions. Line a tortilla press with plastic, place a piece of the topping mixture on top, and top with another piece of plastic. Flatten the mixture, place it on one of the proofed conchas, and make small cuts in the topping that are the same shape as the top of an oyster shell. Repeat with the remaining topping mixture and let the conchas rest for 10 minutes.

11. Place in the oven and bake for 10 minutes. Rotate the pans, lower the oven's temperature to 300°F, and bake for an additional 2 minutes. Remove and let cool before enjoying.

STRAWBERRY SHORTCAKE CON CONCHAS

YIELD: 6 SERVINGS / **ACTIVE TIME:** 10 MINUTES / **TOTAL TIME:** 40 MINUTES

A preparation made to capture the full glory of late spring, and strawberry season.

1. Place the strawberries and ¼ cup of sugar in a large bowl and cover it with plastic wrap. Let the mixture sit until the strawberries start to release their juice, about 45 minutes.

2. Place the remaining sugar, cinnamon, and heavy cream in a mixing bowl and whip until it holds medium peaks. Set the whipped cream aside.

3. Starting at the equator, cut each of the Conchas in half. Place a dollop of the whipped cream on top of one of the halves, followed by a few scoops of the strawberries and their juices. Top with the other half and serve.

INGREDIENTS:

2   LBS. STRAWBERRIES, HULLED AND HALVED

¼   CUP SUGAR, PLUS 2 TABLESPOONS

¼   TEASPOON CINNAMON

1½   CUPS HEAVY CREAM

4   CONCHAS (SEE PAGES 602–603)

BLUE CORN CRUNCHIES

YIELD: 1 CUP / **ACTIVE TIME:** 30 MINUTES / **TOTAL TIME:** 1 HOUR

Lori Sauer: "The blue corn crunchies in the dish were inspired when the restaurant I was working at was nixtamalizing and grinding blue corn into tortillas. I wanted to try a sweet twist on them so that's where this idea came from."

1. Place a piece of parchment beneath a cooling rack. Place the piloncillo, water, cinnamon, and cloves in a small saucepan and warm over medium heat, stirring to dissolve the piloncillo.

2. Strain the syrup into a shallow bowl. Place a single tortilla in the liquid and let it absorb for a few minutes. Flip the tortilla over and soak the other side. Place the tortilla on the cooling rack to drain. Repeat with the remaining tortillas.

3. Add canola oil to a Dutch oven until it is about 2 inches deep and warm it to 350°F. Place the tortillas in the oil and fry until crispy, 1 to 2 minutes. Transfer to paper towel–lined plates to drain and cool.

4. Break the tortillas up and place them in a food processor. Pulse until they are the texture of coarse bread crumbs and use as desired.

INGREDIENTS:

1   LB. PILONCILLO, CHOPPED

2½   CUPS WATER

¼   TEASPOON CINNAMON

⅛   TEASPOON GROUND CLOVES

5   BLUE CORN TORTILLAS

    CANOLA OIL, AS NEEDED

Buñuelos, see page 598

MANGO CON CHILE PATE DE FRUIT

YIELD: 60 CANDIES / **ACTIVE TIME:** 25 MINUTES / **TOTAL TIME:** 3 HOURS AND 30 MINUTES

Lori Sauer: "Mango and chile are one of the best combinations. And since I make all different types of pate de fruit, I figured why not try it out. As you'll see, it turned out to be a very fruitful gamble."

1. Line a baking sheet with a silpat mat and place a silicone candy mold on it. Place the pectin and a little bit of the sugar in a mixing bowl and stir to combine. Add the citric acid to the water and let it dissolve.

2. Place the puree in a saucepan and warm it to 120°F. Add the pectin-and-sugar mixture and whisk to prevent any clumps from forming. Bring the mixture to a boil and let it cook for 1 minute.

3. Stir in the corn syrup and remaining sugar and cook the mixture until it is 223°F. The mixture should have thickened and should cool quickly and hold its shape when a small portion of it is dropped from a rubber spatula.

4. Stir in the lime zest and citric acid-and-water mixture and cook for another minute or so. Remove the pan from heat, strain the mixture, and pour it into the candy mold.

5. Let cool for at least 3 hours before cutting into the desired shapes. Toss in Tajín, sugar, and salt and enjoy.

INGREDIENTS:

3	TABLESPOONS APPLE PECTIN
20.1	OZ. SUGAR, PLUS MORE TO TASTE
1½	TEASPOONS CITRIC ACID
1½	TEASPOONS WATER
17.6	OZ. MANGO PUREE
3½	OZ. CORN SYRUP
	PINCH OF LIME ZEST
	TAJÍN, TO TASTE
	SALT, TO TASTE

CORNCHATA HARD CANDIES

YIELD: 30 TO 60 CANDIES / *ACTIVE TIME:* 30 MINUTES / *TOTAL TIME:* 1 HOUR

Corn's sweetness and availability means one can never cease in the search for preparations that make use of it.

1. Coat a ⅛ silicone candy mold with nonstick cooking spray. Combine the sugar, corn syrup, cream of tartar, and water in a saucepan and bring it to a boil. Cover the pan and let it cook for 2 minutes.

2. Remove the cover and fit the pan with a candy thermometer. Cook until the mixture is 300°F. Remove the pan from heat and let it cool to 275°F.

3. Add the oil and cinnamon to the mixture and stir until just combined. Pour the mixture into the molds with the help of a funnel.

4. Let the candies set for 20 minutes before enjoying.

INGREDIENTS:

2	CUPS SUGAR
⅔	CUP CORN SYRUP
½	TEASPOON CREAM OF TARTAR
¾	CUP WATER
1	TEASPOON HORCHATA OIL
½	TEASPOON CINNAMON

MAYAN CHOCOLATE & BOURBON TRUFFLES

YIELD: 40 TRUFFLES / **ACTIVE TIME:** 40 MINUTES / **TOTAL TIME:** 1 HOUR AND 30 MINUTES

The Mayans' obsession with chocolate, which was so intense that they used cocoa beans as currency, is honored in these rich truffles.

1. Fill a small saucepan halfway with water and bring it to a simmer.

2. Place the cream, chocolates, and cinnamon in a heatproof mixing bowl and place it over the simmering water. Stir until the mixture is smooth.

3. Remove from heat, stir in the bourbon, and strain the mixture into a hotel pan. Place in the refrigerator and let it cool completely.

4. Scoop the desired size for your truffles onto parchment-lined baking sheets. Return to the refrigerator and chill for 10 to 15 minutes.

5. Roll the scoops into balls using your hands. Place them back on the baking sheets and chill in the refrigerator.

6. Fill a small saucepan halfway with water and bring it to a simmer. Place additional chocolate in a heatproof bowl, place it over the simmering water, and stir until melted and smooth. Let the chocolate cool for 5 minutes.

7. Dip the balls into the melted chocolate twice, so that they are completely coated. Place them back on the baking sheets and chill in the refrigerator until set.

8. When set, roll the truffles in the cocoa powder until completely covered and enjoy.

INGREDIENTS:

2	CUPS HEAVY CREAM
1	LB. DARK CHOCOLATE, CHOPPED, PLUS MORE AS NEEDED
3	OZ. MILK CHOCOLATE, CHOPPED
1	TEASPOON CINNAMON
½	CUP BOURBON
¼	CUP COCOA POWDER

MEXICAN WEDDING COOKIES

YIELD: 36 COOKIES / **ACTIVE TIME:** 20 MINUTES / **TOTAL TIME:** 1 HOUR

These buttery, nutty cookies have been beloved across the globe for centuries. In Mexico, they have also been christened with the nickname pedos de monja, which translates to "nuns' farts."

1. Preheat the oven to 325°F. Line two baking sheets with parchment paper.

2. In the work bowl of a stand mixer fitted with the paddle attachment, cream the butter and confectioners' sugar on medium until light and fluffy, about 5 minutes.

3. Add the vanilla and salt and beat until incorporated. Add the flour and pecans and beat the mixture until it comes together as a dough, scraping down the work bowl as needed.

4. Form the dough into 1¼-inch balls, place them in the oven, bake for 10 to 12 minutes. Remove from the oven and let the cookies cool slightly.

5. Roll the cookies in confectioners' sugar until evenly coated. Let them cool completely before enjoying.

INGREDIENTS:

1   CUP UNSALTED BUTTER, SOFTENED

½   CUP CONFECTIONERS' SUGAR, PLUS MORE AS NEEDED

1   TEASPOON MEXICAN VANILLA EXTRACT

¼   TEASPOON KOSHER SALT

2¼   CUPS SIFTED ALL-PURPOSE FLOUR

¾   CUP PECANS, CHOPPED

MEZCAL ICE CREAM

YIELD: 1 QUART / **ACTIVE TIME:** 45 MINUTES / **TOTAL TIME:** 5 HOURS

Here's a bet: you'll soon be trying to incorporate this ice cream into everything.

1. Prepare an ice bath. Place the half & half, sugar, cream, and corn syrup in a medium saucepan and bring it to a simmer.

2. Place the yolks in the work bowl of a stand mixer and whip until pale and thick.

3. Add the milk mixture to the whipped yolks a little bit at a time, whisking constantly. When all of them milk mixture has been incorporated, return the tempered mixture back to the pan and cook over low heat until the mixture is thick enough to coat the back of a wooden spoon.

4. Remove the pan from heat, stir in the mezcal and salt, and strain the mixture into a bowl.

5. Place the bowl in the ice bath until the custard is cool.

6. Churn the custard in an ice cream maker until it reaches the desired consistency. Transfer to an airtight container and freeze for 4 hours before enjoying.

INGREDIENTS:

4	CUPS HALF & HALF
1⅓	CUPS SUGAR
¼	CUP HEAVY CREAM
⅓	CUP CORN SYRUP
⅓	CUP EGG YOLKS
¼	CUP MEZCAL
	PINCH OF KOSHER SALT

MEZCAL & MANGO FLOAT

YIELD: 1 SERVING / **ACTIVE TIME:** 2 MINUTES / **TOTAL TIME:** 2 MINUTES

This smoky, sweet, earthy, and tingly float is elegant and dreamy.

1. Place the puree and ginger beer in a large mason jar and stir to combine.

2. Place the ice cream in a fountain glass and pour the mango soda over the top. Enjoy immediately.

INGREDIENTS:

1   CUP MANGO PUREE

1   CUP GINGER BEER

3-4   SCOOPS OF MEZCAL ICE CREAM (SEE PAGE 620)

MOLE BROWNIES

YIELD: 30 BROWNIES / **ACTIVE TIME:** 15 MINUTES / **TOTAL TIME:** 1 HOUR AND 45 MINUTES

Turns out: you've really never had brownies before.

1. Preheat the oven to 350°F. Coat two 9 x 13–inch baking pans with nonstick cooking spray. In the work bowl of a stand mixer fitted with the paddle attachment, cream the butter, sugar, orange zest, ancho chile, sesame seeds, peanut butter, and cinnamon on medium until the mixture is light and fluffy.

2. Combine the cocoa powder, salt, flour, and cayenne in a separate mixing bowl. Add half of the dry mixture to the creamed butter and beat until incorporated.

3. Add the vanilla and then incorporate the eggs one at a time, scraping down the work bowl as needed. Add the remaining dry mixture and beat until the mixture is a smooth batter.

4. Pour the batter into the pans, place them in the oven, and bake until a knife inserted into their centers comes out clean, 30 to 40 minutes.

5. Remove from the oven, place the pans on cooling racks, and let the brownies cool completely.

6. Run a paring knife along the sides of the pans. Spread the frosting over the brownies, cut them into squares, and enjoy.

INGREDIENTS:

47.6 OZ. UNSALTED BUTTER

79.4 OZ. SUGAR

ZEST OF ½ ORANGE ZEST

1 ANCHO CHILE PEPPER, STEMMED, SEEDED, AND CHOPPED

½ CUP SESAME SEEDS, TOASTED

¼ CUP CREAMY PEANUT BUTTER

⅓ TEASPOON CINNAMON, PLUS A PINCH

20.6 OZ. COCOA POWDER

2½ TEASPOONS FINE SEA SALT

22.2 OZ. ALL-PURPOSE FLOUR

½ TEASPOON CAYENNE PEPPER

3 TABLESPOONS PURE VANILLA EXTRACT

18 EGGS

CHOCOLATE & MEXICAN VANILLA FROSTING (SEE PAGE 628)

MIXED NUT MARZIPAN

YIELD: 36 BARS / **ACTIVE TIME:** 10 MINUTES / **TOTAL TIME:** 20 MINUTES

A quick and delicious take on the traditional Mexican sweet treat.

1. Line two baking sheets with parchment paper and coat with nonstick cooking spray.

2. Place the nuts in a food processor and pulse until coarsely ground. Add the confectioners' sugar and peanut butter and pulse until the mixture is a thick paste.

3. Place the mixture on a flat surface and roll it out to ¾ inch thick. Use cookie cutters to cut the marzipan into the desired shapes and place them on the baking sheets. Enjoy immediately or store in the refrigerator.

INGREDIENTS:

1¼ CUPS ROASTED, UNSALTED PEANUTS

½ CUP SLICED ALMONDS

¼ CUP PECANS

1 CUP CONFECTIONERS' SUGAR

1 TEASPOON CREAMY PEANUT BUTTER

CHOCOLATE & MEXICAN VANILLA FROSTING

YIELD: 4 CUPS / **ACTIVE TIME:** 10 MINUTES / **TOTAL TIME:** 30 MINUTES

Adding a bit of Mexican vanilla to a classic chocolate frosting results in a topping that goes well with the spicy and cinnamon-centric desserts Mexico specializes in.

1. Place the cream in a saucepan and warm it over medium heat. Place the chocolates in a heatproof bowl.

2. When the cream starts to steam, pour it over the chocolates and stir until melted and smooth. Stir in the vanilla and let the mixture cool before using.

INGREDIENTS:

2   CUPS HEAVY CREAM

1   LB. DARK CHOCOLATE, CHOPPED

3   OZ. MILK CHOCOLATE, CHOPPED

½   CUP MEXICAN VANILLA EXTRACT

NO-FRY FRIED ICE CREAM

YIELD: 4 SERVINGS / **ACTIVE TIME:** 30 MINUTES / **TOTAL TIME:** 1 HOUR AND 45 MINUTES

This dessert is served in many Mexican restaurants in the US. This preparation is way easier, less scary, not as messy, and just as good.

1. Place the ice cream on a baking sheet and place it in the freezer for 1 hour.

2. Roll the scoops into balls and place them back in the freezer.

3. Place the cornflakes in a food processor and pulse until finely ground.

4. Place the butter in a medium saucepan and melt it over medium heat.

5. Stir in the cornflake crumbs and the cinnamon and cook until golden brown. Remove from heat and stir in the sugar.

6. Pour the mixture into a shallow pan and let it cool.

7. Roll the ice cream balls in the mixture until evenly coated. Place the coated ice cream balls in the freezer until ready to serve.

INGREDIENTS:

8	SCOOPS OF ICE CREAM
2	CUPS CORNFLAKES
½	CUP UNSALTED BUTTER
2	TEASPOONS CINNAMON
3	TABLESPOONS SUGAR

PAN DE HOJA SANTA

YIELD: 24 ROLLS / **ACTIVE TIME:** 1 HOUR AND 30 MINUTES / **TOTAL TIME:** 24 HOURS

Hoja santa is known as the Mexican pepperleaf, and its flavor is very reminiscent of root beer. As you can imagine, the smell of these rolls when they come out of the oven is intoxicating.

1. To begin preparations for the dough, combine the flour, sugar, and salt in a mixing bowl.

2. Warm the milk to 95°F. Place it in the work bowl of a stand mixer fitted with the dough hook, stir in the yeast, and let the mixture sit until it starts to foam, about 10 minutes.

3. Place the dry mixture in the work bowl, followed by the eggs. Beat until the mixture is combined and let rest for 20 minutes.

4. Incorporate the butter in three increments, folding the mixture three times and then letting it rest for 30 minutes with each addition.

5. Cover the bowl with plastic wrap and let it rest in the refrigerator overnight.

6. To prepare the topping, place the butter in a saucepan and melt it over medium heat. Prepare an ice bath and cool the butter in it briefly. Stir in the cinnamon and hoja santa.

7. Place the pot containing the topping over another pot of hot water to keep the butter from setting up too quickly.

8. Drop small balls of the dough into the butter mixture and toss to coat.

9. Place the balls two-thirds of the way into greased square molds that are on top of a greased and parchment-lined baking sheet. Spread the squares out so they have space to breathe.

10. Sprinkle additional hoja santa over each ball and cover them with plastic wrap.

11. Let the balls rest until they have doubled in size, about 2 hours.

12. Preheat the oven to 325°F. Place the rolls in the oven and bake until golden brown, about 8 minutes. Remove and let cool slightly before enjoying.

INGREDIENTS:

FOR THE DOUGH

35.2 OZ. ALL-PURPOSE FLOUR

3½ OZ. SUGAR

1½ TABLESPOONS KOSHER SALT

8.8 OZ. MILK

4 TEASPOONS ACTIVE DRY YEAST

8 EGGS

17.6 OZ. UNSALTED BUTTER, SOFTENED

FOR THE TOPPING

1 LB. UNSALTED BUTTER

2 TABLESPOONS CINNAMON, PLUS 1 TEASPOON

1 TABLESPOON FINELY CHOPPED FRESH HOJA SANTA, PLUS MORE TO TASTE

THE GENESIS OF CHOCOLATE

It is believed that the ancient Olmec civilization were the first people to discover the magic of chocolate, as they used cacao in a bitter, ceremonial drink, a hypothesis borne out by traces of theobromine—a stimulant that is found in chocolate and tea—being found on ancient Olmec pots and vessels. While the exact role of chocolate in Olmec culture is impossible to pin down because they kept no written history, it appears that they passed their reverence for chocolate onto the Mayans, who valued it to the point that cocoa beans were used as currency in certain transactions.

It is interesting that access to this precious resource wasn't restricted to the wealthy among the Mayans, but was available enough that a beverage consisting of chocolate mixed with honey or chile peppers could be enjoyed with every meal in a majority of Mayan households.

The next great Mexican civilization, the Aztecs, carried things even further. They saw cocoa as more valuable than gold, and the mighty Aztec ruler Moctezuma (also known as Montezuma II) supposedly drank gallons of chocolate each day, believing that it provided him with considerable energy and also served as a potent aphrodisiac.

SWEET CORN PUDDING POPS

YIELD: 12 POPS / **ACTIVE TIME:** 30 MINUTES / **TOTAL TIME:** 24 HOURS

There always seems to be a shortage of preparations when corn season is at its height. This recipe helps keep those anxieties at bay.

1. Prepare an ice bath. Grate the corn kernels into a saucepan and discard the cobs. Add the cream and milk and bring the mixture to a simmer.

2. Place the yolks and sugar in the work bowl of a stand mixer fitted with the whisk attachment and whip until the mixture is pale and thick.

3. Add the milk mixture to the whipped yolks a little bit at a time, whisking constantly. When all of them milk mixture has been incorporated, return the tempered mixture back to the pan and cook over low heat until the mixture is thick enough to coat the back of a wooden spoon.

4. Remove the pan from heat, stir in the vanilla and salt, and strain the mixture into a bowl.

5. Place the bowl in the ice bath until the custard is cool.

6. Pour the custard into popsicle molds and freeze overnight.

INGREDIENTS:

8	EARS OF CORN
4	CUPS HEAVY CREAM
6	CUPS MILK
1½	CUPS EGG YOLKS
2	CUPS SUGAR
2	TEASPOONS MEXICAN VANILLA EXTRACT
⅛	TEASPOON FINE SEA SALT

GLUTEN-FREE SPICY CHOCOLATE COOKIES

YIELD: 12 COOKIES / **ACTIVE TIME:** 15 MINUTES / **TOTAL TIME:** 2 HOURS

Yes, these cookies are gluten-free. No, you won't be able to tell.

1. Combine the flour, cocoa powder, xanthan gum, baking soda, cinnamon, and cayenne pepper in a mixing bowl and set aside.

2. In the work bowl of a stand mixer fitted with the paddle attachment, beat the eggs, sugar, canola oil, and vanilla extract until well combined. Add the dry mixture, set the speed to low, and beat until the mixture is a smooth dough. Fold in the chocolate chips, cover the bowl with plastic wrap, and chill in the refrigerator for 1 hour.

3. Preheat the oven to 325°F. Line a baking sheet with parchment paper. Form the dough into 12 balls and arrange them on the baking sheet, making sure to leave enough space between them. Place in the oven and bake until set, about 12 minutes. Remove from the oven and let the cookies cool on the baking sheets before enjoying.

INGREDIENTS:

⅔ CUP GLUTEN-FREE ALL-PURPOSE FLOUR

¾ CUP COCOA POWDER, PLUS 2 TABLESPOONS

½ TEASPOON XANTHAN GUM (IF MISSING FROM FLOUR)

1 TEASPOON BAKING SODA

2 TEASPOONS CINNAMON

½ TEASPOON CAYENNE PEPPER

2 LARGE EGGS

1 CUP SUGAR

½ CUP CANOLA OIL

1 TABLESPOON PURE VANILLA EXTRACT

1 CUP CHOCOLATE CHIPS

CAJETA

YIELD: 1½ CUPS / **ACTIVE TIME:** 1 HOUR / **TOTAL TIME:** 5 HOURS

The Mexican version of dulce de leche, but it's made with goats' milk, which gives it a slightly tangy finish. Traditionally, cajeta is served over ice cream or fried dough, but it's pretty dang good on anything.

1. Place the goats' milk, sugar, cinnamon stick, and salt in a medium saucepan and bring to a simmer over medium-low heat.

2. In a small bowl, combine the baking soda and water. Whisk the mixture into the saucepan.

3. Continue to simmer for 1 to 2 hours, stirring frequently.

4. When the mixture turns a caramel color and is thick enough to coat the back of a wooden spoon, remove the pan from heat and let the cajeta cool for 1 hour.

5. Transfer to mason jars and refrigerate until set. This will keep in the refrigerator for up to 1 month.

INGREDIENTS:

4	CUPS GOATS' MILK
1	CUP SUGAR
1	CINNAMON STICK
⅛	TEASPOON KOSHER SALT
1½	TEASPOONS WATER
¼	TEASPOON BAKING SODA

MEXICAN CHOCOLATE CRINKLE COOKIES

YIELD: 20 COOKIES / **ACTIVE TIME:** 30 MINUTES / **TOTAL TIME:** 2 HOURS

Spicy, sweet, chocolatey, crunchy, and moist. In other words, a cookie for those who won't rest until they have it all.

1. Line two baking sheets with parchment paper. Fill a small saucepan halfway with water and bring it to a simmer. Place the chocolate in a heatproof bowl, place it over the simmering water, and stir until melted. Remove from heat and set aside.

2. In the work bowl of a stand mixer fitted with the paddle attachment, cream the butter, brown sugar, and vanilla on medium speed until the mixture is very light and fluffy, about 5 minutes. Scrape down the work bowl and then beat the mixture for another 5 minutes.

3. Reduce the speed to low, add the melted chocolate, and beat until incorporated.

4. Add the eggs one at a time and beat until incorporated, again scraping the work bowl as needed. When both eggs have been incorporated, scrape down the work bowl. Set the speed to medium and beat for 1 minute.

5. Add the flour, cocoa powder, baking powder, cinnamon, ancho chile powder, and salt, reduce the speed to low, and beat until the mixture comes together as a dough.

6. Drop 2-oz. portions of the dough on the baking sheets, making sure to leave enough space between them. Place the baking sheets in the refrigerator and let the dough firm up for 1 hour.

7. Preheat the oven to 350°F. Place the confectioners' sugar in a mixing bowl, toss the dough balls in the sugar until completely coated, and then place them back on the baking sheet.

8. Place the cookies in the oven and bake until a cake tester comes out clean after being inserted, 12 to 14 minutes.

9. Remove the cookies from the oven, transfer them to a cooling rack, and let them cool for 20 to 30 minutes before enjoying.

INGREDIENTS:

9	OZ. MEXICAN CHOCOLATE
4½	OZ. UNSALTED BUTTER, SOFTENED
7	OZ. DARK BROWN SUGAR
¾	TEASPOON PURE VANILLA EXTRACT
2	EGGS
7	OZ. ALL-PURPOSE FLOUR
2½	OZ. COCOA POWDER
2	TEASPOONS BAKING POWDER
½	TEASPOON CINNAMON
¼	TEASPOON ANCHO CHILE POWDER
1	TEASPOON KOSHER SALT
2	CUPS CONFECTIONERS' SUGAR, FOR COATING

SOPAIPILLAS

YIELD: 24 SOPAIPILLAS / **ACTIVE TIME:** 35 MINUTES / **TOTAL TIME:** 1 HOUR

The "doughnut of the Southwest" isn't going to meet the expectations of many get when they hear that term, but that doesn't mean it isn't delicious.

1. In the work bowl of a stand mixer fitted with the whisk attachment, combine the flour, baking powder, salt, and sugar. Turn the mixer on low speed and slowly drizzle in the warm water. Beat until the mixture comes together as a soft, smooth dough. Cover the bowl with a kitchen towel and let the dough rest for 20 minutes.

2. Place the vegetable oil in a Dutch oven and warm it over medium heat until it is 325°F. Line a baking sheet with paper towels and place it beside stove.

3. Divide the dough in half and pat each piece into a rectangle. Cut each rectangle into 12 squares and roll each square to ⅛ inch thick.

4. Working in batches of three, place the sopaipillas in the oil and use a pair of tongs to gently submerge them until puffy and golden brown, about 1 minute. Transfer the fried pastries to the baking sheet to drain and cool. When all of the sopaipillas have been fried, dust them with confectioners' sugar and cinnamon and serve with honey.

INGREDIENTS:

3 CUPS SELF-RISING FLOUR

1½ TEASPOONS BAKING POWDER

1 TEASPOON FINE SEA SALT

1 TEASPOON SUGAR

1 CUP WARM WATER (105°F)

4 CUPS VEGETABLE OIL

CONFECTIONERS' SUGAR, FOR DUSTING

CINNAMON, FOR DUSTING

HONEY, FOR SERVING

THE PERFECT FLAN

YIELD: 6 SERVINGS / **ACTIVE TIME:** 30 MINUTES / **TOTAL TIME:** 6 HOURS AND 30 MINUTES

Listen Mamet, you're a great writer, but you're wrong about this: there most definitely *is* a difference between good and bad flan.

1. Preheat the oven to 350°F. Bring 2 quarts of water to a boil and set aside.

2. Place the 1 cup of the sugar and the water in a small saucepan and bring to a boil over high heat, swirling the pan instead of stirring. Cook until the caramel is a deep golden brown, taking care not to burn it. Remove the pan from heat and pour the caramel into a round, 8-inch cake pan. Place the cake pan on a cooling rack and let it sit until it has set.

3. Place the egg yolks, eggs, cream cheese, remaining sugar, condensed milk, evaporated milk, heavy cream, almond extract, and vanilla in a blender and puree until emulsified.

4. Pour the mixture over the caramel and place the cake pan in a roasting pan. Pour the boiling water into the roasting pan until it reaches halfway up the side of the cake pan.

5. Place the flan in the oven and bake until is just set, 60 to 70 minutes. The flan should still be jiggly without being runny. Remove from the oven, place the cake pan on a cooling rack, and let it cool for 1 hour.

6. Place the flan in the refrigerator and chill for 4 hours.

7. Run a knife along the edge of the pan and invert the flan onto a plate so that the caramel layer is on top. Slice the flan and serve.

INGREDIENTS:

2	CUPS SUGAR
¼	CUP WATER
5	EGG YOLKS
5	EGGS
5	OZ. CREAM CHEESE, SOFTENED
1	(14 OZ.) CAN OF SWEETENED CONDENSED MILK
1	(12 OZ.) CAN OF EVAPORATED MILK
1½	CUPS HEAVY CREAM
½	TEASPOON ALMOND EXTRACT
½	TEASPOON PURE VANILLA EXTRACT

MEXICAN VANILLA ICE CREAM

YIELD: 1 QUART / **ACTIVE TIME:** 30 MINUTES / **TOTAL TIME:** 5 HOURS

Adding a slightly spicy vanilla to a rich custard reinvigorates the well-worn classic.

1. In a small saucepan, combine the heavy cream, milk, sugar, salt, and the vanilla seeds and pods and bring to a simmer over medium-low heat, stirring until sugar completely dissolves, about 5 minutes.

2. Remove the saucepan from heat. Place the egg yolks in a heat-proof mixing bowl and whisk them until combined. While whisking constantly, slowly whisk about a third of the hot cream mixture into the yolks. Whisk the tempered egg yolks into the saucepan.

3. Warm the mixture over medium-low heat, stirring constantly, until the mixture is thick enough to coat the back of a wooden spoon (about 170°F on an instant-read thermometer).

4. Strain the custard through a fine-mesh sieve into a bowl and let it cool to room temperature. Cover the bowl, place it in the refrigerator, and let it chill for at least 4 hours.

5. Churn the custard in an ice cream maker until it has the desired consistency. Transfer to an airtight container and freeze for 4 hours before enjoying.

INGREDIENTS:

2	CUPS HEAVY CREAM
1	CUP WHOLE MILK
⅔	CUP SUGAR
⅛	TEASPOON FINE SEA SALT
	SEEDS AND PODS OF 2 MEXICAN VANILLA BEANS
6	LARGE EGG YOLKS

COCKTAILS & BEVERAGES

*M*exico's ascension to the heights of the culinary world have also lifted the spirits associated with the country, tequila and mezcal, to unprecedented levels of appreciation. Of course, almost everyone was acquainted with the former. And for many, due to encounters with subpar offerings, that acquaintance was a trepidatious one.

But as the rich culture of Mexico gained a wider appreciation, people discovered that there were far more varieties of tequila, many of a much better quality, on offer. Tequila, always cool, became a symbol of class, and refinement. And as bartenders and mixologists explored the relatively unknown territory within the agave-based realm, the excitement fostered by tequila carried them to mezcal. Armed with Scotch's smoke, tequila's lift, a process that features unparalelled craft, and enough terroir-based variation to appeal to the wine snob, mezcal has exploded into the public eye, shifting quickly from a curiosity to a mainstay on the shelves at stores around the world.

While they can be appreciated on their own, tequila and mezcal are perhaps best suited to cocktails, a quality we take full advantage of in this chapter. There's the refreshing Paloma (see page 665), the sophisticated air of the Oaxaca Old Fashioned (see page 680), and an ideal version of America's favorite cocktail, the Margarita, a drink firmly entrenched as the symbol that it's time to let the good times roll (see page 658).

A BRIEF OVERVIEW OF TEQUILA & MEZCAL

For starters, all tequila is mezcal. But not all mezcal is tequila. Those of you who are confused, think of it this way: all bourbon is whiskey, but not all whiskey is bourbon.

Both tequila and mezcal are made by distilling the core of the agave plant, known as the piña. There are about 30 different varietals of agave plant that can be used to make mezcals. Only blue agave can be used to produce tequila.

Tequila and mezcal come from different regions of Mexico. Tequila makers can be found in the northern and central parts of the country—Michoacán, Guanajuato, Nayarit, Tamaulipas, and Jalisco, which is where the town of Tequila is located. Oaxaca, which is in southern Mexico, is where 85 percent of mezcal is produced, though it is also made in Durango, Guanajuato, Guerrero, San Luis Potosí, Tamaulipas, Zacatecas, Michoacán, and Puebla.

The separation between the two spirits, in the global imagination, began with Mexico's victory in 1810's War of Independence. Fueled by the energy of that unexpected triumph, those in charge of the burgeoning republic began to look to an increasingly industrialized Europe for inspiration. In Tequila, mezcal producers started to shake off the yoke of the hacienda system, gaining the ability to acquire more capital—resources they had the wisdom to reinvest into their operations. Eventually, Martin Martinez de Castro introduced the copper column still to the town. This innovation, when combined with the development of cooking the agave in a stone oven instead of the traditional earthen pit, bolstered production immensely.

From there, it was little more than a numbers game. Tequila, through sheer quantity and market share, became embedded in most people's minds as Mexico's spirit. And mezcal, by remaining tied to the craft culture that had fostered it, came—until very recently—to be seen as an altogether separate category, a curiosity surrounded by myth, and misunderstanding.

To make tequila, the agave is steamed in ovens before being distilled in copper stills. Once distilled, it is aged in oak barrels, and the amount of time spent in the barrel determines the type of tequila that is bottled. A breakdown of the various types follows:

Plata (no more than 2 months): Also called blanco, silver, joven, or white tequila, this is the purest form of distilled blue agave. Once it has been distilled, it is quickly bottled and distributed. Plata should taste fresh and fruity, with a clean, herbaceous hint. The best way to imbibe plata is on the rocks with a squeeze of fresh lime.

Reposado (2 to 12 months): Extra time in the barrel lets this "rested" tequila mellow out, and imparts a hint of flavors, ranging from oak to vanilla, baking spices, and fruit.

Añejo (1 to 3 years): This tequila has more depth and complexity than both plata and reposado, featuring notes of wood, nuts, and chocolate. While each brand is unique in terms of wood used and resting time, all añejo is going to be soft, smooth, and distinct on the palate.

Extra Añejo (minimum of 3 years): This "extra aged" variety is a relative newcomer to the scene, only becoming an official classification in March 2006.

Tequila, like Champagne, is a designated Appellation of Origin (AO). Like all mezcal, the agave used to produce tequila is tended to by individuals known as jimadors, who still largely perform their work by hand. In order to get a product that is saleable, these jimadors have to plant the agave, care for the plants, and harvest them when they are perfectly ripe. A huge amount of time, energy, and passion gets put into every bottle of pure blue agave tequila. That's even more the case when the tequila is aged.

If you've noticed the continual appearance of "pure" in reference to tequila, that is not an accident. Most everyone knows someone who has tequila firmly on their personal no-fly list. This is undoubtedly due to an encounter with a tequila that was less than 100 percent blue agave, or a mixto. Since they are cheaper to produce, there are many more mixto brands on the market than there are pure agave brands. Legally, these mixto tequilas must be made with at least 51 percent pure blue agave sugar. The other portion of the sugars can be from non-agave sources, like sugarcane, which will affect the taste of the spirit in a negative fashion, and potentially make the aftereffects of an evening much worse. So, in order to make sure you're getting the best experience, carefully read the label of any tequila bottle before you purchase, and say no to mixtos.

To produce mezcal, the agave is cooked over charcoal in basalt-lined pits dug in the ground and distillation happens in clay vessels; this is why most mezcals have a smoky flavor, though, as with Scotch, there are exceptions, with some offerings featuring no smoke at all, and others just a trace to provide balance. Like tequila, mezcal is aged in oak barrels.

Until recently, most people outside of Mexico marked mezcal as "the one with the worm." The existence of this meme appears to be tied to a popular marketing campaign put forth by the Monte Alban brand during the '70s. The worm, or gusano, appeared in every bottle of Monte Alban, but it is not a hallmark of the spirit, as many believed it to be. Though it does still pop up from time to time. The gusano, which feeds upon the agave plant, is believed to be highly nutritious. It can be consumed on its own, or dropped into a bottle, where it does everything from hide unpleasant flavors to add a subtle, pleasant fungal note to a well-crafted mezcal.

Mezcal, due to its association with the rural South and the folk cultures that prevail there, was also misunderstood within Mexico for a long period of time. This began to change when a growing appreciation for craft and heritage entered the national mindset, shifting mezcal from an easily dismissed oddity to a powerfully deep tradition that shifts as one moves from village to village. This rich provincialism contributed much to the lore that surrounds mezcal, including the claim that it will cause those that imbibe to hallucinate. While that is not the case, there is a school that believes the agave sugars in mezcal do produce a stimulating and energizing effect that causes a slightly higher degree of awareness than that which is employed in everyday life.

When selecting a mezcal, much can be determined by looking at the percentage of alcohol. Simply put, the higher the ABV, the less watered down the product is, and the more oils the distillate will contain. These oils provide the spirit with rich flavors and complexity, which is appealing to the aficionado, less so to the entrepreneur looking for global appeal, as they are after a cleaner tasting product with less variance. A good rule of thumb: anything at 40 percent ABV is made for a foreign market, though some of these offerings are designated as single village, meaning they will carry a distinctive character. Anything at 46 percent and up can be trusted to carry the taste of a traditional mezcal.

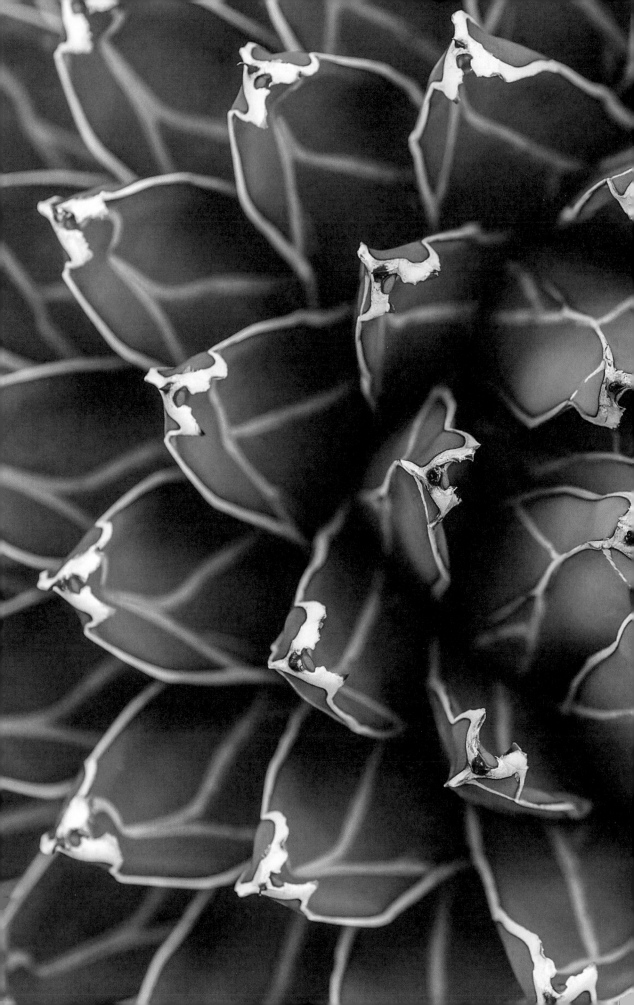

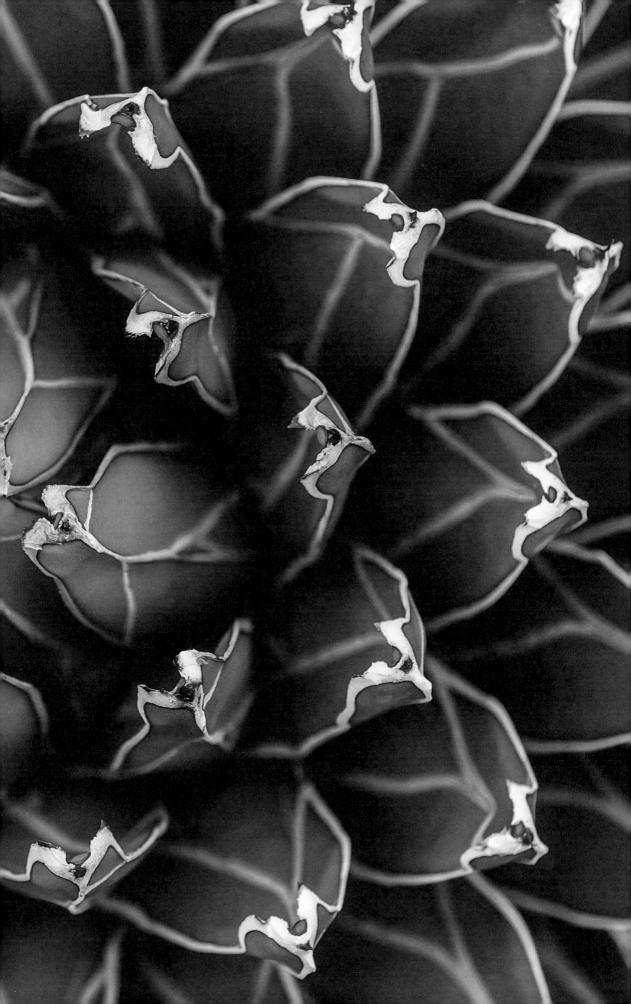

MARGARITA

YIELD: 1 SERVING / **ACTIVE TIME:** 2 MINUTES / **TOTAL TIME:** 2 MINUTES

Everyone should have a perfect Margarita recipe up their sleeve. If you don't yet, your ship has come in.

1. Wet the rim of a double rocks glass and rim half of it with salt.

2. Place all of the ingredients, except for the garnish, in a cocktail shaker, add ice, and shake until chilled.

3. Pour the cocktail into the rimmed glass, add ice if desired, and garnish with the lime wedge.

SALINE SOULTION

1. Place the ingredients in a mason jar, cover it, and shake until the salt has dissolved. For best results, transfer to a bitters bottle.

INGREDIENTS:

	SALT, FOR THE RIM
2	OZ. SILVER TEQUILA
½	OZ. COINTREAU
1	OZ. FRESH LIME JUICE
½	OZ. SIMPLE SYRUP (SEE PAGE 665)
3	DASHES OF SALINE SOLUTIONINGREDIENTS AND PREP FOR THIS?
1	LIME WEDGE, FOR GARNISH

SALINE SOLUTION

⅓	OZ. SALT
3½	OZ. WARM WATER (105°F)

RAY RAY'S MICHELADA

YIELD: 1 SERVING / **ACTIVE TIME:** 10 MINUTES / **TOTAL TIME:** 24 HOURS

The Michelada, a spicy and acidic mix added to beer, is an iconic Mexican drink, and especially refreshing on a warm day. It works with almost any beer, but is best when served with Pacifico, Modelo, Sol, Dos Equis, or Corona.

1. Place all of the ingredients, except for the lager and chamoy, in a mixing bowl and stir to combine. Refrigerate overnight.

2. If desired, rim pint glasses with salt. Fill them halfway with the michelada mix, pour the beer on top, and gently stir to combine. Garnish with chamoy and additional lime juice and Tajín and enjoy.

INGREDIENTS:

2	CUPS CLAMATO
¼	CUP GREEN OLIVE BRINE
1	TABLESPOON TAJÍN, PLUS MORE FOR GARNISH
1	TABLESPOON SOY SAUCE
1	TABLESPOON MAGGI SEASONING SAUCE
1	TABLESPOON CELERY SALT
¼	CUP FRESH LIME JUICE, PLUS MORE FOR GARNISH
1	TEASPOON TABASCO
2	TEASPOONS WORCESTERSHIRE SAUCE
	SALT AND PEPPER, TO TASTE
12	OZ. MEXICAN LAGER
1	OZ. CHAMOY, FOR GARNISH

PLAYA ROSITA

YIELD: 1 SERVING / **ACTIVE TIME:** 2 MINUTES / **TOTAL TIME:** 2 MINUTES

You ever been in a serious cocktail bar on a tropical island? No? Me either, but Aaron Melendrez likes to think this is what a Manhattan would taste like if there was a hidden, high-end palapa serving up agave Manhattans.

1. Combine all of the ingredients, except for the garnish, in a mixing glass, fill it two-thirds of the way with ice, and stir until chilled.

2. Strain into a cocktail glass and garnish with the orange twist.

PINEAPPLE-INFUSED CAMPARI

1. Place the ingredients in a large container and let the mixture steep for 24 to 48 hours.

2. Strain before using or storing.

INGREDIENTS:

¾   OZ. REPOSADO TEQUILA

¾   OZ. JOVEN MEZCAL

½   OZ. PINEAPPLE-INFUSED CAMPARI (SEE RECIPE)

½   OZ. SWEET VERMOUTH

½   OZ. DRY VERMOUTH

DASH OF BITTERMENS ELEMAKULE TIKI BITTERS

1   ORANGE TWIST, FOR GARNISH

PINEAPPLE-INFUSED CAMPARI

12   OZ. PINEAPPLE, FINELY DICED

12   OZ. CAMPARI

VAMPIRO

YIELD: 1 SERVING / **ACTIVE TIME:** 2 MINUTES / **TOTAL TIME:** 2 MINUTES

A Mexican cantina classic. Spicy, smoky, savory, fruity, and boozy, a cocktail that hits all the right notes.

1. Wet the rim of a Collins glass and rim half of it with Tajín.

2. Place the mezcal, Vampiro Mix, juices, and syrup in a cocktail shaker, add 1 ice cube, and whip-shake until chilled.

3. Pour the cocktail into the rimmed glass, add the salt and seltzer, and garnish with the dehydrated blood orange wheel.

VAMPIRO MIX

1. Place all of the ingredients in a blender and pulse until combined.

2. Use immediately or store in the refrigerator, where it will keep for up to 3 days.

INGREDIENTS:

	TAJÍN, FOR THE RIM
2	OZ. MEZCAL
2	OZ. VAMPIRO MIX (SEE RECIPE)
½	OZ. FRESH LIME JUICE
2	OZ. FRESH GRAPEFRUIT JUICE
¾	OZ. SIMPLE SYRUP (SEE PAGE 665)
	PINCH OF KOSHER SALT
2	OZ. SELTZER WATER
1	DEHYDRATED BLOOD ORANGE WHEEL, FOR GARNISH

VAMPIRO MIX

10	OZ. CLAMATO
1	OZ. APPLE CIDER VINEGAR
3	OZ. FRESH LIME JUICE
2	OZ. AGAVE NECTAR
1	TABLESPOON SRIRACHA
2	TEASPOONS BLOOD ORANGE JUICE
2	TEASPOONS SMOKED PAPRIKA
1	TEASPOON GROUND BLACK PEPPER
	SALT, TO TASTE

PALOMA

YIELD: 1 SERVING / **ACTIVE TIME:** 2 MINUTES / **TOTAL TIME:** 2 MINUTES

A Mexican classic that is suitable for any occasion. Name a better duo than grapefruit juice and tequila, I'll wait.

1. Wet the rim of a Collins glass and rim half of it with salt.

2. Place the tequila, juices, and syrup in a cocktail shaker, add 1 to 2 ice cubes, and whip-shake until chilled.

3. Pour the cocktail into the rimmed glass, top with the seltzer, add more ice, and garnish with the grapefruit slice.

SIMPLE SYRUP

1. Place the ingredients in a saucepan and bring to a boil, stirring to dissolve the sugar.

2. Remove the pan from heat and let the syrup cool completely before using or storing.

INGREDIENTS:

	SALT, FOR THE RIM
2	OZ. EL TESORO BLANCO TEQUILA
1	OZ. FRESH GRAPEFRUIT JUICE
½	OZ. FRESH LIME JUICE
½	OZ. SIMPLE SYRUP (SEE RECIPE)
2	OZ. SELTZER WATER
1	GRAPEFRUIT SLICE, FOR GARNISH

SIMPLE SYRUP

1	CUP SUGAR
1	CUP WATER

SPICY MARGARITA

YIELD: 1 SERVING / **ACTIVE TIME:** 2 MINUTES / **TOTAL TIME:** 2 MINUTES

Once you learn the basics of the Margarita, it doesn't hurt to have a couple of tricks up your sleeve. By simply adding chiles to your syrup, you give the cocktail a much spicier look.

1. Wet the rim of a double rocks glass and rim half of it with salt.

2. Place all of the ingredients, except for the garnish, in a cocktail shaker, add ice, and shake until chilled.

3. Pour the cocktail into the rimmed glass, add ice, and garnish with the lime wedge.

BLISTERED JALAPEÑO SYRUP

1. Warm a comal or cast-iron skillet over medium heat. Add the jalapeños and cook until lightly charred, turning them occasionally.

2. Place the jalapeños in a blender, add the water and sugar, and puree on high for 30 seconds.

3. Strain the syrup into a mason jar and use as desired. For best results, use within 48 hours.

INGREDIENTS:

	SALT, FOR THE RIM
2	OZ. SILVER TEQUILA
½	OZ. COINTREAU
1	OZ. FRESH LIME JUICE
½	OZ. BLISTERED JALAPEÑO SYRUP (SEE RECIPE)
3	DASHES OF SALINE SOLUTION (SEE PAGE 658)
1	LIME WEDGE, FOR GARNISH

BLISTERED JALAPEÑO SYRUP

6	JALAPEÑO CHILE PEPPERS, STEMMED AND SLICED
2	CUPS WATER
2	CUPS SUGAR

ÚLTIMA PALABRA

YIELD: 1 SERVING / **ACTIVE TIME:** 2 MINUTES / **TOTAL TIME:** 2 MINUTES

A play on the classic The Last Word cocktail. In subbing mezcal for gin, it becomes what just may be your new favorite cocktail.

1. Place the mezcal, liqueurs, and lime juice in a cocktail shaker, add ice, and shake until chilled.

2. Double-strain into a coupe and enjoy.

INGREDIENTS:

¾ OZ. MEZCAL

¾ OZ. GREEN CHARTRUESE

¾ OZ. LUXARDO MARASCHINO LIQUEUR

¾ OZ. FRESH LIME JUICE

1 LUXARDO MARASCHINO CHERRY, FOR GARNISH

EAST LA

YIELD: 1 SERVING / **ACTIVE TIME:** 2 MINUTES / **TOTAL TIME:** 2 MINUTES

Add a swimming pool and a ceviche and you'll never have a better day.

1. Wet the rim of a double rocks glass and rim half of it with Tajín. Add ice to the glass.

2. Place the cucumber and key lime juice in a cocktail shaker and muddle.

3. Add the tequila and syrup, give the mint leaves a smack, and drop them into the shaker. Add ice and the Saline Solution and shake until chilled.

4. Double-strain into the double rocks glass and garnish with an additional slice of cucumber.

INGREDIENTS:

TAJÍN, FOR THE RIM

4-5 SLICES OF CUCUMBER, PLUS MORE FOR GARNISH

1 OZ. FRESH KEY LIME JUICE

2 OZ. TEQUILA

¾ OZ. SIMPLE SYRUP (SEE PAGE 665)

8 FRESH MINT LEAVES

3 DROPS OF SALINE SOLUTION (SEE PAGE 658)

RANCH WATER

YIELD: 1 SERVING / **ACTIVE TIME:** 2 MINUTES / **TOTAL TIME:** 2 MINUTES

If Texas and Mexico had a baby, and it was a cocktail, it would be this. Keep the bottle of Topo Chico by your side so you can top up your glass.

1. Wet the rim of a highball glass and rim it with salt. Add ice to the glass along with the tequila and lime juice.

2. Top with the Top Chico, add a pinch of salt, and gently stir.

3. Garnish with the lime wedge and enjoy.

INGREDIENTS:

SALT, FOR THE RIM, PLUS MORE TO TASTE

2 OZ. SILVER TEQUILA

½ OZ. FRESH LIME JUICE

4 OZ. TOPO CHICO

1 LIME WEDGE, FOR GARNISH

BATANGA

YIELD: 1 SERVING / **ACTIVE TIME:** 2 MINUTES / **TOTAL TIME:** 2 MINUTES

Originated by Don Javier Delgado Corona, the owner and bartender at La Capilla Bar in Tequila, Mexico. The key is Mexican Coke—breeze right past the canned stuff. Don Javier stirs his gently with a knife and leaves it in the drink, and you'd be wise to follow suit.

1. Wet the rim of a highball glass and rim it with salt.

2. Place the lime juice and salt in the glass and stir until the salt has dissolved.

3. Add the tequila and ice, top with the soda, and gently stir to combine.

4. Garnish with the lime wedge and enjoy.

INGREDIENTS:

2 PINCHES OF KOSHER SALT, PLUS MORE FOR THE RIM

2 OZ. SILVER TEQUILA

½ OZ. FRESH LIME JUICE

3½ OZ. MEXICAN COCA-COLA

1 LIME WEDGE, FOR GARNISH

OAXACA OLD FASHIONED

YIELD: 1 SERVING / **ACTIVE TIME:** 2 MINUTES / **TOTAL TIME:** 2 MINUTES

Originated by Phil Ward at Death & Co. in NYC, this was one of the cocktails that kicked off the agave craze in the US.

1. Place all of the ingredients, except for the garnish, in a mixing glass, add ice, and stir until chilled.

2. Strain into a rocks glass, garnish with the torched orange peel, and enjoy.

INGREDIENTS:

1½ OZ. EL TESORO REPOSADO TEQUILA

½ OZ. DEL MAGUEY MEZCAL

2 DASHES OF ANGOSTURA BITTERS

1 BAR SPOON OF AGAVE NECTAR

1 STRIP OF ORANGE PEEL, TORCHED, FOR GARNISH

COOPER'S CAFÉ

YIELD: 1 SERVING / **ACTIVE TIME:** 2 MINUTES / **TOTAL TIME:** 2 MINUTES

If you want this iced, top up your glass with Topo Chico.

1. Place the espresso, mezcal, and syrup in a cocktail shaker, fill it two-thirds of the way with ice, and shake until chilled.

2. Strain into a Nick & Nora glass and garnish with the strip of orange peel.

INGREDIENTS:

1   OZ. FRESHLY BREWED ESPRESSO

2   OZ. MEZCAL

½   OZ. CINNAMON SYRUP (SEE PAGE 706)

1   STRIP OF ORANGE PEEL, FOR GARNISH

OAXACARAJILLO

YIELD: 1 SERVING / **ACTIVE TIME:** 2 MINUTES / **TOTAL TIME:** 2 MINUTES

Coffee cocktails are always a good idea, unless it's bedtime of course. This play on the very popular Carajillo is how one should order if they happen to find themselves in Oaxaca.

1. Add the Licor 43, mezcal, and agave nectar to a double rocks glass.

2. Add 1 large ice cube. Slowly pour the espresso over the back of a bar spoon positioned as close to the cube as possible so that it floats atop the cocktail.

INGREDIENTS:

1½   OZ. LICOR 43

1   OZ. MEZCAL

1   BAR SPOON OF AGAVE NECTAR

1   OZ. FRESHLY BREWED ESPRESSO

RAMON BRAVO

YIELD: 1 SERVING / **ACTIVE TIME:** 2 MINUTES / **TOTAL TIME:** 2 MINUTES

Transport yourself in front of a trompo serving al pastor in just a couple sips. If you're feeling a little spicy, swap in Tajín for the rim.

1. Wet the rim of a double rocks glass and rim it with salt.

2. Place all of the remaining ingredients in a cocktail shaker, fill it two-thirds of the way with ice, and shake until chilled.

3. Strain into the rimmed glass and enjoy.

CHORIZO-WASHED MEZCAL

1. Place the chorizo in a dry skillet and cook over low heat to render the fat. When the chorizo is cooked through, remove it from the pan and use it in another preparation.

2. Place the rendered fat in a large mason jar. For every 2 oz. of fat, add a 750 ml bottle of mezcal. Let the mixture sit at room temperature for 12 hours.

3. Place the jar in the freezer for 6 to 8 hours.

4. Strain through a fine sieve or cheesecloth and use as desired.

CHARRED PINEAPPLE PUREE

1. Preheat a grill to medium heat (about 400°F). Place the pineapple on the grill and cook until charred on both sides, about 6 minutes.

2. Place the pineapple in a blender and pulse, adding water a tablespoon at a time until the texture of the puree is similar to applesauce. Use immediately or store in the refrigerator, where it will keep for up to 3 days.

INGREDIENTS:

	SALT, FOR THE RIM
1½	OZ. CHORIZO-WASHED MEZCAL (SEE RECIPE)
½	OZ. ANCHO REYES LIQUEUR
1	OZ. CHARRED PINEAPPLE PUREE (SEE RECIPE)
1	OZ. FRESH LIME JUICE
¾	OZ. SIMPLE SYRUP (SEE PAGE 665)
4-5	SPRIGS OF FRESH CILANTRO

CHORIZO-WASHED MEZCAL

8	OZ. MEXICAN CHORIZO
	MEZCAL, AS NEEDED

CHARRED PINEAPPLE PUREE

1	PINEAPPLE, PEELED, CORED, AND CUT INTO RINGS
	WATER, AS NEEDED

JAMAICA COLLINS

YIELD: 1 SERVING / **ACTIVE TIME:** 2 MINUTES / **TOTAL TIME:** 2 MINUTES

Agua fresca and a Tom Collins go together better than you ever imagined. Refreshing floral and botanical notes will carry you till the very last drop of this highball.

1. Place all of the ingredients, except for the Topo Chico and the garnish, in a cocktail shaker, add 2 ice cubes, and shake until the cubes have dissolved.

2. Add the seltzer to the shaker and pour the cocktail over ice into a double rocks glass.

3. Garnish with the lime wedge and enjoy.

JAMAICA SYRUP

1. Place the water in a saucepan and bring it to a boil.

2. Add the hibiscus flowers, salt, star anise, cinnamon stick, and clove and boil for 2 minutes. Reduce the heat and simmer for 10 minutes.

3. Remove the pan from heat, add the sugar, and stir until it has dissolved. Cover the pan and let it sit for 1 hour.

4. Strain before using or storing.

INGREDIENTS:

¾	OZ. JAMAICA SYRUP (SEE RECIPE)
1	OZ. FRESH LIME JUICE
1½	OZ. BOMBAY SAPPHIRE GIN
3	DROPS OF ROSEWATER
2	OZ. TOPO CHICO
1	LIME WEDGE, FOR GARNISH

JAMAICA SYRUP

2	CUPS WATER
1	CUP DRIED HIBISCUS FLOWERS
¼	TEASPOON KOSHER SALT
1	STAR ANISE POD
1	CINNAMON STICK
1	WHOLE CLOVE
2	CUPS SUGAR

EL CHAVO DEL OCHO

YIELD: 1 SERVING / ACTIVE TIME: 2 MINUTES / TOTAL TIME: 2 MINUTES

I'm sure you have had a whiskey sour, but how about a tequila sour? Texture is king in this tropical variation. Pair it with something spicy, or enjoy by itself.

1. Place all of the ingredients, except for the garnish, in a cocktail shaker, add 1 ice cube, and whip-shake until chilled.

2. Strain into a large coupe or a wine glass and garnish with the thyme.

THYME SYRUP

1. Place the sugar and water in a saucepan and bring to a boil, stirring to dissolve the sugar.

2. Add the thyme, remove the pan from heat, and let the syrup cool. Strain before using or storing.

INGREDIENTS:

2	OZ. TEQUILA OCHO BLANCO
½	OZ. LICOR 43
½	OZ. FRESH LIME JUICE
¾	OZ. PASSION FRUIT PUREE
½	OZ. THYME SYRUP (SEE RECIPE)
1	EGG WHITE
1	SPRIG OF FRESH THYME, FOR GARNISH

THYME SYRUP

1	CUP SUGAR
1	CUP WATER
3	SPRIGS OF FRESH THYME

MAYA GOLD

YIELD: 1 SERVING / **ACTIVE TIME:** 2 MINUTES / **TOTAL TIME:** 2 MINUTES

Welcome to the delicate side of mezcal. This light-bodied cocktail is truly a masterpiece.

1. Place all of the ingredients, except for the garnish, in a mixing glass, add ice, and stir until chilled.

2. Strain into a coupe and garnish with the lemon twist.

CHAMOMILE MEZCAL

1. Place the ingredients in a large mason jar and steep for 30 minutes to 1 hour, tasting the mixture every 5 minutes after the 30-minute mark to account for the varying results produced by different mezcals.

2. Strain before using or storing.

INGREDIENTS:

1½ OZ. CHAMOMILE MEZCAL INGREDIENTS AND PREP FOR THIS)

¾ OZ. FINO SHERRY

½ OZ. APEROL

½ OZ. YELLOW CHARTREUSE

1 LEMON TWIST, FOR GARNISH

CHAMOMILE MEZCAL

¼ CUP LOOSE-LEAF CHAMOMILE TEA

8 OZ. MEZCAL

CANOE CLUB

YIELD: 1 SERVING / **ACTIVE TIME:** 2 MINUTES / **TOTAL TIME:** 2 MINUTES

This cocktail brings out the delicate smoky notes of mezcal while staying tropical and fruity. A great drink for both mezcal lovers and those wanting to experiment more with the spirit.

1. Place all of the ingredients in a cocktail shaker and stir to combine. Fill the shaker two-thirds of the way with ice and shake until chilled.

2. Strain over ice into a rocks glass and enjoy.

GINGER & SERRANO SYRUP

1. Place all of the ingredients in a saucepan and bring to a boil, stirring to dissolve the sugar.

2. Remove from heat, let cool completely, and strain before using or storing.

INGREDIENTS:

1½	OZ. MEZCAL
½	OZ. CRÈME DE MURE
¾	OZ. GINGER & SERRANO SYRUP (SEE RECIPE)
½	OZ. FRESH LIME JUICE
3	DASHES OF PEYCHAUD'S BITTERS

GINGER & SERRANO SYRUP

1	CUP SUGAR
½	CUP WATER
3	SERRANO CHILE PEPPERS, SLICED
2	LARGE PIECES OF FRESH GINGER, CHOPPED

FLOR DE JALISCO

YIELD: 1 SERVING / **ACTIVE TIME:** 2 MINUTES / **TOTAL TIME:** 2 MINUTES

This creation strikes the perfect balance between sweet and smoky thanks to the strawberry jam.

1. Place all of the ingredients, except for the garnishes, in a cocktail shaker, fill it two-thirds of the way with ice, and shake until chilled.

2. Strain over ice into a rocks glass and garnish with pineapple leaves, a lime wheel, and a marigold blossom.

BLACK LAVA SOLUTION

1. Place the ingredients in a saucepan and bring the mixture to a boil, stirring until the salt has dissolved.

2. Remove the pan from heat and let it cool completely before serving.

INGREDIENTS:

1½	OZ. REPOSADO TEQUILA
½	OZ. MEZCAL
½	OZ. STRAWBERRY JAM
½	OZ. AGAVE NECTAR
½	OZ. FRESH LIME JUICE
	DASH OF BLACK LAVA SOLUTION (SEE RECIPE)
3	DASHES OF BITTERMENS HELLFIRE HABANERO SHRUB
2	PINEAPPLE LEAVES, FOR GARNISH
1	LIME WHEEL, FOR GARNISH
1	MARIGOLD BLOSSOM, FOR GARNISH

BLACK LAVA SOLUTION

½	CUP WATER
¼	CUP BLACK LAVA SALT

LAVAGAVE

YIELD: 1 SERVING / **ACTIVE TIME:** 2 MINUTES / **TOTAL TIME:** 2 MINUTES

A refreshingly tart cocktail that is made for those days where you can't seem to leave the shade.

1. Place all of the ingredients, except for the garnish, in a cocktail shaker, fill it two-thirds of the way with ice, and shake until chilled.

2. Strain, discard the ice in the shaker, return the cocktail to the shaker, and dry shake for 15 seconds.

3. Pour the drink into a coupe and garnish with grated lavender buds.

LAVENDER AGAVE

1. Place the lavender buds in a piece of cheesecloth and use kitchen twine to fashion a sachet.

2. Place the agave in a saucepan and bring it to a boil.

3. Remove the pan from heat, add the sachet, and let it steep for 2 hours. Remove the sachet before using or storing.

INGREDIENTS:

1½	OZ. TEQUILA
½	OZ. MEZCAL
¾	OZ. LAVENDER AGAVE (SEE RECIPE)
½	OZ. GRAPEFRUIT JUICE
½	OZ. FRESH LIME JUICE
¾	OZ. EGG WHITE
	DASH OF BITTERCUBE CHERRY BARK VANILLA BITTERS
	DRIED LAVENDER BUDS, GRATED, FOR GARNISH

LAVENDER AGAVE

1	TEASPOON DRIED LAVENDER BUDS
4	CUPS AGAVE NECTAR

BLACKER THE BERRY, THE SWEETER THE JUICE

YIELD: 1 SERVING / **ACTIVE TIME:** 2 MINUTES / **TOTAL TIME:** 2 MINUTES

This beauty sings with picante and sugary notes, and is perfect beside a simple dinner of tacos.

1. Place blackberries in a highball glass and muddle. Add crushed ice to the glass.

2. Place the mezcal, St-Germain, syrup, lime juice, and agave in a cocktail shaker, fill it two-thirds of the way with ice, and shake until chilled.

3. Strain into the highball glass and garnish with a lime wheel and sage leaves.

INGREDIENTS:

5	BLACKBERRIES
1½	OZ. MEZCAL
¾	OZ. ST-GERMAIN
½	OZ. GINGER SYRUP (SEE PAGE 767)
2	DASHES OF BITTERMENS HABANERO HELLFIRE SHRUB
¾	OZ. FRESH LIME JUICE
½	OZ. AGAVE NECTAR
1	LIME WHEEL, FOR GARNISH
2	FRESH SAGE LEAVES, FOR GARNISH

DRUNKEN RABBIT

YIELD: 1 SERVING / **ACTIVE TIME:** 2 MINUTES / **TOTAL TIME:** 2 MINUTES

If you can, serve these in an empty pineapple shell. If not, a tumbler or rocks glass will work.

1. Place all of the ingredients, except for the garnishes, in a blender with one scoop of crushed ice and puree until smooth.

2. Pour the cocktail into a pineapple shell, tumbler, or rocks glass and garnish with pineapple leaves, an orange slice, mint, and Tajín.

CINNAMON SYRUP

1. Place the sugar and water in a saucepan and bring to a boil, stirring to dissolve the sugar.

3. Add the cinnamon sticks, remove the pan from heat, and let the syrup cool completely. Strain before using or storing.

INGREDIENTS:

2   OZ. MEZCAL

1   OZ. ANCHO REYES

1½   OZ. PINEAPPLE JUICE

1½   OZ. GUAVA JUICE

1   OZ. CINNAMON SYRUP (SEE RECIPE)

     PINEAPPLE LEAVES, FOR GARNISH

1   ORANGE SLICE, FOR GARNISH

     FRESH MINT, FOR GARNISH

     TAJÍN, FOR GARNISH

CINNAMON SYRUP

1   CUP SUGAR

1   CUP WATER

3   CINNAMON STICKS

SHAKE YOUR TAMARIND

YIELD: 1 SERVING / **ACTIVE TIME:** 2 MINUTES / **TOTAL TIME:** 2 MINUTES

The tamarind brings some tangy notes that highlight the blend of tequila and mezcal.

1. Place all of the ingredients, except for the garnishes, in a mixing glass, fill it two-thirds of the way with ice, and stir until chilled.

2. Double-strain into a glass and garnish with mint leaves and a cinnamon stick.

INGREDIENTS:

1½	OZ. RESPOSADO TEQUILA
¼	OZ. MEZCAL
¼	OZ. CAMPARI
¾	OZ. TAMARIND CONCENTRATE
¾	OZ. CINNAMON SYRUP (SEE PAGE 706)
¼	OZ. FRESH LIME JUICE
	FRESH MINT, FOR GARNISH
1	CINNAMON STICK, FOR GARNISH

PINEAPPLE EXPRESS

YIELD: 1 SERVING / **ACTIVE TIME:** 2 MINUTES / **TOTAL TIME:** 2 MINUTES

Finished off with mezcal mist and fresh pineapple juice, this has the perfect amount of froth.

1. Place the tequila, agave, lime juice, and pineapple juice in a cocktail shaker, fill it two-thirds of the way with ice, and shake until chilled.

2. Double-strain over ice into a rocks glass.

3. Using a spray bottle filled with mezcal, mist the cocktail. Garnish with the salt and pineapple and enjoy.

THAI CHILI AGAVE

1. Place the chiles and water in a saucepan and bring to a boil.

2. Add the agave nectar and simmer the mixture for 1 hour.

3. Let the mixture cool completely. Strain before using or storing.

INGREDIENTS:

2	OZ. TEQUILA
1	OZ. THAI CHILE AGAVE (SEE RECIPE)
1	OZ. FRESH LIME JUICE
2	OZ. PINEAPPLE JUICE
	MEZCAL, TO MIST
	PINCH OF SALT, FOR GARNISH
1	PINEAPPLE RING, FOR GARNISH

THAI CHILE AGAVE

2	OZ. THAI CHILE PEPPERS
2	CUPS WATER
2	CUPS AGAVE NECTAR

BRUJERA

YIELD: 1 SERVING / **ACTIVE TIME:** 2 MINUTES / **TOTAL TIME:** 2 MINUTES

The marriage of tequila, salty, and spicy give this gorgeous cocktail a dynamic flavor profile. Activated charcoal can be purchased online. In this recipe, it is there for color only, so you can forgo it if you wish.

1. Place all of the ingredients, except for the garnish, in a mixing glass, fill it two-thirds of the way with ice, and stir until chilled.

2. Strain over a large ice cube into a rocks glass. Express the strip of orange peel over the cocktail and then use it as a garnish.

INGREDIENTS:

- 1½ OZ. REPOSADO TEQUILA
- ½ OZ. RUM
- 2 DASHES OF ANGOSTURA BITTERS
- ¼ OZ. AGAVE NECTAR

  DASH OF ACTIVATED CHARCOAL
- 1 STRIP OF ORANGE PEEL, FOR GARNISH

EL VATO SWIZZLE

YIELD: 1 SERVING / ACTIVE TIME: 2 MINUTES / TOTAL TIME: 2 MINUTES

An elevation of the Margarita that features fresh watermelon juice and the homemade Mexican pepper reduction.

1. Place the tequila, juices, reduction, and cilantro in a Pilsner glass, add some crushed ice, and use the swizzle method to combine. To use the swizzle method, place a swizzle stick between your palms and rub them together to rotate the stick, while also moving it up and down in the cocktail to aerate it.

2. Top with the bitters and more crushed ice. Garnish with a slice of watermelon and additional cilantro and enjoy.

MEXICAN PEPPER REDUCTION

1. Make sure to prepare this in a well-ventilated kitchen, as the fumes from cooking the reduction will make the air extremely peppery. Place all of the ingredients, except for the sugar, in a saucepan, bring to a boil, and cook for 20 minutes.

2. Strain into a mixing bowl, add the sugar, and stir until dissolved. Let the mixture cool completely before using or storing.

INGREDIENTS:

- 1½ OZ. TEQUILA
- 1 OZ. FRESH LIME JUICE
- ¾ OZ. FRESH WATERMELON JUICE
- ¾ OZ. MEXICAN PEPPER REDUCTION (SEE RECIPE)
- LARGE PINCH OF FRESH CILANTRO, PLUS MORE FOR GARNISH
- DASH OF PEYCHAUD'S BITTERS
- 1 SLICE OF WATERMELON, FOR GARNISH

MEXICAN PEPPER REDUCTION

- 4 CUPS WATER
- 2 DRIED CHILES DE ARBOL
- 2 ANCHO CHILE PEPPERS
- 1½ JALAPEÑO CHILE PEPPERS, SLICED LENGTHWISE
- 6 CUPS SUGAR

714 | MEXICAN FOOD

THE FIFTH ELEMENT

YIELD: 1 SERVING / **ACTIVE TIME:** 2 MINUTES / **TOTAL TIME:** 2 MINUTES

When tequila and avocado come together, you know you're in for a treat. This well-balanced cocktail has a wonderful mouthfeel and the striking color wows all who encounter it.

1. Wet the rim of a coupe and rim it with the Citrus Salt.

2. Place all of the remaining ingredients, except for the garnish, in a cocktail shaker, fill it two-thirds of the way with ice, and shake until chilled.

3. Strain into the coupe and garnish with the dehydrated lemon slice.

CITRUS SALT

1. Combine all of the ingredients in a mixing bowl and store in an airtight container.

AVOCADO MIX

1. Place all of the ingredients in a blender and puree until smooth.

INGREDIENTS:

	CITRUS SALT (SEE RECIPE), FOR THE RIM
2	OZ. TEQUILA
2	OZ. AVOCADO MIX (SEE RECIPE)
¾	OZ. FRESH LIME JUICE
½	OZ. AGAVE NECTAR
1	EGG WHITE
1	DEHYDRATED LEMON SLICE, FOR GARNISH

CITRUS SALT

	ZEST OF 2 LEMONS
	ZEST OF 2 LIMES
½	CUP KOSHER SALT

AVOCADO MIX

	FLESH OF 3 AVOCADOS
2	LBS. PINEAPPLE, PEELED AND CORED
12	OZ. FRESH CILANTRO

DESERT DAISY

YIELD: 1 SERVING / **ACTIVE TIME:** 2 MINUTES / **TOTAL TIME:** 2 MINUTES

A stunning, complex cocktail sure to wow anyone, even if you don't have the handblown glass in the picture.

1. Place all of the ingredients, except for the garnish, in a cocktail shaker, fill it two-thirds of the way with ice, and shake until chilled.

2. Strain over ice into a glass and garnish with an edible flower.

ORANGE BELL PEPPER & BEET SYRUP

1. Juice the pepper and beets separately. Strain the remaining pulp, pressing down on it to extract as much liquid as possible.

2. Place the juices and sugar in a saucepan and bring the mixture to a boil, stirring until the sugar has dissolved. Remove the pan from heat and let the syrup cool completely before using.

INGREDIENTS:

1½   OZ. TEQUILA

½   OZ. AVERNA AMARO

¾   OZ. FRESH LIME JUICE

¾   OZ. ORANGE BELL PEPPER & BEET SYRUP (SEE RECIPE)

4   DROPS OF SALINE SOLUTION (SEE PAGE 658)

10   DASHES OF BITTERMENS HELLFIRE HABANERO BITTERS

1   EDIBLE FLOWER, FOR GARNISH

ORANGE BELL PEPPER & BEET SYRUP

½   CUP CHOPPED ORANGE BELL PEPPER

½   CUP CHOPPED BEETS

1   CUP SUGAR

LA DIOSA

YIELD: 1 SERVING / **ACTIVE TIME:** 2 MINUTES / **TOTAL TIME:** 2 MINUTES

If you've yet to discover how well tropical fruit goes with a bit of chili powder and Tajín, allow this cocktail to usher you into your new obsession.

1. Place all of the ingredients, except for the egg white and garnishes, in a cocktail shaker, fill it two-thirds of the way with ice, and shake until chilled.

2. Strain, discard the ice, and return the mixture to the shaker. Add the egg white and dry shake for 15 seconds.

3. Strain into a coupe and garnish with the Tajín and flowers.

PINEAPPLE MARMALADE

1. Place all of the ingredients in a large saucepan and bring to a simmer. Simmer for 5 hours, until the liquid has reduced by at least half.

2. Remove the cinnamon sticks and chiles. Place the remaining mixture in a blender and puree until smooth. Let cool before using or storing.

INGREDIENTS:

- 1½ OZ. TEQUILA
- ¾ OZ. TRIPLE SEC
- ½ OZ. FRESH LIME JUICE
- 1 TABLESPOON PINEAPPLE MARMALADE (SEE RECIPE)
- ½ BAR SPOON CHILI POWDER

  SMALL BUNCH OF FRESH CILANTRO
- 1 EGG WHITE

  TAJÍN, FOR GARNISH

  EDIBLE FLOWERS, FOR GARNISH

PINEAPPLE MARMALADE

- 4 PINEAPPLES, PEELED, CORED, AND CUBED
- 8 CINNAMON STICKS
- ¼ CUP PURE VANILLA EXTRACT
- 4 ORANGE PEELS
- 2 GUAJILLO CHILIES, STEMMED AND SEEDED
- 1 CUP SWEET VERMOUTH
- 1 CUP LILLET
- 4 CUPS SUGAR

RISING SUN

YIELD: 1 SERVING / **ACTIVE TIME:** 2 MINUTES / **TOTAL TIME:** 2 MINUTES

An exceptional cocktail that is rolling with waves of flavor.

1. Rim a coupe with salt and place the cherry in the bottom of the glass.

2. Place the tequila, Chartreuse, and lime cordial in a cocktail shaker, fill it two-thirds of the way with ice, shake until chilled, and strain into the rimmed coupe.

3. Top with the sloe gin, allowing it to slowly filter through the cocktail.

INGREDIENTS:

SALT, FOR THE RIM

1   MARASCHINO CHERRY

1½   OZ. TEQUILA

⅔   OZ. YELLOW CHARTREUSE

½   OZ. LIME CORDIAL

1   BAR SPOON SLOE GIN

DONS OF SOUL

YIELD: 1 SERVING / **ACTIVE TIME:** 2 MINUTES / **TOTAL TIME:** 2 MINUTES

A cocktail so good that Jose Cuervo gave it a gold medal at its 2015 cocktail competition.

1. Place all of the ingredients, except for the garnish, in a blender and pulse until combined.

2. Strain the mixture into a cocktail shaker, fill it two-thirds of the way with ice, and shake until chilled.

3. Strain into a cocktail glass and garnish with the strip of lime peel.

INGREDIENTS:

1⅔ OZ. TEQUILA

1 OZ. FRESH TOMATO, CHOPPED

⅔ OZ. PAPRIKA

2 BAR SPOONS FRESH LIME JUICE

2 BAR SPOONS FRESH LEMON JUICE

1 BAR SPOON AGAVE NECTAR

¼ TEASPOON CHILI POWDER

PINCH OF PINK PEPPER

DASH OF BOB'S CORIANDER BITTERS

1 STRIP OF LIME PEEL, FOR GARNISH

HAY ZEUS

YIELD: 1 SERVING / **ACTIVE TIME:** 2 MINUTES / **TOTAL TIME:** 2 MINUTES

A cocktail that highlights those wonderful grassy, green, and vegetal vibes you get from high-land tequila and mezcal.

1. Place all of the ingredients, except for the garnish, in a cocktail shaker, fill it two-thirds of the way with ice, and shake until chilled.

2. Strain over a block of ice into a ceramic bowl or cup.

3. Garnish with the cornflower leaves.

ZEUS JUICE CORDIAL

1. Place the hay, celery juice, and caster sugar in a blender and pulse until combined.

2. Strain through cheesecloth and stir in the Simple Syrup, mezcal, wine, Saline Solution, and toasted coconut drops.

INGREDIENTS:

½ OZ. TEQUILA

½ OZ. FRESH LIME JUICE

1¾ OZ. ZEUS JUICE CORDIAL (SEE RECIPE)

CORNFLOWER LEAVES, FOR GARNISH

ZEUS JUICE CORDIAL

⅜ OZ. CRUSHED HAY

5¼ OZ. CELERY JUICE

3½ OZ. CASTER SUGAR

⅞ OZ. SIMPLE SYRUP (SEE PAGE 665)

8 OZ. MEZCAL

3½ OZ. GIK BLUE WINE

½ OZ. SALINE SOLUTION (SEE PAGE 658)

2 DROPS OF MSK TOASTED COCONUT FLAVOUR DROPS

SUNDAY MORNING COMING DOWN

YIELD: 1 SERVING / **ACTIVE TIME:** 2 MINUTES / **TOTAL TIME:** 2 MINUTES

This is a sipping drink designed with tequila lovers in mind. It's strong and citrusy while retaining a smooth, balanced flavor.

1. Place all of the ingredients, except for the garnish, in a mixing glass and fill it two-thirds of the way with ice. Using another, empty mixing glass, pour the cocktail back and forth between the glasses until combined.

2. Strain over two ice cubes into a cocktail glass. Express the strip of orange peel over the cocktail and use it as a garnish.

INGREDIENTS:

1⅜ OZ. TEQUILA

½ OZ. DRY VERMOUTH

⅜ OZ. APEROL

1 TEASPOON AGAVE NECTAR

5 DROPS OF CHILE PEPPER EXTRACT

1 STRIP OF ORANGE PEEL, FOR GARNISH

PEACH TEA

YIELD: 1 SERVING / **ACTIVE TIME:** 2 MINUTES / **TOTAL TIME:** 2 MINUTES

This recipe is for a single serving, but it is also a good batch cocktail, because of the preparation involved.

1. Add the ingredients, except for the club soda and garnish, to a highball glass filled with ice and stir until chilled.

2. Top with the club soda and garnish with the lemon wedge.

SILVER NEEDLE–INFUSED TEQUILA

1. Place the ingredients in a mason jar and steep for 24 hours.

2. Strain before using or storing.

PEACH CORDIAL

1. Place the peaches and pectin in a blender and puree for about 5 minutes.

2. Strain through a coffee filter, add the remaining ingredients, and stir until the sugar has dissolved.

INGREDIENTS:

½ OZ. SILVER NEEDLE–INFUSED TEQUILA (SEE RECIPE)

½ OZ. TEQUILA

¾ OZ. PEACH CORDIAL (SEE RECIPE)

1 DROP OF CLARY SAGE TINCTURE

DASH OF MERLET CRÈME DE PÊCHE

CLUB SODA, TO TOP

1 LEMON WEDGE, FOR GARNISH

SILVER NEEDLE–INFUSED TEQUILA

10½ OZ. TEQUILA

⅛ OZ. LOOSE-LEAF SILVER NEEDLE TEA

PEACH CORDIAL

4½ LBS. PEACHES, PITTED

2 TEASPOONS PECTIN

53 OZ. CASTER SUGAR

1 OZ. CITRIC ACID

10 DROPS OF GALBANUM TINCTURE

CHAMPAGNE PALOMA

YIELD: 1 SERVING / **ACTIVE TIME:** 2 MINUTES / **TOTAL TIME:** 2 MINUTES

A delicious, sparkling variation on the beloved classic.

1. Place the tequila, juice blend, and syrup in a mixing glass, fill it two-thirds of the way with ice, and stir until chilled.

2. Strain into a champagne flute, top with the Champagne, and garnish with the grapefruit twist.

INGREDIENTS:

¾   OZ. TEQUILA

2½   OZ. PINK-AND-WHITE GRAPEFRUIT JUICE BLEND (1:1 RATIO)

DASH OF CINNAMON SYRUP (SEE PAGE 706)

CHAMPAGNE, TO TOP

1   GRAPEFRUIT TWIST, FOR GARNISH

DIABLO OTOÑO

YIELD: 1 SERVING / ACTIVE TIME: 2 MINUTES / TOTAL TIME: 2 MINUTES

A light but surprisingly complex drink, thanks to the fig cordial and the slight bitterness added by the tonic.

1. Add all of the ingredients, except for the tonic water, to a highball glass containing three ice spheres and stir until chilled.

2. Top with the tonic water.

FIG CORDIAL

1. Preheat the oven to 350°F. Place the figs on a parchment-lined baking sheet, cover them with the honey, and then sprinkle the walnuts around the pan. Bake for 10 minutes.

2. Pour all of the Fig Leaf Syrup in a saucepan and warm it over medium heat. When the figs are done, add them to the syrup and simmer for 10 minutes.

3. Strain, stir in the citric acid and Rosé, and let cool completely before using or storing.

FIG LEAF SYRUP

1. Place the fig leaves in a container and pour the syrup over them. Steep for 30 minutes.

2. Strain before using or storing.

INGREDIENTS:

1	OZ. TEQUILA
1	OZ. FIG CORDIAL (SEE RECIPE)
1	TEASPOON FIG LIQUEUR
	TONIC WATER, TO TOP

FIG CORDIAL

15	FIGS, QUARTERED
3½	OZ. HONEY
1¾	OZ. WALNUTS
	FIG LEAF SYRUP (SEE RECIPE)
1	TABLESPOON CITRIC ACID
7	OZ. ROSÉ

FIG LEAF SYRUP

30	FIG LEAVES
3	CUPS SIMPLE SYRUP (SEE PAGE 665), WARM

LOST IN THE RAIN IN JUÁREZ

YIELD: 1 SERVING / ACTIVE TIME: 2 MINUTES / TOTAL TIME: 2 MINUTES

A cocktail that can brighten even the darkest days.

1. Place all of the ingredients, except for the garnish, in a cocktail shaker and dry shake for 15 seconds.

2. Add ice and shake until chilled.

3. Double-strain into a coupe and garnish with the chunk of dehydrated pineapple.

RICH DEMERARA SYRUP

1. Place the ingredients in a saucepan and bring to a boil, stirring to dissolve the sugar.

2. Let cool before using or storing.

INGREDIENTS:

1   OZ. MEZCAL

¾   OZ. APEROL

⅞   OZ. FRESH LIME JUICE

½   OZ. RICH DEMERARA
        SYRUP (SEE RECIPE)

1¼   OZ. PINEAPPLE JUICE

3   DASHES OF ABSINTHE

1   EGG WHITE

1   DEHYDRATED PINEAPPLE
        CHUNK, FOR GARNISH

RICH DEMERARA SYRUP

2   CUPS DEMERARA SUGAR

1   CUP WATER

UNSCALPE

YIELD: 1 SERVING / **ACTIVE TIME:** 2 MINUTES / **TOTAL TIME:** 2 MINUTES

This follows a fairly typical bittersweet blueprint for an aperitivo cocktail. However, this one has a subtle, smoky twist, courtesy of the mezcal and the unique Islay Cask bitters.

1. Place the mezcal, bitters, and Aperol in a mixing glass, fill it two-thirds of the way with ice, and stir until chilled.

2. Strain into a goblet and garnish with the strip of orange peel.

INGREDIENTS:

1½ OZ. MEZCAL

1 OZ. KAMM & SONS ISLAY CASK

1 OZ. APEROL

1 STRIP OF ORANGE PEEL, FOR GARNISH

PIÑA FUMADA

YIELD: 1 SERVING / **ACTIVE TIME:** 2 MINUTES / **TOTAL TIME:** 2 MINUTES

Sharp, smoky, honey-sweet, and very unique in overall flavor, this puts a refreshing tiki twist on a Mexican staple.

1. Place all of the ingredients, except for the club soda and garnishes, in a cocktail shaker, fill it two-thirds of the way with ice, and shake until chilled.

2. Strain over crushed ice into a highball glass and top with the club soda.

3. Add more crushed ice, garnish with the pineapple leaf and lemon wedges, and enjoy.

INGREDIENTS:

1¼	OZ. MEZCAL
¾	OZ. FRESH LEMON JUICE
2	TEASPOONS VELVET FALERNUM
½	OZ. HONEY
	CLUB SODA, TO TOP
1	PINEAPPLE LEAF, FOR GARNISH
1	LEMON WEDGE, FOR GARNISH

MEZCAL SURVIVOR

YIELD: 1 SERVING / **ACTIVE TIME:** 2 MINUTES / **TOTAL TIME:** 2 MINUTES

You'll still feel the smokiness of the mezcal, but it interacts beautifully with the other ingredients.

1. Place the mezcal, Cocchi Americano, syrup, and lemon juice in a cocktail shaker, fill it two-thirds of the way with ice, and shake until chilled.

2. Strain into a cocktail glass and mist the cocktail with absinthe. If desired, light it on fire and then garnish with the maraschino cherries, speared on a toothpick.

LIME SYRUP

1. While the syrup is still warm, stir in the lime zest and lime juice. Steep for 15 minutes.

2. Strain and let cool completely before using.

INGREDIENTS:

1¾ OZ. MEZCAL

⅞ OZ. COCCHI AMERICANO

¾ OZ. LIME SYRUP (SEE RECIPE)

⅞ OZ. FRESH LEMON JUICE

ABSINTHE, TO MIST

3 MARASCHINO CHERRIES, FOR GARNISH

LIME SYRUP

RICH DEMERARA SYRUP (SEE PAGE 737)

ZEST OF 3 LIMES

1 CUP FRESH LIME JUICE

CANTARITOS

YIELD: 1 SERVING / **ACTIVE TIME:** 2 MINUTES / **TOTAL TIME:** 2 MINUTES

In Jalisco, Mexico, this drink would be mixed and imbibed in a charming clay pot like the one in the photo. A Cantaritos is so refreshing that this delightful touch isn't essential, but it can't be argued that a Collins glass carries the same charm.

1. Add the ingredients, except for the garnish, to a Collins glass filled with ice in the order they are listed.

2. Gently stir to combine and garnish with the lime wedge.

INGREDIENTS:

2	OZ. REPOSADO TEQUILA
1½	OZ. FRESH ORANGE JUICE
¾	OZ. FRESH PINK GRAPEFRUIT JUICE
½	OZ. FRESH LIME JUICE
2	PINCHES OF SALT
2	OZ. PINK GRAPEFRUIT SODA
1	LIME WEDGE, FOR GARNISH

NAKED & FAMOUS

YIELD: 1 SERVING / **ACTIVE TIME:** 2 MINUTES / **TOTAL TIME:** 2 MINUTES

The salmon pink color is a bit deceptive, as the drink is smoky thanks to the mezcal and bittersweet thanks to the Aperol.

1. Chill a coupe in the freezer.

2. Place all of the ingredients in a cocktail shaker, fill the shaker two-thirds of the way with ice, and shake until chilled.

3. Strain into the chilled coupe.

INGREDIENTS:

¾   OZ. MEZCAL

¾   OZ. YELLOW CHARTREUSE

¾   OZ. APEROL

¾   OZ. FRESH LIME JUICE

KINDA KNEW ANNA

YIELD: 1 SERVING / **ACTIVE TIME:** 2 MINUTES / **TOTAL TIME:** 2 MINUTES

Don't mistake crème de mure as some exotic ingredient—it's simply blackberry liqueur.

1. Place the tequila, liqueur, and lime juice in a cocktail shaker, fill it two-thirds of the way with ice, and shake until chilled.

2. Strain over ice into a double rocks glass, top with the ginger beer, and garnish with the sage leaf.

INGREDIENTS:

1	OZ. TEQUILA
1	OZ. CRÈME DE MURE
1	OZ. FRESH LIME JUICE
2	OZ. GINGER BEER
1	SAGE LEAF, FOR GARNISH

JALISCO SOUR

YIELD: 1 SERVING / **ACTIVE TIME:** 2 MINUTES / **TOTAL TIME:** 2 MINUTES

Slipping a bit of tequila into a Pisco Sour adds considerable depth to the beguiling classic.

1. Place the tequila, pisco, lime juice, and syrup in a cocktail shaker, fill it two-thirds of the way with crushed ice, and shake until chilled.

2. Strain into a coupe and garnish with the bitters.

INGREDIENTS:

1 OZ. TEQUILA

1 OZ. PISCO

¾ OZ. FRESH LIME JUICE

¾ OZ. SIMPLE SYRUP (SEE PAGE 665)

3 DASHES OF ANGOSTURA BITTERS, FOR GARNISH

SHE'S A RAINBOW

YIELD: 1 SERVING / **ACTIVE TIME:** 2 MINUTES / **TOTAL TIME:** 2 MINUTES

If you remember Midori as being too sweet, you should try it again. Suntory has recently cut back the sugar content by 20 percent.

1. Place the ingredients in a cocktail shaker, fill it two-thirds of the way with ice, and shake until chilled.

2. Strain over ice into a highball glass and garnish with the slice of grapefruit.

INGREDIENTS:

2	OZ. TEQUILA
1	OZ. MIDORI
5	OZ. WHITE GRAPEFRUIT JUICE
1	GRAPEFRUIT SLICE, FOR GARNISH

TRUE ROMANCE

YIELD: 1 SERVING / **ACTIVE TIME:** 2 MINUTES / **TOTAL TIME:** 2 MINUTES

Fresh, zesty, and bittersweet, this one is love at first sight.

1. Place the mezcal, Chartreuse, and amaro in a rocks glass containing one large ice cube and stir until chilled.

2. Garnish with the lime twist and the pinch of sea salt.

INGREDIENTS:

1½ OZ. MEZCAL

1 OZ. YELLOW CHARTREUSE

¾ OZ. AVERNA AMARO

1 LIME TWIST, FOR GARNISH

PINCH OF SEA SALT, FOR GARNISH

FIRE WALK WITH ME

YIELD: 1 SERVING / **ACTIVE TIME:** 2 MINUTES / **TOTAL TIME:** 2 MINUTES

A damn fine cocktail that has many more faces and facets than it appears.

1. Place the lime juice, orgeat, and jalapeño in a cocktail shaker and muddle.

2. Add ice, the tequila, and falernum and shake until chilled.

3. Strain into a coupe, garnish with the strip of orange peel, and enjoy.

INGREDIENTS:

½ OZ. FRESH LIME JUICE

½ OZ. ORGEAT

2 SLICES OF JALAPEÑO CHILE PEPPER

2 OZ. REPOSADO TEQUILA

½ OZ. FALERNUM

1 STRIP OF ORANGE PEEL, FOR GARNISH.

PAN

YIELD: 1 SERVING / **ACTIVE TIME:** 2 MINUTES / **TOTAL TIME:** 2 MINUTES

A beautiful drink that should be reserved for moments of extreme revelry.

1. Place the tequila, vermouth, syrup, and puree in a cocktail shaker, fill it two-thirds of the way with ice, and shake until chilled.

2. Strain into a goblet and garnish with the dill and ginger.

LEMONGRASS SYRUP

1. Place the ingredients in a saucepan and bring to a boil, stirring to dissolve the sugar.

2. Remove from heat, let cool completely, and strain before using or storing.

INGREDIENTS:

1	OZ. TEQUILA
⅓	OZ. DRY VERMOUTH
⅓	OZ. LEMONGRASS SYRUP (SEE RECIPE)
⅔	OZ. PEAR PUREE
1	SPRIG OF FRESH DILL, FOR GARNISH
1	PIECE OF FRESH GINGER, FOR GARNISH

LEMONGRASS SYRUP

1	CUP WATER
1	CUP SUGAR
3	LEMONGRASS STALKS, PEELED AND BRUISED

MÁMÙ VIDA

YIELD: 1 SERVING / **ACTIVE TIME:** 2 MINUTES / **TOTAL TIME:** 2 MINUTES

When eaten, the Szechuan flower provokes a multisensory experience, including mouth tingling, numbness, and increased salivation, making it an unusual, yet exciting surprise in the drink.

1. Place the honey, lemon juice, and mezcal in a cocktail shaker, fill it two-thirds of the way with ice, and shake until chilled.

2. Strain over ice into a double rocks glass and garnish with the Szechuan flower and pinch of salt.

SZECHUAN & CHIPOTLE HONEY

1. Place the Szechuan peppercorns in a saucepan and toast until fragrant.

2. Add the chiles and water and bring to a boil. Reduce the heat and simmer for 5 minutes.

3. Strain, add the honey, and stir until combined. Let cool completely before using or storing.

INGREDIENTS:

- ¾ OZ. SZECHUAN & CHIPOTLE HONEY (SEE RECIPE)
- ¾ OZ. FRESH LEMON JUICE
- 2 OZ. MEZCAL
- 1 SZECHUAN FLOWER, FOR GARNISH
- PINCH OF FLAKY SEA SALT, FOR GARNISH

SZECHUAN & CHIPOTLE HONEY

- ½ OZ. SZECHUAN PEPPERCORNS
- 4½ OZ. CHIPOTLE MECO CHILE PEPPERS, TORN
- 2 CUPS WATER
- 2 CUPS HONEY

LA SANTA

YIELD: 1 SERVING / **ACTIVE TIME:** 2 MINUTES / **TOTAL TIME:** 2 MINUTES

If a verde agua fresca had a sophisticated, sober cousin, this would be it. So perfectly balanced you'll forget it doesn't have alcohol.

1. Place the cucumber and lime juice in a cocktail shaker and muddle.

2. Add the remaining ingredients and 2 to 3 ice cubes and shake until chilled.

3. Strain over ice into a Collins glass and garnish with an additional slice of cucumber.

SNAP PEA SYRUP

1. Place the ingredients in a mason jar and shake until the sugar has dissolved. You do not want to heat the syrup, as it will negatively impact the flavor of the fresh juice. Use immediately or store in the refrigerator, where it will keep for up to 1 day.

INGREDIENTS:

- 4 SLICES OF CUCUMBER, PLUS MORE FOR GARNISH
- 2 OZ. FRESH LIME JUICE
- 4 OZ. GREEN APPLE JUICE
- 1¼ OZ. SNAP PEA SYRUP INGREDIENTS AND PREP FOR THIS)
- ½ OZ. SIMPLE SYRUP (SEE PAGE 665)
- 4 SMALL PIECES OF HOJA SANTA

SNAP PEA SYRUP

- ½ FRESH SNAP PEA JUICE
- ½ CUP CASTER SUGAR

LA CURA

YIELD: 1 SERVING / **ACTIVE TIME:** 2 MINUTES / **TOTAL TIME:** 2 MINUTES

If Abuelita's cold remedy was a nonalcoholic cocktail. If you're feeling good and tempted to turn this into nightcap, add 2 oz. of tequila.

1. Place all of the ingredients in a cocktail shaker, add 1 ice cube, and whip-shake until chilled.

2. Pour the cocktail into a Collins glass, add more ice, and garnish with additional mint.

GINGER SYRUP

1. Place the sugar and water in a saucepan and bring to a boil, stirring to dissolve the sugar.

2. Add the ginger and cook for another minute.

3. Remove the pan from heat and let the syrup cool. Strain before using or storing.

INGREDIENTS:

4	OZ. MINT ICED TEA
½	OZ. GINGER SYRUP (SEE RECIPE)
½	OZ. SIMPLE SYRUP (SEE PAGE 665), MADE WITH HONEY
1	OZ. FRESH LEMON JUICE
6	SPRIGS OF FRESH MINT, PLUS MORE FOR GARNISH

GINGER SYRUP

1	CUP SUGAR
1	CUP WATER
	2-INCH PIECE OF FRESH GINGER, SLICED

HORCHATA

YIELD: 6 SERVINGS / **ACTIVE TIME:** 1 HOUR / **TOTAL TIME:** 24 HOURS

Any long-grain rice will work, but an offering from Mahatma seems to produce the best results.

1. Place the rice in a large skillet and toast over medium heat until fragrant and lightly browned, about 15 minutes, stirring frequently. Let the rice cool completely; if immersed in water while hot, the rice will cook and become too mushy.

2. Transfer the rice to a large container and cover it with the water. Add the cinnamon sticks, cover the container with a linen towel, and let the mixture sit at room temperature overnight.

3. Add the mixture to a blender in batches and pulse 10 times. You want to break the rice down, not completely pulverize it. Strain the mixture through a fine-mesh sieve, pressing down on the solids to extract as much liquid and flavor as possible.

4. Add the condensed milk, coconut milk, and cinnamon and stir until incorporated. Add simple syrup to taste and refrigerate until cold.

INGREDIENTS:

4¼ CUPS LONG-GRAIN RICE

8½ CUPS WATER

6 CINNAMON STICKS

1 (14 OZ.) CAN OF SWEETENED CONDENSED MILK

1 (14 OZ.) CAN OF COCONUT MILK

1 TEASPOON CINNAMON

SIMPLE SYRUP (SEE PAGE 665), TO TASTE

CORNCHATA

YIELD: 6 SERVINGS / **ACTIVE TIME:** 10 MINUTES / **TOTAL TIME:** 45 MINUTES

Lori Sauer: "This drink was, obviously, inspired by the traditional horchata. It happened to be corn season, and I really wanted to try it out." Per usual, Lori's willingness to experiment paid off handsomely.

1. Place all of the ingredients in a blender and puree until smooth.

2. Strain the mixture into a container, pressing down on the solids to extract as much liquid as possible. Chill in the refrigerator for 30 minutes and serve over ice.

INGREDIENTS:

4	CUPS CORN
1½	CUPS WATER
2	TABLESPOONS SUGAR
3	PINCHES OF CINNAMON

HORCHATA CON RUM

YIELD: 1 SERVING / ACTIVE TIME: 2 MINUTES / TOTAL TIME: 2 MINUTES

Any spirit can be used here, but rum is best with the creamy and nutty qualities of horchata.

1. Place the Horchata and rum in a cocktail shaker, add ice, and shake until chilled.

2. Strain over crushed ice into a Collins glass, grate some of the cinnamon stick over the top, and garnish the cocktail with it and the lime zest.

INGREDIENTS:

¾ OZ. HORCHATA (SEE PAGE 768)

2 OZ. RUM

1 CINNAMON STICK, FOR GARNISH

ZEST OF 1 LIME, FOR GARNISH

HORCHATA CON ESPRESSO

YIELD: 1 SERVING / **ACTIVE TIME:** 2 MINUTES / **TOTAL TIME:** 2 MINUTES

Iced is best here, but if you are fortunate enough to have an espresso machine with a good steam wand, don't hesitate to turn this into a latte.

1. Pour the horchata over ice into a glass. Add the syrup and stir until combined.

2. Pour the espresso over the back of a spoon to float it on top.

VANILLA SYRUP

1. Place the ingredients in a saucepan and bring to a boil, stirring to dissolve the sugar.

2. Remove from heat, let cool completely, and strain before using or storing.

INGREDIENTS:

8   OZ. HORCHATA (SEE PAGE 768)

     VANILLA SYRUP, TO TASTE (SEE RECIPE)

2   OZ. FRESHLY BREWED ESPRESSO

VANILLA SYRUP

1   CUP WATER

1   CUP SUGAR

3   VANILLA BEANS, SPLIT

XOCOLATL

YIELD: 4 SERVINGS / **ACTIVE TIME**: 10 MINUTES / **TOTAL TIME**: 10 MINUTES

X ocolatl is a slightly bitter, spiced chocolate drink that can be served hot or cold. It dates back to the Mayans, who served it to warriors for energy.

1. Place the milk in a small saucepan and warm over medium heat.

2. When the milk starts to simmer, add the chocolate. Stir until the chocolate has melted, making sure the mixture does not come to a boil.

3. Pour the mixture into a blender and puree until frothy. Pour into mugs and enjoy.

INGREDIENTS:

4   CUPS MILK

6   OZ. MEXICAN CHOCOLATE, CHOPPED

AGUA DE MELON

YIELD: 4 TO 6 SERVINGS / **ACTIVE TIME:** 10 MINUTES / **TOTAL TIME:** 10 MINUTES

Agua frescas are beloved throughout Mexico. This sweet melon water is best served cold over ice.

1. Cut the melon into quarters and remove the rind.

2. Place half of the melon, water, and honey in a blender and puree until smooth.

3. Strain through a fine-mesh sieve into a pitcher.

4. Place the remaining melon, water, and honey in the blender, puree until smooth, and strain into the pitcher.

5. Stir until thoroughly combined and serve over ice.

INGREDIENTS:

1 WHOLE CANTALOUPE OR HONEYDEW MELON, HALVED AND SEEDED

6 CUPS WATER

1 TABLESPOON HONEY

AGUA DE TAMARINDO

YIELD: 4 TO 6 SERVINGS / **ACTIVE TIME:** 1 HOUR / **TOTAL TIME:** 4 HOURS

Tamarind originated in parts of Asia and Africa, but it is widely used in Mexican kitchens. It has a beguiling flavor that changes as it moves across the tongue, shifting from sour to sweet.

1. Place half of the water in a medium saucepan and bring it to a boil.

2. Remove the tamarind from its shells, remove the strings, and discard.

3. Add the tamarind, sugar, and brown sugar to the boiling water. Reduce the heat and simmer for 20 minutes.

4. Turn off the heat and let the mixture steep for 2 hours.

5. Once the mixture has cooled, use your hands to remove the tamarind seeds, and squeeze the pulp back into the mixture.

6. Place the mixture in a blender and puree until smooth.

7. Strain the puree through a fine sieve. Add the remaining water and stir to combine.

8. Chill in the refrigerator for 1 hour and serve over ice.

INGREDIENTS:

8	CUPS WATER
15	TAMARIND PODS
¾	CUP SUGAR
¼	CUP BROWN SUGAR

AGUA DE JAMAICA

YIELD: 4 TO 6 SERVINGS / **ACTIVE TIME:** 15 MINUTES / **TOTAL TIME:** 2 HOURS

This sweet and tangy hibiscus flower (jamaica) water is the perfect beverage during a barbecue, where its refreshing essence leavens the effects of the sun and heavy foods.

1. Place all of the ingredients in a saucepan and bring to a boil, stirring to dissolve the sugar.

2. Reduce the heat and simmer for 20 minutes.

3. Remove the pan from heat and let cool completely.

4. Strain through a fine-mesh sieve and refrigerate for at least 1 hour before serving over ice.

INGREDIENTS:

2	CUPS HIBISCUS BLOSSOMS
½	OZ. CINNAMON STICKS, CRUSHED
	PINCH OF CARDAMOM
2	WHOLE CLOVES
4	ALLSPICE BERRIES
½	CUP SUGAR
12	CUPS WATER

ATOLE

YIELD: 6 SERVINGS / **ACTIVE TIME:** 30 MINUTES / **TOTAL TIME:** 30 MINUTES

Piloncillo is an unrefined cane sugar mainly found in Mexico that is treasured for its rich, caramel-like flavor.

1. Place the milk, piloncillo, and cinnamon stick in a medium saucepan and cook over medium-low heat, stirring until the piloncillo has dissolved. Remove from heat, strain the mixture, and set it aside.

2. Combine the warm water and masa in a bowl and whisk until smooth. Place the mixture in the saucepan and stir in the milk mixture, vanilla, and salt.

3. Bring the mixture to a simmer, stirring constantly. Reduce the heat and cook until the mixture has thickened and is smooth and velvety. Pour into mugs and sprinkle a little cinnamon on top.

INGREDIENTS:

4   CUPS MILK

4   OZ. PILONCILLO

1   CINNAMON STICK

1½ CUPS WARM WATER (105°F)

½   CUP MASA HARINA

2   TEASPOONS MEXICAN VANILLA EXTRACT

    PINCH OF KOSHER SALT

    CINNAMON, FOR GARNISH

CHAMPURRADO

YIELD: 6 SERVINGS / **ACTIVE TIME:** 30 MINUTES / **TOTAL TIME:** 30 MINUTES

This drink and the Atole on page 787 are also wonderful poured over a scoop of ice cream.

1. Place the milk, piloncillo, cinnamon stick, and chocolate in a medium saucepan and cook over medium-low heat, stirring until the piloncillo has dissolved. Remove from heat, strain the mixture, and set it aside.

2. Combine the warm water and masa in a bowl and whisk until smooth. Place the mixture in the saucepan and stir in the milk mixture, vanilla, and salt.

3. Bring the mixture to a simmer, stirring constantly. Reduce the heat and cook until the mixture has thickened and is smooth and velvety. Pour into mugs and sprinkle a little cinnamon on top.

INGREDIENTS:

4   CUPS MILK

4   OZ. PILONCILLO

1   CINNAMON STICK

6   OZ. MEXICAN CHOCOLATE

1½   CUPS WARM WATER (105°F)

½   CUP MASA HARINA

2   TEASPOONS MEXICAN VANILLA EXTRACT

     PINCH OF KOSHER SALT

     CINNAMON, FOR GARNISH

TEJUINO

YIELD: 32 SERVINGS / **ACTIVE TIME:** 10 MINUTES / **TOTAL TIME:** 4 TO 7 DAYS

This fermented beverage is perfect to make when you look at the weather and see a heat wave on the horizon.

INGREDIENTS:

32	CUPS WATER
10	OZ. PILONCILLO
1	CINNAMON STICK
1	LB. PREPARED MASA (SEE PAGE 352)
	SIMPLE SYRUP (SEE PAGE 665), TO TASTE
1	CUP FRESH LIME JUICE
	SALT, FOR SERVING
	LIME WEDGES, FOR SERVING

1. Place the water, piloncillo, and cinnamon stick in a large saucepan and bring to a simmer, whisking to dissolve the piloncillo.

2. Whisk in the masa and remove the pan from heat.

3. Pour the mixture into a large glass container, cover with cheesecloth, and secure it with a rubber band. Let the mixture ferment at room temperature for 4 days.

4. Taste the tejuino. The flavor should be slightly sour and sweet, with the aroma of sourdough. If desired, add simple syrup to taste. If you want a more robust fermented taste, let the tejuino ferment for another 3 days.

5. Add the lime juice and ice and stir to incorporate. Serve over crushed ice with salt (a pinch per glass should be the right amount) and lime wedges. The tejuino will keep in the refrigerator for up to 2 weeks.

PINEAPPLE TEPACHE KOMBUCHA

YIELD: 6 SERVINGS / **ACTIVE TIME:** 10 MINUTES / **TOTAL TIME:** 5 TO 10 DAYS

This carbonated drink is a take on the traditional tepache beverage, which came about in pre-Hispanic Mexico. Before the use of pineapple for tepache, maize was the core of the drink. It is best enjoyed cold.

1. While wearing gloves, combine the water and syrup in a large mason jar. Add the SCOBY liquid and make sure that the pH level of the mixture is under 4.2. Add more SCOBY liquid if needed.

2. Add the SCOBY, cover the container with a paper towel, and secure it with a rubber band. Let the mixture ferment for 5 to 10 days, tasting the kombucha every day to see if the flavor has developed to your liking.

3. Bottle once you are happy with the flavor.

TEPACHE SYRUP

1. Place all of the ingredients, except for the brown sugar, in a large container and stir to combine.

2. Cover the container with a paper towel, secure the paper towel with a rubber band, and let the mixture ferment for 4 to 5 days at room temperature.

3. Strain and place the liquid in a saucepan. Cook over medium heat until it has reduced by half.

4. Add the brown sugar and continue to cook, stirring to dissolve the sugar, until approximately 4 cups of syrup remain.

5. Remove the syrup from heat and let cool before using or storing. While this is intended for use in the kombucha, it is also lovely over pancakes and waffles.

INGREDIENTS:

12	CUPS WATER
13½	OZ. TEPACHE SYRUP (SEE RECIPE)
21	OZ. SCOBY LIQUID (STARTER KOMBUCHA)
	5-7 INCH SCOBY

TEPACHE SYRUP

1	PINEAPPLE, CHOPPED
8	WHOLE CLOVES
10	ALLSPICE BERRIES
1	CINNAMON STICK, TORCHED
5	DRIED CHILES DE ARBOL
3	BAY LEAVES, CRUSHED
20	CUPS WATER
2	TABLESPOONS BLACK PEPPERCORNS, TOASTED
21	OZ. BROWN SUGAR

TEPACHE DE PIÑA

YIELD: 6 TO 8 SERVINGS / **ACTIVE TIME:** 15 MINUTES / **TOTAL TIME:** 4 TO 7 DAYS

This fermented beverage uses the whole pineapple to create a refreshing and salubrious tonic.

INGREDIENTS:

32	CUPS WATER
4	OZ. PILONCILLO
1	LARGE STICK OF MEXICAN CINNAMON
3	WHOLE CLOVES
1	PINEAPPLE

1. Place half of the water, the piloncillo, cinnamon, and cloves in a large saucepan and warm over medium heat, stirring to dissolve the sugar.

2. Cut the top and bottom off of the pineapple and rinse it well. Cut it into 4-inch pieces, leaving the skin on. Place the chopped pineapple in the warm liquid and turn off the heat.

3. Strain the liquid into a bowl. Place the pineapple in a large, 3- to 4-gallon glass jar or vessel and add the remaining water along with the warm syrup and spices. Use a plate to keep the pineapple submerged in the liquid and cover the container with cheesecloth. Hold the cheesecloth in place with a rubber band or tie.

4. Let the pineapple ferment for anywhere from 4 to 7 days, depending on the time of the year. Hotter months will result in a faster ferment and therefore less time is necessary. Colder months may require 7 days to fully ferment. While wearing a pair of gloves, gently stir the contents of the jar with your hands each day.

5. Fermenting should begin the second day, and bubbling or foaming inside the container is perfectly normal. You will begin to sense a sweet and sour smell emanating from the mixture.

6. As the fourth day approaches, taste the beverage. It should taste similar to a pineapple mineral water, and should have developed tiny bubbles and gas. If mold begins to form on the side of the jar at any point, do not drink any of the liquid and discard it.

7. When the tepache is fully fermented and the desired taste has been reached, strain the liquid and reserve in the refrigerator. Serve over ice on its own, or with your favorite tequila or mezcal.

NOTE: Tepache can be made with other fruits if pineapple is not available.

MEXICAN HOT CHOCOLATE

YIELD: 4 SERVINGS / **ACTIVE TIME:** 15 MINUTES / **TOTAL TIME:** 15 MINUTES

Incorporating a bit of spice into a simple cup of hot chocolate will wake up more than just the drink.

1. Place the milk, half-and-half, cinnamon sticks, and chile in a saucepan and warm it over medium-low heat for 5 to 6 minutes, making sure the mixture does not come to a boil. When the mixture starts to steam, remove the cinnamon sticks and chile.

2. Add the sweetened condensed milk and whisk until combined. Add the chocolate chips and cook, stirring occasionally, until they have melted. Stir in the vanilla, nutmeg, and salt.

3. Ladle into warmed mugs and top with whipped cream.

INGREDIENTS:

- 3   CUPS WHOLE MILK
- 1   CUP HALF-AND-HALF
- 3   CINNAMON STICKS
- 1   RED CHILE PEPPER, STEMMED AND SEEDED
- ¼   CUP SWEETENED CONDENSED MILK
- 1½   LBS. SEMISWEET CHOCOLATE CHIPS
- ½   TEASPOON PURE VANILLA EXTRACT
- 1   TEASPOON FRESHLY GRATED NUTMEG
- ½   TEASPOON FINE SEA SALT
-    WHIPPED CREAM, FOR GARNISH

CONVERSION TABLE

WEIGHTS

1 oz. = 28 grams
2 oz. = 57 grams
4 oz. (¼ lb.) = 113 grams
8 oz. (½ lb.) = 227 grams
16 oz. (1 lb.) = 454 grams

VOLUME MEASURES

⅛ teaspoon = 0.6 ml
¼ teaspoon = 1.23 ml
½ teaspoon = 2.5 ml
1 teaspoon = 5 ml
1 tablespoon (3 teaspoons) = ½ fluid oz. = 15 ml
2 tablespoons = 1 fluid oz. = 29.5 ml
¼ cup (4 tablespoons) = 2 fluid oz. = 59 ml
⅓ cup (5 ⅓ tablespoons) = 2.7 fluid oz. = 80 ml
½ cup (8 tablespoons) = 4 fluid oz. = 120 ml
⅔ cup (10 ⅔ tablespoons) = 5.4 fluid oz. = 160 ml
¾ cup (12 tablespoons) = 6 fluid oz. = 180 ml
1 cup (16 tablespoons) = 8 fluid oz. = 240 ml

TEMPERATURE EQUIVALENTS

°F	°C	Gas Mark
225	110	¼
250	130	½
275	140	1
300	150	2
325	170	3
350	180	4
375	190	5
400	200	6
425	220	7
450	230	8
475	240	9
500	250	10

LENGTH MEASURES

1/16 inch = 1.6 mm
⅛ inch = 3 mm
¼ inch = 1.35 mm
½ inch = 1.25 cm
¾ inch = 2 cm
1 inch = 2.5 cm

IMAGE CREDITS

Cover, Back Cover, Pages 4–5, 6–7, 8, 10–11, 12, 14–15, 16, 19, 24–25, 26, 29, 30–31, 41, 42–43, 57, 66, 68–69, 78–79, 86–87, 94–95, 96, 99, 102, 108, 112–113, 115, 116–117, 124–125, 132–133, 134, 137, 139, 142, 144–145, 148–149, 150, 152–153, 154, 156–157, 160, 162–163, 174, 176–177, 185, 188, 194, 200, 202–203, 204–205, 206–207, 208, 211, 212–213, 220, 227, 228–229, 230, 232–233, 234, 236–237, 238, 240–241, 244, 246–247, 250, 252–253, 256, 264, 266–267, 273, 274–275, 276, 278–279, 284–285, 286, 289, 290–291, 292, 296–297, 319, 320–321, 322, 324–325, 328–329, 348–349, 350, 353, 354–355, 358–359, 361, 369, 372, 375, 378, 383, 384–385, 391, 392, 396–397, 398, 413, 414–415, 425, 426–427, 438, 445, 446–447, 449, 450–451, 453, 454, 466, 478–479, 481, 482, 488, 493, 494–495, 496, 503, 510, 512–513, 520, 524, 538–539, 540, 543, 567, 568–569, 580, 582–583, 592, 594–595, 611, 612–613, 618, 634, 650, 689, 762–763, 796–797, 798, and 800 courtesy of Jim Sullivan.

Pages 305, 306, 340, 343, 344, 347, 464, 637, 699, 700, 703, 704, 707, 708, 711, 712, 715, 716, 719, 720, 723, 724, 727, 728, 731, 732, 735, 736, 739, 740, 743, 747, 748, 759, 760 courtesy of Cider Mill Press.

Pages 120–121 and 500–501 courtesy of Diego Delso, Creative Commons Attribution-Share Alike 3.0

Pages 249, and 376–377 courtesy of Brett Hodnett, Creative Commons Attribution-Share Alike 2.0

Pages 100–101 courtesy of Alan Ruiz, Creative Commons Attribution-Share Alike 4.0 International

Pages 218–219 courtesy of JMndz, Creative Commons Attribution-Share Alike 4.0 International

Pages 262–263 courtesy of Ariadne Delgado, Creative Commons Attribution-Share Alike 4.0

Pages 332–333 and 624–625 courtesy of Tomas Castelazo, Creative Commons Attribution-Share Alike 3.0

Pages 338–339 courtesy of Gzzz, Creative Commons Attribution-Share Alike 3.0

Pages 402–403 courtesy of Ruben Poncia, Adry del Rocio, and Carlos Alberto, Creative Commons Zero

Pages 550–551 courtesy of Gobierno CDMX, Creative Commons Zero

Pages 596–597 courtesy of Sharon Hahn Darlin, Creative Commons 2.0

Pages 608–609 courtesy of Christian Cariño, Creative Commons Attribution-Share Alike 4.0

All other photos used under official license from Shutterstock.com

Illustrations courtesy of Christina Hess

CONTRIBUTORS

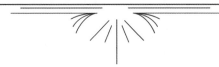

GABE ERALES

Hailing from the culturally rich border town of El Paso, Texas, Chef Gabe Erales has a passion for preserving Mexican corn and culture, and has infused that passion into everything he creates in the kitchen. His cooking philosophy focuses on locality through strong relationships with local farmers. Erales also seeks honesty in his roots by sourcing unique varieties of landrace corn, chiles, and other ingredients from different regions of Mexico. Married with four children, Erales recently launched his scholarship program, Niños de Maíz, with The Culinary Institute of America. He was also a contestant on Season 18 of Bravo's *Top Chef*. To learn more about what projects he is working on, visit gabeerales.com.

LUIS ROBLES

Chef Luis Robles is a graduate of Culinary Arts at the Los Angeles Trade-Technical College, where he is currently an Associate Professor teaching whole animal butchery and overseeing the school's public restaurant. Born and raised in East Los Angeles to Mexican immigrants, he began as a dishwasher in 1999 and worked his way up the ranks in restaurants serving classical French cuisine. Chef Robles has worked with chefs across America and abroad, and has held chef positions at the Disneyland Hotel, Patina Restaurant Group, Bon Appétit, and Wolfgang Puck Catering. Throughout the years he has had the privilege to cook for special events such as the Food & Wine Festival, the 2010 Winter Olympics, and the annual Governor's Ball at the Academy Awards. In 2016, he was invited to speak at the MAD Symposium in Copenhagen to present the findings of his research on kitchen violence. Teaching the future generations of cooks fuels his drive and motivation, especially the resiliency of those students whose upbringing closely mirrors his.

BALO OROZCO

Chef Balo Orozco grew up in Guadalajara, Jalisco, Mexico. His first job in the industry was working at a Japanese-run sushi restaurant at age 16. During a trip to Tulum in the Yucatan, he met Eric Werner of Hartwood, the famous, off-the-grid destination restaurant, which is an absurd yet accurate phrase; they worked together for five years, fishing together twice a week to supply the restaurant. Chef Orozco was recruited by Danny Bowien for Mission Cantina, the utterly bonkers and sometimes transcendent Mexican restaurant he opened (and then closed) on New York's Lower East Side. Orozco also worked briefly cooking with Thai grandmothers. He has also worked at Sqirl, and Cála with Gabriela Camara. As the Chef de Cuisine at Onda, he made Mexican-inspired food using California-grown produce from local farmers markets. After developing a close relationship with local farmers and understanding the impact of food waste, he partnered with Jacqui Harning to launch Sunset Cultures, making preserves and raw kombucha with seasonal produce from Los Angeles farmers markets.

AUGIE SAUCEDO

Chef Augie is a classically French trained Executive Chef with over 26 years of experience. He has worked in various environments, from hotels and restaurants to catering and as an in-home personal chef. Chef Augie's versatile and global creations are both beautifully presented and delicious. In his most recent position at Hotel Republic, Chef Augie successfully improved the Marriott food score from 59 to 75, proving that his recipes are palate pleasing to most guests. He enjoys donating his talents to benefit worthy causes. Not only is Chef Augie a talented professional, he also loves what he does.

LORI SAUER

Growing up, I knew that I wanted to be a pastry chef. I started working in the industry at 16, and had a few kitchen jobs before I went to a culinary academy. My first real pastry job was at Pechanga Resort and Casino in 2003, where I worked for Executive Pastry Chef Jean Marie Verhoven. In 2006, I moved to San Diego from the Inland Empire to help Chef Bradley Ogden and Chef Jim Phillips open the Anthology Supper Club. Shortly after, I went to work at The Lodge at Torrey Pines for Chef Jeff Jackson. After three years, I accepted my first Executive Pastry Chef title when I joined the exclusive members' only resort The Bridges at Rancho Santa Fe. It was a little over a year later that I felt it was time to move onto a more challenging role and push the boundaries with my culinary skills. So, I stepped into the role as Executive Pastry Chef at George's at the Cove in 2011, and worked for Chef Trey Foshee for six years. During this period, I also created desserts at Galaxy Taco for about a year. In 2017, I became the Executive Pastry Chef of Blue Bridge Hospitality and their collection of restaurants. In 2019, I decided to return to the Lodge at Torrey Pines as the Executive Pastry Chef, and continue to work in this role.

AARON MELENDREZ

For San Gabriel Valley native Aaron Melendrez, it all started in his family's kitchen. He would stand there as a young boy watching his Abuelita and Tías prepare traditional Mexican dishes while he soaked in the flavors, scents, and recipes of his heritage. This immersive experience would later influence his signature approach to creating cocktails and beverage programs all over the city.

Melendrez got his start in some of LA's best restaurants: the Soho House West Hollywood, Gordon Ramsey's at the London Hotel during its Michelin-starred tenure, and the reopening of the illustrious Hotel Bel-Air. Melendrez went on to create and revitalize beverage programs for some of the best bars and restaurants in the city, including Salazar, which led to accolades such as Best New Restaurant Los Angeles.

At the beginning of 2018, while working with Illegal Mezcal, Aaron became a founding partner in Va'La Hospitality. The team of industry all-stars immediately went on to work with such clients as Starz Network, Heineken, Bacardi, and Showtime's hit show *The L Word*. In 2019, the team was recognized by *Esquire* for their work overhauling Here & Now, which secured the bar's placement on the publication's annual "Top 50 Bars in America" list. Additional credits include restoring the historic Prince Bar in Koreatown; creating beverage programs both for Guerrilla Tacos and Escala Koreatown; and working on the team at Normandie Club when it was named one of the World's Best Bars.

Melendrez, alongside side his wife Sarah, is now back in his hometown of Whittier, where he is sixth generation. Here he is transforming his passion for food and products into his dream of opening the farm-to-table, chef-driven deli and specialty market Uptown Provisions. He believes in investing in the livelihood of his community, and after experiencing the limited availability of ingredients locally, he is excited to bring increased access to the quality this community has been asking for.

JOSÉ LUIS HINOSTROZA

A native of Southern California, José Luis Hinostroza grew up in a Mexican household in the heart of one of the richest agricultural regions in America and the birthplace of the farm-to-table movement. He first ventured from home to work at Alinea in Chicago, where he became kitchen manager at 21 and was exposed to the high-intensity world of fine dining. He moved to Spain to work under Jordi Roca at El Celler de Can Roca, and by age 24 he was named Chef de Cuisine at the 2 Michelin-star restaurant De Kromme Watergang in The Netherlands. Until recently, he was at Rene Redzepi's culinary mecca, Noma in Copenhagen, and formed part of the research and development team of Noma Mexico. His product-driven menú at ARCA brings together the bold and explosive flavors of Mexico, executing a casual fine-dining experience with the technique and knowledge of a chef who has spent the past 10 years working in some of the best fine-dining kitchens in the world.

VANESSA CECEÑA

Vanessa Ceceña, a daughter of Mexican immigrants, grew up in San Diego, California, along the US-Mexico border. She writes about life on the border, migration, and about the intersections between food, policy, and community. As a transfronteriza, her writing is influenced by her bicultural identity and travels in Mexico and Asia, giving her work a transnational flair. Vanessa received her master's degree in Social Work from USC and an undergraduate degree in International Development Studies. The early years of her career were spent working alongside Oaxacan indigenous communities, where she was taught the importance of food and language as a tool for cultural preservation. In 2015, Vanessa received an award from the Society of Professional Journalists, San Diego chapter, for her piece on deportation and family separation. When she isn't eating or writing, she can be found on the dance floor, dancing salsa and bachata.

JIM SULLIVAN

Jim is a graduate of the Art Institute of California's culinary program and a self-taught photographer. His work has a strong focus in the culinary field as well as portraiture and lifestyle. His publications range from *Food and Wine* to *Leica Camera* and *Art Culinaire*. His clientele ranges from Californios, Michelin-starred restaurants, Birdie G's, and Liholiho Yacht Club. When he isn't traveling for work, he can be found in Southern California spending time with his family and their little French Bulldog, Mochi.

INDEX

absinthe
  Lost in the Rain in Juárez, 737
  Mezcal Survivor, 742
Abuela's Sopes, 357
Abuelita's Chocolate Pots de Crème, 552
agave nectar
  Blacker the Berry, The Sweeter the Juice, 705
  Brujera, 713
  Dons of Soul, 725
  The Fifth Element, 717
  Flor de Jalisco, 701
  Habanero Agave, 216
  Lavender Agave, 702
  Oaxaca Old Fashioned, 680
  Oaxacarajillo, 683
  Sunday Morning Coming Down, 729
  Thai Chile Agave, 710
Agua de Jamaica, 784
Agua de Melon, 778
Agua de Tamarindo, 783
Aguachile Verde de Camarón, 171
Albondigas Soup, 334
almonds
  Charred Pepper Tartare, 400–401
  Chiles en Nogada, 85
  Mexican Chocolate Sauce, 584
  Mixed Nut Marzipan, 627
  Mole Negro, 440–441
  Mole Poblano, 119

  Moscovy Duck Breast Mole, 98
  Puerco en Pipian Verde, 75
  Salsa Macha, 521
Anaheim chile peppers
  Pavo en Escabeche, 111
ancho chile peppers
  Barbacoa Adobo, 483
  Chile Colorado, 452
  Chilorio, 89
  Coffee & Ancho Roasted Carrots with Chile Toreado Mayo, 226
  Mexican Pepper Reduction, 714
  Mextlapique de Callo de Hacha, 164
  Mixiotes de Pollo, 110
  Mole Brownies, 623
  Mole Manchamanteles, 455
  Mole Negro, 440–441
  Moscovy Duck Breast Mole, 98
  Mushroom Barbacoa, 239
  Pescado Zarandeado, 196
  Pierna de Puerco, 71
  Pipian Rojo, 484
  Salsa Macha, 521
Ancho Reyes liqueur
  Drunken Rabbit, 706
  Ramon Bravo, 688
Aperol
  Lost in the Rain in Juárez, 737
  Maya Gold, 695
  Naked & Famous, 746

  Sunday Morning Coming Down, 729
  Unscalpe, 738
apples
  Mole Blanco, 458
  Mole Manchamanteles, 455
Arbol Macha, Pork Toro with, 428
Arroz a la Mexicana
  Chilorio, 89
  recipe, 529
Arroz con Leche, 554
Atole, 787
Averna Amaro
  Desert Daisy, 718
  True Romance, 754
avocado leaves
  Barbacoa Adobo, 483
avocados
  Aguachile Verde de Camarón, 171
  Avocado Mix, 717
  Ceviche de Pescado, 195
  Cocktail de Marisco, 184
  Dzik de Res, 51
  The Fifth Element, 717
  Guacamole, 432
  Gulf Rock Shrimp Aguachile with Avocado Panna Cotta, 138
  Salsa Cruda Verde, 525
  Salsa de Aguacate, 503
  Sweet Corn & Pepita Guacamole, 449
  Tetelas de Aguacate con Requesón y Nopales, 382

Vuelva la Vida Coctel de
Camarones, 151
ayocote beans
Frijol Ayocote with Pasilla
Yogurt, 248
Sopa de Chorizo, Ayocotes y
Acelgas, 298

bacon
Carne en Su Jugo, 90
Baja Lobster & Street Corn
Salad, 143
Baja Tortilla Soup, 301
banana
Mole Poblano, 119
banana leaves
Cochinita Pibil, 28
Mushroom Barbacoa, 239
Ostiones al Tapesco, 161
Pescado Adobado en Hoja
de Platano, 191
Puritos de Platano Macho
Relleno de Frijoles Negros
y Mole Negro, 221
Tamales de Chulibu'ul, 368
barbacoa
Barbacoa Adobo, 483
Mushroom Barbacoa, 239
Batanga, 679
Bay Leaf Oil, 526
beans
about, 21
Abuela's Sopes, 357
Beef Machaca with Potatoes
& Eggs, 91
Carne en Su Jugo, 90
Chicken Tinga Sopes, 393
Chilaquiles Rojos, 417
Chilibul, 32
Costilla Corta de Res con
Chile Colorado, 70
Frijol Ayocote with Pasilla
Yogurt, 248
Frijoles de la Olla, 257
Frijoles Negros Refritos, 254
Huaraches with Wild

Mushrooms & Epazote,
356
Huevos Motuleños, 394
Huevos Rancheros, 387
Memelas de Chicharron,
390
Molotes de Frijol y Queso,
360
Pan de Cazon, 165
Puritos de Platano Macho
Relleno de Frijoles Negros
y Mole Negro, 221
Sopa de Chorizo, Ayocotes y
Acelgas, 298
Sopa de Frijol Colado, 317
Tacos Dorados de Frijol,
Chorizo y Camote, 386
Tostadas de Cueritos, 59
beef
Albondigas Soup, 334
Beef Barbacoa Tacos,
412
Beef Cheeks with Salsa
Verde, 52
Beef Machaca with Potatoes
& Eggs, 91
Beef Stock, 342
Caldo de Res, 336
Carne Asada, 58
Carne en Su Jugo, 90
Chilibul, 32
Costilla Corta de Res con
Chile Colorado, 37
Dzik de Res, 51
Milanesa de Res y Mole
Blanco, 33
Picadillo de Res, 73
Puchero de Tres Carnes,
318
Beef Stock
Costilla Corta de Res con
Chile Colorado, 37
Dzik de Res, 51
recipe, 342
beef tongue
Lengua en Salsa Roja, 56

beer
Michoacán-Style Carnitas,
46
Ray Ray's Michelada, 661
Salsa Borracha, 508
beets
Betabel with Salsa Macha y
Queso Fresco, 234
Guanajuato Strawberry &
Beet Salad, 210
Orange Bell Pepper & Beet
Syrup, 718
berries
Blacker the Berry, The
Sweeter the Juice, 705
Guanajuato Strawberry &
Beet Salad, 210
Raicilla-Soaked Berries, 594
Strawberry Hot Sauce, 460
Strawberry Shortcake con
Conchas, 606
Betabel with Salsa Macha y
Queso Fresco, 234
beverages
Agua de Jamaica, 784
Agua de Melon, 778
Agua de Tamarindo, 783
Atole, 787
Batanga, 679
Blacker the Berry, The
Sweeter the Juice, 705
Brujera, 713
Canoe Club, 698
Cantaritos, 745
Champagne Paloma, 733
Champurrado, 788
Cooper's Café, 682
Cornchata, 770
La Cura, 767
Desert Daisy, 718
Diablo Otoño, 734
Dons of Soul, 725
Drunken Rabbit, 706
East LA, 673
El Chavo del Ocho, 694
El Vato Swizzle, 714

The Fifth Element, 717
Fire Walk with Me, 755
Flor de Jalisco, 701
Horchata, 768
Horchata con Espresso, 774
Horchata con Rum, 771
Jalisco Sour, 750
Jamaica Collins, 691
Kinda Knew Anna, 749
Lavagave, 702
Lost in the Rain in Juárez, 737
Mámù Vida, 761
Margarita, 658
Maya Gold, 695
Mexican Hot Chocolate, 794
Mezcal Survivor, 742
Naked & Famous, 746
Oaxaca Old Fashioned, 680
Oaxacarajillo, 683
Paloma, 665
Pan, 758
Peach Tea, 730
Piña Fumada, 741
Pineapple Express, 710
Pineapple Tepache Kombucha, 790
Playa Rosita, 662
Ramon Bravo, 688
Ranch Water, 674
Ray Ray's Michelada, 661
Rising Sun, 722
La Santa, 764
Shake Your Tamarind, 709
She's a Rainbow, 753
Spicy Margarita, 668
Sunday Morning Coming Down, 729
Tejuino, 789
Tepache de Piña, 791
True Romance, 754
Última Palabra, 669
Unscalpe, 738
Vampiro, 664
Xocolatl, 777

Birria de Chivo, 67
black beans
    Chilibul, 32
    Frijoles de la Olla, 257
    Frijoles Negros Refritos, 254
    Pan de Cazon, 165
    Sopa de Frijol Colado, 317
Black Lava Solution, 701
Blacker the Berry, The Sweeter the Juice, 705
black-eyed peas
    Chulibu'ul, 534
Blue Corn Crunchies
    Horchata Ice Cream, 542
    recipe, 607
bolillo
    Tortas Ahogadas, 423
    Tortas de Lomo, 418
Bonbonaise, 560
Bone Marrow
    Momma's Sopa de Conchitas, 294
    recipe, 294
Bourbon Truffles, Mayan Chocolate &, 615
Brujera, 713
Brussels Sprouts, Fried, 216
Buñuelos
    Coffee Flan with Buñuelos, 562
    recipe, 598
Butternut Squash & Chorizo Bisque, 307

cabbage
    Caldo de Res, 336
    Carnitas de Atun, 168
    Chicken Tinga Sopes, 393
    Empanadas de Picadillo, 80
    Gorditas de Picadillo de Res, 77
    Puchero de Tres Carnes, 318
    Taquitos de Papa, 281
cactus
    Ensalada de Nopales, 272
    Mixiotes de Pollo, 110

Tetelas de Aguacate con Requesón y Nopales, 382
Cajeta, 639
Calabacitas con Elote y Queso Fresco, 265
Caldo de Espinazo de Puerco, 326
Caldo de Pescado, 331
Caldo de Res, 336
California chile peppers
    Caldo de Espinazo de Puerco, 326
    Caldo de Pescado, 331
    Mole Poblano, 119
Camarones a la Diabla, 197
Camarones en Adobo, 158
Camote con Mole Blanco, 222
Campari
    Pineapple-Infused Campari, 662
    Shake Your Tamarind, 709
Canoe Club, 698
Cantaritos, 745
Carne Adobada, 311
Carne Asada, 58
Carne en Su Jugo, 90
Carnitas de Atun, 168
carrots
    Albondigas Soup, 334
    Arroz a la Mexicana, 529
    Beef Stock, 342
    Caldo de Pescado, 331
    Caldo de Res, 336
    Charred Escabeche, 470
    Chicken Stock, 341
    Coffee & Ancho Roasted Carrots with Chile Toreado Mayo, 226
    Escabeche, 518
    Fish Stock, 345
    Picadillo de Res, 73
    Puchero de Tres Carnes, 318
    Smoked Trout Tostadas, 183
    Sopa de Lentejas, 337
    Vegetable Stock, 346

cascabel chile peppers
    Pierna de Puerco, 71
cauliflower
    Escabeche, 518
    Tortitas de Coliflor, 268
Cecina de Cerdo, 40
celery
    Beef Stock, 342
    Caldo de Pescado, 331
    Chicken Stock, 341
    Fish Stock, 345
    Sopa de Lentejas, 337
    Vegetable Stock, 346
Ceviche de Pescado, 195
Chamomile Mezcal
    Maya Gold, 695
    recipe, 695
Champagne Paloma, 733
Champurrado, 788
Chantilly Cream
    Mexican Hot Chocolate,
        794
    Strawberry Shortcake con
        Conchas, 606
Charred Escabeche, 470
Charred Pepper Emulsion,
    400–401
Charred Pepper Tartare,
    400–401
Charred Pineapple Puree, 688
chartreuse, green
    Última Palabra, 669
chartreuse, yellow
    Maya Gold, 695
    Naked & Famous, 746
    Rising Sun, 722
    True Romance, 754
Chavo del Ocho, El, 694
chayotes
    Chayote en Pipian Rojo,
        245
    Pipian Rojo, 484
cheese. See individual cheese
        types
chicharron
    Chicharron en Salsa Roja, 62

Chocolate-Covered
    Chicharron, 566
    Memelas de Chicharron,
        390
chicken
    Chicken Chorizo, 109
    Chicken en Salsa Cremosa
        de Champiñones, 104
    Chicken Stock, 341
    Chicken Tinga Sopes, 393
    Enchiladas de Mole, 126
    Masa-Battered Fried
        Chicken, 122
    Milanesa de Pollo, 131
    Pollo Veracruzano, 123
    Pozole Blanco, 288
    Puchero de Tres Carnes, 318
Chicken Chorizo
    Abuela's Sopes, 357
    Chilaquiles Rojos, 417
    recipe, 109
chicken livers
    Higados en Salsa Chipotle
        de Adobo, 53
Chicken Stock
    Arroz a la Mexicana, 529
    Chayote en Pipian Rojo,
        245
    Chilaquiles Rojos, 417
    Chile Colorado, 452
    Chileatole Verde, 514
    Frijol Ayocote with Pasilla
        Yogurt, 248
    Higados en Salsa Chipotle
        de Adobo, 53
    Joroches de Chorizo y
        Frijoles Colados, 373
    Masa for Tamales, 365
    Mole Blanco, 458
    Mole Manchamanteles, 455
    Mole Negro, 440–441
    Momma's Sopa de
        Conchitas, 294
    Moscovy Duck Breast Mole,
        98
    Pig Ear Salad, 405

Pipian Rojo, 484
Pollo Veracruzano, 123
Puchero de Tres Carnes, 318
Pulpo al Pastor, 155
Puritos de Platano Macho
    Relleno de Frijoles Negros
    y Mole Negro, 221
recipe, 341
Sopa de Chile Poblano, 310
Sopa de Chorizo, Ayocotes y
    Acelgas, 298
Sopa de Flor de Calabaza,
    314
Sopa de Frijol Colado, 317
Sopa de Lentejas, 337
chickpeas
    Caldo de Espinazo de
        Puerco, 326
    Puchero de Tres Carnes, 318
chihuacle negro chile peppers
    Mole Negro, 440–441
Chihuahua cheese
    Molotes de Frijol y Queso,
        360
chilaca peppers
    about, 22
Chilaquiles Rojos, 277
Chilaquiles Verdes, 417
Chile Colorado
    Costilla Corta de Res con
        Chile Colorado, 37
    recipe, 452
Chile Toreado Mayo
    Masa-Crusted Sardines with
        Pickled Manzano, 201
    recipe, 226
Chileatole Verde, 514
chiles, about, 21–23. See also
        individual chiles
chiles de arbol
    Arbol Macha, 428
    Beef Cheeks with Salsa
        Verde, 52
    Calabacitas con Elote y
        Queso Fresco, 265
    Camarones a la Diabla, 197

Cecina de Cerdo, 40
Chilaquiles Rojos, 277
Chile Colorado, 452
Esquites con Longaniza, 424
Frijoles Negros Refritos, 254
Huaraches with Wild
    Mushrooms & Epazote,
    356
Menudo, 293
Mexican Pepper Reduction,
    714
Mixiotes de Pollo, 110
Mole Poblano, 119
Pipian Rojo, 484
Pork Toro with Arbol
    Macha, 428
Preserved Limes with Chile
    de Arbol & Spices, 459
Pulpo al Pastor, 155
Quesadillas de
    Champiñones, 251
Salsa de Arbol, 498
Salsa Macha, 521
Sere de Pescado, 300
Sopa de Camarón Seco, 323
Strawberry Hot Sauce, 460
Tinga de Pollo, 114
Tomato Aguachile, 231
Tortas Ahogadas, 423
Tostadas de Cueritos, 59
Chiles en Nogada, 85
Chiles Rellenos, 269
Chiles Toreados, 489
Chilibul, 32
Chilorio, 89
chipotle chile peppers
    Barbacoa Adobo, 483
    Mole Poblano, 119
    Mushroom Barbacoa, 239
    Pozole, 304
    Tinga de Pollo, 114
chipotle meco chile peppers
    Mole Manchamanteles, 455
    Mole Negro, 440–441
    Szechuan & Chipotle
        Honey, 761

chipotle mortia chile
    peppers
    Charred Pepper Tartare,
        400–401
    Costilla Corta de Res con
        Chile Colorado, 70
    Fermented Chile Adobo,
        504
    Mole Poblano, 119
    Morita Salsa, 505
    Pierna de Puerco, 71
    Pig Ear Salad, 405
    Pulpo al Pastor, 155
    Salsa Borracha, 508
    Smoked Morita Oil, 401
    Sopa de Chorizo, Ayocotes y
        Acelgas, 298
    Verdolagas en Salsa Verde,
        242
chipotle peppers
    about, 22
    Chilibul, 32
chipotles en adobo
    Camarones en Adobo, 158
    Chilibul, 32
    Higados en Salsa Chipotle
        de Adobo, 53
Chocoflan, 563
chocolate
    Abuelita's Chocolate Pots de
        Crème, 552
    Champurrado, 788
    Chocolate & Mexican
        Vanilla Frosting, 628
    Chocolate Mole Profiteroles,
        571
    Chocolate Tamarind
        Truffles, 576
    Chocolate-Covered
        Chicharron, 566
    Cinnamon & Chocolate
        Cake, 587
    Dark Chocolate Ganache,
        590
    Gluten-Free Spicy
        Chocolate Cookies, 636

Mayan Chocolate &
    Bourbon Truffles, 615
Mexican Chocolate Sauce,
    584, 794
Mole Negro, 440–441
Mole Poblano, 119
Moscovy Duck Breast Mole,
    98
Spicy Chocolate Truffles,
    577
Xocolatl, 777
See also cocoa powder
Chocolate & Mexican Vanilla
    Frosting
    Mole Brownies, 623
    recipe, 628
Chocolate Ice Cream
    Chocolate Mole Profiteroles,
        571
    recipe, 572
Chocolate Mole
    Chocolate Mole Profiteroles,
        571
    recipe, 575
chorizo/sausage
    Abuela's Sopes, 357
    Butternut Squash &
        Chorizo Bisque, 307
    Chicken Chorizo, 109
    Chilaquiles Rojos, 417
    Chorizo-Washed Mezcal,
        688
    Esquites con Longaniza, 424
    Huevos Motuleños, 394
    Joroches de Chorizo y
        Frijoles Colados, 373
    Queso Fundido, 429
    Sopa de Chorizo, Ayocotes y
        Acelgas, 298
    Tacos Dorados de Frijol,
        Chorizo y Camote, 386
Chulibu'ul
    recipe, 534
    Tamales de Chulibu'ul, 368
Churros, 581
cilantro

Aguachile Verde de
    Camarón, 171
Arbol Macha, 428
Avocado Mix, 717
Beef Cheeks with Salsa
    Verde, 52
Birria de Chivo, 67
Caldo de Pescado, 331
Carne Asada, 58
Carne en Su Jugo, 90
Ceviche de Pescado, 195
Chilaquiles Rojos, 417
Chileatole Verde, 514
Cilantro Pesto, 210
Cocktail de Marisco, 184
Coconut Dressing, 147
Coctel de Camaron, 190
Cumin & Cilantro
    Vinaigrette, 473
La Diosa, 721
Dzik de Res, 51
Dzikil P'aak, 511
Empanadas de Picadillo, 80
Enchiladas de Mole, 126
Ensalada de Nopales, 272
Guacamole, 432
Guanajuato Strawberry &
    Beet Salad, 210
Gulf Rock Shrimp
    Aguachile with Avocado
    Panna Cotta, 138
Huevos Rancheros, 387
Lengua en Salsa Roja, 56
Memelas de Chicharron,
    390
Mole Verde, 492
Ostiones al Tapesco, 161
Pescado Adobado en Hoja
    de Platano, 191
Picadillo de Res, 73
Puerco en Pipian Verde, 75
Salsa de Aguacate, 503
Salsa Verde Tatemada, 480
Sopa de Chile Poblano, 310
Sopa de Lentejas, 337
Sopa de Papa, 327

Striped Sea Bass Ceviche,
    146–147
Sweet Corn & Pepita
    Guacamole, 449
Taquitos de Papa, 281
Tikin Xic, 175
Tomato Aguachile, 231
X'nipek, 487
Cinnamon & Chocolate
    Cake, 587
Cinnamon Syrup
    Champagne Paloma, 733
    Cooper's Café, 682
    Drunken Rabbit, 706
    recipe, 706
    Shake Your Tamarind, 709
Citrus Salt, 717
Clamato
    Cocktail de Marisco, 184
    Coctel de Camaron, 190
    Ray Ray's Michelada, 661
    Vuelva la Vida Coctel de
        Camarones, 151
Cocchi Americano
    Mezcal Survivor, 742
Cochinita Pibil, 28
Cocktail de Marisco, 184
cocktails. See beverages
cocoa powder
    Chocoflan, 563
    Chocolate Ice Cream, 572
    Chocolate Mole, 575
    Gluten-Free Spicy
        Chocolate Cookies, 636
    Mayan Chocolate &
        Bourbon Truffles, 615
    Mexican Chocolate Crinkle
        Cookies, 640
    Mexican Chocolate Sauce,
        584
    Mole Brownies, 623
    Spicy Chocolate Truffles,
        577
    See also chocolate
coconut
    Bonbonaise, 560

Coconut Dressing
    Striped Sea Bass Ceviche,
        146–147
coconut milk
    Coconut Dressing, 147
    Coconut Tres Leches, 593
    Horchata, 768
    Sere de Pescado, 300
    Striped Sea Bass Ceviche,
        146–147
Coctel de Camaron, 190
Codorniz a la Parilla, 103
coffee/espresso
    Chocoflan, 563
    Coffee & Ancho Roasted
        Carrots with Chile
        Toreado Mayo, 226
    Coffee Flan with Buñuelos,
        562
    Cooper's Café, 682
    Horchata con Espresso, 774
    Oaxacarajillo, 683
Cointreau
    Margarita, 658
    Spicy Margarita, 668
Conchas
    Concha Bread Pudding, 555
    recipe, 602–603
conversion tables, 799
Cooper's Café, 682
corn
    Baja Lobster & Street Corn
        Salad, 143
    Calabacitas con Elote y
        Queso Fresco, 265
    Chileatole Verde, 514
    Chulibu'ul, 534
    Cornchata, 770
    Esquites con Longaniza, 424
    Sweet Corn & Pepita
        Guacamole, 449
    Sweet Corn Pudding Pops,
        635
corn husks
    Mextlapique de Callo de
        Hacha, 164

Pescado Zarandeado, 196
Corn Tortillas
   Baja Tortilla Soup, 301
   Chilaquiles Rojos, 277
   Enchiladas de Mole, 126
   Huevos Motuleños, 394
   Huevos Rancheros, 387
   Moscovy Duck Breast Mole, 98
   Pipian Rojo, 484
   Sopa de Camarón Seco, 323
   Sopa de Chile Poblano, 310
   Taquitos de Papa, 281
   Taquitos de Requesón con Rajas, 280
Cornchata, 770
Cornchata Hard Candies, 614
Costilla Corta de Res con Chile Colorado, 37
Costillitas de Puerco en Chile Rojo, 70
cotija cheese
   Empanadas de Picadillo, 80
   Esquites con Longaniza, 424
   Gorditas de Picadillo de Res, 77
   Joroches de Chorizo y Frijoles Colados, 373
   Taquitos de Papa, 281
   Tostadas de Cueritos, 59
crab
   Baja Tortilla Soup, 301
   Cocktail de Marisco, 184
cream cheese
   Coffee Flan with Buñuelos, 562
   The Perfect Flan, 644
crème de mure
   Canoe Club, 698
   Kinda Knew Anna, 749
cucumber
   Aguachile Verde de Camarón, 171
   Ceviche de Pescado, 195
   Cocktail de Marisco, 184
   Coctel de Camaron, 190

East LA, 673
Gulf Rock Shrimp
   Aguachile with Avocado Panna Cotta, 138
   La Santa, 764
   Tomato Aguachile, 231
Cumin & Cilantro Vinaigrette, 473
Cura, La, 767
Cured Sardines, 406
curry leaves
   Pig Ear Salad, 405
Custard Ice Cream Base, 647

Dark Chocolate Ganache
   Cinnamon & Chocolate Cake, 587
   recipe, 590
Desert Daisy, 718
desserts
   Abuelita's Chocolate Pots de Crème, 552
   Arroz con Leche, 554
   Blue Corn Crunchies, 607
   Bonbonaise, 560
   Buñuelos, 598
   Cajeta, 639
   Chocoflan, 563
   Chocolate & Mexican Vanilla Frosting, 628
   Chocolate Ice Cream, 572
   Chocolate Mole, 575
   Chocolate Mole Profiteroles, 571
   Chocolate Tamarind Truffles, 576
   Chocolate-Covered Chicharron, 566
   Churros, 581
   Cinnamon & Chocolate Cake, 587
   Coffee Flan with Buñuelos, 562
   Concha Bread Pudding, 555
   Conchas, 602–603
   Cornchata Hard Candies, 614

   Custard Ice Cream Base, 647
   Dark Chocolate Ganache, 590
   Gluten-Free Spicy Chocolate Cookies, 636
   Horchata Ice Cream, 542
   Leche Quemada, 544
   Mango con Chile Pate de Fruit, 610
   Mayan Chocolate & Bourbon Truffles, 615
   Mexican Chocolate Crinkle Cookies, 640
   Mexican Chocolate Sauce, 584
   Mexican Wedding Cookies, 619
   Mezcal & Mango Float, 622
   Mezcal Ice Cream, 620
   Mixed Nut Marzipan, 627
   Mole Brownies, 623
   No-Fry Fried Ice Cream, 630
   Orejas, 549
   Pan de Hoja Santa, 631
   Perfect Caramel, 601
   The Perfect Flan, 644
   Piloncillo Syrup, 557
   Raicilla-Soaked Berries, 594
   Sopaipillas, 643
   Spicy Chocolate Truffles, 577
   Strawberry Shortcake con Conchas, 606
   Sweet Corn Pudding Pops, 635
   Sweet Empanadas, 545
Diablo Otoño, 734
Diosa, La, 721
Dons of Soul, 725
Drunken Rabbit, 706
Duck Breast Mole, Moscovy, 98

Dzik de Res, 51
Dzikil P'aak, 511

East LA, 673
eggs
  Beef Machaca with Potatoes
    & Eggs, 91
  Chilaquiles Rojos, 417
  Coffee Flan with Buñuelos,
    562
  Huevos Motuleños, 394
  Huevos Rancheros, 387
  Milanesa de Res y Mole
    Blanco, 33
Empanadas de Picadillo, 80
Enchiladas de Mole, 126
Ensalada de Nopales
  Milanesa de Pollo, 131
  recipe, 272
epazote
  about, 225
  Chileatole Verde, 514
  Epazote Oil, 467
  Frijol Ayocote with Pasilla
    Yogurt, 248
  Huaraches with Wild
    Mushrooms & Epazote,
    356
  Langosta al Mojo de Ajo,
    136
  Mextlapique de Callo de
    Hacha, 164
  Mole Verde, 492
  Molotes de Frijol y Queso,
    360
  Pan de Cazon, 165
  Pulpo al Pastor, 155
  Quesadillas de
    Champiñones, 251
  Sopa de Camarón Seco, 323
  Sopa de Chorizo, Ayocotes y
    Acelgas, 298
  Sopa de Flor de Calabaza,
    314
  Sopa de Frijol Colado, 317
  Sopa de Hongos, 295

Verdolagas en Salsa Verde,
  242
Escabeche
  Charred Escabeche, 470
  Chilibul, 32
  Costilla Corta de Res con
    Chile Colorado, 37
  Pavo en Escabeche, 111
  recipe, 518
  Tortas de Lomo, 418
  Tostadas de Cueritos, 59
espresso/coffee
  Chocoflan, 563
  Coffee & Ancho Roasted
    Carrots with Chile
    Toreado Mayo, 226
  Coffee Flan with Buñuelos,
    562
  Cooper's Café, 682
  Horchata con Espresso, 774
  Oaxacarajillo, 683
Esquites con Longaniza, 424

falernum
  Fire Walk with Me, 755
fennel
  Mole Blanco, 458
Fermented Chile Adobo, 504
Fifth Element, The, 717
Fig Cordial
  Diablo Otoño, 734
  recipe, 734
Fig Leaf Syrup, 734
Fire Walk with Me, 755
fish
  Caldo de Pescado, 331
  Carnitas de Atun, 168
  Ceviche de Pescado, 195
  Cured Sardines, 406
  Fish Stock, 345
  Koji-Fried Sardines, 407
  Masa-Battered Fish Tacos,
    178
  Masa-Crusted Sardines with
    Pickled Manzano, 201
  Pan de Cazon, 165

Pescado Adobado en Hoja
  de Platano, 191
Pescado Veracruz, 189
Pescado Zarandeado, 196
Sere de Pescado, 300
Smoked Trout Tostadas, 183
Striped Sea Bass Ceviche,
  146–147
Tikin Xic, 175
See also seafood
fish sauce
  Arbol Macha, 428
  Striped Sea Bass Ceviche,
    146–147
  Vuelva la Vida Coctel de
    Camarones, 151
Fish Stock
  recipe, 345
  Sere de Pescado, 300
Flor de Calabaza con Queso
  Fresco y Hierbabuena,
  260
Flor de Jalisco, 701
Flour Tortillas
  Beef Machaca with Potatoes
    & Eggs, 91
  Costilla Corta de Res con
    Chile Colorado, 37
  Smoked Trout Tostadas, 183
Fried Brussels Sprouts, 216
Fried Tortilla Strips
  Baja Tortilla Soup, 301
  Sopa de Chile Poblano, 310
Frijol Ayocote with Pasilla
  Yogurt, 248
Frijoles de la Olla
  Beef Machaca with Potatoes
    & Eggs, 91
  Costilla Corta de Res con
    Chile Colorado, 70
  Huevos Rancheros, 387
  recipe, 257
Frijoles Negros Refritos
  Abuela's Sopes, 357
  Chicken Tinga Sopes, 393
  Chilaquiles Rojos, 417

Huaraches with Wild
Mushrooms & Epazote,
356
Huevos Motuleños, 394
Memelas de Chicharron,
390
Molotes de Frijol y Queso,
360
Puritos de Platano Macho
Relleno de Frijoles Negros
y Mole Negro, 221
recipe, 254
Tacos Dorados de Frijol,
Chorizo y Camote, 386

garlic
Barbacoa Adobo, 483
Birria de Chivo, 67
Camarones en Adobo, 158
Carne Adobada, 311
Carne en Su Jugo, 90
Cecina de Cerdo, 40
Charred Pepper Emulsion,
400–401
Charred Pepper Tartare,
400–401
Chilaquiles Verdes, 417
Chile Colorado, 452
Chilorio, 89
Costilla Corta de Res con
Chile Colorado, 70
Dzikil P'aak, 511
Fermented Chile Adobo,
504
Frijol Ayocote with Pasilla
Yogurt, 248
Langosta al Mojo de Ajo,
136
Lengua en Salsa Roja, 56
Luis's Carnitas, 76
Michoacán-Style Carnitas,
46
Mixiotes de Pollo, 110
Mole Manchamanteles, 455
Mole Negro, 440–441
Mole Poblano, 119

Mole Verde, 492
Morita Salsa, 505
Mushroom Barbacoa, 239
Pan de Cazon, 165
Pavo en Escabeche, 111
Pescado Veracruz, 189
Pierna de Puerco, 71
Pig Ear Salad, 405
Pipian Rojo, 484
Pozole Blanco, 288
Puchero de Tres Carnes, 318
Puerco en Pipian Verde, 75
Pulpo al Pastor, 155
Recado Rojo, 497
Salsa Borracha, 508
Salsa de Aguacate, 503
Salsa de Arbol, 498
Salsa de Chiltomate, 477
Salsa Verde Tatemada, 480
Sere de Pescado, 300
Smoked Trout Tostadas, 183
Sopa de Camarón Seco, 323
Sopa de Chile Poblano, 310
Sopa de Chorizo, Ayocotes y
Acelgas, 298
Sopa de Flor de Calabaza,
314
Sopa de Frijol Colado, 317
Sopa de Hongos, 295
Striped Sea Bass Ceviche,
146–147
Verdolagas en Salsa Verde,
242
Vuelva la Vida Coctel de
Camarones, 151
Gik blue wine
Zeus Juice Cordial, 726
gin
Jamaica Collins, 691
ginger
Canoe Club, 698
Coconut Dressing, 147
Ginger & Serrano Syrup,
698
Ginger Syrup, 767
Striped Sea Bass Ceviche,

146–147
ginger beer
Kinda Knew Anna, 749
Mezcal & Mango Float, 622
ginger juice
Pig Ear Salad, 405
Ginger Syrup
Blacker the Berry, The
Sweeter the Juice, 705
La Cura, 767
recipe, 767
Gluten-Free Spicy Chocolate
Cookies, 636
goat
Birria de Chivo, 67
Goats' milk
Cajeta, 639
Gorditas de Picadillo de Res,
77
green onions
Puerco en Pipian Verde, 75
Guacamole
recipe, 432
Sweet Corn & Pepita
Guacamole, 449
Taquitos de Requesón con
Rajas, 280
guajillo chile peppers
about, 22
Barbacoa Adobo, 483
Beef Cheeks with Salsa
Verde, 52
Birria de Chivo, 67
Camarones a la Diabla, 197
Camarones en Adobo, 158
Cecina de Cerdo, 40
Chicken Chorizo, 109
Chilaquiles Rojos, 277
Chile Colorado, 452
Chilorio, 89
Costilla Corta de Res con
Chile Colorado, 70
Menudo, 293
Mixiotes de Pollo, 110
Mole Manchamanteles, 455
Mole Negro, 440–441

Mole Poblano, 119
Moscovy Duck Breast Mole, 98
Mushroom Barbacoa, 239
Pescado Adobado en Hoja de Platano, 191
Pescado Zarandeado, 196
Pierna de Puerco, 71
Pineapple Marmalade, 721
Pipian Rojo, 484
Pulpo al Pastor, 155
Salsa de Arbol, 498
Sopa de Camarón Seco, 323
Sopa de Chorizo, Ayocotes y Acelgas, 298
Spicy Chocolate Truffles, 577
Tomato Aguachile, 231
Guanajuato Strawberry & Beet Salad, 210
guero chile peppers
Sopa de Flor de Calabaza, 314
Gulf Rock Shrimp Aguachile with Avocado Panna Cotta, 138

Habanero Agave
Fried Brussels Sprouts, 216
recipe, 216
habanero chile peppers
Dzik de Res, 51
Dzikil P'aak, 511
Habanero Honey, 533
Huevos Motulenos, 394
Mole Blanco, 458
Pan de Cazon, 165
Recado Rojo, 497
Salpicon de Rabano y Chile Habanero, 486
Salsa de Chiltomate, 477
Tikin Xic, 175
X'nipek, 487
halibut
Sere de Pescado, 300
Ham Stock

Carne Adobada, 311
recipe, 311
Hay Zeus, 726
hierbabuena
Albondigas Soup, 334
Flor de Calabaza con Queso Fresco y Hierbabuena, 260
Higados en Salsa Chipotle de Adobo, 53
hoja santa
Chileatole Verde, 514
Mixiotes de Pollo, 110
Mole Negro, 440–441
Mole Verde, 492
Pan de Hoja Santa, 631
La Santa, 764
Tortilla Gruesa de Hoja Santa y Queso, 374
hominy
Menudo, 293
Pozole, 304
Pozole Blanco, 288
honey
Fig Cordial, 734
Habanero Honey, 533
Lomo y Manchamanteles, 45
Piña Fumada, 741
Szechuan & Chipotle Honey, 761
Horchata
Horchata con Espresso, 774
Horchata con Rum, 771
Horchata Ice Cream, 542
recipe, 768
Huaraches with Wild Mushrooms & Epazote, 356
Huauzontles Relleno de Queso con Chiltomate, 223
Huevos Motuleños, 394
Huevos Rancheros, 387

ice cream
Chocolate Ice Cream, 572

Custard Ice Cream Base, 647
Horchata Ice Cream, 542
Mezcal Ice Cream, 620
No-Fry Fried Ice Cream, 630

jalapeño chile peppers
Baja Tortilla Soup, 301
Beef Machaca with Potatoes & Eggs, 91
Ceviche de Pescado, 195
Charred Escabeche, 470
Chilaquiles Rojos, 417
Chiles Toreados, 489
Cocktail de Marisco, 184
Escabeche, 518
Fire Walk with Me, 755
Gulf Rock Shrimp Aguachile with Avocado Panna Cotta, 138
Lengua en Salsa Roja, 56
Mexican Pepper Reduction, 714
Mextlapique de Callo de Hacha, 164
Puerco en Pipian Verde, 75
Sopa de Chile Poblano, 310
Taquitos de Papa, 281
Vuelva la Vida Coctel de Camarones, 151
Jalisco Sour, 750
Jamaica Collins, 691
Jamaica Syrup, 691
Joroches de Chorizo y Frijoles Colados, 373

kale
Mole Verde, 492
Sopa de Chile Poblano, 310
Kinda Knew Anna, 749
Koji-Fried Sardines, 407
Koji-Marinated Sweet Potatoes with Salsa Macha, 215

lamb
    Birria de Chivo, 67
Langosta al Mojo de Ajo, 136
Lavagave, 702
Lavender Agave
    Lavagave, 702
    recipe, 702
Leche Quemada, 544
leeks
Fish Stock, 345
Vegetable Stock, 346
lemongrass stalks
    Lemongrass Syrup, 758
    Pan, 758
    Striped Sea Bass Ceviche,
      146–147
lemons/lemon juice
    Citrus Salt, 717
    Coconut Dressing, 147
    Flor de Calabaza con Queso
      Fresco y Hierbabuena,
      260
    Smoked Trout Tostadas, 183
    Striped Sea Bass Ceviche,
      146–147
    Vuelva la Vida Coctel de
      Camarones, 151
Lengua en Salsa Roja, 56
lentils
    Sopa de Lentejas, 337
Licor 43
    El Chavo del Ocho, 694
    Oaxacarajillo, 683
Lillet
    Pineapple Marmalade,
      721
lime cordial
    Rising Sun, 722
Lime Crema
    Baja Tortilla Soup, 301
    Momma's Sopa de
      Conchitas, 294
    recipe, 294
Lime Syrup
    Mezcal Survivor, 742
    recipe, 742

limes/lime juice
    Aguachile Verde de
      Camarón, 171
    Arbol Macha, 428
    Barbacoa Adobo, 483
    Carnitas de Atun, 168
    Ceviche de Pescado, 195
    Chiles Toreados, 489
    Citrus Salt, 717
    Coctel de Camaron, 190
    Codorniz a la Parilla, 103
    Dzik de Res, 51
    Dzikil P'aak, 511
    Guacamole, 432
    Gulf Rock Shrimp
      Aguachile with Avocado
      Panna Cotta, 138
    Lime Syrup, 742
    Michoacán-Style Carnitas,
      46
    Mixiotes de Pollo, 110
    Mushroom Barbacoa, 239
    Ostiones al Tapesco, 161
    Pan de Cazon, 165
    Pescado Zarandeado, 196
    Pig Ear Salad, 405
    Preserved Limes with Chile
      de Arbol & Spices, 459
    Ray Ray's Michelada, 661
    Recado Rojo, 497
    Salpicon de Rabano y Chile
      Habanero, 486
    Striped Sea Bass Ceviche,
      146–147
    Tomato Aguachile, 231
    X'nipek, 487
lobster
    Baja Lobster & Street Corn
      Salad, 143
    Langosta al Mojo de Ajo,
      136
Lomo y Manchamanteles, 45
Longaniza, Esquites con, 424
Lost in the Rain in Juárez, 737
Luis's Carnitas, 76

maize, 23
Mámù Vida, 761
mango puree
    Mango con Chile Pate de
      Fruit, 610
    Mezcal & Mango Float, 622
manzana chile peppers
    Pickled Manzano Pepper,
      528
    Sopa de Flor de Calabaza,
      314
maraschino liqueur
    Última Palabra, 669
Margarita, 658
marrow bones
    Menudo, 293
masa/masa harina
    Abuela's Sopes, 357
    Atole, 787
    Champurrado, 788
    Chicken Tinga Sopes, 393
    Chileatole Verde, 514
    Empanadas de Picadillo,
      80
    Gorditas de Picadillo de
      Res, 77
    Huaraches with Wild
      Mushrooms & Epazote,
      356
    Huauzontles Relleno de
      Queso con Chiltomate,
      223
    Joroches de Chorizo y
      Frijoles Colados, 373
    Masa for Tamales, 365
    Masa-Battered Fish Tacos,
      178
    Masa-Battered Fried
      Chicken, 122
    Masa-Crusted Sardines with
      Pickled Manzano, 201
    Memelas de Chicharron,
      390
    Mole Blanco, 458
    Molotes de Frijol y Queso,
      360

Quesadillas de
Champiñones, 251
Tacos Dorados de Frijol,
Chorizo y Camote, 386
Tamales de Chulibu'ul, 368
Tejuino, 789
Tetelas de Aguacate con
Requesón y Nopales, 382
Tlacoyos de Hongos, 379
Tomato Aguachile, 231
Tortilla Gruesa de Hoja
Santa y Queso, 374
Tortillas de Masa Harina,
352
Maya Gold, 695
Mayan Chocolate & Bourbon
Truffles, 615
Melon, Agua de, 778
Memelas de Chicharron, 390
Menudo, 293
metates, 23
metric conversions, 799
Mexican Chocolate Crinkle
Cookies, 640
Mexican Chocolate Sauce,
584
Mexican cuisine
history of, 13–15
regional differences in,
17–21
staple ingredients of, 21–23
Mexican Hot Chocolate, 794
Mexican Pepper Reduction
El Vato Swizzle, 714
recipe, 714
Mexican Wedding Cookies,
619
Mextlapique de Callo de
Hacha, 164
mezcal
Blacker the Berry, The
Sweeter the Juice, 705
Canoe Club, 698
Chamomile Mezcal, 695
Chorizo-Washed Mezcal,
688

Cooper's Café, 682
Drunken Rabbit, 706
Flor de Jalisco, 701
Lavagave, 702
Lost in the Rain in Juárez,
737
Mámù Vida, 761
Maya Gold, 695
Mezcal & Mango Float, 622
Mezcal Ice Cream, 620
Mezcal Survivor, 742
Naked & Famous, 746
Oaxaca Old Fashioned, 680
Oaxacarajillo, 683
Pierna de Puerco, 71
Piña Fumada, 741
Pineapple Express, 710
Playa Rosita, 662
Ramon Bravo, 688
Salsa Borracha, 508
Shake Your Tamarind, 709
True Romance, 754
Última Palabra, 669
Unscalpe, 738
Vampiro, 664
Zeus Juice Cordial, 726
Michoacán-Style Carnitas, 46
Midori
She's a Rainbow, 753
Milanesa de Pollo, 131
Milanesa de Res y Mole
Blanco, 33
mint
La Cura, 767
East LA, 673
Flor de Calabaza con Queso
Fresco y Hierbabuena, 260
Mole Verde, 492
Mixed Nut Marzipan, 627
Mixiotes de Pollo, 110
molcajete, 434
Mole Blanco
Camote con Mole Blanco,
222
Milanesa de Res y Mole
Blanco, 33

recipe, 458
Mole Brownies, 623
Mole Manchamanteles
Lomo y Manchamanteles,
45
recipe, 455
Mole Negro
Enchiladas de Mole, 126
Puritos de Platano Macho
Relleno de Frijoles Negros
y Mole Negro, 221
recipe, 440–441
Mole Poblano, 119
Mole Spice
Masa-Crusted Sardines with
Pickled Manzano, 201
recipe, 201
Mole Verde, 492
Molotes de Frijol y Queso,
360
Momma's Sopa de Conchitas,
294
Monterey Jack cheese
Chiles Rellenos, 269
Queso Fundido, 429
Morita Salsa
recipe, 505
Tacos Dorados de Frijol,
Chorizo y Camote, 386
Moscovy Duck Breast Mole,
98
mulato chile peppers
Mole Poblano, 119
mushrooms
Chicken en Salsa Cremosa
de Champiñones, 104
Huaraches with Wild
Mushrooms & Epazote,
356
Mushroom Barbacoa, 239
Quesadillas de
Champiñones, 251
Sopa de Hongos, 295
Tlacoyos de Hongos, 379

Naked & Famous, 746

negro chile peppers
  Mole Poblano, 119
New Mexico chile peppers
  Beef Barbacoa Tacos, 412
  Caldo de Espinazo de
    Puerco, 326
nixtamalization process, 23
No-Fry Fried Ice Cream, 630
nuts. *See individual nut types*

Oaxaca cheese
  Beef Barbacoa Tacos, 412
  Chicken en Salsa Cremosa
    de Champiñones, 104
  Chiles Rellenos, 269
  Huauzontles Relleno de
    Queso con Chiltomate,
    223
  Memelas de Chicharron,
    390
  Molotes de Frijol y Queso,
    360
  Quesadillas de
    Champiñones, 251
  Queso Fundido, 429
  Tortilla Gruesa de Hoja
    Santa y Queso, 374
Oaxaca Old Fashioned, 680
Oaxacarajillo, 683
octopus
  Cocktail de Marisco, 184
  Pulpo al Pastor, 155
olives
  Pescado Veracruz, 189
  Pollo Veracruzano, 123
  Smoked Trout Tostadas, 183
onions
  Barbacoa Adobo, 483
  Beef Stock, 342
  Chicken Stock, 341
  Cocktail de Marisco, 184
  Fish Stock, 345
  Frijol Ayocote with Pasilla
    Yogurt, 248
  Frijoles de la Olla, 257
  Mushroom Barbacoa, 239

Pan de Cazon, 165
Pescado Veracruz, 189
Pickled Red Onion, 515
Puchero de Tres Carnes, 318
Pulpo al Pastor, 155
Smoked Trout Tostadas, 183
Sopa de Flor de Calabaza,
  314
Sopa de Frijol Colado, 317
Vegetable Stock, 346
Verdolagas en Salsa Verde,
  242
X'nipek, 487
Orange Bell Pepper & Beet
  Syrup
  Desert Daisy, 718
  recipe, 718
orange juice
  Barbacoa Adobo, 483
  Carnitas de Atun, 168
  Chilorio, 89
  Codorniz a la Parilla, 103
  Dzik de Res, 51
  Dzikil P'aak, 511
  Luis's Carnitas, 76
  Michoacán-Style Carnitas,
    46
  Mixiotes de Pollo, 110
  Mushroom Barbacoa, 239
  Pan de Cazon, 165
  Recado Rojo, 497
  Salpicon de Rabano y Chile
    Habanero, 486
  Vuelva la Vida Coctel de
    Camarones, 151
  X'nipek, 487
Orejas, 549
Ostiones al Tapesco, 161
ox tongue
  Lengua en Salsa Roja, 56
oxtail
  Rabo de Res en Salsa Roja,
    84
oysters
  Ostiones al Tapesco, 161

Paloma, 665
Pan, 758
Pan de Cazon, 165
Pan de Hoja Santa, 631
Panna Cotta, Gulf Rock
  Shrimp Aguachile with
  Avocado, 138
parsley
  Albondigas Soup, 334
  Mole Verde, 492
pasilla chile peppers
  about, 22
  Barbacoa Adobo, 483
  Chicken Chorizo, 109
  Costilla Corta de Res con
    Chile Colorado, 70
  Frijol Ayocote with Pasilla
    Yogurt, 248
  Mextlapique de Callo de
    Hacha, 164
  Mole Negro, 440–441
  Mole Poblano, 119
  Mushroom Barbacoa, 239
  Puerco en Pipian Verde, 75
  Puritos de Platano Macho
    Relleno de Frijoles Negros
    y Mole Negro, 221
  Salsa Borracha, 508
  Sopa de Hongos, 295
pasta
  Momma's Sopa de
    Conchitas, 294
  Sopa de Fideo, 330
Pavo en Escabeche, 111
peaches
  Lomo y Manchamanteles,
    45
  Mole Manchamanteles, 455
  Peach Cordial, 730
  Peach Tea, 730
peanut butter
  Chocolate Mole, 575
  Mixed Nut Marzipan, 627
  Mole Brownies, 623
peanuts
  Arbol Macha, 428

Mixed Nut Marzipan, 627
Puerco en Pipian Verde, 75
Striped Sea Bass Ceviche,
    146–147
pears
    Mole Manchamanteles, 455
peas
    Arroz a la Mexicana, 529
    Picadillo de Res, 73
    Snap Pea Syrup, 764
pecans
    Mexican Wedding Cookies,
        619
    Mixed Nut Marzipan, 627
    Mole Negro, 440–441
peppers, bell
    Chulibu'ul, 534
    Orange Bell Pepper & Beet
        Syrup, 718
    Pescado Veracruz, 189
    Pollo Veracruzano, 123
    See also individual chile
        peppers
pequin chile peppers
    Chilaquiles Rojos, 417
Perfect Caramel
    Coffee Flan with Buñuelos,
        562
    recipe, 601
Perfect Flan, The, 644
Pescado Adobado en Hoja de
    Platano, 191
Pescado Veracruz, 189
Pescado Zarandeado, 196
Picadillo de Res
    Chiles en Nogada, 85
    Empanadas de Picadillo, 80
    Gorditas de Picadillo de
        Res, 77
    recipe, 73
Pickled Manzano Pepper
    Masa-Crusted Sardines with
        Pickled Manzano, 201
    recipe, 528
Pickled Pineapple, 465
Pickled Red Onion

Beef Barbacoa Tacos, 412
Birria de Chivo, 67
Chicken Chorizo, 109
Enchiladas de Mole, 126
Gorditas de Picadillo de
    Res, 77
Huaraches with Wild
    Mushrooms & Epazote,
    356
Memelas de Chicharron,
    390
Mole Poblano, 119
Pescado Adobado en Hoja
    de Platano, 191
recipe, 515
Tinga de Pollo, 114
Tortas Ahogadas, 423
Pico de Gallo
    Carnitas de Atun, 168
    Masa-Battered Fish Tacos,
        178
    recipe, 281
Pierna de Puerco, 71
Pig Ear Salad, 405
piloncillo
    Arroz con Leche, 554
    Atole, 787
    Blue Corn Crunchies, 607
    Champurrado, 788
    Mole Manchamanteles, 455
    Piloncillo Syrup, 557
    Tejuino, 789
    Tepache de Piña, 791
Piña Fumada, 741
pine nuts
    Mole Blanco, 458
pineapples/pineapple juice
    Avocado Mix, 717
    Charred Pineapple Puree,
        688
    Pickled Pineapple, 465
    Pineapple Express, 710
    Pineapple Marmalade, 721
    Pineapple Tepache
        Kombucha, 790
    Pineapple-Infused Campari,

662
    Playa Rosita, 662
    Pulpo al Pastor, 155
    Tepache de Piña, 791
pinto beans
    Carne en Su Jugo, 90
Pipian Rojo
    Chayote en Pipian Rojo,
        245
    recipe, 484
pisco
    Jalisco Sour, 750
plantains
    Huevos Motuleños, 394
    Mole Blanco, 458
    Mole Manchamanteles,
        455
    Mole Negro, 440–441
    Puchero de Tres Carnes, 318
    Puritos de Platano Macho
        Relleno de Frijoles Negros
        y Mole Negro, 221
Playa Rosita, 662
poblano chile peppers
    about, 22
    Charred Pepper Emulsion,
        400–401
    Charred Pepper Tartare,
        400–401
    Chiles en Nogada, 85
    Chiles Rellenos, 269
    Sopa de Chile Poblano, 310
    Taquitos de Requesón con
        Rajas, 280
Pollo Veracruzano, 123
pomegranate seeds
    Chiles en Nogada, 85
    Sweet Corn & Pepita
        Guacamole, 449
pork
    Caldo de Espinazo de
        Puerco, 326
    Carne Adobada, 311
    Cecina de Cerdo, 40
    Chilorio, 89
    Cochinita Pibil, 28

Costilla Corta de Res con
Chile Colorado, 70
Lomo y Manchamanteles, 45
Luis's Carnitas, 76
Michoacán-Style Carnitas,
46
Pierna de Puerco, 71
Pork Toro with Arbol
Macha, 428
Pozole, 304
Pozole Blanco, 288
Puchero de Tres Carnes, 318
Puerco en Pipian Verde, 75
Tortas Ahogadas, 423
Tortas de Lomo, 418
pork belly
Chicharron en Salsa Roja,
62
Tostadas de Cueritos, 59
potatoes
Beef Machaca with Potatoes
& Eggs, 91
Caldo de Pescado, 331
Caldo de Res, 336
Picadillo de Res, 73
Puchero de Tres Carnes, 318
Sopa de Papa, 327
Taquitos de Papa, 281
Pozole, 304
Pozole Blanco, 288
Preserved Limes with Chile de
Arbol & Spices, 459
Puchero de Tres Carnes, 318
Puerco en Pipian Verde, 75
Pulpo al Pastor, 155
pumpkin puree
Sweet Empanadas, 545
pumpkin seeds
Dzikil P'aak, 511
Mole Verde, 492
Moscovy Duck Breast Mole,
98
Pipian Rojo, 484
Puerco en Pipian Verde, 75
Sweet Corn & Pepita
Guacamole, 449

Puritos de Platano Macho
Relleno de Frijoles Negros
y Mole Negro, 221
purslane
Verdolagas en Salsa Verde,
242
puya chile peppers
Rabo de Res en Salsa Roja,
84

quail
Codorniz a la Parilla, 103
Quesadillas de Champiñones,
251
queso enchilado
Abuela's Sopes, 357
Baja Lobster & Street Corn
Salad, 143
Cilantro Pesto, 210
Queso Fresco
Betabel with Salsa Macha y
Queso Fresco, 234
Calabacitas con Elote y
Queso Fresco, 265
Chicken Tinga Sopes, 393
Chilaquiles Rojos, 277
Chiles en Nogada, 85
Enchiladas de Mole, 126
Ensalada de Nopales, 272
Flor de Calabaza con Queso
Fresco y Hierbabuena,
260
Guanajuato Strawberry &
Beet Salad, 210
Huaraches with Wild
Mushrooms & Epazote,
356
Huevos Motuleños, 394
Huevos Rancheros, 387
Puritos de Platano Macho
Relleno de Frijoles Negros
y Mole Negro, 221
Quesadillas de
Champiñones, 251
recipe, 522
Sopa de Flor de Calabaza,

314
Sopa de Papa, 327
Tinga de Pollo, 114
Tomato Aguachile, 231
Verdolagas en Salsa Verde,
242
Queso Fundido, 429
queso panela
Tortas de Lomo, 418

Rabo de Res en Salsa Roja, 84
radishes
Chicken Tinga Sopes, 393
Lengua en Salsa Roja, 56
Salpicon de Rabano y Chile
Habanero, 486
Raicilla-Soaked Berries
Coconut Tres Leches, 593
recipe, 594
raisins
Mole Blanco, 458
Mole Manchamanteles, 455
Mole Negro, 440–441
Moscovy Duck Breast Mole,
98
Ramon Bravo, 688
Ranch Water, 674
Ray Ray's Michelada, 661
Recado Rojo
Chicken Chorizo, 109
Cochinita Pibil, 28
Pescado Adobado en Hoja
de Platano, 191
Pulpo al Pastor, 155
recipe, 497
Tikin Xic, 175
red snapper
Caldo de Pescado, 331
refried beans
Tostadas de Cueritos, 59
See also Frijoles Negros
Refritos
regional cuisines, 17–21
requesón
Taquitos de Requesón con
Rajas, 280

Tetelas de Aguacate con
    Requesón y Nopales, 382
rice
    Albondigas Soup, 334
    Arroz a la Mexicana, 529
    Arroz con Leche, 554
    Horchata, 768
    Horchata Ice Cream, 542
rice flour
    Pig Ear Salad, 405
Rich Demerara Syrup
    Lime Syrup, 742
    Lost in the Rain in Juárez,
        737
    recipe, 737
ricotta cheese
    Taquitos de Requesón con
        Rajas, 280
    Tetelas de Aguacate con
        Requesón y Nopales, 382
Rising Sun, 722
rum
    Brujera, 713
    Horchata con Rum, 771

salads
    Guanajuato Strawberry &
        Beet Salad, 210
    Pig Ear Salad, 405
Saline Solution
    East LA, 673
    Margarita, 658
    recipe, 658
    Spicy Margarita, 668
    Zeus Juice Cordial, 726
Salpicon de Rabano y Chile
    Habanero
    Milanesa de Res y Mole
        Blanco, 33
    Puchero de Tres Carnes, 318
    recipe, 486
Salsa Borracha
    Mixiotes de Pollo, 110
    Mushroom Barbacoa, 239
    recipe, 508
Salsa de Chiltomate

Chilibul, 32
Cochinita Pibil, 28
Tikin Xic, 175
Salsa Cruda Verde
    Beef Cheeks with Salsa
        Verde, 52
    Gorditas de Picadillo de
        Res, 77
    Luis's Carnitas, 76
    Molotes de Frijol y Queso,
        360
    recipe, 525
    Verdolagas en Salsa Verde,
        242
Salsa de Aguacate
    Pulpo al Pastor, 155
    recipe, 503
    Tlacoyos de Hongos, 379
Salsa de Arbol
    recipe, 498
    Tortilla Gruesa de Hoja
        Santa y Queso, 374
Salsa de Chiltomate
    Huauzontles Relleno de
        Queso con Chiltomate,
        223
    recipe, 477
    Tamales de Chulibu'ul, 368
Salsa Macha
    Betabel with Salsa Macha y
        Queso Fresco, 234
    Koji-Marinated Sweet
        Potatoes with Salsa
        Macha, 215
    recipe, 521
Salsa Quemada
    Abuela's Sopes, 357
    Codorniz a la Parilla, 103
Salsa Verde Tatemada
    Chicken Chorizo, 109
    Michoacán-Style Carnitas,
        46
    recipe, 480
    Tetelas de Aguacate con
        Requesón y Nopales, 382
Santa, La, 764

sardines
    Cured Sardines, 406
    Koji-Fried Sardines, 407
    Masa-Crusted Sardines with
        Pickled Manzano, 201
sauerkraut
    Smoked Trout Tostadas, 183
sausage/chorizo
    Abuela's Sopes, 357
    Butternut Squash &
        Chorizo Bisque, 307
    Chicken Chorizo, 109
    Chilaquiles Rojos, 417
    Chorizo-Washed Mezcal, 688
    Esquites con Longaniza, 424
    Huevos Motuleños, 394
    Joroches de Chorizo y
        Frijoles Colados, 373
    Queso Fundido, 429
    Sopa de Chorizo, Ayocotes y
        Acelgas, 298
    Tacos Dorados de Frijol,
        Chorizo y Camote, 386
scallops
    Mextlapique de Callo de
        Hacha, 164
SCOBY liquid, 790
Sea Bass Ceviche, Striped,
    146–147
seafood
    Aguachile Verde de
        Camarón, 171
    Baja Lobster & Street Corn
        Salad, 143
    Caldo de Pescado, 331
    Camarones a la Diabla, 197
    Camarones en Adobo, 158
    Carnitas de Atun, 168
    Ceviche de Pescado, 195
    Cocktail de Marisco, 184
    Coctel de Camaron, 190
    Gulf Rock Shrimp
        Aguachile with Avocado
        Panna Cotta, 138
    Langosta al Mojo de Ajo,
        136

Masa-Battered Fish Tacos, 178

Masa-Crusted Sardines with Pickled Manzano, 201

Mextlapique de Callo de Hacha, 164

Ostiones al Tapesco, 161

Pan de Cazon, 165

Pescado Adobado en Hoja de Platano, 191

Pescado Veracruz, 189

Pescado Zarandeado, 196

Pulpo al Pastor, 155

Sere de Pescado, 300

Smoked Trout Tostadas, 183

Sopa de Camarón Seco, 323

Striped Sea Bass Ceviche, 146–147

Tikin Xic, 175

Vuelva la Vida Coctel de Camarones, 151

See also fish

Sere de Pescado, 300

serrano chile peppers

Aguachile Verde de Camarón, 171

Carne en Su Jugo, 90

Chicharron en Salsa Roja, 62

Chileatole Verde, 514

Chiles Toreados, 489

Coctel de Camaron, 190

Coffee & Ancho Roasted Carrots with Chile Toreado Mayo, 226

Ginger & Serrano Syrup, 698

Guacamole, 432

Huevos Rancheros, 387

Mole Verde, 492

Ostiones al Tapesco, 161

Pescado Adobado en Hoja de Platano, 191

Picadillo de Res, 73

Puerco en Pipian Verde, 75

Salsa Cruda Verde, 525

Salsa Verde Tatemada, 480

Sere de Pescado, 300

Sopa de Chile Poblano, 310

Striped Sea Bass Ceviche, 146–147

Tetelas de Aguacate con Requesón y Nopales, 382

Tomato Aguachile, 231

sesame seeds

Chocolate Mole, 575

Mexican Chocolate Sauce, 584

Mole Blanco, 458

Mole Brownies, 623

Mole Manchamanteles, 455

Mole Negro, 440–441

Mole Poblano, 119

Mole Verde, 492

Moscovy Duck Breast Mole, 98

Pipian Rojo, 484

Salsa Macha, 521

Shake Your Tamarind, 709

sherry

Maya Gold, 695

She's a Rainbow, 753

short ribs

Costilla Corta de Res con Chile Colorado, 37

Puchero de Tres Carnes, 318

See also beef

shrimp

Aguachile Verde de Camarón, 171

Caldo de Pescado, 331

Camarones a la Diabla, 197

Camarones en Adobo, 158

Cocktail de Marisco, 184

Coctel de Camaron, 190

Gulf Rock Shrimp Aguachile with Avocado Panna Cotta, 138

Sopa de Camarón Seco, 323

Vuelva la Vida Coctel de Camarones, 151

Silver Needle-Infused Tequila, 730

Simple Syrup

La Cura, 767

East LA, 673

Fig Leaf Syrup, 734

Horchata, 768

Jalisco Sour, 750

Paloma, 665

Ramon Bravo, 688

La Santa, 764

Tejuino, 789

Vampiro, 664

Zeus Juice Cordial, 726

sloe gin

Rising Sun, 722

Smoked Morita Oil

Charred Pepper Tartare, 400–401

recipe, 401

Smoked Trout Tostadas, 183

Snap Pea Syrup, 764

Sopa de Camarón Seco, 323

Sopa de Chile Poblano, 310

Sopa de Chorizo, Ayocotes y Acelgas, 298

Sopa de Fideo, 330

Sopa de Flor de Calabaza, 314

Sopa de Frijol Colado

Joroches de Chorizo y Frijoles Colados, 373

recipe, 317

Sopa de Hongos, 295

Sopa de Lentejas, 337

Sopa de Papa, 327

Sopaipillas, 643

sorrel

Betabel with Salsa Macha y Queso Fresco, 234

soups

Albondigas Soup, 334

Baja Tortilla Soup, 301

Beef Stock, 342

Butternut Squash & Chorizo Bisque, 307

Caldo de Espinazo de
Puerco, 326
Caldo de Pescado, 331
Caldo de Res, 336
Carne Adobada, 311
Chicken Stock, 341
Fish Stock, 345
Menudo, 293
Momma's Sopa de
Conchitas, 294
Pozole, 304
Pozole Blanco, 288
Puchero de Tres Carnes, 318
Sere de Pescado, 300
Sopa de Camarón Seco, 323
Sopa de Chile Poblano, 310
Sopa de Chorizo, Ayocotes y
Acelgas, 298
Sopa de Fideo, 330
Sopa de Flor de Calabaza,
314
Sopa de Frijol Colado,
317
Sopa de Hongos, 295
Sopa de Lentejas, 337
Sopa de Papa, 327
Vegetable Stock, 346
Spicy Chocolate Truffles, 577
Spicy Margarita, 668
spinach
Puerco en Pipian Verde, 75
Sopa de Chile Poblano, 310
Sopa de Lentejas, 337
squash
Butternut Squash &
Chorizo Bisque, 307
Calabacitas con Elote y
Queso Fresco, 265
Caldo de Res, 336
Puchero de Tres Carnes, 318
Sopa de Flor de Calabaza,
314
squash blossoms
Flor de Calabaza con Queso
Fresco y Hierbabuena,
260

Sopa de Flor de Calabaza,
314
staple ingredients, 21–23
St-Germain
Blacker the Berry, The
Sweeter the Juice, 705
strawberries
Guanajuato Strawberry &
Beet Salad, 210
Strawberry Hot Sauce, 460
Strawberry Shortcake con
Conchas, 606
Striped Sea Bass Ceviche,
146–147
Sunday Morning Coming
Down, 729
sunflower seeds
Cilantro Pesto, 210
Mole Blanco, 458
Sweet Corn & Pepita
Guacamole, 449
Sweet Corn Pudding Pops,
635
Sweet Empanadas, 545
sweet potatoes
Camote con Mole Blanco,
222
Koji-Marinated Sweet
Potatoes with Salsa
Macha, 215
Puchero de Tres Carnes, 318
Tacos Dorados de Frijol,
Chorizo y Camote, 386
Swiss chard
Sopa de Chorizo, Ayocotes y
Acelgas, 298
Szechuan & Chipotle Honey
Mámù Vida, 761
recipe, 761

tacos
Beef Barbacoa Tacos, 412
Tacos Dorados de Frijol,
Chorizo y Camote, 386
tamales
Masa for Tamales, 365

Tamales de Chulibu'ul, 368
tamarind concentrate
Shake Your Tamarind, 709
tamarind paste
Chocolate Tamarind
Truffles, 576
tamarind pods
Agua de Tamarindo, 783
Taquitos de Papa, 281
Taquitos de Requesón con
Rajas, 280
Tejuino, 789
Tepache de Piña, 791
Tepache Syrup, 790
tequila
Batanga, 679
Brujera, 713
Cantaritos, 745
Champagne Paloma, 733
Desert Daisy, 718
Diablo Otoño, 734
La Diosa, 721
Dons of Soul, 725
East LA, 673
El Chavo del Ocho, 694
El Vato Swizzle, 714
The Fifth Element, 717
Fire Walk with Me, 755
Flor de Jalisco, 701
Hay Zeus, 726
Jalisco Sour, 750
Kinda Knew Anna, 749
Lavagave, 702
Margarita, 658
Oaxaca Old Fashioned, 680
Paloma, 665
Pan, 758
Peach Tea, 730
Pineapple Express, 710
Playa Rosita, 662
Ranch Water, 674
Rising Sun, 722
Salsa Borracha, 508
Shake Your Tamarind,
709
She's a Rainbow, 753

Silver Needle-Infused
    Tequila, 730
Spicy Margarita, 668
Sunday Morning Coming
    Down, 729
Tetelas de Aguacate con
    Requesón y Nopales,
    382
Thai Chile Agave
    Pineapple Express, 710
    recipe, 710
Thyme Syrup
    El Chavo del Ocho, 694
    recipe, 694
Tikin Xic, 175
Tinga de Pollo
    Chicken Tinga Sopes, 393
    recipe, 114
Tlacoyos de Hongos, 379
tomatillos
    Arbol Macha, 428
    Baja Tortilla Soup, 301
    Carne en Su Jugo, 90
    Chilaquiles Rojos, 417
    Dzikil P'aak, 511
    Mole Blanco, 458
    Mole Negro, 440–441
    Mole Verde, 492
    Puerco en Pipian Verde, 75
    Salsa Borracha, 508
    Salsa Cruda Verde, 525
    Salsa de Aguacate, 503
    Salsa Verde Tatemada, 480
    Striped Sea Bass Ceviche,
        146–147
Tomato Aguachile, 231
tomato juice
    Cocktail de Marisco, 184
    Vuelva la Vida Coctel de
        Camarones, 151
tomatoes
    Albondigas Soup, 334
    Baja Tortilla Soup, 301
    Beef Machaca with Potatoes
        & Eggs, 91
    Birria de Chivo, 67

Calabacitas con Elote y
    Queso Fresco, 265
Caldo de Pescado, 331
Camarones a la Diabla, 197
Ceviche de Pescado, 195
Chicharron en Salsa Roja,
    62
Chilaquiles Rojos, 277
Chiles Rellenos, 269
Chulibu'ul, 534
Coctel de Camaron, 190
Dzik de Res, 51
Dzikil P'aak, 511
Ensalada de Nopales, 272
Guacamole, 432
Huevos Motuleños, 394
Huevos Rancheros, 387
Lengua en Salsa Roja, 56
Mextlapique de Callo de
    Hacha, 164
Mole Manchamanteles, 455
Mole Negro, 440–441
Momma's Sopa de
    Conchitas, 294
Morita Salsa, 505
Pan de Cazon, 165
Pescado Veracruz, 189
Picadillo de Res, 73
Pipian Rojo, 484
Pollo Veracruzano, 123
Quesadillas de
    Champiñones, 251
Rabo de Res en Salsa Roja, 84
Salsa de Chiltomate, 477
Sopa de Fideo, 330
Sopa de Papa, 327
Taquitos de Papa, 281
Tinga de Pollo, 114
Tomato Aguachile, 231
Tortas Ahogadas, 423
Tortitas de Coliflor, 268
X'nipek, 487
Topo Chico
    Huauzontles Relleno de
        Queso con Chiltomate,
        223

Jamaica Collins, 691
    Ranch Water, 674
Tortas Ahogadas, 423
Tortas de Lomo, 418
Tortilla Gruesa de Hoja Santa
    y Queso, 374
Tortillas de Harina de Trigo,
    444
Tortillas de Masa Harina,
    352
Tortitas de Coliflor, 268
Tostadas
    Tinga de Pollo, 114
Tostadas de Cueritos, 59
tripe
    Menudo, 293
triple sec
La Diosa, 721
Trout Tostadas, Smoked, 183
True Romance, 754
tuna
    Carnitas de Atun, 168
turkey
    Pavo en Escabeche, 111
turnips
    Mole Blanco, 458

Última Palabra, 669
Unscalpe, 738

Vampiro, 664
Vanilla Syrup, 774
Vato Swizzle, El, 714
Vegetable Stock
    Baja Tortilla Soup, 301
    Butternut Squash &
        Chorizo Bisque, 307
    Chile Colorado, 452
    Frijol Ayocote with Pasilla
        Yogurt, 248
    Masa for Tamales, 365
    Moscovy Duck Breast Mole,
        98
    Pipian Rojo, 484
    recipe, 346
    Sopa de Chile Poblano, 310

Sopa de Chorizo, Ayocotes y
  Acelgas, 298
Sopa de Flor de Calabaza, 314
Sopa de Frijol Colado, 317
Velvet Falernum
  Piña Fumada, 741
Verdolagas en Salsa Verde, 242
vermouth, dry
  Pan, 758
  Sunday Morning Coming
    Down, 729
vermouth, sweet
  La Diosa, 721
  Pineapple Marmalade, 721
  Playa Rosita, 662
  Sunday Morning Coming
    Down, 729

Vuelva la Vida Coctel de
  Camarones, 151

walnuts
  Chiles en Nogada, 85
  Fig Cordial, 734
watercress
  Caldo de Espinazo de
    Puerco, 326
wine, white
  Chicken en Salsa Cremosa
    de Champiñones, 104
  Pollo Veracruzano, 123

xcatic chile peppers
  Pavo en Escabeche,
    111

X'nipek
  Cochinita Pibil, 28
  Joroches de Chorizo y
    Frijoles Colados, 373
  recipe, 487
Xocolatl, 777

yogurt
  Frijol Ayocote with Pasilla
    Yogurt, 248
  Sopa de Chile Poblano, 310
yucateca achiote paste
  Recado Rojo, 497

Zeus Juice Cordial, 726
zucchini
  Albondigas Soup, 334

ABOUT CIDER MILL PRESS BOOK PUBLISHERS

Good ideas ripen with time. From seed to harvest, Cider Mill Press brings fine reading, information, and entertainment together between the covers of its creatively crafted books. Our Cider Mill bears fruit twice a year, publishing a new crop of titles each spring and fall.

"Where Good Books Are Ready for Press"

Visit us online at

cidermillpress.com

or write to us at

PO Box 454
12 Spring St.
Kennebunkport, Maine 04046